*A Sign for Cain*

## By Fredric Wertham

*The Brain as an Organ*
*Dark Legend: A Study in Murder*
*The Show of Violence*
*Seduction of the Innocent*
*The Circle of Guilt*
*A Sign for Cain: An Exploration of Human Violence*

# A SIGN FOR CAIN

An Exploration of Human Violence

FREDRIC WERTHAM, M.D.

NEW YORK: THE MACMILLAN COMPANY
LONDON: COLLIER-MACMILLAN LIMITED

ACKNOWLEDGMENTS ARE DUE TO THE FOLLOWING
FOR PERMISSION TO QUOTE:

Bob Dylan, "Blowin' in the Wind." Copyright 1962 by M. Witmark & Sons. Used by permission.

H. W. Nevinson, *Visions and Memories,* Oxford University Press, London. Used by permission.

George Bernard Shaw, "So We Lay Down the Pen." Used by permission of the Public Trustee and the Society of Authors.

Library of Congress Catalog Card Number: 66-20825

FIRST PRINTING

The Macmillan Company, New York
Collier-Macmillan Canada Ltd., Toronto, Ontario

Printed in the United States of America

# CONTENTS

# A Sign for Cain

And Jehovah appointed a sign for Cain, lest any finding him should smite him.

—GENESIS 4:15

If a way to the better there be, it exacts a full look at the worst.

—THOMAS HARDY

# CHAPTER ONE

# The Goddess of Violence

How many deaths will it take 'til he knows
That too many people have died?
                    —Bob Dylan

BIRTH is the beginning of life, death is its end. But violent death is an end before the end. Often it is an end with great physical pain and suffering. It is this latter aspect that has motivated me, as a physician, to make a comprehensive study of the subject of violence. It was in the course of these studies that I learned that violence is not only physical suffering and annihilation, as it is in such catastrophes of nature as an earthquake or the eruption of a volcano. Violence has far greater effects on the lives of the survivors and on society. Whether the victims are forgotten or not (and they are often not even properly counted), violent deaths have deeper and more enduring consequences than we like to concede. Violence corrupts. We need to realize how insidious it is. We also have to make clear to ourselves the connections between the manifold phenomena related to it.

If I had to compare violence with a medical disease, I would compare it with cancer. Cancer can start insidiously in any part of the body. It becomes known to us through a local manifestation, but it can spread all over the body. It is deadly if not arrested in time. And it requires all the ingenuity of science to diagnose early, to treat, and to prevent.

There is an old saying that "nothing matters until a fool starts violence." That has a certain validity, except that before anybody starts violence, many others must have prepared the ground. The aggressor is not the only, and sometimes not even the chief, transgressor. He comes onstage and fires the shot, but the script has been written long before. One single actor does not make a play.

According to the legend, which, whatever else it may constitute, embodies some element of anthropological truth, the earliest family—Adam, Eve, and their children—was beset by three major troubles: first, what has been described as a "turmoil of thought," especially about good and evil (the tree of the knowledge of good and evil); secondly, sex (the serpent of lust); thirdly, violence (Cain's murder of Abel).

It is an interesting fact that the philosophers, the scientists, and the theologians have focused their attention on the first two. There are innumerable treatises on moral philosophy and, of course, on sex. But violence as a general subject has been neglected. This despite the fact that we are today nearer to mass violence than ever in the history of the world. Even the sign of Cain, or mark of Cain, is sometimes misunderstood. I have heard district attorneys asking for the death penalty while pointing to the "sign of Cain" on the accused's forehead. They did not realize that this sign does not stamp a man as one fit for the death penalty, but on the contrary is a device *against* continued violence: "a sign for Cain, lest any finding him should smite him."

The chain of the continuity of violence reaches from the most ancient times to today's headlines. Can we break this chain?

Recently two middle-aged women in Brooklyn on a summer evening were walking on a side street toward one of the larger avenues, after visiting a friend nearby. They intended to take a taxi home. About 250 feet from the avenue, a group of boys came up, crowding the sidewalk. The women drew back to let them pass. The last boy grabbed the right arm of one woman, to take her purse, then knocked her down on the sidewalk and jumped on her again and again. When she was taken to the hospital, it was found that she had a broken shoulder, broken elbow, broken arm, and a compound fragmented fracture of her right thighbone, for which an elaborate operation was necessary. She needed three nurses around the clock. And when she recovers, she will have to wear a brace from her hip to her heel and will be permanently crippled, with one leg shorter than the other. In my professional contact with this case, I learned what terrible pain and shock were caused—and that the expenses involved wiped out a family's savings. There was no sexual connotation to this attack. Since the boy had the pocketbook, there was no reason for pure gain to explain his stomping the woman so mercilessly.

Twenty-five years ago this would have been an exceptional case and would have caused a sensation. Now it did not raise a ripple and was not even reported as news. It happens too often. The boys were never caught; if they had been caught, the authorities would not have known what to do with them. This is today's violence in pure culture. I have known a number of similar cases. They are as a rule not fully reported, far less solved or resolved. Those who use the fashionable explanations for violence, that it is due to domineering mothers or inadequate ones, to pent-up aggressive instincts or a revolt against early toilet training, do not know the current facts of life in big American cities. They try to reduce ugly social facts to the level of intriguing individual psychological events. In this way they become part of the very decadence in which present-day violence flourishes.

Psychology has an important role to play, in its place, but no violent act can be fully explained by psychology alone. We must take into account the society, the various influences which surround the individual and family. Violence is always a historical fact; that is to say, it is always relative to the prevailing social-historical conditions. It is futile to try to translate it into some superhistorical principle in individual human nature. If on the streets of Brooklyn a young boy wantonly stomps a woman, much more is at work than a little imp in his brain.

Violence is destructive physical action against another person. But there is another kind of violence in the broadest sense which may be called figurative violence. It may be somewhat intangible, but it is neither invisible nor inaudible. We say smilingly, "I'll break your neck," or "I'll punch you in the nose," or speak of giving somebody a "tongue-lashing." It is merely verbal, but it has psychological implications. A prominent writer just now advocates in a column printed in many papers that youths who commit violent crimes be "fried" (meaning electrocuted). We use as a matter of course such crude and almost obscene expressions as "population explosion."

Language itself helps us to trace the ramifications of figurative or symbolic violence. We speak of "doing violence" to a text, an idea, or a principle. That means to misrepresent it or distort it unscrupulously. Disagreements are necessary, but they are often expressed in violent invective. The noise of loudspeakers, overshrill music, leaving the radio turned on very loudly, overloud commercials on television—they all belong to this violence in the broader sense. What corresponds to it is a kind of ruthlessness in thought and feeling.

This radiates into many spheres: politics, economic life, art and literature, and the ordinary relations between human beings. Henry James spoke of the American business scene as characterized by a "boundless ferocity of battle." We are becoming so enveloped by this whole atmosphere that we hardly realize it any more.

The influence of figurative violence on actual physically violent occurrences is hard to trace in detail, but as a matter of social psychology this influence undoubtedly exists. When the environment tolerates, approves, propagates, or rewards violent expressions, violent behavior is more apt to happen.

Figurative violence also implies a larger issue, the dominance in our society of the principle of success-at-any-price. This ruthless striving for success is permeated with violencelike elements. As James Baldwin has expressed it, "The American equation of success with the big time reveals an awful disrespect for human life." To put something over on the other person, to overpower him, is rewarded socially and economically. There is a whole philosophy of self-expression and "self-actualization" popular in some academic and intellectual circles which in part teaches the young to live out their aggressive drives regardless of what that may do to other people. In a book that is part of a series edited by a professor of psychology at Harvard University, we find this revealing statement: "Necessary to the concept of self-actualization is a certain selfishness and self-protectiveness, a certain promise of necessary violence, even of ferocity." It is significant for the spirit of our time that the same term, "ferocity," which was used by Henry James in condemnation is used here by a modern psychologist with scientific approval.

The success-at-any-price principle debases man. Rabindranath

Tagore, whose thinking was much occupied with questions of violence and nonviolence, wrote in one of his last poems of

> This play of losing and winning
> This false magic of life

The magic of losing and winning, of success-at-any-price, is closely related to violence. For anybody who wishes to help stem the tide of physical violence in the world, great effort is required to escape the standardized ways of success-thinking in our social life.

It is a paradox that while physical violence is such a definite, decisive, and irrevocable act, writing about it is often evasive and unrealistic. Violence, individual or multiple, is not an idea, not a psychological-philosophical abstraction. It is not an eternal, universal constituent of all human existence, as some philosophers seem to assume. It is part of the harsh reality of our historically developed social life.

There is not one scientific or scientifically oriented book in any language on the general subject of physical violence as such and its prevention. This is a significant gap. And if you look over recent books in fields like sociology, social science, psychology, and psychopathology, the word "violence" is usually not in the index. In school and college courses and textbooks, violence is presented only in patriotic garb, with heavy emphasis on dates, geographical places, names of rulers and commanders. We learn a lot in school about the violence of conquest, but little about the conquest of violence.

The fact that no scientific book on violence has been written is a problem that itself becomes a part of the study of violence. There are a number of significant reasons for this neglect. Violence is an emotionally loaded subject. It has more extensive implications than are apparent on the surface. The details that lead up to it are even more disconcerting because they concern us all. Its distant roots and runners reach into the life space of almost everybody, in the form of ultimate gain from it or responsibility for it. This is dimly felt by many people, though not often fully realized or easily admitted. Sweeping and comforting generalizations replace concrete research. Do we perhaps, as the columnist Henry

Butler expressed it, "privately cling to the promise of some kind of magic fulfillment through savagery"?

We need to keep in mind the critical role of violence in human affairs. An important aspect of human development, past and present, could be outlined by the history of the occurrence of violence, the reasons for it, and the evolution of ideas about it. When we look beneath the surface for the causes of violence, including seemingly remote ones, we are apt to find raw truths not easily acceptable. We may learn that less lofty forces are at work than we thought. In chemistry, if you put sulfuric acid on a lump of sugar, it becomes black and you reveal the carbon coal underneath. No feelings are hurt, no interests impinged upon. But if you investigate violence, you are likely to trespass on touchy ground.

The study of violence may, in a restricted way, begin in the laboratory. You can put mice in a cage with an electrically wired floor. When you send a painful electric current through the wires, the mice begin to fight and bite one another. That, by analogy, may be some clue to why men fight. But the study has to reach much further, away from the laboratory and into the home, the street, the forum.

One reason for the neglect of violence is that it is regarded as too isolated and restricted a subject. We have learned about the many disguises, pre-stages, and finer ramifications of sex. We have not yet learned that the murder drive also has many masks, that temptation, seduction, and many other influences play a role, that its causes and its effects are as widespread as those of sex.

Another obstacle to seeing violence concretely and frankly is the aspect of its so-to-say official standing. When the government wants to prevent violence, it speaks of law and order. But law and order are themselves maintained by the potential threat of violence. As Barbara Wootton expressed it, our society, and every civilized society, is in the last resort founded on violence. According to the sociologist Max Weber, the state is the monopoly for all legitimate physical violence, and all political structures are structures of violence. Surely that is insufficient for explaining either the state or violence, but it is a view, widely held, which has done it part to prevent our seeing violence as a whole. After

all, there is a prospect—not an illusion, but a scientific prognosis—
that with the progress of science and morality, nonviolent structures of society will be built.

Perhaps the strongest reason for the neglect of the subject of
violence is a growing disregard for the victim. Surely when a murder is committed we owe it to the victim to settle it properly, either
showing our condemnation by punishment or our understanding
by psychiatric or social treatment—all in an effort to prevent future
violence. When a war is ended we owe it to the victims to build
quickly a proper peace and at least try to prevent thereby a repetition. This is all far from the reality around us. Rarely is a murder
case fully studied in its complete context. As for wars, the creation of the Polish Corridor after the First World War is a good
example of a settlement which any schoolboy who could look at a
map would know was dangerously unstable. Two decades after the
Second World War, there was no peace settlement. Again, any
schoolboy could see by a glance at a map that the island of Taiwan
can no more represent the whole of China than the tail can wag
the dog and that the current fashion of dividing countries in half
is in the long run unworkable. Such arrangements are permanent
invitations to violence.

Monuments to the Unknown Soldier may assuage our conscience, but they do not fulfill our duty to the victims. The Soldier
has no name, and his death becomes something impersonal, distant, and general. Actually his death was anything but impersonal.
He did have a name, and an address, and people who loved him.
Were he to come back to life, would we be able to answer his
legitimate questions about violence? Moreover, considering London, Hiroshima, Dresden, and many other cities and villages,
there should also be monuments to the Unknown Civilian, especially to the Unknown Children, the greatest and most innocent
sufferers. Is it not significant, considering the thousands of child
victims, that nobody seems ever to have thought of erecting a
monument to the Unknown Child?

In the light of the number of victims and the reality of their
suffering, writers' discussions of subtle differences about what
anxiety really is or what existence really means become less important. These abstruse disquisitions have lost a good deal of

their meaning for us. It is as if nothing had happened and all these dead had not really died. The disregard for victims is related to a general lack of feeling for the average man. We have become interested in the elites, the exceptional, the specially gifted, the consumer, the glamorously neurotic, *et al.,* but not in the average man, his wife, and his child.

The lack of serious concern for the victim is illustrated by a recent case. A young man of prominent family in New York was accused of drunken driving, reckless driving, and leaving the scene of an accident in which five people, including a six-year-old child, were killed. Some witnesses said he was driving ninety miles an hour and later was unsteady on his feet. He had previously been guilty of thirteen traffic violations and had been deprived of his driver's license once. Yet it took a panel of three criminal-court judges only five minutes of deliberation to acquit him. *One minute per victim* is not enough. Young people who read about this in the newspapers or hear about it on the radio or on television can learn from this neither respect for law nor sympathy for victims.

Another point has contributed to the neglect of violence as a subject of scientific and serious literature. With regard to violence we are apt to deceive ourselves—and be deceived—about the degree of civilization we have reached. It seems a small error, but it may be a fatal one, to believe that we are already living in an era of nonviolence or even that a time of true nonviolence has begun. Most of the victims of the First World War had not the faintest idea, and would not have believed, that another big war could break out and last for more than four years. The countless civilians who perished prior to and during the Second World War in bombardments, concentration camps, euthanasia proceedings, extermination camps, jails, and slave-labor camps could not imagine that such a development was possible in the modern world. Far less could these victims believe that this would happen to their children. This is their tragic guilt. Their disbelief made them even more defenseless. They listened to those who in the early labor movement were called the "all-righters," those who say that everything is all right or at any rate by itself soon will be all right. The study of violence as such should help to dispel these illusions in the future.

We live at present in an era of the greatest potential violence in the history of the world. No, it has *not* always been so. There are many symptoms from diverse fields to bear that out. This is an age when a postwar period has drifted imperceptibly into a prewar period. The name we give it is peace. Wedged between the barbarism of yesterday and that of the morrow, we can kill more and faster than any previous generation.

The study of violence cannot rely merely on the historical data known prior to two decades ago. There are entirely new facts from which we can learn. Violence is not history, it is the present. First, of course, are the technological advances, atomic bombs, and missiles, which have made violence a mass threat of hitherto unimagined proportions. But we have learned (or maybe it is better to say we have had a chance to learn) about other circumstances which a generation ago would have seemed inconceivable; for example, even before the advent of atomic arms, unprecedented large-scale killings, especially of civilians, took place with what are called conventional weapons, like fire bombs. Related to this there have been changes in psychological and sociological attitudes which are not yet recognized officially and academically. These changes have played a part in bringing about the events, and the events in turn have reinforced the changes. These new attitudes can be easily summed up: the readiness for violence and brutality has increased in recent years. Not to recognize this is a form of social blindness. That is true technologically, socially, psychologically, and politically.

It is often said that the real danger lies in the unalterable nature of man. Recent history disproves that. Since it can be documented that the readiness to violence has increased, man can evidently be conditioned either upward or downward. When a serious modern playwright like Arthur Miller writes of "human nature as the only source of violence" and François Mauriac (referring to Nazi massacres) speaks of "the inherent ferocity of human nature," they unwittingly make themselves part of the atmosphere of violence of our time. For if it is all in human nature, and if we are all guilty, then nobody is guilty. And if we are all responsible, no man is responsible. We make it too easy for ourselves. We want to confess and participate at the same time. Such authors are in effect reverting to Spengler, a prophet of violence, who told the German people two years before Hitler came to power: "The tactics of man's life is that of a splendid, brave, cunning, cruel beast of prey. He lives attacking, killing, destroying. He has wanted to be master as long as he has existed."

Others like to isolate in their minds those who act brutally or violently and put them into ready-made categories—psychological, sociological, political, geographical, national, ethnic, racial. The facts of our time do not bear out such facile generalizations. The labels prevent us from seeing the often less palatable truths.

Romantic poets and dogmatic psychoanalysts believe that everybody who kills has severe guilt feelings afterward, consciously or unconsciously. That may have been true for some times and some places. It certainly is not always true today. Justification feelings bolstered by false social-philosophical ideas frequently replace guilt feelings. Freud described unconscious guilt feelings in a very restricted sense. He did not generalize them for almost all crime and violence as is often done now.

It has been widely stated by psychiatrists and lay writers that in our culture every killer must be psychopathic. That implies a rosy view of our society. It leaves out the terrible aspects of normality (however defined) in a violent age. We flatter ourselves if we believe that our social conditions are so far above reproach that only mentally ill adults and children can commit violence.

In trial after trial of men who committed mass murder during the Nazi regime, it has now been ascertained, some fifteen or twenty years after the crime, that the perpetrators were educated, respected citizens who lived typical, ordinary, successful lives with their wives and happy children. They were well-adjusted family men. To label them psychopathic personalities merely serves to obscure the issue. We come much closer to the truth if we realize with historian James Parks that the facts of these mass murders show "what man could organize and do, could watch and plan, and could find allies for in the whole operation among all the civilized countries of Europe." A British Member of Parliament, Maurice Edelman, expresses it this way: "The plague of our generation is this passion to give pain: to torture as in Algeria; to mass extermination as in Hitler's Germany; to mass obliteration, as in the preparations for atomic war."

Nor can one still say that mass murders and atrocities were committed only by violence-indoctrinated party fanatics. We learn differently from eyewitnesses. For example—and this is by no means an isolated or exceptional instance—when the German Army had to evacuate a Russian village, they herded all the inhabitants who had been left behind, old men and women, children, the disabled, into houses and set the houses afire. One little boy jumped from a window through the flames to the ground. He wept, terrified. He was picked up by the legs and tossed back into the flames. All this was not carried out by the specially trained SS troops, as is so often assumed, but was done by ordinary soldiers. In civilian life they were workers, peasants, artisans, clerks, businessmen.

To subsume this under the convenient term "individual sadism" would mean to misunderstand its essential nature. To label it "mob action" would also be misleading. It was routine. As a matter of fact, one of the German soldiers later stated quite truthfully that they had acted on orders. If you have to destroy a village with all its inhabitants, you cannot let one little boy escape. It would be like appearing at parade with unpolished shoes. What propaganda had been put into these men's heads, from cradle to Krupp, that they were able and willing to do this? A concrete study of that is necessary to understand them. However, what obedience to orders means in an ordinary soldier's head was clearly expressed about another mass killing in Poland. A corporal stated: "I did not think about my orders. I thought that they must be right and everything in order because they came from the highest quarters." The vast majority of those who committed such acts have never been called to account. They still think they acted right.

We bar the way to understanding if we assume that this can be explained by national characteristics. We may not be willing to concede this—until it is too late—but a very similar type of violence-thinking pervades our own "highest quarters," and a similar type of propaganda influences those who will think it right to obey orders. What is being thought of and prepared today is not only the destruction of villages, but that of large cities and whole provinces. No child will be able to crawl through those flames. The prediction of Michael Innes is about to become true: "We scrap a generation by violent and costly means, and very soon it is the cost and not the scrapping that troubles us."

Force and violence are deeply embedded in our whole economic process. A very substantial part of production, employment, economic planning, and research is devoted to the means of violence. We live in a violence economy. If this were to cease suddenly, the greatest economic dislocation would follow. The fear of violence is counterbalanced unconsciously by a fear that the production of the means for it would also cease. We are drawn into this stream and will continue to be until we have learned to dam it and put its water to better use.

Our cultural and psychological atmosphere is charged with the electricity of violence. The old know about death because they have seen their friends and acquaintances die. But many of them have not been exposed to violence. The young know all about violence but nothing about death. The big manifestations of violence, such as the mass killings of the recent past or those prepared for the future, are too big for us to visualize. Who can see in his mind's eye the reality of a million killed? Yet the statistical knowledge of this reality makes the little manifestations of violence seem too banal and insignificant. In large cities young salesgirls living in reputable neighborhoods have learned to keep revolvers in their apartments for protection. They feel they have to guard themselves not only from robbery or sexual attacks but also from the fierce cruelty so frequently shown on the streets and in the buildings. Perpetrators of these acts are usually very young. These youngsters in turn have been exposed through mass media to violent images continuously and relentlessly, in every context and every costume. No previous civilization can equal the amount or the degree of brutality.

We are victims of the hydrogen bomb before it is ever used, for the psychological fallout comes far in advance of the physical one. We are entering an era in which overnight the innocent become guilty, the murderer and the victim become one. Poets have called this the age of anxiety. More accurately but less poetically, one can say it is an age of complacence. It has also been called the age of space flight, but that has as a prerequisite that we stay alive to go there. According to my diagnosis, this is the age of violence.

The goddess of violence is a strong and alluring woman. She stands on a pedestal of granite, the granite of human indifference. Her emblem is not the sword, for she will use any weapon. Her eyes are not bandaged, for she chooses her victims. In one hand she holds a smoking, smoldering torch of hate. In the other she has a graven tablet with an inscription that reveals the secret of her power: "Let mankind continue in the false belief that violence will cease by itself."

From my psychiatric and sociological studies I have arrived at a double thesis. On the one hand, violence is becoming much more entrenched in our social life than people are willing to believe. On the other hand, it is in our power eventually to conquer and abolish it.

The following propositions may be formulated:

Violence is not so complicated and difficult a subject as those who do not want to do anything about it would have us believe. We must learn to understand it, not in its complexity but in its simplicity. Violence has to be seen as a whole. That is to say, all its manifestations have to be taken seriously, from little toy guns, military toys, and violent mass media to political murders, riots, and wars. These are very different matters, but they are not entirely unrelated. All forms of human violence are in some way connected with one another. The task is to trace the connections and to uncover the violence potential in whatever disguise it appears.

Violence and violence-mindedness are deeply embedded in our whole social life. Explosions of violence occur because we live in a peaceful dream about ourselves and permit the explosive material to accumulate. None of our traditional safeguards against violence have kept pace with the reality of violence.

Violent acts cannot be explained by human nature alone. Their roots reach further than the individual. All psychological forces operate in a social environment, and it is necessary in scientific studies to achieve a balance between the psychological and the social.

Violence is not over when it is over. It is always part of a process. If the process is not halted and the violence resolved, it will break out again, maybe in a different place or at a different time.

We underestimate the extent of violence in our time, do not give sufficient recognition to its inconspicuous prestages, and neglect decisive and rational measures afterward.

In different periods of history, the pattern of violence changes and the factors leading up to it change too.

The whole fabric of our civilization rests in the last analysis on the avoidance of violence.

# CHAPTER TWO

# Can Violence Be Studied Scientifically?

A fact, in science, is not a mere fact, but
an instance.
—BERTRAND RUSSELL, *The Scientific
Outlook*

THE wife of a thirty-six-year-old man and mother of four children
decided that she had to leave her husband and move out of the
house. There had been endless quarreling, and her husband had
often physically abused her and beaten her. He drank a lot. Just
as she finished packing the essential things for herself and her
children, her husband walked in, fired three bullets, and killed her.
Then he walked into the neighboring apartment, where he fired
some more shots, critically wounding his brother and killing his
brother's wife. He went on to another home, where he shot and
seriously wounded a woman. On the street he saw a man washing
his car, and he shot and wounded him critically. Then he walked
several blocks and invaded another family's home. For more than
three hours he terrorized them at gunpoint, drinking the beer he
had found there and tearfully talking about his unhappy marriage.
Finally he took the eighteen-year-old daughter of the house at
gunpoint to this family's car. He put her in the front seat next
to him and drove away. Every once in a while he pistol-whipped
her; finally he raped her in the most brutal fashion.

Such a case is part of the raw material for the scientific study
of violence. It raises many questions. Could it have been prevented?
By psychiatry? By social-service procedures? By the domestic-
relations court? By a combination of all three? Can it teach us any

lessons about other, less spectacular cases? What could have been done to straighten out this marriage? Where could the wife have found help? How important was alcohol in leading to the final killing spree? How accurate are newspaper reports, which influence public opinion in this field? Often (as in this case) they report mostly about the exciting chase that led to the arrest of the killer. Who will help the surviving victims? Invading a home and terrorizing a family sadistically is a frequent theme of stories on television and in comic books. That is a very minor point but can we ignore it completely if we want to generalize about violence? Does not *every* factor need to be taken seriously? Can we draw conclusions from such a gross and obvious case about minor outbursts of violence? Does the mere recital of the violent spree of such a man, unrelieved by everyday details of his life, give us a realistic picture of the man—and of the event itself?

I had to ask a judge once for permission to visit a murderer in jail. My purpose, I told him, was a follow-up study after a psychiatric examination which I had carried out long before. The judge exploded, "That is absurd! You want to study one murderer to prevent another man from murdering!" The judge's reaction was a little hasty, but the question whether violence can be studied scientifically is a very legitimate one.

To carry out such studies, we need not start entirely without premises. In any study of human violence, that would be impossible, because there is some value judgment even in the best-intentioned objectivity. Even if we are not conscious of these premises, they enter subconsciously. Cain and Abel cannot both be right. Instead of making a claim of no premises, we have to start from reality-based ones, arrived at by scientific reasoning. At a later stage of inquiries, these premises can be translated into hypotheses which we must verify and prove.

If we do not start from sound premises, we leave the door open to false ones. The influential German philosopher Karl Jaspers, now professor of philosophy in Basel, Switzerland, writes that "the impulse to the application of violence," . . . "the pleasure in violence," . . . "the impulse to sacrifice oneself in such violence, to die or to be victorious"—all these are "fundamental human instincts" which cannot be abolished. It is most significant, not to say ominous, that he makes such a statement in his lecture on "The Atom Bomb and the Future of Man." But there is no scientific evidence for this. If human nature is permitted and helped to develop properly, it is not compelled or even inclined to violence or destructive aggression. The claim is also often made that violence is an integral part of human life. That is what the producers of mass media and their experts say, defending stories of torture, mutilation, and murder for children. These stories are supposed to teach children what human life is really like and to prepare them for it. But violence is no more an integral part of human life than tuberculosis, syphilis, or cancer. We study these afflictions to prevent them. This is part of the medicoscientific approach to the study of violence. It has as a definite aim the prediction, reduction, and prevention of violence.

Science requires the isolation of a problem. With violence, that is difficult. On the one hand, it is a special phenomenon; on the other, it has many different manifestations and connections. To circumscribe the concept of violence too narrowly or to diffuse it too much may lead to error. It has been said, for example, that war is in all things and that Mars, the god of war, does not exist any more as an entity but is present everywhere. That means diluting a problem to such an extent that it disappears, and such overgeneralization can lead to nothing. If we want to destroy Mars, we have to localize him a little better.

We must distinguish between individual killing, such as murder, and collective killing in war. War is not a mere addition of aggressive acts by individuals. It is on an entirely different plane. It is a collective action to be understood only if we consider the objective social and economic laws that determine it. The causes that lead to war lie deeper than any probing of the individual unconscious can reveal. They belong to much deeper Plutonic levels of historico-economic processes. What goes on in the "dark recesses of the mind" is often easier to find and less relevant than what goes on in the dark recesses of society, and to try to explain war by the subjective psychology of individuals alone is futile. War is not an individual aberration. If Hitler had been analyzed by Freud, the Second World War would not have been avoided.

But the distinction between individual and collective killing is not an absolute one. All manifestations of violence are related. This does not mean that there is an abstract essence of violence. It means that there are concrete connections, ramifications, and similarities. A comprehensive study of violence can be done only by taking these diverse manifestations into account. Recently when an adolescent who had committed a violent delinquency was asked why he had gotten into trouble, he answered quite truthfully, "There will probably be an atomic war in the near future, and I don't expect to survive."

✓ Even to compare murder and war is controversial. To regard murder as war may seem uncivic; to view war as murder, unpatriotic. But that should not deter us from tracing some of the connections.

In some primitive clan societies, a murder committed for whatever reason was tantamount to a declaration of war between two clans. It could last for years. It could spread to whole villages and districts. In some parts of the world—for example, in the Balkans —such wars still occurred in the early nineteenth century. Gradually, with the progress of civilization, measures were introduced to reduce these warlike outbreaks of violence. Sometimes the number of those permitted to participate was limited, or a free interval, what we now would call a cooling-off period, was decreed between the original murder and the ensuing war. In France, for instance, a "King's forty days" was enforced. If any warlike act occurred during these forty days, the warrior was treated like a common murderer. In the eleventh century, a *treuga dei* (armistice of God) was decreed. According to this, any violent, warlike self-help was forbidden from Wednesday night until Monday morning—except in case of real war.

One of my patients was at the front in several battles of the First World War. He had never been interested in politics and knew nothing about conscientious objectors, but he felt deeply that any killing was murder. He was considered a good soldier and got promoted; but he told me that during the whole time, he never did anything that might wound or kill anybody. When he was in command of soldiers, he deliberately directed them so that nobody would get hurt. Once when he was in charge of a number of enemy prisoners, he arranged it so they could escape and get back to their own side. None of them escaped. They probably felt as he did.

This abstention from violence (which is not at all infrequent in wars) is in contrast to the opposite, wanton violence. During the civil war in France in 1848, citizens erected barricades in Paris from which they exchanged shots with soldiers. A bystander watched the men on one of the barricades and finally told them that their way of handling a gun was all wrong. He took a gun and showed them how to do it expertly: he aimed the gun, fired, and killed an officer at the end of the street. The men on the barricade were delighted and asked him to stay with them and join in the fight. He refused, explaining, "I am not interested in politics." This episode is reminiscent of another which occurred almost a hundred years later. After the fall of France during the Second World War, P. G. Wodehouse, the famous creator of Jeeves, was royally installed by the Nazis in the Hotel Adlon in Berlin and broadcast for the Nazi Propaganda Ministry. He extolled the Nazis as "a fine body of men." When asked about this later, he said in his defense, "I never was interested in politics."

In studying an individual who has committed a serious violent act, we sometimes find there was a long preparatory period. During that time, psychological and social forces driving toward the act and opposing it were contending. Finally a stage was reached where the counterforces proved too weak and the violent act became unavoidable and predictable. A similar process exists in nations. The socioeconomic and political forces driving toward war become stronger and the physical preparations for war achieve a momentum of their own. In addition, the vilification of the opponent makes ever more headway. The counterforces are overcome. A stage is reached—just as in the individual—when national violence has become no longer avoidable.

Individual and collective violence have this in common, that in their scientific study, three phases or periods have to be distinguished:

1. The action phase itself
2. The previolence phase
3. The postviolence phase

This is the pattern of violence. All three phases are important and illuminate one another.

The third phase is the most likely to be neglected, but what society does with a murder case afterward often throws light on how it could have occurred in the first place. If the past is minimized in the postviolence phase, the seeds of future violence are sown. For example, the village of Putten, in Holland, is widely known as the "village of widows and orphans." In retaliation for partisan activity (which the villagers had nothing to do with) the village was destroyed and the male population of Putten was sent to concentration camps, where 540 perished. Nazi Air Force general Christiansen, who ordered this retaliation, spent three years in prison as a war criminal. Today he is still an honorary citizen of the town where he was born, and a street is still named after him. Recently he was honored with a gold medal for his services to aviation. Instead of becoming a symbol of a new dedication to humaneness, the "village of widows and orphans" casts a dark shadow over the future.

Wherever violence is disregarded and forgotten, it perpetuates itself. Wherever it remains unresolved, it persists as a focus of infection. He who helps to hush up a murder case becomes himself an associate in guilt for the next murder.

To resolve violence in the postviolence phase means to elucidate and explain those factors, direct or indirect, near or distant, which led to it in the first place and to condemn, counteract, or abolish them. Paradoxical as it may seem, we have a responsibility not only for the present and future but also for the past. If we leave past violence unsettled, unlamented, and often even unrecorded, we make ourselves accomplices to it.

A war without a proper peace is very much like a murder which remains undetected, unpunished, and ununderstood. What "properly resolved" or "unresolved" means in concrete instances has to be studied, but it is often clear enough if the facts are adequately investigated and faced. The Treaty of Versailles was bad enough; the no-treaty after the Second World War is worse.

All the sciences that have any relation to human behavior, especially violent behavior—from neurophysiology and anthropology to sociology and psychology—are pertinent to the scientific study of violence. Criminology has a role to play. So has history, if it is not restricted to just diplomatic history. But these sciences cannot be added to one another like eggs in a basket. It is the task of what is called today interdisciplinary research to strive for a comprehensive view without sacrificing the discipline of each separate science. This will enable researchers in various fields to study violence from different angles. The danger is that questionable methods and speculative tenets of one science may be taken over by another. In this way, some sociologists have become amateur psychoanalysts, and some psychopathologists amateur sociologists, without concrete data.

There are some people who believe that it is scientific to devise methods for killing, but "not scientific" to try to avoid it. Naturally the scientific study of violence cannot be a "pure" science. We the observers ourselves live in an atmosphere that breeds the spirit of violence actually and figuratively, in a thousand ways. Moreover, it is difficult to define the limitations of this field or to turn the findings into figures and measurements. However, science is not only curves and tables. Michael Swann, professor of natural history at Edinburgh University, expresses it like this: "Science in the last resort is not figures or experiments, but a way to understand things."

A number of years ago I was asked by a magazine to write an article on the race factor in contemporary life. I had just done a study of white and colored children from the state of Delaware as part of the preparation for the famous 1954 U.S. Supreme Court decision abolishing segregation. In this paper, I said that this racial discrimination "is in the deepest sense anti-educational" and that racial slights produce the deepest emotional wounds, much deeper than is realized. The magazine refused the article (which was later published in a psychiatric journal), for the reason that I had not "proved" my point. Indeed, I had not in the manner of the physical sciences. One cannot prove that with graphs, statistics, and experiments. I had relied on clinical judgment about concrete cases. Clinical science is a science too. Without it, very little of modern psychiatry and psychoanalysis would exist.

It is widely recognized that the physical sciences, especially nuclear physics, exact as they are, have close connections with politicomilitary situations. It is apt to be overlooked that psychology and the social sciences also have connections with political matters even though they may be submerged. If this is not clearly understood and recognized, it introduces sources of bias and error. Just as we use the physical sciences to perfect killing, we should use the social sciences to prevent killing. Admittedly the behavioral and social sciences lag far behind the physical ones. We know more about the movement of an electron than about that of money, more about the speed of distant stars than about the beginning and end of a depression or of industrial cycles, and more about the courses of celestial bodies and the possibilities of clashes between them than about those of neighboring nations.

For the study of problems of individual violence, a combination of what may be called dynamic clinical psychiatry and sociology is the most fruitful approach. In both these sciences, it is often harder to obtain all the data of violence accurately than it is to interpret them. Description comes before analysis. And in the field of violence, the task of description is not by any means done.

Psychiatry is a potent instrument. The danger is that it is sometimes applied to explain brutal and sadistic acts in a way that actually amounts to condoning them. We are apt to use psychiatry the way a drunk uses a lamppost: not for the light but to lean against. To talk about violence within the confines of individual psychology or pathology alone means tearing the act away from all its complex social connections. This aspect of violent death is well realized in J. B. Priestley's play *An Inspector Calls*. Following the tragic death of a young working girl, we are shown the lives and involvement of her fiancé and of the other members of a well-to-do middle-class family—father, mother, son, and daughter. Nobody specifically wanted this girl's death, but objectively existing social conditions make them all factors in its causation. They are no longer innocent bystanders but have become guilty participants.

Looked at superficially, it may appear that there is a lot of inevitability about violence. But the more we concentrate scientifically on a concrete question in the general stream of violence, the more do we find that pure coincidence, accident, and chance disappear and causal sequences of events emerge.

# CHAPTER THREE

# Why Men Kill

Have you explored the inner relations of
an act? Do you know the causes with
certainty, why it happened, why it had to
happen? If you had, you would not be so
hasty with your judgments.
—GOETHE

Terrible are the weaknesses of violence.
—STANISLAW J. LEC

## Some Basic Considerations

### NEUROPATHOLOGY

IN the brain of animals and man there is a mechanism situated
in lower brain centers which is intimately connected with readiness
for violence. Special events in the outside world can stimulate it.
These events have something to do with the survival of the animal
or its species. This mechanism is the substrate of what may be
spoken of as rage. The animal gets ready to threaten or carry out
an attack. Once the mechanism is stimulated, it can still be in-
hibited by the higher centers in the brain, the cerebral cortex.
Closely connected with this neurological stimulation are chemical
changes in the blood which add to the quick preparedness of the
animal. We know so much about this physiological process because
we can reproduce it or imitate it closely in experiments—for
example, with rats. This can be done without any events which
threaten the animals' survival. We remove the higher brain centers
or separate them from the lower ones. This creates a state in which
almost any strong enough stimulus creates a ragelike reaction.

This is called sham rage. We can make these outbursts of rage disappear by inactivating certain lower brain centers, namely, the posterior part of the hypothalamus.

Very rarely, a primitive rage mechanism is set in motion in human beings with definite pathological brain conditions. It is always accompanied by a disorder of consciousness and subsequent amnesia. A young patient in Johns Hopkins Hospital, while talking amiably to his doctor, suddenly grabbed a lamp from the desk and tried to hit a nurse over the head. Afterward he had no recollection at all of having done this and no idea as to why he had. Before such a pathological rage is accepted as a plea for lack of responsibility in court, however, the clinical diagnosis of a definite pathological condition must be carefully and firmly established.

Violence is always based on physical movements. These tendencies to movement, which we call motor drives, can be greatly increased in rare instances through specific damage to the brain. In the early 1920's, for example, there was an outbreak of epidemic encephalitis. Children were observed who had a tremendous tendency to overactivity and who in some cases committed violent acts. Their destructive aggressiveness was beyond the control of their willpower. They suffered from a specific brain infection. In occasional instances, milder forms of this disease are a factor in otherwise unexplainable outbursts of juvenile violence.

The fact that we can isolate in the brain an ancient preformed readiness for violence does not mean that there is in man an inborn, unalterable, eternal instinct for violence. Nor is there any evidence in neurophysiology or in clinical psychopathology that we have an inborn, fixed amount of instinctive, destructive aggressiveness which must be given vent to in one way or another. We do not have to behave like rats. Primitive mechanisms have been modified via the higher centers in the cerebral cortex whose functions, according to Pavlov, are socially determined. And with the progress of civilization, they will be further modified. There is no reason to postulate an eternal contrast between the rage-ready individual and a curbing society. On the contrary, everything points to a future time when with respect to violence the interests of the individual and those of society will be identical. It is only in that distant future that one can say that anybody who starts violence must have something wrong with his brain.

## ANIMAL PSYCHOLOGY

In the animal kingdom, violence is the rule. For many animals, to be nonviolent is not natural. In fact, nature sacrifices one creature to the other with fearful pain. A fitch will bite through the spine of a number of smaller animals so that they cannot run away and keep them as a living larder. "Cruel, brutal, horrible," comments the nature writer Hermann Loens. The philosophers and theologians have a hard time with nature's violence, when they consider it at all. Before the suppressed parts of his autobiography were published, it was generally assumed that Darwin had lost his religious faith—he had once intended to become a country clergyman—because of his doctrine of evolution. But it is now known that this came from something else. A keen and sympathetic observer, Darwin could never get over nature's infliction of pain on little animals. He asked: "What advantage can there be in the sufferings of millions of the lower animals throughout almost endless time?" The question has never been answered.

But this is not the whole story. By and large, animals kill for only one reason: survival. Violence is not identical with hate and hostility. Animals do not kill for hate, spite, revenge, sadism, or greed. They are generally averse to killing members of their own species. Most important of all, they never systematically kill large numbers of the same species. That is a prerogative of man. So when we speak of massacres, extermination camps, mass bombings, and so on, we should not refer to the "bestial" in man. It isn't the beast, it is man himself—or better, perhaps, superman.

Some modern studies of animal psychology, especially by L. D. Clark of the University of Utah, throw an interesting light on human violence. Even animals well equipped for attack and predisposed to it may never display destructive aggression unless it is elicited by specific environmental conditions. In contrast to hunger and sex, destructive aggression is not an instinct or even a drive, in the usual sense of these terms. It is not reduced by being expressed or acted out. It is greatly influenced by learning. These careful investigations should be kept in mind when the facile argument is used that violent stories help children to act out their aggressions.

### ANTHROPOLOGY

The existence of a "golden age" of nonviolence among primitive people is not borne out by research. Primitive man was not nonviolent. From the scattered anthropological evidence, we must conclude, on the contrary, that there was a lot of violence: cruel punishments, mutilations, torture, infanticide, selling children of other tribes into slavery, accusations of witchcraft, with consequent retaliations, flagellation, human sacrifices, and so on. Myths give us an indication. According to an ancient Greek myth, for example, Zagreus, son of Zeus and Persephone, was killed by the Titans, who tore him to pieces and devoured him. Athena rescued his heart, which Zeus then swallowed. The Titans were killed by Zeus. Very similar stories existed in different parts of the world. It has been inferred with some justification that such stories have a parallel in ancient primitive practices. So if we want to study violence from the point of view of eventually creating a non-violent world, we must look not backward but forward.

It would be wrong, however, to conclude that primitive men had an instinctive pugnacity or natural ferocity. Their violence grew out of their circumstances and living conditions, the corresponding social institutions, and the fact that the outside world was full of threats. Infanticide was not due to cruelty or absence of feeling. Primitive as well as aboriginal parents were very kind and indulgent to their children. But they lived under such adverse conditions and had to be on the move so often and for so long that their babies had to be sacrificed sometimes for the common good. Social checks were invented to prevent this practice as time went on. For instance, girls were betrothed in infancy so that the infants could be preserved.

Human sacrifice is another example contradicting the theory of a natural, instinctive cruelty and savageness. That was not the expression of any individual instinct of brutality. At a given stage of civilization, such sacrifices were considered necessary social measures, and, as H. J. Massingham has pointed out, they were sponsored by "science, national security, state policy, official morality and the Divine Blessing."

What primitive man did not know and practice is the deliberate, emotionless, systematized, mechanical violence in the form of mass killings and bombings which modern history has made us acquainted with. This mass violence, it may be interesting to note, has been sponsored by the same social institutions that sponsored the old practice of human sacrifice.

Anthropology teaches us that violence represents the growing pains of mankind. This growth is an arduous path.

## The Structure and Dynamics of Murder

In New York City there is more than a murder a day. It is difficult to translate such an impersonal statistic into common human experience. What arouses our emotion is the individual case, and some particularly atrocious murder occasionally does that. For a while then the public is troubled. Lincoln Steffens, an experienced editor and reporter, said that the news usually lasts no more than eleven days, whatever the crime is. The most typical response of the man in the street, the person who appears in the judicial process in the role of juror, is the question, "Why did he kill?" It is a key question.

In some of the most primitive societies, this question was never raised. If a man killed a stranger, it was not considered a crime; if he killed a member of the tribe, he drew the severest punishment. Why he did it made little difference. As a matter of fact, if it was accidental the punishment was the same as if he had done it with intent. The revulsion against murder was so great and so emotional that only the event itself—not the mentality of the agent —was regarded as important. As a scientific problem to be solved by scientific means, the question of why is not yet a hundred years old. The Italian psychiatrist Cesare Lombroso (1836-1909) went beyond the purely moralistic approach and directed scientific attention to the study of violent crime. We no longer believe in his findings or methods, but he was one of the first to search for a scientific answer to the question of why men kill. His answer, that the physical constitution and heredity explain cold-blooded murder, was not confirmed, although it is occasionally revived in some new garb, even to explain juvenile violence. Lombroso's theory is an evasion of unwelcome psychological and social questions. We now have other sciences, other methods, and other answers. In the forefront is the study of the life and mind of the murderer and his social environment. The quest is difficult and laborious.

Acts of violence are rarely investigated well enough to bring to light all the causal factors. It is usually more difficult to collect all the facts than to analyze them. Sometimes what seems to be a good enough reason turns out on closer study to be superficial, neglecting deeper motives. At other times, a well-sounding depth-psychological speculation turns out to be wrong when other objective details about a person's life become known. The more concrete our analysis, the more valid our generalizations. That very plausible explanations may mislead is well known in the history of science. It was universally assumed that when a very big stone and a little stone were dropped from a height, the big stone would drop faster. Galileo proved by concrete investigation that this was not so. When two organisms mated, it seemed only reasonable that the characteristics of their offspring would be intermediate between those of their parents. Mendel and Darwin showed that the results were different. In the same way facile interpretations by analogy and not by analysis have been given for acts of violence. Usually motives come in bundles and are deflected by circumstances. Whenever a single traumatic childhood experience is incriminated or an explanation propounded which is too pat and leaves no room for other significant details we should—like good detectives—suspect the conclusion.

This can be best demonstrated with literary works where we have at our disposal all the details that were available to the person who made the interpretation. For example Fritz Wittels, a leading psychoanalyst and biographer of Freud, in interpreting Theodore Dreiser's *An American Tragedy,* came to the conclusion that an unconscious incestuous wish for his sister was the effective motive of Clyde Griffiths' murder of his pregnant girl friend. Granted that such an unconscious motive may have existed, it was only a very small part of the story and could be effective only in conjunction with much more potent causes and concrete social circumstances. What is so important in this is that this type of speculative one-factor interpretation has influenced a large part of the public, especially writers. It has also affected the legal profession, which is becoming inclined to credit psychiatry with an omniscience it does not possess. *An American Tragedy* is an antiviolence book of deep social significance. Fancy and misleading interpretations are an ingredient of the smog of violence in which we live.

In the study of murderers, there are two pitfalls we have to guard against. One is to regard murder as a mystery. We hear and read a lot about elementary, irrational forces, about mysterious interstices of the human mind, and about deeply hidden aggressive drives which in obscure ways make a man a murderer. It sounds fine after dinner to speak of these unfathomable depths from which violence comes, unexpected and unpredictable. According to such speculations, murder is not murder but is always something else. Not only does such mystification cover up the real issues, it provides a kind of justification for not assuming responsibility, and it even lends a touch of glamour and romance to murder. There is nothing glamorous or romantic about murder; it is a catastrophic event in the life of man. It is also not true, as is so often said, that there is something very mysterious about war. There is no "war impulse." In our time the very clarity of the causes and effects of war is terrifying, especially in view of mankind's unclear helplessness up to now to prevent it. There is nothing obscure about war. Nowadays it is a calculated risk. That it often turns out to be a miscalculated risk does not make it mysterious.

The second fallacy about murderers is the generalization from our knowledge of adult neurotics which assumes that every murderer must be suffering from some individual pathological condition. That is supposed to be an enlightened and humanitarian point of view. It is just the opposite. Actually, in the study of individual violence, we need more precision in distinguishing between what is an individual pathological mental condition and what are social phenomena whose main cause does not lie in individual morbidity. Of course, we have learned, largely from Freud, that the normal reaches far into the abnormal and that the abnormal can be understood to a large extent in terms of the normal. But not to distinguish between those who are ill and those who are not is as crude as the error the primitives made in not distinguishing between accident and intent. That is not the way to protect society or to safeguard the rights of genuinely ill individuals. As Sir Norwood East pointed out in his study of male murderers, a person may be maladjusted without being a "pathological case."

I spent many hours examining Raymond Fernandez and Martha Beck of the famous Lonely Hearts case. The pair had made it a practice to become acquainted with lonely women who had money, through a Lonely Hearts Club correspondence. Usually they posed as brother and sister. Fernandez would court the women and propose marriage to them. Under some ingenious and elaborate pretext, they would induce a woman to turn over to them all her money and property. Then they would kill her and leave the locality for new pastures. Their murderous operations reached over a number of states and even into Europe. During my examination of her, I turned over in my mind several theories about Martha Beck. She might, for instance, be a neurotic person who had fallen under a hypnoticlike spell of Fernandez. But the cold facts—and "cold" is the proper word—dispelled all my theories. In one instance, after they had killed a woman and were about to leave the house, Martha Beck killed the two-year-old daughter of the slain woman as an extra precaution. I was talking very seriously with her one day in the Women's House of Detention in the Jefferson Market Court Building in Manhattan. The adult victims in the case up for trial were one thing, I said; but what about the baby? "Tell me about drowning the little child in the bathtub." The recollection did not disturb her in the least. She burst into a hearty laugh. "No!" she said. "It was not in a *bathtub*. It was in a *washtub* in the basement." She explained that a crying baby would have drawn attention to the house and that, if questioned, the child might have identified her, at least to the extent of saying that a woman had been there. This was a careful calculation. I had to admit to myself that it was rational, not irrational. Despite all my probing, I found no evidence that I could interpret as symptoms of pathology. The motive of naked greed overshadowed everything else.

Greed led directly to this cold-blooded cruelty. And anyone who says that excessive greed is a mental disease in our society does not know that society. He may have read Freud, but he skipped Balzac and the early Upton Sinclair.

In the public consciousness, however, this case, which is so significant for the understanding of one type of violence, appears in the guise of the alibi of abnormality. Popular writers who do not know the psychiatric facts describe the case differently, one widely read account being announced as "one of the most complete case studies of a crime on record." It reaches the conclusion that both partners were severely mentally diseased and suffered from "compulsions"! Are there compulsions to kill a two-year-old baby to cover up tracks of other murders? The explanation given is that there were "blind motivations based on obsessive urges hidden deep within the subconscious minds of the slayers." Money was only a "relatively minor factor." Sometimes when I think of the heartless scene at the basement washtub, I ask myself how decadent a society must be to excuse such a callous deed as a compulsion emanating from a mysterious, unspecified, and unexamined unconscious. Again, as so often happens in the postviolence phase, light is thrown on the atmosphere in which these crimes (not all of which, in this case, were cleared up) could develop in the first place: the public is offered and accepts an abstruse, unrealistic pseudopsychological explanation, and the abuses of some of the Lonely Hearts Clubs continue.

The general factors entering into the causation of violent crime are very similar to those in other crimes. They do not operate singly or directly, but form part of a multidimensional whole. They interact with one another and with more specific factors. The relative importance of each has been much discussed, with inconclusive results. The main factors are clear, however. They have been outlined by those with much experience in this field, from Clarence Darrow to Justice Curtis Bok, both of them jurists with advanced knowledge and conscience. Among these factors are poverty, including need for money in special emergency situations; adverse conditions in the home, which accounts for the predominance of domestic homicide; failure to capture criminals (only one felon in five is caught); failure to settle a case properly so that the educational function of the law can come into play; unwise legislation, *i.e.,* harsh treatment of minor offenses or differences in law in neighboring states; glorification of crime and violence in shows, publications, and mass media; vindictiveness in the penal system. These items have to be related to specific situations, persons, localities, and other more special causes. In violent crime the geographic factor, which covers complex economic and cultural conditions, is very important. For example, according to the Cambridge Studies in Criminal Science series, crimes of violence are insignificant in both incidence and gravity in London as compared with New York, Chicago, or any other major city in America. And Professor Leon Radzinowicz, director of the Institute of Criminology of Cambridge University, has written that the crime reports of the Federal Bureau of Investigation read to him like war communiqués. The United States homicide rate is six times that of England. Any attempt at individual psychology has to take this perspective into account.

There is no unitary type, psychologically or pathologically, of persons who commit violence. The old saying, often quoted, that men don't commit murder for a reason but because they are murderers is certainly wrong. Nor can we be satisfied with saying that every person is different from every other. In one respect, that is of course true; but if we think only of differences, we cannot arrive at scientific conclusions. Every single rose is different from any other; but if we restricted ourselves to that, there would be no botany.

Our knowledge is limited because we know the psychology only of the unsuccessful murderers. It has been estimated that one person in thirty-five in the United States must be an uncaught criminal. Sometimes he may be a murderer. I have had occasion to study several patients who had committed murder but were unarraigned, but that is exceptional. Usually they are not available for study.

Despite these limitations and difficulties, we can indicate some personality traits which seem to recur in individuals who commit violent acts. Of course, these traits are not direct causes, nor are they in any way specific. They occur also in individuals who have nothing to do with violence, just as the symptom of coughing occurs in people without tuberculosis as well as in those who have it. Under certain circumstances, however, and through unhappy conjunction with other factors, they may play a certain aggravating or precipitating role. As a supplement to psychiatric examinations and tests, I have sometimes carried out field studies in the neighborhood and spoken to friends, girl friends, clergymen, employers, fellow employees, neighbors, and relatives. In this way, I obtained a fuller picture of a person's objective life situation and his characteristics. While traits so discovered may not help us to explain a murder, knowledge of them may help us to understand it.

The violent cannot by any means be summed up as the vicious. Their traits cannot be subsumed under any common denominator. It is not usually the case that several of these traits combine to lead to a certain result. What happens is rather that one trait becomes more potent in the presence of other traits and circumstances. The violence-prone may have a readiness to hate. That does not mean that they desire or like to hate, but that they have developed a habit of reacting with hate. Hating is disagreeable and painful. Overwhelming hate is always allied to fear. In the same way, overwhelming fear of other people is always allied to hate. This emotional combination is hard to bear. The building up of hate, which is in itself a complex phenomenon based on contradictory feelings, can occur under very different circumstances and from very different motivations. Rarely does it erupt into violence, but sometimes it does. When the object of the hate-fear is dead, the painful feelings cease. That is part of the magic of murder.

The cycle of murder and release may be repeated. A young man was found in school to be a gifted violinist and became a musician. His parents were divorced when he was five. As a result he was shuttled back and forth between his parents and among other relatives. When he was twelve, his father drowned in a heroic attempt to rescue a girl. His son admired him for this and greatly mourned his death. He was very ambitious about his music, and as an adolescent, after a not very successful performance, he attempted suicide. People who knew him described him as having a very likable disposition. His mother was beautiful. Of his relationship with her, he said, "We did not have that formality that is usual between mother and son. We were more like brother and sister."

On another occasion, he said, "The best way I could tell it to you is to tell you that I felt towards her the same way that Hamlet felt towards his mother." He feared his mother's disapproval and resented her interference. He felt she was responsible for the divorce, although he knew no details. Both his father and mother remarried after the divorce. He resented this on the part of his mother but not his father. He had very few and only minor fights with other boys, but when he did he reacted with considerable hate toward his opponents.

He married at eighteen. "I was too young, not biologically but financially." The marriage was not successful. There were jealousies and disagreements. One day, after many arguments, he shot and killed his wife. Then he put her on a couch and said a prayer over her body. Immediately afterward, he went to his mother and told her the whole story. She advised him to surrender to the police, which he did. He was spared the death penalty, and the judge, who was impressed that there was "good in him," gave him a sentence from twenty years to life in prison.

His prison record was excellent. He was in only one minor fight, and in that he was on the defensive. He continued his musical education by correspondence so successfully that he started arranging classical pieces for popular music and also wrote original compositions. Some of his work became known on the outside and gained wide recognition. As a result, the Court of Pardons, after an investigation, felt that there was "every evidence of rehabilitation and that there is every probability that upon his release he shall never again commit any serious breach of the criminal law." After nineteen years in jail, he was paroled.

He was very successful professionally in the outside world, got a job arranging music, and kept on composing. He had become a celebrity and met other celebrities. He was now thirty-eight. After only a few months of liberty, it all ended. Headlines blazed:

MUSIC FREES HIM, MURDER JAILS HIM

He had stabbed and killed a young woman with whom he had had a love affair. A friend of his who knew him well told me, "She was more than a girl for him, she was a symbol, a symbol of the world."

It was after this second murder that I examined him. Closer analysis of the processes, nature, and motives of his conduct revealed an element of symbolic matricide in both murders. In any case, it was possible to demonstrate to the satisfaction of the District Attorney a strong pathological aspect in this quiet, soft-spoken man. He was not charged with first-degree murder, for which the death penalty would have been certain, but was permitted to plead murder in the second degree. By what seemed simple arithmetical reasoning, the court arrived at the sentence: whereas he had received twenty years to life for the first murder, he received forty years to life for the second. 1366354

In acts of violence, there is often something that is supremely arrogant. The persons are habitually disposed to lift themselves, not by work or thought but by some quick action against others, to something that is higher in their eyes. This is closely related to feelings of inferiority. They may not necessarily be merely imaginary. Frequently, overaggressive action is rooted in a sense of passivity. Violence is often connected with incompetence and sexual violence always means sexual incompetence. When committed alone or in collaboration with others an act of violence may mitigate or remove a man's habitual feelings of inferiority. It frees him from the burden of his own personality.

Another personality trait is a tendency to ruminate and give in to feelings of uncertainty and indecision. There may then be a habitual tendency to think of a violent act as a means to rehabilitate himself in the eyes of others and himself. There are people who from their early years on have an aversion to thinking things out slowly and carefully and to weighing facts as they arise. They don't like to deliberate. They seek a quick way out and violence may be one. One may say paradoxically, that what is called a deliberate act of violence is sometimes due to habitual evading of deliberation. These are people who desire fast, magic effects and want to escape from having to make a choice. They may have more inhibitions about some minor unconventional act than about seriously injuring somebody.

Other individuals have a tendency to use their hands or fists readily in and as an argument. In minor disagreements with playmates when they were children, or in adult life with roommates, waiters, or taxi drivers, they are prone to threaten to strike. They often get into fistfights over trivial causes. Frequently these are individuals who are not verbally expressive. There is an analogy with observations in animal psychology. Some cats which are otherwise good-natured and affectionate express disapproval if petted in a wrong way or a wrong place by striking out quickly with a paw. That is not intended to injure, but merely means no. Other cats of equally friendly temperament never do that, but express their disapproval vocally by some almost articulate sound which also means no.

The readiness to fight comes sometimes from the influence of violence in the home, the street, or the mass media. Sometimes no such influences can be traced. These persons may never get into serious trouble, but I have found this trait in the history of individuals who have committed homicide, especially in cases where there was a large impulsive element. One young man killed his girl friend, who had rejected him. After a long argument, he hit her and finally strangled her. Those who knew him well could not imagine him capable of such an act. But they recalled how often he got into minor, innocuous fistfights. When he told me the story of the crime, he did not in his own mind consciously connect the crime with his previous fights; but his account of it sounded much like all the others, except that this one was a fight to the finish.

The most important point to realize about personality traits of the murderer is that it is not possible to characterize him by one single, pervading trait. Contradictory ones can exist side by side in the same person. That is as true of murderers as it is of others. As the Swiss poet Conrad Ferdinand Meyer put it:

> I am not a figured-out book of fiction,
> I am a man with his contradiction.

During psychotherapy of delinquent youths, I have found that what may appear as elementary character qualities (and are frequently described as such in the literature on juvenile delinquency) can often be not only modified but turned into the opposite. Children whose sensitivity was blunted and who committed brutal acts without scruples became friendly and considerate. Some individuals are oversensitive and may react destructively when their feelings are hurt. Others are just the opposite, cool and insensitive. Frequently both sets of traits are present in the personality structure (as the psychiatrist Kretschmer pointed out for adults and the child psychiatrist Kramer for children). Environmental influences determine which will be dominant in a given situation and in their general development.

The grounds for why men kill are not so different from those for other wrong things they do. They are based on all kinds of negative emotions: greed, jealousy, fear and the persisting memory of fear, distortion and frustration of sexual development, hunger for revenge, petty angers and irritations, hostility, wild ambition, sadistic fixations, resentment, unforgiven humiliations, rivalries in almost any sphere. These emotions are kindled by very different circumstances always in close relation to the mores and customs of the time. For example, it was to be expected that the frequent irritations and frustrations with the upkeep of household appliances could lead in an extreme case to violence. Recently a thirty-two-year-old TV repairman had a disagreement with a man whose set he had repaired. And soon afterward, the customer walked into the repair shop and shot and killed him.

Nobody is immune to negative emotions. We have to learn to live with them. But when they become isolated and exaggerated, and when the individual becomes separated from common bonds, active death wishes against others may appear. Ask yourself whether you have never had pleased feelings when you read an obituary. Why did you wish that person dead? Fear? Envy? Self-righteousness, condemning in another what you subconsciously would like to have had or done yourself?

Fear, not only of physical injury, but social fear, can be an overpowering negative emotion. Cause fear and you sow the idea of violence. An instructive example is blackmail. Blackmail does not consist only of the simple setup of a letter making certain demands with the threat of divulging something hidden. A blackmail situation may exist, and very often does, in which the threats and demands are only hinted at or are merely implied. This is especially true in our era of blacklists and the linking of sex and security in investigatory and public exposures. In all blackmail, the idea of violence, the death wish against the tormentor, comes up. The blackmailed person, once he realizes the situation he is in (which sometimes takes quite a while), has only three alternatives. He can pay or do what is wanted of him; he can resist and refuse and accept the prospect of the consequences; he can think of eliminating the one who harasses him. The last alternative invariably forces itself into consciousness. A judge of a high court was given to understand, by a professional man who was also a politician, that certain judicial decisions were expected from him. The hint was dropped that otherwise the exposure of some moral indiscretion in his life might interfere with his next nomination and election. It was contrary to his usual temperament, but the judge became consumed with the idea of getting rid of the man who was causing him so much mental anguish. He sought psychiatric advice. It was difficult to help him to free himself from that painful preoccupation with violence. Eventually a solution was found: he confided the whole matter to a very influential friend whose political power protected him. A blackmail situation is always potentially a situation of violence. Usually blackmail is handled much too leniently by the law.

Why such death wishes are translated into action is more difficult to answer. It is, I believe, the crux of the whole matter. Why people wish to commit violence is easier to understand than why they actually do it. As in any complex chemical reaction, there are always several operative factors, and often there is a cataylst. Alcohol is such a catalyst. So is poverty, sometimes, and race prejudice and general excitability and irritability, and easy accessibility of methods and weapons. Any of these may enter into the final reaction. As the gentle princess Sita says in the *Ramayana,* the great antiviolence epic of ancient India, "The very bearing of weapons changeth the mind of those that carry them."

Sometimes a catalyst consists of the unhappy chance that at the time of greatest emotional tension a person reads or hears of or sees on the screen a crime that somehow seems to fit his own situation. This detail may seem trivial. Psychiatrists have not paid much attention to it because it is not "deep" enough. Lawyers do not credit it because it may sound like a made-up excuse. But a great writer like Theodore Dreiser knew that a seemingly unsolvable personal dilemma and the incidental suggestion of an easy solution by violence may become fused in a fateful union. Clyde Griffiths in *An American Tragedy* wants to marry a wealthy girl, but is confronted with the fact that his own girl friend is pregnant. No thought of murder has entered his mind. Then he comes across an item in a newspaper recounting how an upturned canoe was found in a lake and later the unidentified body of a girl recovered. Her male companion was missing. After reading this, he cannot dismiss the thought from his mind. What if he and his girl friend were in a boat and the boat should capsize. "What an escape! What a relief from a gigantic and by now really destroying problem!" He fights the idea: "He must not, he must not, allow such a thought to enter his mind. Never, never, never! . . . A thought of murder, no less! Murder!" Eventually he succumbs. Dreiser, of course, does not offer this episode as an explanation of the crime but he shows that it is a factor in the dynamics of murder.

I have observed similar minor previolence influences in forensic psychiatric cases. A teenager who stabbed his mother to death saw shortly before the deed a movie showing a life situation similar to his own. It confirmed his determination. A woman who killed her young daughter happened to read about the Hindenburg disaster shortly before. The report said that some of the victims were so badly burned that they could not be identified. She tried to burn the child after killing her. It is difficult to evaluate how important such experiences are, but it is certain that in some cases they tip the scales. We do not sufficiently realize how easy it would have been sometimes for a murder *not* to have been committed.

A general atmosphere of violence is very important, for violence is as contagious as the measles. The more we inculcate in young people via the mass media and in other ways the false idea that there is something courageous about killing, the more we are fostering it in susceptible individuals. One can say that just as suicide is that cowardly act for which one has to have the most courage, so murder is that courageous act in which there is most cowardice.

Given the negative emotions and the death wish and a catalyst, there must still be one more important factor: the whole personality and the whole life situation of the individual. The difference between one who murders and one who does not is never in a single impulse or in a single mental attitude, however destructive. Pushkin expressed this best when he described the contrast between the two personalities in his play *Mozart and Salieri*. The play is based on the story that Mozart was poisoned by Salieri, another composer. As a matter of fact, even today medical histories discuss the question of whether Mozart died of mercury poisoning. Salieri craved virtuosity and narrowed his whole life down to achieving his ambition. Envy, therefore, could fill his heart to such an extent that he committed murder. For Mozart, on the other hand, music and the rest of life were inseparable. He was passionately devoted to both. It is quite possible that at one time or another he, like the rest of mankind, had passing feelings of envy; but he could never have become their slave. He could never have committed murder.

For murder is never a superficial event. It always requires an enormously strong impulse, an overcoming of resistances and inhibitions, and a building up of rationalizations. There are always counterforces against the negative emotions, death wishes, catalysts, and personality patterns which culminate in the drive to kill. That is why murder is the greatest conflict a man can have with himself or with society.

These counterforces of reason and sympathy may come successfully into play in a mature person even when he is on the verge of violence. In *The Cricket on the Hearth,* Dickens has described this conflict in John Peerybingle: "Some shadowy idea that it was just to shoot this man like a Wild Beast, seized him, and dilated in his mind until it grew into a monstrous demon in complete possession of him, casting out all milder thoughts and setting up its undivided empire." Murderers whom I have examined have sometimes described just such a state of mind, although they were not so articulate. Is this "empire" really "undivided"? John suddenly hears the chirping of the cricket on the hearth, symbolizing and representing all the counterforces. As a result, as in a man awakening from a frightful dream, "his better nature awoke into life and action." Unfortunately, sometimes the conflict ends in the opposite way. Instead of the chirping of the cricket, we supply the shrill voices of modern life.

The existence of such an emotional conflict is not always apparent on the surface. At present, for example, we see more and more juveniles who commit violence. James D. C. Murray, the eminent attorney who has defended and understood many of them, has described a typical sequence of events: the youth likes to have a girl; in order to have a proper standing with her, he has to have a car; he steals one; to entertain her, he needs money; he sees all around him false prototypes of what a real girl wants; he learns about guns; he shoots. I have found that when young people appear on arraignment, they may give a superficial impression that is entirely misleading. They seem unconcerned and conflictless. Again and again it is reported in the newspapers that they are indifferent and "show no emotion." How are they supposed to behave? This kind of behavior is frequently misunderstood as indicating obduracy and hardness of heart. And this attitude is supposed to be the reason why they kill. Or sometimes the psychiatric phrase "flat affect" is applied to them, and on that basis the wrong diagnosis of schizophrenia is made.

Beneath the surface, things are very different. These boys may have absorbed some callousness from the street and the mass media, which are their hidden educators, and from other influences. But they have good, decent, and loyal inclinations too. They find themselves confronted with an overwhelming psychological and social reality. They are too immature to digest it or work it out. To go to the other extreme and say of such a boy that he is driven by deep, impenetrable, unconscious, destructive instincts may satisfy our need for biological theories and our aversion to facing unpleasant social inequities, but it does not help us to understand young people. What they need and rarely get is help for their problems—they usually need it long before.

Scientifically, it is misleading to emphasize the isolated phenomenon of an impulse. What we see instead is a human being in whom such an impulse works. The decisive point is often not why one does it, but how one justifies it, rationalizes it, to oneself. The impulse is individual, the rationalization is social. This is where the individual and the socal meet. If the environment itself is ruthless, it is easy to take a cue from that and find a plausible rationalization for violent behavior. The idea that an impulse to murder may arise momentarily in and by itself is not tenable. Nothing has a longer preparation than an impulsive violent act. There are always several factors, and the seemingly most insignificant may, in the presence of others, become the most potent and decisive one. Without this factor, the murder might not have been committed.

A violent act is always a triangle. A study of one person can never explain it. Nor a study of two. We always have to visualize the potential influence on one another of first, the perpetrator; second, the victim; third, the reaction of the other people in a smaller or wider circle. This applies not only to the deed itself but also to the pre- and postviolence phases. The perpetrator and the victim cannot be fully understood in isolation. It is different with animals. If a cat kills a mouse, we do not need to know how other cats think about it, either during the act or long before or after. We know the species of cats and against this background can evaluate the individual cat. The same is true of the victim, the mouse. But knowledge of the species *human being* is not sufficient to explain, far less predict, the incidence and form of his violence. There is a continuing influence of the social environment, family, class, and nation on the development of the individual. Not only what the victim but what others thought in the past enters into the act; what they think afterward may help to explain it.

This does not mean a restriction on individual psychology. On the contrary, considering concretely the wider perspective will help make psychopathology and psychoanalysis more realistic and less speculative. If present-day physics were as speculative as a large part of psychology still is, no rocket would go into orbit. We need to consider concretely the three points of the triangular stucture of murder.

The reason why men kill, in short, is always to be found in negative factors in the personality and in society. For a murder to be committed, it takes two people *and* their social environment.

# CHAPTER FOUR

# Fostering Factors

He who wants to present a corrective
must know thoroughly what the existing
weaknesses are.
—Søren Kierkegaard

VIOLENCE is not a neutral subject. There are many ways to evade
facing it. One is the prevalent practice of passing it over entirely
in many discussions of human, psychological, and social matters,
when a closer or broader look would reveal that it has a bearing
on them, in one way or another. Another form of evasion is a
superscientific attitude which tries to reduce everything to a quantitative level, where it can be characterized by measurements and
numbers. Each phenomenon is then just a little more or less than
something else. In sociological problems, this method can advance
us only part of the way. Applied to the problem of violence, it leads
to a pseudoexactness which leaves out vital qualitative factors. We
can produce violence today with exact mathematical precision, but
we cannot prevent it that way.

To study violence without examining the concrete conditions
which may help to bring it about leaves the subject hanging in the
air. We cannot afford to be "pure" scientists and look at just part
of it. We must view the whole. That includes anybody who commits violence and anybody who causes it or permits it to be
committed. And we have to deal not only with maladjusted persons, but also with maladjusted social conditions. Because violence
reaches into our daily social, emotional, and political life, we should
not be surprised to find a number of very heterogeneous things—
social customs, institutions, theories, and beliefs—playing a role as

violence-fostering factors. (Grouping these factors together does not mean that these factors have equal value or significance.) Violence-fostering factors are those which stand in the way of our education toward a nonviolent world or help to retard the laying of social foundations for it. Violence itself is one such factor, for it is like drug addiction: if you use a drug and tolerate it, you have to increase the dose. That is very evident in political terror. Unfinished business after individual or collective violence is another example, for it creates a momentum for further violence.

Violence and the factors leading up to it confront us episodically. We must try to find the more general meaning behind the episodic character of violence and its manifold causes. If one discusses some of the very diverse items which contain built-in pro-violence forces one seems to be digressing and putting incommensurables together. But this very diversity is made necessary by the insidious nature of violence. We must envisage these very dissimilar conditions which are conducive to violence, because prevention will not be possible if we leave out any of them and restrict our perspective according to a one cause–one effect formula. We cannot abolish rain in a climate of rain or violence in a climate of violence. To discuss these various items only from the point of view of their pro-violence potential is, of course, one-sided. But it may, like a concentrated beam of light, reveal aspects otherwise obscured or not emphasized.

## Alcohol

Alcohol is the lubricant of violence. How closely alcohol and violence are related can be seen from the fact that among alcoholics, violence, including accidents and suicides, is the most frequent— and preventable—cause of death. Many violent acts would not occur at all or would not take the particular form they do if alcohol did not enter as a factor. This is especially true of acts committed with particular brutality and recklessness. Again and again when we study carefully cases of assault and murder, we find that alcohol played a role. How important its role is depends on the individuals and on the circumstance. Frequently it seems minor but nevertheless it is a potent, even a decisive factor for the end result. It has been estimated that 50 percent of violent crimes today are connected with alcohol.

Any discussion of the social effects of drinking is apt to come up against a defensive attitude, not only on the part of the person who drinks, but from influential distillers, alcohol merchants, and advertisers. It is of course not a question of drinking, but of *over*-drinking. We cannot understand an abuse if we confuse it with a use.

Because of the different susceptibility of different individuals, overdrinking is not easy to define. There has been a lot of quibbling about what is excessive and what harm alcohol can do. So much has been written about alcohol that it may confuse even the sober. It is well known that disturbed chronic alcoholics and severely drunk persons may beat their wives and children and commit other violent acts. But the main and very frequent problem of alcohol-furthered violence is not that people are drunk but that they may drink a little too much at the wrong time, in the wrong place, in the wrong frame of mind. It is frequently a problem not of heavy drinking but of drinking that is sufficient under the circumstances to be excessive for that particular person. This type of drinking, and its effect on health and behavior, is not diagnosed often enough. The trouble is not that it cannot be cured but that it is not recognized. Too frequently we permit the patient to make his own diagnosis. He may say, "I am not a drinker. I can stop anytime." Maybe he can. But does he?

Even excessive drinkers, including those who have committed violent acts, can be greatly helped and rehabilitated; in fact, the fight against violence has to include this help. An obstacle to it is the widespread pessimism about whether this can be done. For example, the Research Council on Problems of Alcohol, whose board of directors and scientific committee include many prominent members of the psychiatric and social establishment, says in a pamphlet addressed to the general public about "problem drinkers": "Is there any known cure for this disease? No! Further and continued research is necessary if such a cure or cures are to be found." Actually, with modern methods of psychiatry and psychotherapy, many can be cured.

It is being more and more recognized that alcohol plays a tremendous role in automobile accidents. This vehicular violence, as it may be called, is not in the main a matter of the heavily drunk person (although, of course, in the individual case, he is a great danger) but of the driver who has had just a little too much. Those who would like to minimize the danger in the combination of alcohol and driving like to point out that teetotalers also have traffic accidents. This does not disprove the fact that alcohol is frequently a causal or contributing factor. For New York City in 1962, it was found that in 75 percent of all fatal automobile and fatal pedestrian accidents, alcohol was a factor.

In contrast to our knowledge about accidents, the contribution of alcohol to acts of violence is still underestimated. It is often repeated that a man under the influence of alcohol will not do anything he would not do when sober. Clinical psychological studies tell a different story. Some people under the influence of alcohol will commit an act—especially a brutal act—which they would otherwise never do.

The thirty-two-year-old wife of a well-to-do businessman lived in a happy marriage. She had three young children, whom she was bringing up very well. She was conscientious, but not overconscientious. At times her duties as housewife became a little too much for her: chauffeuring the children to school, doctor, dentist, music lessons; dealing with the repairmen for the various laborsaving (but not emotion-saving) devices in the home; and so on. She had developed one of the pleasant customs of gracious living: a cocktail with her husband when he came home from work. This increased to two, and often more. The time between five and six o'clock gradually turned out to be the most trying: the husband getting home tired, wishing for but not bringing peace; the children around at the same time; the preparations for dinner. Sometimes she took highballs during the day. Once there was an unfortunate concatenation of circumstances. She had had a most trying day; she had a little more alcohol than usual; there was a minor argument with her husband about what would be the most suitable financial planning. Suddenly in the midst of it she left the room, came back with a knife from the kitchen, and stabbed her husband in the chest. It was not a very serious injury, but it was a wound nevertheless. It might have been serious. She had never before thought or done anything remotely like that.

It does not make a great deal of difference whether we label such a young woman a problem drinker, an excessive social drinker, a true or not really true alcoholic addict, a minor alcoholic, a near alcoholic, or a prealcoholic (all these terms abound in the literature). The important point is that it is the alcohol which has to be eliminated from her life. Of course, there were deeper motives for her conduct, but the symptom of drinking had to be treated. With modern psychotherapeutic, medical, and social measures, we can cure such an individual and save the marriage and family. Marriage counseling is not enough for that. Cases like this do not appear in statistics. They often don't even receive treatment because neither the alcohol nor the violence is taken seriously enough. But the sequence of events is characteristic for one type of case. There are four phases:

1. Drinking according to the mores of the group.
2. It becomes a habit.
3. The dose is increased so that it becomes excessive.
4. Under certain circumstances, loss of self-control occurs.

Often there is nothing seriously wrong with these individuals' super-ego, or conscience. The trouble is that conscience is soluble in alcohol.

Alcohol may lead to violence in a number of different ways. There is no special type of personality that may be adversely affected by it. Some factors that lead people to undisciplined drinking and to violence are very similar. That applies also to the underlying emotional conflicts. To seek escape in a drink is an easy method; so is violence. Fear, especially fear of social inadequacy, may lead to either. There is always a bit of fear where there is a bit of excessive drinking. The effects of alcohol, that is to say, of too much for that person under particular circumstances, may subtly create a readiness for violence. He becomes somewhat overstimulated—which amounts not to a real stimulation but to a depression of the highest faculties of will, intellect, and inhibition. There is a degree of emotional instability and an impairment of the sense of caring for things or for people. A blunting of self-criticism occurs early. Irritability may be released or increased. In these ways, dangers of violence are created, which in most cases do not lead to actual deeds.

As a telling example of alcohol as a contributing factor, one particularly brutal display of violence can be cited. It has been given the medical name of "battered-baby syndrome" or "battered-child syndrome" or "maltreatment syndrome." Some parents, usually young ones, treat their infant or very young children with almost unbelievable brutality and cruelty. It has been estimated that as many as 10,000 such cases occur annually in the United States and that the number of them is growing. These children have been found to have burns, wounds, ruptured internal organs, broken ribs, arms, and legs. According to the American Humane Association, parents have beaten their children with straps, electric cords, TV aerials, ropes, rubber hose, fan belts, sticks, pool cues, bottles, broom handles, baseball bats, chair legs, a sculling oar. More than half of the children so abused were under four years old. More than a quarter of them died of their injuries. According to this same report, the children were kicked, burned in open flames or with electric irons or hot pokers, scalded by hot fluids, strangled, suffocated with pillows or plastic bags, drowned in bathtubs, stabbed, bitten, shot, subjected to electric shock, stamped on, had pepper forced down their throats. One child was buried alive.

In a recent case, a four-year-old girl had her hands tied behind her and was plunged into cold water. Children have also been found starved to death. In another case, a young father beat his seventeen-week-old son because he could not tolerate his crying. The baby was found with injuries that included sixteen broken bones. In still another case, a young man disciplined his three-year-old daughter "by seating her on a hot stove." Infants as young as seven weeks have been admitted to hospitals with fractured ribs and head injuries. Some children have been admitted to hospitals several times.

This is a recent phenomenon; it is increasing and it seems to occur as a mass phenomenon only in the United States. Different factors are responsible for this. The parents belong to a generation which has grown up with crime and horror comic books and the violence of other mass media. They live in a time when war and foreign policy are almost interchangeable terms and nonviolence is regarded as a radical invention. In a considerable proportion of the cases, alcohol plays a very important causal or contributing role, in both fathers and mothers. Without the lubrication with alcohol, some of the cases would not have happened.

Even though in the individual case, alcohol may play a decisive role, it is only a part of the whole picture of the battered-baby syndrome. The syndrome itself, in all its aspects, is a most important symptom of our time. It is a link in the documentation of my thesis that the spirit of violence is rampant in our society. It is a matter not only of the occurrence of these heartless cruelties against defenseless children, but of the inadequacy of the steps taken so far to prevent them. Physicians, legislators, and child-care agencies have taken up the question belatedly. Even now no proper solution has been found. This is one of those forms of violence which society calls "incredible" and is unequipped to deal with. Why, in an orderly society, should this be such a baffling medical, social, and legal problem?

Perhaps there are clues in the extraordinary statements that some child psychiatrists have made. One stated that there is, in fact, a danger that pediatricians and those who work with children "will identify themselves too closely with the child." How can one possibly identify too closely with children so abused? Another, from the National Institute of Mental Health, accuses the child and points to the child's role in precipitating and prolonging the battered-child syndrome: ". . . the children are involved in some cases in furthering their own continued beatings." A third, a professor of psychiatry, told a psychiatric convention that the underlying cause is the child-beating parents' "lack of awareness of the basic personality" of the infant, that "these parents are not bad people. They have a neurosis in the same manner that many people have a neurosis, and they deserve punishment no more than the person who has a fear of heights." Theories like this expressed by acknowledged child experts are an obstacle to doing something realistic about such multiple violence. They indicate that these horrible examples of cruelty against children are not merely brutal individual defaults, but part of a decadent attitude about violence in our society.

In the now so frequent brutal juvenile violence, committed by individuals or gangs, alcohol is a very important though much overlooked factor. When Michael Farmer, a fifteen-year-old boy handicapped by infantile paralysis, was beaten, kicked, and stabbed to death in a Manhattan park by a group of boys, one of the boys said later, "I didn't wanna hit him at first. Then I kicked him twice. He was laying on the ground looking up at us. I kicked him on the jaw or someplace. Then I kicked him in the stomach. . . . I stabbed him with the bread knife. You know, I was drunk, so I just stabbed him [giggling]. He was screaming like a dog. He was screaming there. And then I took the knife out, and I told the other boys to run." "Drunk" and "giggling" are the important words here.

A more indirect connection between alcohol and violence is seen in some particularly violent and brutal young individuals. It often happens that they have seen or experienced much violent behavior on the part of their parents, and this parental violence itself is not infrequently connected with alcohol.

Naturally alcohol is not the only substance that has a relation to violence, but it is by far the most important one. Drugs like heroin may lead to violence in very different, more indirect ways. Drug addicts sometimes commit crimes in desperation to obtain the drug. Undoubtedly some especially violent robberies could be prevented if the prevention of drug addiction were more efficient. For marihuana the relationship to violence has been greatly exaggerated. Its greatest danger at present among young people is that it often leads to the taking of heroin and therefore indirectly to possible violence. I have often seen the chain of events: use of marihuana, transition to heroin for a greater thrill, violent crime to get a supply of the expensive drug.

## Communications

Communication is the opposite of violence. Where communication ends, violence begins. Why, then, is there so much violence or threat of violence in the world today, when the technical means of communication have been so perfected?

Part of the answer lies in the discrepancy between what is actu-

ally done with these means and what could be done. We have the
greatest opportunity for communication that any civilization has
ever had. We can reach millions of people in the remotest places
with the greatest speed. But we do not make constructive use of
this ability.

When individuals fully communicate with one another, they do
not use violence. But if we cannot get a response to our egos by
communication of words and feelings, we are tempted to evoke in
fantasy a response by violent means. When violence does erupt, it
comes from a breakdown of communication. This is shown glar-
ingly in the sexual sphere. The study of violent sex criminals often
shows a long history of noncommunication, sexually and emotionally.

Several observers have pointed out that real communication with
young people is harder today than it used to be. Here is one of the
roots of juvenile violence. It also seems that adults in general find
it more difficult to communicate with their fellowmen. When
discussion touches fundamental issues, it stops at vital points.
Despite the technical extent of mass interchange, we have an
international communication gap.

Communications are the nervous system of society. One of the
criteria which distinguish man from animals is the way in which
needs are satisfied. Most animals satisfy their needs in a direct,
immediate manner. Human beings have to do this in a mediate
manner, by way of the detour of social production. That is to say
that one of the concrete foundations of human life is cooperation.
This in turn must be based on the means of communication. Never
before in the history of mankind was mass cooperation more possible than it is today. What prevents it? Just as the earth's atmosphere can be poisoned by nuclear fallout, so the atmosphere of
cooperation can be affected by psychological fallout from the media
of mass communication. Max Born, one of the greatest and most
conscientious atomic physicists, who received the Nobel Prize in
1954, sees a dark shadow over the future. He ascribes it on the
one hand to the methods of mass destruction, on the other to the
abuse of the means of mass communication, which influence the
ideas in the heads of men.

For the difficult task of building a nonviolent world, the individual has to receive information so that he can use it according to his best critical judgment. For this he must rely on communications. The more the mass media of communication become slanted, clogged, abused, transformed into a vast machinery of hate, the greater is the danger that the mass methods of physical destruction will come into play. When in the spring of 1963 in Birmingham, Alabama, the demonstrations of Negroes against segregation and discrimination took place, the white community was largely unaware of what was really going on, for what reason, and with what effects. There were only very brief notices in the newspapers, buried on inside pages. The day after the biggest demonstration, early in May, the Birmingham *News* featured a banner headline on its front page:

SYRIA IN SIXTH DAY OF RIOTING

Thus the dangers of violence are not averted but increased by barriers of nonunderstanding.

This kind of miscommunication is typical of what happens in other places and under different circumstances. Newspapers are apt to give us not the news that is fit to print, but the news that is printed to fit. The Birmingham example also illustrates the old device of diverting attention from domestic affairs to what goes on in distant countries about which the reader knows little, so that he cannot form his own judgment.

There is a wasteland of noncommunication between nations. Communication at the summit is not enough when the valleys are so separated. In this wasteland a lot of goodwill that might help in the cause of antiviolence gets lost, while the weeds of suspicion and denigration grow. When the first woman space traveler, Valentina Tereshkova, circled the earth, it was a milestone in the emancipation of women, of all women in the world. It created a new image of woman as the real equal of man. The American news media reduced a human achievement to a political problem. They looked for negative things: that she was not fully trained, not a real pilot but just a parachute jumper; that according to the "U.S. space experts," she did not accomplish what she was really supposed to do. The day following her historic flight, *The New York Times* had an article with this headline:

### SOVIET SPACE FAILURE?

The media of communication can be a powerful force for violence or against it. The broadcasts of Lord Haw-Haw and P. G. Wodehouse for the Nazis, of Ezra Pound for the Italian Fascists helped to induce ordinary people to think of themselves as heroes in a good cause, willing later to commit any violence asked of them. In the preelectronic era, such announcements could not have been spread so quickly or so widely.

For years in the midst of peace, mass communications have been used to sow and increase hostility among people. We put the worst interpretations on any utterances or actions by possible opponents. This has spread over all the fields of information, entertainment, and learning. We have become so used to it that we hardly notice it any more when whole nations are regularly regarded as inferior, as potential enemies, or as always acting in bad faith. This is more dangerous than direct appeals to violence, because it supplies advance justification for violence by continually vilifying those against whom it might be directed. With comic books we have taught this to a whole generation of children. The other media are a little more subtle. There is what may be called an inflammatory index: the higher the degree of vilification, the greater the possibility of violence. At present, this index is certainly not favorable.

Vilification of whole groups, with its continuous stream of insinuations, is especially dangerous for one reason: the ideas can very quickly and suddenly turn into action. This vilification, paving the way to violence, need not consist of crude terms of abuse. It can be done in a refined way. In a poem that was recently read on a British radio broadcast, Erich Fried pointed this out:

> One doesn't say "we want to slaughter them,"
> That doesn't make a good impression.
> It is enough to regret
> That "one can't negotiate with them."
> Also "they are not human beings"
> Sounds obsolete and is not necessary.
> "They are different from us"
> Sounds much better.
> Not to swear death and destruction,

Only to shake one's head and shrug one's shoulder—
"They understand only one language."
The slaughter will follow by itself.

Real signals of understanding and humaneness have great difficulty in coming through or cannot come through at all. One of the best methods for communication among all nations and all ages is through the arts. To quite an extent independent of the social and political ideas of the artist or the society in which he functions, there are some qualities in works of art to which human sensibility responds. This is true not only of an aesthetic elite but of masses of people. We can communicate with dead civilizations like that of the Etruscans through the works of art found in their tombs, works admired by such diverse persons as Freud, D. H. Lawrence, and D'Annunzio. Why not cultivate communication with the living? For years there has been a deficiency in the showing and reporting of specific foreign movies and plays. When they are reviewed or discussed, it is done with a self-righteousness combining picayune formal criticisms, cold-war sentiments, and political prejudice; and if anything is shown except a boy kissing a girl, accusations of propaganda are added. This has become so routine that we can almost predict what reviews will say about a show from specific countries.

We hear a great deal about the "Berlin wall." But there are other, bigger walls in the world which, though invisible, are much more extensive and divisive. They divide, for instance, the many millions of Chinese and American people. Must we accept the fact that the sociopolitical differences are so paramount that all communications have to be cut off? The millions of people involved know at present as little about one another as if they were living on different planets.

That communications and violence are opposites was dramatically shown by a historical event, when more than 200,000 people, Negro and non-Negro, marched on Washington in the summer of 1963. Many had anticipated that there would be some violence. Some thought this partly from prejudice, partly from the unconscious wish that some violence would frustrate the march and its results. They were wrong. Even minor episodes of violence were completely absent. A young construction inspector for the city of

Detroit who participated in the march expressed its meaning very clearly: "The whole thing was an attempt to communicate." It was indeed a gigantic group communication, the very opposite of violence.

What interferes with the free flow of communication in news and entertainment is not so much overt, official censorship. More insidious and far-reaching is so-called self-censorship. It consists in multiple, continual pressures from commercial, social, religious, and political sources. Plainspokenness is so hazardous that it is relatively rare to hear or express unfiltered opinions. This pressuring stifles communications, especially those that try to help (and not just in pious generalities) to bring about a more peaceful world.

One of the obstacles to communication in the mass media is that news is treated as entertainment, and entertainment is made into news. A lot of news is far too serious to be presented just for its entertainment value. If in ten minutes a variety of information for all tastes cannot be presented constructively, it might be better to present only one or two items in necessary detail and perspective. Violence prevention in the world of today needs a better grasp and communication of today's realities.

Also important for world communications is the choice of what is translated and how it is translated. By and large, books that can help in education for a nonviolent world do not fare very well.

A particularly sensitive area of communication from which sparks of violence may fly is that between leaders and masses. Signals can go from leaders to masses and from masses to leaders. Many good and peaceable ideas on the part of potential leaders get lost because they are not distributed to the masses; many decent attitudes of the masses come to nothing because they are not communicated to the leaders.

The term "masses" is often used in a depreciative, status-conscious way. It is taken for granted that assembled groups, as such (if we don't like them, we call them mobs), are always inferior, in comparison with the individual, and that they have certain unalterable bad qualities. But masses are made up of average, normal men, and their reactions depend on many factors, one of them being communication with leaders. More often than not, what is designated as mob violence is really leader violence.

This leadership role is related to the problem of power, for one way excessive power corrupts is by creating isolation and thus the temptation to use violence. Dostoevski, speaking of corporal punishment in *The House of the Dead,* has described from his own prison experiences how "this immense power over the body and soul of a fellow-man like himself" leads to insensitiveness, cruelty, and violence. On a different level, absolute political power leads to estrangement from the masses and creates the danger of off-with-his-head methods for a solution of vexing problems. There can be no doubt that Stalin, who in the words of John Gunther was "probably the most powerful single human being in the world," was isolated and corrupted by the excessive absolute power concentrated in one person.

A classic example of the breakdown of interchange between leaders and masses occurred in Germany after the First World War, in January, 1919. A large number of people, estimated at many thousands, appeared in the thoroughfares near the Brandenburg Gate. They assembled at nine in the morning to demonstrate against militarism and violence. What they wanted exactly, they did not know, except to change the old order that had led them into a bloody war. There were no banners or signs. The people were good-natured but did not know what to do with their goodwill. Occasionally some voices would cry out, "Never again war!" In the meantime, their leaders sat somewhere else, no one knew where, and debated and deliberated, nobody knew what. The masses waited for a message or for just a word. It got cold, and a heavy fog descended. Midday came, and hunger was added to the cold. The leaders kept on deliberating. The people continued to wait patiently on the streets and in the park. No message from their leaders, not a word. Finally dusk fell—and the masses went sadly home. It became known later that the leaders had sat in council all day, all evening, all through the night, and on into the next morning, leaving and returning, deliberating and deliberating. Nothing of all this had reached the masses on the streets. This episode had enduring results. There was an understandable disappointment and withdrawal on the part of the common people, who wanted a democratic, nonbloody, nonviolent Germany. Masses and leaders had completely failed to communicate.

Even at that early date, in 1919, some young men in Germany wore bright and shiny emblems in their lapels—swastikas, symbols of a new elite and a new kind of communication. Fourteen years later, after a period of political strife, communication by command came into full being. On May Day in 1933, another large demonstration and procession took place in Berlin. Many of the participants were workers, because the chief of the General German Trade Union League, Theodor Leipart, for many years a prominent union leader, had ordered all union members to join the demonstration. There were many bands, uniformed Nazi formations, and Nazi banners in the march. It snowed and later rained. Despite this, everything went as scheduled.

Communication by order seemed to have worked. It was, of course, not a genuine two-way communication. It was more like a faulty computer without feedback. It was also a prelude to violence. The very next day, May 2, 1933, at ten o'clock in the morning, armed and uniformed storm troopers occupied all trade-union headquarters. On that day the free trade unions and the trade-union movement in Germany ceased to exist.

One-sided communication by command spread through all walks of life and all sections of the population. Psychiatry was no exception. A few months after the first of May demonstration in Berlin, a message appeared in the *Journal of Psychotherapy,* whose newly appointed editor was C. G. Jung. The message, which was in fact an order, was worded by a cousin of Marshal Hermann Goering, Dr. M. H. Goering. It instructed psychotherapists to make "a serious scientific study of Adolf Hitler's fundamental work, *Mein Kampf,* and to recognize it as a basic work." They did. Communication by order, *i.e.,* one-way communication, became the rule. The violence followed.

People who do not communicate do not know each other; people who do not know each other can be stirred up to hate. Good communications are an antidote to violence. Any interference with them therefore causes or increases the danger of violence. One way in which this can happen is the creation of doubt or fear or, especially, ill will.

The science of cybernetics can help us to understand how a failure of communication can have very serious results. A cybernetic system, like an electronic computer, depends on the free flow of information. If there is a breakdown in the smoothly functioning information system, there will be a sudden breakdown in the machine. Similarly—of course, on a much higher level of organization—if there is failure in communication in human societies, their peaceful development is interfered with. The average citizen does not know how much interference there is—unnecessarily.

One typical example is the Allied (NATO) Travel Office in West Berlin. This agency was founded at the end of the Second World War and originally performed a useful function. In the sixties, however, some of its feats of interference would be ludicrous if the general consequences for peace in our time were not so serious. The Brecht Theatre Ensemble, which one of the most outstanding modern critics, Kenneth Tynan, has called the most significant stage in the world today, was prevented from performing in Denmark and in Scotland at the Edinburgh Festival. A children's choir from East Germany was not permitted to accept an invitation to sing in England. Scientists living in East Germany, even when they were completely apolitical, were prevented from taking part in congresses: one geneticist could not attend the International Genetics Congress at the Hague, though he was slated to be vice-president of it; a diabetes specialist could not give a lecture on diabetes in Modena, Italy, which he had been invited for; an authority on Zola could not attend a Zola conference at the British Institut Français or give a guest lecture at a London college; the director of the Berlin Zoo was not permitted to participate in the congress of zoo directors in Chester, England; a famous linguist could not go to the University of Ghent in Belgium to accept an honorary doctor's degree; the International Association for Mass Communication (*sic*) had to transfer a scheduled congress to a place where attendance by all the participants was possible. These may be small signs and signals, but no cybernetic system could function like this.

The relation of failure of communication to violence is illustrated by some events in 1965 which constituted something entirely new on the American scene. As a protest against war and violence, three persons—a woman in Detroit, a young man in Washington, and another in New York—set fire to themselves and burned themselves to death. All three had tried in vain to communicate their convictions to the public, the government, or both. This failure of communication turned to violence against themselves. The widespread response in the postviolence phase in these hardened times was typical and indicative of what drove them to their deed in the first place. The news media reported that they were or must have been "insane," "crazy," "not rational," "emotionally unstable," "probably psychotic," "nuts," "deeply disturbed," "demented," "confused." The U.S. Ambassador to the United Nations said their action was "terribly unnecessary." A prominent psychiatrist said of the self-immolation by the man in Washington that it belonged to the category of any other suicide attempt and that the reason a person gives for his self-destruction is not necessarily the factor that led to it. In other words, he does not really know what he is doing.

However, these acts were not just suicides by mentally disordered persons. They were signals. We cannot afford to nullify them and write them off as irrational. That would be a kind of cynicism like that of Paul Valéry, who wrote about martyrs that they would "rather die than reflect." We have to decode these signals. Whatever we may think of the ideas or the methods employed, they impart a message against violence. At the very least they are a fiery question mark urging us to "reflect." It seems a sound social-psychological assumption that when three different people take such actions on account of their convictions, there are many others who have the same ideas without expressing them in such extreme measures. These acts of self-immolation were supreme assertions of what James Fenimore Cooper called Principle over Interest. Have we gone so far as to say that if a man sacrifices himself for a principle, he must be out of his mind?

## Commercial Disrespect for Human Life

Violence does not exist in a vacuum. The Spanish philosopher José Ortega y Gasset has said that man is himself and his circumstance. That is true also of those who commit violent acts or are tempted to do so. If we want to understand them, we cannot afford to neglect their "circumstance," however trivial some of it may seem. Among the factors which may influence them are all those which create an atmosphere in which respect for human life is lowered. We are inclined to think of this as something entirely separate from what people actually do, but in life no such separateness exists. Nearly all the murderers I have examined had in various degrees a disrespect for human life, that of others and their own. They were not born that way. It was an acquired attitude.

Under different social and historical circumstances, different influences contribute to this disregard. In our time, certain segments of advertising play a very important role in the negation of the value of human life. This abuse of communication can be documented in these three areas:

1. Cigarette advertising
2. Alcohol advertising
3. Arms advertising for the nursery

### CIGARETTE ADVERTISING

It is now scientifically well established that too much cigarette smoking (and inhaling) is a causal contributing factor in lung cancer, cancer of the respiratory system, disorders of the cardio-vasculatory system (including coronary heart disease), and certain respiratory diseases. This conclusion is based on published clinical, pathological, and statistical studies. There are not so very many medical diseases, outside of infectious ones, in which the connection between an injurious agent and the pathological result is better established than the connection between cigarette smoking and cancer of the lungs. Here is a large field for mass medical prevention. More people have died from lung cancer than from automobile accidents. In 1961, 37,500 people died from traffic accidents; as many as 42,230 died from respiratory cancer. In New York State in 1963, one of five men between the ages of forty-five and sixty-four who died from all causes died because of cigarette smoking. This has been called mass murder. Is it caused by things or by people, by the forces of nature or by the forces of society?

Adequate prevention, which would be so important for the

nation's health, has been made practically impossible, principally because of the large amount of money spent on cigarette advertising. The total for television and radio alone amounted to $134,-000,000 in 1961. At present, it is reported to be even higher. More than half of the cigarette commercials appear in young people's viewing time, before 9 P.M. There are special college representatives who promote specific brands and give away free packs or even cartons of cigarettes. Much of the advertising is especially persuasive to young people. They are presented with false images of male virility and female glamour. The idea conveyed is that every manlike, adventurous occupation needs the smoking of cigarettes: mountain climbing, athletics, every sport, piloting an airplane, and so on. The message for girls is that attractiveness and romance require the help of cigarettes. Dr. S. I. Hayakawa, expert on language communication, quotes an especially ingenious and poetic advertisement: "Take a puff . . . it's springtime! Gray rocks and the fresh green leaves of springtime reflected in a mountain pool . . . where else can you find air so refreshing? And where can you find a smoke as refreshing as [brand name]?"

The belief in the much-touted filters has no more scientific validity than the medieval superstition that a substance from the horn of a unicorn had healing power. There were no unicorns, and there is no safe filter. An experienced psychiatrist, Dr. Henry A. Davidson, found in an interesting study that a considerable percentage of cigarette smokers gave as their reason for smoking the belief that filter tips have removed the harmful material.

The smoking habit, with real dependence on cigarettes, is increasing, especially among young people, including high-school children. To a large extent, advertising is responsible for that.

There are definite underlying psychological motives for excess cigarette smoking. But that does not explain the social phenomenon. The reasons for the absence of legal and administrative protection of the public, especially the young, are political and economic. Many senators and congressmen are from tobacco-growing states and are reluctant to do anything about the $4,000,000,000 tobacco industry. An encouraging sign occurred recently, however. The chairman of the world's second largest advertising agency resigned his position because he did not want to "have anything do with any advertising agency which promotes the sale of cigarettes anywhere in the world." This was not a rash action, but an informed one. Emerson Foote had been active in both the American Cancer Society and the American Heart Association. Young people can learn from this example that the disrespect for human life shown by cigarette advertising is not universal.

### ALCOHOL ADVERTISING

Apart from being a lubricant of violence, alcohol is often a contributing factor to premature death. This is true not only of the severe forms of alcoholism but also for every kind of habitual overdrinking. The life expectancy of excessive drinkers is less than in the general population. Diseases of the heart and liver take an especially heavy toll. Many conditions are aggravated by alcohol —gastric disorders, for example.

Alcoholism is the country's No. 3 health problem, coming right after heart disease and cancer. The nation spends about as much money on liquor as on all hospital and physicians' services. On an average, every American fifteen years of age and older spends $80 a year on beer, wine, and liquor. There are counties where 6 percent of all adults are alcoholics. In some counties, 80 percent of the fourteen-year-olds have been introduced to drinking. Alcoholism among women and teenagers is increasing.

In the field of alcoholism, preventive medicine has a very important and essentially promising task. What is the greatest obstacle? The disregard for human life as shown by alcohol over-advertising. Much of this advertising is not designed to inform (communicate) but is meant to seduce. We are urged to believe that whatever we do, alcohol will help us do it better. This is expressly stated for all spheres of life: parties, homemaking, family life, Christmas, friendship, sports, patriotism, gracious living, romance, status, travel. A typical illustrated advertisement (a young man and a girl on a ship): "The night lights glimmer with a holiday happiness, and moment by moment care slips away. Now is the time, and anywhere is the place, for the smooth elegance of [brand name] (86.8 proof)." Some radio and television stations now carry commercials for hard liquor, although formerly there was a tradition to exclude them. Another breakthrough is that more and more alcohol advertising is addressed to women. You are shown a glamorous young woman, glass in hand, or with a highball on the table or tray beside her. You see her in a glowing mood, and you are given to understand where the glow comes from—alcohol. This sort of promotion is in part responsible for the current increase in alcoholism among women, especially harassed housewives. There used to be a tradition that the national women's magazines did not carry alcohol advertisements. Now we see ads advising home-makers to serve liquor "always, with any meal." In the weeks before Christmas, one liquor firm alone recently spent $6,000,000 on advertising and sales promotion.

Apologists for alcohol commercials have stated that the advertisers do not show a person, especially a girl, actually drinking, but "only pouring it into a glass." That is the same as if a person who advertises pornography were to say in his defense that he does not show actual sexual intercourse but merely the final preparations for it.

Overdrinking is related to overadvertising. It is futile to try to do something about excessive drinking if we don't care about excessive advertising. In countries where there is less alcohol over-advertising, there is less overdrinking. Public health activity against alcoholism can be effective only if it makes use of the means of mass communication to impart scientific information to the public. At present, these media through their advertisements work strongly and successfully in the opposite direction, evincing a disrespect for human life and an unconcern for it which fertilize the soil for violence.

ARMS ADVERTISING FOR THE NURSERY

One day in the fall of 1964, I visited an acquaintance in one of the more affluent suburbs near New York City. As I was looking through a window with a view of adjoining gardens, I saw children playing near a wall. The youngest were just toddlers; some were three or four years old; the oldest were not more than twelve. They were playing war. It was really a savage game, with rough infighting, throwing one another to the ground, and shouting and yelling. They had pistols, rifles, machine guns, and bazookas. Most of the boys had two guns, and some had pseudobayonets. All the arms looked very real. They wore helmets and other warlike headgear. I heard one boy yell out, directing two others, "You mow them down when I wave!" The fighting was so rough that first one little boy, then another ran away in tears. The others laughed at this. One boy was tied to a tree, his clothes half torn off. He was facing execution. One girl was led away into captivity. I have often seen children playing on the sidewalks in New York, but never a group so heavily armed with all the instruments of violence and destruction.

I remember the date of this occasion, because it was the day the President had declared a day of dedication in memory of President Kennedy's assassination one year before. What tools had we given these children to dedicate themselves with? It seemed to me that President Kennedy was being killed a second time, this time in spirit. As far as these gun-carrying children were concerned, instead of Kennedy Day, this day might just as well have been called Lee Harvey Oswald Day.

Toys of violence teach disrespect for human life. Children learn the fascinating feeling of power that comes from aiming even a toy weapon. The first person we know of who spoke up against violent toys for children was a very intelligent woman, Goethe's mother, who refused to buy a toy guillotine which the poet wanted to give to his six-year-old son. We have not learned that lesson yet. Advertising plays a most important role in the domestic arms race for the children's market. These advertisements—or, more correctly, pervertisements—have planted in the child's mind, and that of his parents, the idea that hardly anything is more important in a child's life than a collection of guns, knives, and any conceivable variety of warlike toys. With ingenious methods, including the mobilization of experts, a whole generation of parents and children has been persuaded that playing with weapons (or exact replicas thereof) has nothing whatever to do with violence. For toy guns alone, parents spend millions of dollars every year. We delude ourselves if we continue to believe that play with toy weapons, especially by preschool children, is entirely harmless. The enticing advertisements for weapons, combined with the violence seen on television, condition children to enjoy violence. A toy gun is an invitation to play-killing. The youngsters in my group-therapy sessions have a simple term for all these weapons and war toys. They call them "kill toys."

It is a strange paradox of our time that you see intelligent parents voicing opposition to nuclear war while their children at home are absorbed in play with missiles that have toy atomic warheads. A country that gives its children so many war toys, toys with war.

In a recent humanitarian French movie, *Taxi for Tobruk,* the widow of a German officer killed in the war in Africa shows her young child, while he is playing, photographs of his ancestors who had died for their country: the great-grandfather in the Franco-Prussian war of 1870–1871, the grandfather in the First World War, the father in the Second World War. The little boy keeps on playing with his wooden toy gun. The mother takes it away from him and throws it in the fireplace. The message is that the idea of violence is the same, from toy guns to war. It is generally recognized that construction toys and tools serve wholesome ends and may give children constructive ideas which they may not have had before. Destructive toys suggest and encourage destructive trends in the same way.

To speak of toy guns in the atomic age may sound incongruous. But even small signs have to be taken seriously, because they may influence the individual and may give us hints about the mood and mores of a society.

We can distinguish four types of guns that have been widely advertised for years in magazines and newspapers, on radio and television, and in many millions of the comic books which are especially merchandised for children:

1. Toy guns that cannot be easily mistaken for or converted into real guns
2. Toy guns that look exactly like real guns but cannot be converted
3. Toy guns that can be converted into real weapons that are dangerous and lethal
4. Real guns (pistols and rifles)

Children can obtain all four categories directly though these advertisements. They can, of course, also pressure their parents into buying them.

Guns in the first category are an introduction to play with violence. Thirty-five years ago if a boy of three or four insisted on having two big guns in a holster so that he could carry them with him, it might have been suspected that there was something wrong with him. Today—thanks to advertising—it is just the opposite. The boy without a gun may be suspected of being a sissy by his classmates in kindergarten; his parents may have been told in skillfully devised promotional material: "There's a right time for the right toy," and the right time for guns and "two-holster belts" is the age group "two to four years" for both sexes. Even toys in this first category are not so harmless physically. In an extreme case, a four-year-old boy who loved to play with them had a whole collection. Once when he was in a grocery store with his mother, he spotted an old revolver which the woman who owned the store kept on a shelf. He did some more playing. He took this revolver, pointed it at the woman, and pulled the trigger. She died from a bullet wound in the stomach.

Another variety of toy gun is the widely advertised gunbrush. It is a toothbrush in a container in the form of a gun. "At gunpoint, a toothbrush!" says the advertisement, promising that this toothbrush will make your boy positively "trigger-happy"! Another advertisement says: "Pull the trigger and you get a satisfying realistic click." Such toothbrush guns will not make a child a murderer, but they show that every opportunity is taken to suggest to children the pleasure of playing with violence.

With the imitation pistols in the second category, many holdups and burglaries have been and are being committed. The police commissioner of New York City reported in 1962 that there was a tremendous rise in crimes perpetrated with the aid of these weapons. A typical advertisement for one of the multitude of these says: "Not only does it smoke like a real gun—it looks like one, too!"

Many of these guns are made from molds of real pistols. In 1965, particularly realistic-looking guns were found in the hands of children as young as ten. They resemble .38-caliber pistols so closely that they fool even experienced police officers. This can have tragic consequences. When a fifteen-year-old boy recently entered a store carrying one of these toys, two police officers tried to question him. He playfully pointed his toy gun at them. They mistook it for a real one and shot him dead.

When children are found with these realistic toy guns, they are apt to be turned over to the juvenile bureau of the police department. What about the advertisers?

With toys in the third category, which can be converted into zip guns and similar weapons, serious injury and death can be inflicted. Often adults have no idea that what seem to be harmless toy guns can do real harm. A three-year-old girl, playing, fired a genuine .32-caliber cartridge from a toy gun. She had found a real bullet and inserted it in a cap gun which was designed to fire plastic bullets and small percussion caps. Some of the toy guns eject a bullet or slug with such force that they can put out an eye.

Advertisements and commercials for these three categories condition the youngest children and their parents to believe that shooting is a part of the growing-up process. The demilitarization of the nursery has to begin here.

Having for years advocated such a disarmament on the basis of clinical studies, I have learned what the many obstacles are. They are not the destructive instincts in children or the lack of good sense on the part of parents. The major obstacle is the high-pressure advertising of the manufacturers. Another is the rationalizations supplied by psychologists, psychiatrists, and child experts. In Freud's peaceful Vienna a dream about a gun may have been a harmless sex symbol, but in our civilization it is more likely to be a crystallized intention to kill, in play or in earnest. Again and again it has been stated that guns are good for building a boy's character. One psychiatrist has observed that "as small boys shoot each other without mercy, their faces glow with excitement." He upholds the notion that this kind of excitement is all right because "the boys are working through their ancestral past," "they are as innocent as the kittens pouncing on each other's tail." Such opinions, propounded in the name of psychiatry, are part of the intellectual decadence and violence-mindedness of our time. Some child experts have declared that gunplay in childhood can have nothing to do with later behavior because delinquency is due to bad social influences. They do not seem to realize that the toy-gun industry itself is a social phenomenon—and an influential one.

One of the most widely known child experts has stated that "depriving American boys of toy pistols" "would be tampering with precious traditions." Is it an American tradition precious enough to be preserved, to give millions of children even an inkling of disregard for human life? In the very month when President Kennedy was killed, the expert presented this image to American parents: "The 6-year-old boy who hasn't yet learned how to stand up to the other boys on the block . . . brandishing a toy pistol. . . ." The idea conveyed is that a city boy needs a toy gun to gain self-confidence and maintain himself on the block. That can be looked at from a very different angle. A boy should gain self-confidence with less artificial means than a gun. The self-confidence derived from weapons often leads to arrogance. To use a gun for individual self-assertion and to improve one's self-image is just what we should eliminate. Moreover, why should we take for granted that there always has to be conflict and hostility on the block, for the children to fight out while brandishing toy guns? It is our civic responsibility to decrease and abolish it where it does exist.

The real guns, in the fourth category, have been advertised for years to children, and boys of thirteen and fourteen have obtained deadly .22-caliber rifles just by answering these advertisements. In cities there is nothing for boys to hunt except other boys.

A full-page advertisement by a firearms manufacturing company in *Parents' Magazine* shows how parents are pressured by ads addressed to their most earnest desires for the best for their children. The text is as persuasive as it is fallacious. It warns parents that "overprotection is harmful"; that playing with toy guns and watching Westerns on television is a "healthy outlet"; that both boys and girls "want to progress from toy guns to real guns as they want to progress from kiddy-cars to automobiles" (surely an odd comparison); that denying a real gun to a child is a "prejudice based on the harm a gun might do"; that firearms are a means to the "teaching of maturity and responsibility to children."

The harm, psychological and physical, that real guns can do in the hands of children is greatly underrated. The temptation (a word that occurs rarely in modern psychological texts) to use them experimentally is great, the danger of accident even greater. The father of two boys, aged five and nine, responded to advertising by buying the nine-year-old a .22-caliber rifle so that the boy could possess a gun of his own. He intended to take the boy that same evening to a rod-and-gun club for instructions in safe use of the rifle. That afternoon, the two boys played with the gun in the living room of their home. They inserted cartridges in the rifle and ejected them, trying to see how far the shells would fly when ejected. While the gun was in the hands of the younger boy, it accidentally discharged and the older boy was killed.

Such a typical case raises a number of questions. Through what influences does a decent and intelligent boy get the desire to own a gun of his own? Can a rod-and-gun club really instruct a young child in the safe use of firearms? And, most important, does it not show disrespect for human life to advertise guns for children? An editorial in the magazine *Pennsylvania Game News* recently stated that sooner or later every American boy wants a real gun that shoots real bullets. If that is true the advertisers carry a real load of responsibility for it. For a gun represents violence. Children are no more born with a desire for a gun than adults are born with a desire for an atom bomb. While crediting the fact that under special circumstances an adolescent may put a gun to useful purposes on a farm in the country, we should remember that the frontier has long since vanished from most of America. It is not fair to let our children be seduced by our own dreams of a rugged pioneer past.

A particularly clear example of the disrespect for human life in advertising directed at children is furnished by ads for switchblade knives. For years, illustrated advertisements for them appeared in tens of millions of comic books. In England, where they are called flick knives, they are forbidden by a law well named the Offensive Weapons Act. These knives have no constructive use whatsoever. They serve only as weapons for threats or very sudden attacks. They can also be easily concealed. They have been used by adolescents for assaults, extortions, rapes, burglaries. All attempts to stop this advertising in the United States were fruitless. They were answered by the rationalization that these knives are the expression of youth's natural instinct of aggression. The advertising did not stop until finally switchblade knives were forbidden by law —for adults.

How far this disrespect for life goes can be seen from the games advertised directly to children. A full-page ad in a recent comic book promotes one called Missile Attack. With this game, children get "enough nuclear battle equipment for maximum effect and massive counterattack." The description announces: "You deliver the nuclear knockout." Children's minds are sufficiently filled with talk and images of war as it is. Recently a teacher asked in class, "What is a mushroom?" And a little boy answered, "It looks exactly like the explosion of an atom bomb."

The Christmas season of 1965–1966 was a high point in toy weaponry. As the *New Yorker* expressed it, the toy manufacturers "loosed the dogs of war on the counters." Children could have a camera which opens to form a pistol, a transistor radio which forms a rifle, a briefcase which conceals a dagger, and a toy called Seven Guns in One. If children are not destruction-minded, the toy industry is doing its best to make them so. For these weapon-toys are not only merchandise, but also carry a message: Murder is fun, and war is a pleasure.

In rebuttal to criticism of war toys and games, it is sometimes said that they do no "specific harm." That is quite true. Children don't start wars. The damage is not that children are being made belligerent and want to invade and bomb other nations. The harm done consists primarily in the fact that they unlearn respect for life and become conditioned to accept violence and war. Recently the advertising manager of a big toy corporation stated that war toys are beneficial. They stimulate children "to keep up with current events." One can only hope that current events will not keep up with what the children play.

# CHAPTER FIVE

# Climates for Violence

Where illegality reigns by law
The rule of reason must withdraw.
—GOETHE

We have strewn cruelty upon the earth.
—H. W. NEVINSON

## Fascism

THE term "fascism" should not be bandied about lightly and used where it does not strictly apply. Not every modern reactionary government is fascist. When fascism comes to power it is not merely the development of one government into another essentially similar one. There is a sharp break leading to a regime characterized by open violence. Other regimes, democratic, socialist, and communist, have committed violence and applied terror. But they have regarded it as an aberration or a temporary expedient and looked forward to a nonviolent time and have not advocated violence in principle. For fascism, violence is the ideal and the reality. That is the difference. According to fascism, peace is a degrading utopia, and war is for men what maternity is for women. "In all Fascist thinking," as the *Times Literary Supplement* puts it, "war was a good thing."

Violence is the politics of fascism. We can express it this way: violence is an immanent part of fascism, and fascism is the apotheosis of mass violence. Countless people have lost their lives because they did not recognize this fundamental truth but instead harbored all sorts of social illusions. Millions who were declared politically, racially, nationally, socially, or productively inferior were killed. It was not merely violence in the form of terrorism; it also included calculated genocide, as we now call it. As Djuma Mbogo of Rwanda (where thousands died in massacres) has written: "Genocide in Rwanda as elsewhere follows logically on fascism."

How little the essential violence character of fascism was recognized can be seen from two examples. Even the leftist political parties did not realize the radical and extensive use the Nazis would make of violence and what tremendous power (whether we like to admit it or not) that gave them. On January 30, 1933, when Hitler was named Chancellor, the official Communist newspaper in Berlin, *The Red Flag,* had this banner headline:

HITLER REIGNS—COMMUNISM MARCHES ON!

And the *Workers Newspaper,* the official Socialist organ in Vienna, wrote: "Hitler could not wait any longer. Every day made him weaker. He chose the other eventuality: the chancellorship—in truth, surrender."

As these two quotations show, the ruthlessness, the extent, and the effectiveness of violence had been greatly underestimated—as is so often the case.

What was in essence, though not in name, the first fascist regime in the modern world was established by the victorious Allies after the First World War in Hungary. It started a reactionary political pattern of persuasion by open violence and the typically fascistic combination of bureaucratic and sadistic violence. The term "fascism" itself first came up in Italy in the early twenties. For a long time, people did not know what it really represented. The Italian writer Emilio Marinetti expressed most clearly what fascism means: daily heroism, love of danger, glorification of force and war, and, most characteristic, "violence considered as an argument."

Although it may have different features in different countries, the political-historical essence of fascism is always the same, whether it is the Action Française, Italian fascism, German national socialism, or Falangist fascism in Spain.

When fascism, under the deceptive name of national socialism, was advocated in Germany, it was not readily recognized that Nazism is fascism. Yet the Nazi program had stated very clearly that what was needed—and coming forthwith—was the "iron fist of a dictator," that there would be a "folk battle for power," and that "battle means war against many." When Hitler came to power, it was a mortal blow to any prospect of a peaceful world. Collective security became collective insecurity. He had begun by instilling fear, threatening force, and practicing and preaching sporadic violence. Now violence became the law of the land. As late as the middle thirties, few writers, including correspondents, understood the violent substance of German fascism as well as Thomas Wolfe. The population, he wrote, is "infested with the contagion of an ever-present fear" and shows a "plague of the spirit—invisible but as unmistakable as death."

Why does a modern nation write violence on its banner? Most facile and noncommittal are the purely and exclusively psychological explanations. They do not stand up under scientific scrutiny. For a psychological study of Nazi violence, we would have to include a variety of agents: those who directly commit the acts and supervise them (executioners, concentration-camp guards, soldiers who kill civilians, police, *et al.*); those who command these acts; those who organize them (the Eichmann type); the upper echelon of leaders, civilian and military; those who backed the Leader or Il Duce financially from the beginning; the thousands of followers who participated in various ways or applauded or acquiesced for years; the many professionals and intellectuals who approved the violence, compromised with it, or supplied made-to-order theories to justify and support it. All these were necessary for the fascist regime to stay in power and continue its violence. Obviously it would be futile to look for common psychological characteristics in the individual among such diverse people. Psychological factors did, of course, enter; but they can be properly evaluated only together with the social matrix in which they operated. In the light of the hard economic and political facts, psychological speculations about whether the individual fascist follower had a "character structure" with "authoritarian" or "masochistic" tendencies seem farfetched. The individualistic psychoanalytic speculations about fascism offer no remedy, and their practical consequences are not action but inaction. The responsibility is transferred from the social to the individual and from the individual to nowhere.

To put all the onus of fascist mass violence on individual leaders like Hitler means to ascribe to them a personal greatness and power (even for evil) which they did not possess. Hitler did not set blind forces into motion. On the contrary, very conscious ones set him in motion. To explain what happened by the irrationality of the leaders means to ignore the very rational forces that brought them to power. It is a most convenient evasion. It narrows down the responsibility to something one could have done nothing about. Psychopathological diagnoses of fascist leaders are mostly based on speculation and facile analogies. For instance, one psychoanalyst writes in all seriousness: "Life in the dark forests affected the thinking of the German tribes," and, "It apparently did not occur [to Hitler] that he was conquering an entire country [Austria] in order to revenge himself on his father."

Similarly, in 1947 the Commissioner of Mental Health in the state of Massachusetts described Hitler's case history as an example of mental disease, stressing that he had an overbearing father and an indulgent mother, that he was unable to make a successful economic adjustment, that he had delusions of grandeur, that at the last he imagined commanding nonexistent armies, that his program of aggression and sadism offered an answer to the neurotic needs of people. To reduce a sociopolitical problem to a cliché of mental pathology in this way is a disservice to the cause of antiviolence.

Hitler, Goebbels, and Goering were not exceptional or demonic characters. Except for Hitler's oratorical gifts, these men were not different from multitudes of others. Of course, Hitler was more fanatical than the ordinary man or he would not have become the leader; but, in fact, the trick was to be just like the others and so to merge with the crowd and facilitate identification with the leaders. Mediocrity was one of the Nazi leaders' assets, one of the foundations of their power. Hitler was an easily recognizable lower-middle-class type, fanatically patriotic, full of indignation, ready to serve financially powerful masters, and finally dying a fiery, violent death, like a comic-book criminal-hero. Goebbels was a shallow, vain journalist and resourceful publicity man with a dash of Heidelberg University training. Goering was a typical officer with political and financial ambitions. They all had energy and no scruples, and knew (as did many others) that violence is an easy method against the unwary.

Explanation of history by the individual psychology of leaders is a hazardous undertaking. Psychological evaluations vary and change according to the times and circumstances. Winston Churchill, certainly a connoisseur of men, spoke in Rome after Il Duce had been in power for five years of "Signor Mussolini's gentle and simple bearing and his calm, detached poise." Arnold Toynbee was convinced of Hitler's sincerity in desiring peace. A leading educator, George N. Shuster, president of Hunter College in New York, wrote in 1934 that "Hitler is destined to go down to history as a cross between Hotspur and Uncle Toby and to be as immortal as either." André Gide, an acknowledged psychological author, wrote: "He [Hitler] behaves like a genius. I particularly admire the diversity of his methods. . . . Soon even those he vanquishes will feel compelled, while cursing him, to admire him." And many others wrote in a like vein. Even if individual psychological summing up of personalities were undertaken more scientifically and objectively, it could not explain the development of fascism. Nor can social psychology alone help us by studying national character, considering how many nations at one time or another have espoused the cause of fascism and how many people of different nationalities have helped fascists in operation. If we do not want to be led astray by fancy psychological theories, we must pry wider and deeper.

✓Fascism, with its politics of physical force, is not accidental, nor is it a symptom of individuals. It is a historical event, the outcome of concrete, objectively demonstrable socioeconomic processes. One small statistical detail can help to introduce us to the social reality of prefascist Germany. By the spring of 1932, about one-half of all trade-union members were unemployed, one-fourth only partially employed. These figures have added significance because a large percentage of German workers were in trade unions; they mean that every second family in Germany was hit by unemployment or semiemployment. In peacetime, some degree of unemployment is almost always present in a capitalist economy. When it reaches such catastrophic proportions, however, it results in profound changes in attitude. Most important, the hope of employment dies out. The gulf between those denied participation in the process of production, which they experience as a denial of the right to live, and those who resent having to pay more taxes to keep the idle going gets wider and wider. Those who profit from the system as it is want to maintain it at all costs. Here is one of the chief roots of fascism. The bulk of the people looking for a way out become ready to accept and believe in two things: a false savior and a false scapegoat. In Germany the industrial magnates supplied both. Seconded by big bankers and landed nobility, they selected Adolf Hitler, who had made a name for himself by advocating ruthless methods, and brought him to power. They gave him the commission to bring about a strongly rearmed Germany and muzzle the labor movement. That could be achieved and maintained only with the aid of violence.

We have all seen and heard Hitler in newsreels and in television documentaries addressing large crowds. We are less familiar with the important early occasions when he met small august groups of economic leaders. For example, in February, 1926, he was invited to address the National Club of 1919 at Hamburg. This was a conservative club of industrialists, big businessmen, and high officials and officers. His methods were approved by the audience. In the autumn of 1931, he was invited by a leading steelman, Fritz Thyssen, to speak at Essen, the heart of an important industrial region, before the Club of Industrialists. He was fully accepted, and his large financial support was assured. In January, 1932, Thyssen introduced Hitler to a group of 600 major industrialists at the Manufacturers Club in Düsseldorf. There Hitler outlined his programs and plans: ruthless dictatorship at home, war adventures abroad. His audience cheered. In February, 1933, Hitler was invited to speak before the commanding officers of the army. He presented his ideas, including war plans and the plan to Germanize ruthlessly the occupied countries. The Krupp and Thyssen concerns were among the earliest financial supporters of the Nazis. As Alfred Krupp stated in 1946: "We are realists, we wanted to produce and therefore put our efforts behind the man who made our work secure." Hitler kept his promises and executed the plans that were financed by the industrial leaders: violence at home and abroad.

Here we come face to face with one of the crucial problems of violence. This certainly sounds like irrational violence. Can it be at all understood from an individual angle alone? We like to flatter ourselves and indulge in the belief that this kind of cold-blooded cruelty is far from us and from our modes of life. Is it? The truth is that when Krupp and Thyssen and others endorsed Hitler and heavily invested in his plans, their investment was commercially sound. It paid. The Thyssen industrial concern is today one of the biggest in Europe. And Krupp, who also used slave labor extensively, became one of the richest men in Europe. The victims do not appear on the ledgers any more. In the long run, the investment in fascism by the higher industrial and banking strata proved a good one. German industry did not lose the Second World War; it won.

What people were told and thought they were doing was another story. Long before the rule of fascism, a whole literature had laid the groundwork, hypernationalistic and superman-oriented. The young people especially were conditioned to violence by being told in high-sounding books that they were by birth an elite whose duty it was to expand and conquer. In this way, decent people who loved their homes and children were brought around to picture themselves as heroes. They became willing to kill others who loved theirs. The permissible victims were all those within the country who were declared officially to be inferior or subhuman and any opponents in a foreign country. If we do not include this long-standing indoctrination, the chain of causality of fascistic mass violence cannot be fully understood. Justification of violence, which is really exhortation to violence, occurred in the most unlikely places. For example, in an introduction to Plato's *Dialogues* the psychiatrist and philosopher Kurt Hildebrandt wrote "The creative spirit justifies war and destruction."

Fascism cannot be changed. It cannot be "liberalized." Murder is not only its weapon but its real emblem. In August, 1936, the poet and playwright Federico García Lorca, whom Dr. Félix Martí-Ibáñez has called "the great modern popular Spanish poet," was taken at midnight from his bed in Granada by a detachment of fascist guards, the Escuadra Negra, as the people called them. He was taken first to the building of the *gobernador civil* and then by force to a lonely country house, La Colonia, a Fascist Party headquarters. On the first floor of that building, dances were held in a brothellike atmosphere; in the cellar, prisoners were tortured. The following day, Lorca was removed to a lonely ravine, forced to dig his own grave, and shot. His plays were not performed in Madrid until 1960. Then one of them was performed there, to frenetic applause from the audience. But the Franco government forbade any extensive reviews in the newspapers, and a magazine which did print a long review could be distributed only after the review was cut out. As Lorca's recent biographer Guenter Lorenz writes: "Murder has still to be called murder, even if the murderers have long since been accepted in good society."

Fascism is by its very nature violent and regressive. It would be naïve to think that it affects only the lives of those in countries where it is in power or where attempts are being made to install it. On the contrary, it can have far-reaching influences on other countries. It is a focus of infection. And like any focal infection in the body, it can have distant effects. As long as a fascist regime exists in a great country like Spain and is accepted and helped by other nonfascist countries, the idea of banishing violence from the world remains an idle dream.

## Colonialism

All colonialism is fundamentally based on violence. Just as fascism can be seen as the application of colonial methods to one's own country, so colonialism can be looked at as the application of fascistic methods to a foreign country. In some respects, fascism is a kind of colonialism at home, while colonialism is fascism abroad. The violence as such is the same, and even the economic motives have a lot in common. Of course, this is not an identity but a similarity. The historical-political circumstances are different. Some phenemona have a striking resemblance nonetheless. Long before the unto-death slave-labor camps in Germany, in which so many perished, forced labor under the most cruel conditions existed in the Congo. This was not only as long as the Congo Free State belonged to King Leopold, but also under the rule of the Belgian Parliament. As Mark Twain expressed it: "In many countries we have taken the native's land from him and made him our slave, and lashed him every day, and broken his pride and made death his only friend, and overworked him till he dropped in his tracks."

Colonies are created by violence. They are distant territories which the stronger nation has conquered by the use or threat of arms, annexed, and continues to maintain in subjection in the same way. No state has willingly become a colony. The purposes of colonization are essentially four: to extract as much wealth as possible, partly by cheap labor; to obtain raw materials and foods; to find markets for manufactured products; to establish military, naval, and air stations. In the course of time, the colonizing nation acquires what it considers permanent property rights.

The incidence and form of violence and brutality vary with different nations, countries, and periods. But the over-all record shows that physical force is a common denominator. In 1761, William Law, famous for his defense of human nature against the charge of essential vileness, wrote against the Europeans "sailing around the globe with fire and sword and every murdering art of war to seize the possessions and kill the inhabitants of both the Indies." Almost two hundred years later, Ananda Coomaraswamy, the great authority on Indian art and philosophy, could deplore the colonial massacres, the firing on unarmed crowds, the floggings, the imprisonments without trials in colonial India. In the beginning of this century, Anatole France spoke out against the brutal wars of expansion and annexation against the Chinese on the part of European nations. Have the Chinese, he asked in his ironic manner, the right to defend themselves with their porcelain cannons against our modern artillery? The European nations, he wrote, restore order in China by robbery, rape, plundering, murder, and arson. And he added the statement that those who profit from "violent colonization" deceive themselves if they think it will last forever.

"Colonialism," in the words of the psychiatrist Dr. Frantz Fanon, "is violence in its natural state." The wholesale killing of native populations in colonies may seem to us to be a thing of the past. But it is part of my thesis that the spirit of this violence is anything but dead—quite apart from the still-existing colonies. In 1962 a German professor of international law was reported to have told his students: "The Negro is incapable of self-control and self-discipline. It was the greatest mistake of Western colonial policy that the sovereign race did not deport or exterminate the Negroes fifty years ago." In the same year, U.S. Senator Allen J. Ellender of the Senate Appropriations Committee made a ninety-day tour of the continent of Africa. He concluded that the average Africans are "unprepared for self-government" and incapable of governing without white help. He defended the role of the Portuguese in their African colonial possessions, where notoriously violent methods have been used. The shadow of colonial and post-colonial violence still hangs over the world.

The natives of colonies have a pervasive subconscious fear of physical harm from their masters. This is not a neurotic anxiety but a realistic attitude based on what they have experienced and on what their parents, grandparents, and relatives have told them. It is transmitted from generation to generation. Usually a rosy picture is painted, for home consumption, of all the benefits the rulers bestow on their colonial subjects. The violence is concealed. Occasionally humane and courageous writers lift the veil—E. D. Morel, Sir Roger Casement, Mark Twain. Often the truth about the cruelties becomes known only after the sovereignty of the colonial power has ended, as in the German "model colony" Togo in West Africa, described by Manfred Nussbaum.

The colonial powers do not like to talk about violence. They prefer to talk about schools rather than prisons, missionaries rather than the military, education rather than forced labor, roads and railways instead of road gangs, the money they put in but not the wealth they extract. They boast of bringing civilization to the savage, religion to the heathen, hospitals to the sick. They leave out that it is the threat of force and brutality in their daily life that keeps the population willing. We must be on guard against the propaganda that anywhere in the world the colonial powers have given more than they have taken away or that they have acted without the threat or use of violence.

Colonial power corrupts not only those whom it affects but the colonizers themselves. They become infected with smug superiority. However well disguised and rationalized it may be, what their real underlying feeling toward their subject people is has been well described by Rudyard Kipling:

> Your new-caught, sullen peoples,
> Half-devil and half-child.

It is on this sociopsychological basis that the bureaucracy of brutality flourishes.

When cruelties in a colony become public, the authorities prefer to call it a transgression of one specific individual official. But that sort of facile explanation, blaming one individual sadist, usually does not hold when the general policy relies on physical oppression as the instrument of power. Torture is the worst form of violence. Its use is more rampant in colonies than in home countries. It is one of the methods of colonial suppression. Jean-Claude Paupert, a Frenchman who was one of the first to document the tortures in colonial Algeria and was imprisoned by his government as a result, has pointed out that torture is so closely allied to colonialism that it is impossible to fight the one without fighting the other. At his trial he stated: "I have learned that the good souls are wrong to protest each time against torture, for torture in a colonial regime is legitimate."

Even those who have the greatest sympathy for oppressed populations may sometimes underestimate or overlook the influence of the violence factor on the state of mind of native people. For example, as outstanding and humanitarian a writer as Leonard Woolf, whose *Diaries in Ceylon,* about his time as colonial administrator, was recently published, does not seem to be really conscious of how much four hundred years of physical oppression and pillage by Portuguese, Dutch, and British rulers had directly caused the state of the people as he found them.

The close association of colonialism to brutality is well illustrated by the history of aerial bombings. The isolated dropping of bombs from fighter planes in World War I was relatively minor. Deliberate air bombing of civilian populations was first practiced on colonial people—"captives," as Rudyard Kipling called them. It meant, of course, massacres of women and children. One of the first civilian air massacres, the bombing of villages, was carried out in what is now Yemen in about 1923 by the Royal Air Force. Later the British bombed civilians in northern India; the French bombed the recalcitrant Riff population; and under the colonial ministry of Paul Reynaud, women and children were air-bombed in Indochina. All these incidents were directed against colonial peoples.

The slave trade, carried out with fearful brutality and cruelty and approved of in its time by both the secular and the spiritual establishments, was of course closely allied to colonialism. It has been estimated that the slave trade cost the continent of Africa 150,000,000 lives. The effects on the whole economic and cultural development were enormous. In fact, this is one of the reasons why countries in Africa are underdeveloped today. We like to explain away these consequences of violence by ascribing the underdevelopment to a supposed racial inferiority.

In addition to the violence of the original conquest, the continuing "pacification," and the violence applied in the daily life and labor of the natives, there is another kind: *hidden* violence, or what may be called social murder. A large percentage of colonial populations die prematurely, from neglect, curable and preventable diseases, and, especially, hunger and malnutrition. The social conditions leading to this mass hunger are maintained by the threat or use of open physical force. Hunger has the same power over man that violence has, the power of life and death. In fifty years of French rule in Madagascar, the population was reduced by more than a half (from 10,000,000 to 4,500,000). We must try to visualize the misery involved in such figures. According to reports for the British Colonial Office, a very large proportion of peasants in Bengal subsisted on a diet on which rats could not survive more than five weeks. In 1930 there was a great famine in the colonial provinces of Tonkin and Annam (now part of Vietnam). When unarmed processions of natives appealed for relief, they were mowed down with machine guns by the French Foreign Legion. Thus hidden violence led to overt violence.

One of the greatest tragedies of humanity was the famine of 1943–1944 in India, when 3,000,000 people perished within a year. It was not what was called a "normal" famine, that is, one due to natural catastrophes, but was caused by mismanagement and black-market operations. The Indian painter Chittaprasad, a pupil of Abindranath Tagore, called it "an avalanche of mass murders."

The relationship of colonization to violence is threefold:

1. The threat or use of open physical force against colonial people
2. The hidden violence in the form of hunger, malnutrition, and overwork
3. The division of colonial possessions among the great powers

The last named has been a great war-producing factor. For example, few people in 1914 expected the outbreak of a world war. And yet during the four decades preceding 1914, the groundwork was laid for a major conflict of interests and spheres of influence. In that relatively short period, the great powers—England, Russia, France, Germany, Japan, and the United States—obtained sovereignty over distant territories two and a half times the size of the whole of Europe. It meant the imposition of colonial status on 523,000,000 people. The division of these possessions is an important feature of the previolence phase of World War I.

Elements of some of the economic-social features of colonialism persist today in other political relations. Sociologists and political scientists speak of half-colonies and of neocolonialism, of indirect colonialism and hidden colonialism. This means that an industrially and economically stronger nation penetrates an economically weaker one. Some French authors speak of *les nations prolétaires* in contrast to the developed, affluent countries. It is only recently that these weaker nations have been called underdeveloped countries. Their underdevelopment is in large part due to previous colonial overexploitation. All these relationships have great potentialities for ill will and possible violence. Latin America is an example. It has been estimated that of 192,000,000 people living there, 100,000,000 suffer from hunger and malnutrition. At the same time, big U.S. firms made on the continent of Latin America in a five-year period $3,479,000,000 profit.

In Brazil, 750,000 children die yearly; 6,000,000 children

do not reach the age of sixteen; one-half of all newborn do not complete the first year of life. This is a country in which North American firms have a decisive economic position, having invested there more than three-quarters of a billion dollars. And of the aid to underdeveloped countries of the Alliance for Progress, fully three-quarters went to the rich miniature state Guanabara, which is the smallest state of the Estados Unidos do Brasil. It may not be entirely without significance that at President Kennedy's funeral, the Governor of Puerto Rico and the President of the Philippines were present, but not a single Latin American chief of state.

We have many advantages over the underdeveloped countries—economic, educational, cultural. One main advantage is that, as the philosopher and historian Theodor Lessing expressed it, we have "a murder science, a murder technique, a murder industry." It will be a basic problem of the future whether these under-developed countries have a chance to develop full equality without first having to develop our proficiency in these spheres.

In front of one of the buildings of the University of Hamburg in Germany, there stands today an elaborate monument. The realistic statue represents a German colonial officer, Hermann von Wissmann. Below him and reaching up to their master in gestures of obedient submissiveness are two Negroes. The monument does not say how many natives were killed and wounded when Wissmann bloodily suppressed their resistance to the harsh colonial rule in German East Africa.

Colonialism is historically a school for ruthlessness. A world without violence will be a world without colonies. Maybe someday, monuments like that of Wissmann will disappear—this one should have disappeared long ago. Maybe they will be replaced by monuments not to violence and subjection but to nonviolence and freedom.

## Race Prejudice

Race prejudice of any kind is potential violence. Even in its mildest forms, a violence potential is immanent. Racism is the belief that one group of people is by virtue of innate physical and inevitably linked mental characteristics decisively different from another group. This concept of inherent differences is never neutral but leads directly to the idea that one race is superior to another. Race-thinking means in essence that we really disregard what an individual is or does, that we do not identify him as a person, but instead substitute racial biological judgments.

Not only may race discrimination lead to violence; it is in itself latent violence. If we exclude an individual from significant human relationships because of race—that is to say, for biological or alleged biological reasons—we deprive him of his identity. We deny his right to be an individual. That means, in the last analysis, that we are denying him his right to life. Usually this idea is deeply hidden and not recognized, but sometimes it crops up into the open. For example, not so many years ago, testimony was given in open U.S. Senate discussion that "a Negro has no right to live anyhow unless a white man wants him to live." This thought is embedded in all race prejudice. Such prejudice may be operative without the word "race" being mentioned, but wherever it exists, it singles out those who, when other factors come up, may become ready targets. Historically they always have. When in 1938 during an outbreak of Nazi violence the synagogue of Worms, Germany, was completely destroyed, it was the *seventh time* that this had happened since the building was first erected in 1034.

To judge human beings by biological or zoological criteria is a primitive way of thinking. We should therefore not be surprised to find it so intimately linked with the primitive idea of violence. Of course, there is a biological heritage; but an exclusively biological orientation concerning human beings reduces man to an impersonal natural phenomenon. It means that a group is denied not as a representative of ideas or principles but as a biological entity, a creation of nature.

A biological orientation is common to all racists. It is a most convenient method to avoid acknowledgment of unwelcome socioeconomic factors. If everything is due to nature, society is blameless. If, for example, such a large proportion of nonwhite people in the world live in poverty, that is regarded not as a social phenomenon but as a natural one. In this way, both poverty and violence are perpetuated. Even racial discrimination and segregation, which so clearly are socially determined, are represented as a purely biological matter. A member of the U.S. Senate stated: "The colored people have congregated in Harlem. That is due to an inborn instinct. . . . They want to be together. . . . That is nothing but human nature." The full flavor of prejudice represented in this statement is brought out by the fact that in the forties the population density in Harlem was more than six hundred persons per acre, while for Manhattan generally the density was about two hundred per acre. According to the New York Housing Authority, one block in Harlem between Seventh and Eighth Avenues "is reputed to be the most crowded dwelling area in the world."

References to the "soul" of a race—the "Slavic soul" or the "inscrutable Oriental mind"—have led to great confusion and countless cruelties. It would be well if they were replaced by more concrete terms—and thinking—such as tradition, national heritage, or historical development. In our time, a fundamental contrast is supposed to exist between East and West, based on innate and unalterable racial characteristics. It is made to appear that these groups of mankind are totally different. Wide generalizations abound. Western man is supposed to have a "basic personality" all his own—a term purely subjective and speculative. The Eastern-mind-versus-Western-mind contrast is assumed to affect decisively all spheres of human activity. The well-known art critic Roger Fry once wrote: "According to C. G. Jung, Western art implies an extrovert attitude and Eastern art an introvert attitude. Anyone who knows Oriental and Western art at all intimately must shudder at the temerity of any such generalization."

"Western man" is not a scientific category, although it is presented as such. Do Richard Wright, Sigmund Freud, Joseph Conrad, Chopin, S. I. Hayakawa, Kandinski, and Guillaume Apollinaire come under this designation? And what is the "Oriental mind"? The great linguist Dr. Hayakawa has written: "Since Buddha, Confucius, General Tojo, Mao Tse-tung, Syngman Rhee, Pandit Nehru and the proprietor of the Golden Pheasant Chop Suey House all have 'Oriental minds,' it is hard to imagine what is meant."

False contrasts between Western and Oriental minds have

adversely affected communication in all spheres of intellectual life. And in this instance, as in all others, interference with communication fosters violence. The eminent philosopher E. A. Burtt has pointed this out for the realm of philosophy, writing that the "Occidental superiority complex has blocked any genuine cooperation between Western and Eastern thinkers. . . . This complacency is one of the causes of war."

Whatever widens the artificial breach between races smooths the path to violence. Most of the literature on the psychology of races is folklore. In probably no other field is there so much pseudoscientific writing. Mental qualities are enumerated as representing the innate character of a whole race. The superior race is idealistic, knightly, and gifted for leadership; the inferior race is treacherous, oversexed, and unstable. However, the racial image changes when political and social circumstances change. Before their entry on the side of Italy in the First World War, the Rumanians were described in the newspaper *Popolo d'Italia* like this: they have nothing to do with the noble race of Romans; they are a mixture of barbaric tribes subjected by the Romans, namely, Slavs, Tatars, Mongols, Huns, and Turks; they are a riffraff of barbarian, inferior people. When Rumania joined Italy in the war, the same newspaper had this to say: the Rumanians are the worthy offspring of the noble Roman race; having the honor of belonging to the Latin race, it was to be expected that they would join the fight for freedom. It was Schopenhauer who criticized these facile generalizations and wrote: "Human narrow-mindedness, perversity, and baseness appear in every country, only in different form. One calls that national character."

Racism is linked not only with overt but also with hidden violence. In the Union of South Africa, the life-span of colored and native people is thirty years, that of the white population sixty years. The psychoanalyst Dr. Wulf Sachs, who pioneered in psychiatry in South Africa, reported that not one single case of syphilis among black South Africans was properly treated. Senile dementia is unknown among them because they do not live long enough. And yet Heinrich Luebke, Food Minister in the Adenauer government and subsequently President of West Germany, has congratulated the South African government on its racial policy and urged that it be extended to the whole of Africa. "The native problem," he said, "is in good hands here." He recommended the South African government's racial policy as "useful for other countries of the African continent."

In the United States, tuberculosis ranks second as a cause of death among Negroes, whereas it is in fourteenth place among whites. In 1960 the infant mortality among Negroes was more than five times that of the white population. That means that we who tolerate these conditions or defend them are ourselves in fact baby killers. In the same year, 1960, three Negro mothers died in childbirth for every white one. The life expectancy of American Indians is more than twenty years less and that of American Negroes five years less than that of the general population. It has been estimated that of all the people on earth, less than half have a chance to remain alive above the age of ten. Racism plays a large role in this hidden violence.

Postulating innate mental qualities from a physical race concept always implies that there are superior and inferior races. Characterizing a race or an "ethnic group" by mental and emotional qualities may sound scientific and objective, but it is always subjective and evaluative. We need to see the deep inroads that race prejudice, especially in scientific garb, has made in our culture. The Nazis did not invent it; they exploited it. The potential violence is inherent in it in the first place. Dr. A. A. Brill, for many years the leading American psychoanalyst, stated in a postgraduate lecture at Columbia University that "if you go to a neighborhood like Harlem where the colored race predominates, you will be immediately impressed, even infected, by the vivid emotional emanation. The Negroes as a race . . . are very accessible, very ready to talk if you give them the slightest encouragement." Dr. Brill's observations may sound harmless, but quite apart from being patronizing and condescending, they are false and based on pure prejudice. That is very much like what the white people in the Union of South Africa say of Negroes: "Can't you see how happy they are? They even sing and dance." Race-thinking is international. Dr. C. G. Jung stated in a paper read at a congress in the presence of Freud that "the causes for the [sexual] repression can be found in the specific American Complex, namely in the living together with lower races, especially with Negroes. Living together with barbaric races exerts a suggestive effect on the laboriously tamed instinct of the white race and tends to pull it down."

Killing, especially mass killing, does not come naturally to modern man. It needs psychological preparation. There are different ways in which brutalization can be instilled and maintained. The arousal of an impulse, an impetus, to destructive aggression may be enough for fantasy, but it is not enough for action. What is required is a rationalization, an acceptable reason for taking life. One of the best rationalizations is the vilification of the victim. And among all the possible rationalizations, the best and most convenient is race prejudice. If a person is condemned and denied by race alone, which is supposed to affect his whole personality, the vilification can become complete and unanswerable. There is nothing he can do for himself or that society can do for him. The supersocial and superhistorical category of race enables us to conceal from ourselves and others the underlying (usually material) driving forces.

We must make clear to ourselves that there is an easy transition from this belief to the idea that the racially inferior person is not fully human. The first step is that he is no longer considered an individual, but is seen as a type or a stereotype. The second step is that he is regarded as subhuman. Even as generally liberal-minded a poet as Swinburne in a poem called Boer children and women "whelps and dams." The victim may be read out of the human race and regarded as a lower form of life. He is consigned to nonhuman status and is no longer entitled even to mercy. In this way, violence is made acceptable to the respectable man. What is aroused in him is not so much hatred or hostility, although that, of course, is instigated too, but indifference. By this dehumanization, violence can be explained, justified, and propagated. Ananda Coomaraswamy, who opposed both violence and racism, was not believed when he wrote, long before the era of genocide, that if one race considers itself human and another "an essentially inhuman force," it desires not only its complete subordination but its extermination.

The first writer who propounded a modern theory of race-thinking and racialism was a French aristocrat who wrote in the early eighteenth century, Henri de Boulainvilliers. He is hardly recalled today, although his ideas live on. His book contains all the main ingredients of present-day racism: the socioeconomic basis; the idea that one race is biologically completely different from another; the superiority of one race over the other; the dependence of all civilization on the superior race (the Franks over the Gauls); most important, the justification for violence. At its very inception, as this shows, racism was inseparable from violence.

In all the later voluminous literature of racialism, these same elements can be detected. And wherever it became really dominant, in Czarist Russia, Nazi Germany, or the American South, overt violence followed. The many writers and speakers—French, German, American, and others—who preach philosophical and supposedly scientific racialism do not as a rule openly advocate violence. But studying their utterances carefully, we find that occasionally they make statements showing very plainly the close connection between race prejudice and physical force. For example, Eugen Duehring (d. 1921), an influential economist and philosopher against whom Engels wrote his treatise *Anti-Duehring,* wrote: "Nordic man, matured under a cooler sky, has the duty to exterminate the parasitic races in the same way that one just has to exterminate poisonous snakes and wild beasts of prey."

In a unique clinical experiment, the link between race prejudice and violence became unexpectedly evident. In preparation for expert psychiatric opinion later submitted to the U.S. Supreme Court in Washington in 1954, for its historic decision on desegregation, my colleagues and I at the Lafargue Clinic in Harlem examined groups of white and Negro children from Delaware, aged nine to fifteen. They were brought to the clinic from Delaware for that purpose. In psychodiagnostic tests and group discussions with some of the white children, tendencies to violence came out. One of their fantasies was to force Negro children to work while they played. They wanted the colored children "to do all the work while we are playing." Forcing the Negro children meant tying them up with their hands behind their backs: "They shouldn't be tied up all the time, but only when they don't work." The sadistic element was unmistakable. Some of the revealing information came from the children talking not only about themselves, but also about what other children had told them. The readiness for violence was linked to ideas of racial superiority. It became clear that these ideas were not spontaneous with the children, but were suggested by the adult world, including mass media, especially crime comic books in which darkskinned people have been depicted as savages to be beaten and hanged. (The children had some of these comic books with them.)

Lynchings on racial grounds are one of the worst expressions of race prejudice. Between 1882 and 1939, more than 5,000 Negroes were lynched in the United States, more than 1,800 since the year 1900. These statistics are incomplete, inasmuch as they do not include the countless and uncounted persons who have been lynched in a clandestine way and just disappeared without getting into the statistics. They also do not include the many cases in which a Negro is killed by a single white man and also just disappears. In accordance with local custom, almost as a rule these lynchings have not been solved.

When the National Association for the Advancement of Colored People (NAACP) was founded in 1909, its main aim was a federal antilynch law. No clearer indication of the high violence content of our society exists than the fact that such urgent legislation has not been passed to this day. The reason given is that it would infringe on states' rights and be unconstitutional. The states of the Deep South have not prosecuted the overwhelming majority of these cases. It would be hard to believe that it is not the spirit of the Constitution to protect the lives of innocent people. According to William Bradford Huie, who described the "police-assisted" Schwerner-Chaney-Goodman lynch murder, so much violence has been used since the 1954 Supreme Court school decision that "some federal action seems imperative." In the field of water and air pollution, control under states' rights has proved a complete failure. The head of the U.S. Senate Subcommittee on Conservation, Senator Gaylord Nelson, therefore sees federal controls as the only remedy. This comparison is not farfetched. For just as water and air are polluted by poisonous substances, so the social atmosphere is contaminated by uncontrolled murder.

The political-constitutional problem of a national antilynch law may be difficult; the social-ethical problem is simple. Violence tolerated is violence encouraged.

Ghettos are monuments to racism. In Nazi-occupied Warsaw, thousands of German tourists drove in sight-seeing buses through the ghetto. For them it was like an excursion to the zoo. The wretched inhabitants could see their curious faces staring through the bus windows. In New York City, people used to go slumming in the Harlem ghetto, in nightclubs located in blocks where the inhabitants lived in tenements infested by rats which bit sleeping children. (Today the rats are still there.)

One cannot discuss the long history of ghettos without including violence or the history of violence without referring to ghettos. In a ghetto the value of every life is lowered. This is an objective social law. Ghettos are violence prone. On the one hand, the inhabitants are less well protected; on the other, the authorities are much more apt to use violent methods to keep law and order in what is, in a truly democratic sense, essentially an unlawful and disordered setup. Outbreaks of violence in a ghetto are like bouts of fever in the course of a chronic disease. What is important is the chronic disease of discrimination and deprivation. In 1954 the U.S. Supreme Court in Washington ordered the abolition of school segregation, which is intimately related to the persistence of ghettos. If this law is obeyed as little and as slowly as it has been up to now, it will take no less than a hundred years before its aim is accomplished. Every act of racial violence, open or hidden, during that period will be connected by invisible threads with this civic failure. As Harry Golden said in his Jeffrey Lecture at Johns Hopkins University: "It's not a question of whether Negroes can go to school with whites; it is a question of death."

Race riots are a most important violent social phenomenon. They are not simple but complex in structure. Every major race riot is an abortive revolution. That does not mean that any leaders or organizations are involved. All race riots have great similarities with one another, but there are also significant differences, dependent on the locality and the historical period in which they occur. Superficially they represent a break in peace and quiet, unforeseeable and unexpected. Actually, study of the previolence phase shows that they are an outbreak of latent violence. I had occasion at the Lafargue Clinic to examine a number of persons— youths and adults—who participated in riots. They could tell me about themselves, their motives and their feelings before and after, and also about other persons who were involved.

Study of the postviolence phase shows that these riots are generally not resolved. Fundamentally responsible circumstances are not changed, reforms remain on the verbal level. It is therefore not justified for the public and for officials always to be surprised when and where riots occur. The recent riots in Harlem, Brooklyn, Rochester, Elizabeth, and Philadelphia were especially instructive. Almost a year before the most destructive race riot in United States history, in the Watts district of Los Angeles, I wrote in the British magazine *XXth Century:* "They [the recent race riots] were predicted and predictable, just as we can now predict that there will be further riots. Their violence has remained unresolved."

The attempt to "pinpoint" the specific blame for a race riot poses a pseudoproblem. A number of factors are involved, as cause and as determining the nature of the occurrences. The remote factors are much more important than the immediate precipitating ones. The fires lit in race riots were lit long before the riots started. We can dispense with some of the announced theories that race riots are just outbreaks of "hooliganism" caused by "criminals bent on plunder," that they are "emanations of the unconscious" due to "inborn hostilities in all human beings," that they come from "self-alienation" or are just "irrational." The much-blamed "breakdown in Negro family life" is merely a result of other conditions.

The concrete factors, social and psychological, involved in the violence of race riots are varied. Among them are:

1. The despair and morale-shattering effect of chronic unemployment on racial grounds. In the Watts district of Los Angeles, the unemployment rate was twice that of the rest of the county.
2. Poor housing. In Watts the population density was three times the county rate.

3. Violence draws national and worldwide attention, whereas nonviolence evidently doesn't: who ever heard of Watts before the riots? Some of the reasons and descriptions given by rioters resemble those given by participants in prison riots.

4. Legal demonstrations, illegal (forbidden) ones, and riots are not such totally different phenomena as we would like to assume. While legal marches are very different from riots, there are transitions between them; they all are forms of protest and have similar causations. Often a legal demonstration which occurs in a place where it is not wanted is officially called a riot and treated as such.

5. Inadequate social services.

6. Absence of trade-union discipline. Negroes are widely not accepted for union apprenticeship and are compelled to find work outside of trade-union jurisdiction.

7. Vandalism in a group is highly infectious as has been shown by Alex Comfort under totally different circumstances.

8. Poor people take advantage of the situation and start looting.

9. Drug pushers order addicts to loot so that they can get paid and also get more heroin, which runs short during riots anyhow; the addicts do organized looting of entire stores with valuable merchandise.

10. Looting and destruction of stores owned by Negroes has to do with the class angle—for instance, the deep class distinctions among Negroes.

11. Lack of communication between the leaders and the masses.

12. Echoes of overseas events with racial overtones, like the Vietnamese war.

13. Memories of violence done to members of the family or friends and acquaintances in the South.

14. The gospel of violence as preached by the mass media. In a recent television spectacular, the command was shrieked: "Burn! Kill! Devastate! Take their women!

Loot their homes!" (The rape part of the script was not followed in any of the riots.)

15. Ghettos and ghettolike conditions in an environment of affluence are maintained by force and violence (of which the police are a symbol). Rioters see their violence as the obverse of the complacency of the ordinary citizen. If a man in Harlem sees his infant child being bitten by the descendants of the same rats that bit him when he was a child, it is hard for him to have a firm belief in nonviolence.

16. Consciously or unconsciously, rioters intend to express a message. According to the playwright Loften Mitchell, author of *Land Beyond the River,* it is a double one: a cry for help and for recognition.

The diffusion of race prejudice in our cultural environment is greatly underestimated. Violence is its inevitable outcome. It is inherent in the smallest beginnings. Race prejudice is not restricted to any groups or personality types. It does not arise from any innate feature of our human nature. It is imbibed from the environment. That is where it has to be corrected, refuted, and counteracted.

Over the years, race prejudice has penetrated and found a harbor in many phases of our intellectual life, even in the very highest and most unexpected regions. Everybody knows Beethoven's Ninth Symphony as a paean to human brotherhood. As the text for the famous choral part, Beethoven chose an inspiring ode by the idealistic poet Schiller:

> Free and joyful once again,
> All mankind unites fraternal. . . .
> We embrace you, countless millions!
> This embrace for all the world!

Yet this same poet expressed for generations of students to read what amounts to a most prejudiced exclusion of a large part of mankind: "It seems incomprehensible that the life-giving power in man is effective only in such a small part of the world and that those immense masses of people [outside Europe] do not count at all for human progress. It is especially curious that all these nations and altogether all non-Europeans on this earth completely lack moral and aesthetic qualities."

Complacence about race prejudice is complacence about violence. If we do not stem the one, we cannot completely conquer the other. At best we remain content with an adjournment of violence.

# CHAPTER SIX

# The Malthus Myth

The state of our civilization is such that
mankind would already possess all the
means to be exceedingly rich, but as a
whole is still stricken with poverty.
—BERTOLT BRECHT

A HISTORIC meeting took place in Venice in 1958, the Twelfth
International Congress of Philosophy. It was memorable because
it was attended by delegates from more countries (West and East)
than at any time since World War II. The atmosphere was one of
peace, and the delegates made serious attempts to find common
ground for constructive discussions. In a paper addressed to this
congress, an American professor of philosophy maintained that
the problem of population increase was a greater threat to humanity than the atomic bomb. In a later article, he wrote: "In the long
run 'the population bomb,' unless controlled, may prove a greater
threat to mankind than the hydrogen bomb." A research professor
of theology at a well-known university stated in an article (which
was printed and reprinted in three popular magazines) that overpopulation confronts "the civilized world with the threat of an
explosion second only to atomic warfare in destructiveness." In a
similar turn of mind, the distinguished liberal writer Bruce Bliven,
former editor of the *New Republic,* describes our epoch as "these
days of the population explosion and the hydrogen bomb." And
John D. Rockefeller III sums it up when he writes in a popular
magazine article: "Both nuclear weapons and population growth
endanger mankind."

The atomic bomb is the symbol, the incarnation, of modern
mass violence. Are we justified in even speaking in the same vein

of violent death and of the birthrate? And is it not a perverse idea to view population destruction and population growth as twin evils?

To advise birth control for an individual family is, of course, totally different from saying that overpopulation is the cause of major social problems and that its control is their only solution. The idea that the restriction of population is a panacea goes back a long time, to a book by the Rev. Thomas Robert Malthus. The title of the first edition of this book, published in 1798, was *An Essay on the Principle of Population as it affects the Future Improvement of Society, with Remarks on the Speculations of Mr. Godwin, M. Condorcet, and other Writers*. The men mentioned in the subtitle whose "speculations" were criticized, are significant: William Godwin, author of *Enquiry Concerning Political Justice* (1793), was a progressive writer who stressed the effect of environment on moral character. He had great influence on Shelley, who was his son-in-law. His wife, Mary Wollstonecraft, was a pioneer in the emancipation-of-women movement. The Marquis de Condorcet was a mathematician and philosopher, one of the chief figures of the French Enlightenment and one of the great theoreticians of the French Revolution. In his *Sketch of the Historic Picture of the Progress of the Human Mind* (1794), he wrote inspiringly about the future progress of human society. He had wide influence on sociology. Condorcet was the first great writer who said that war can and will be abolished.

The second edition of Malthus' book, published in 1826, had the more confident and outspoken title *An Essay on the Principle of Population; or a view of its past and present effects on Human Happiness; with an inquiry into our prospects respecting the future removal or mitigation of the evil which it occasions*. Malthus wrote a great deal on economic subjects until his death in 1834. He was an Anglican clergyman and for many years professor of political economy and history at a college founded by the East India Company, which had made such immense profits out of India. He was a member of the Political Economy Club, the Royal Society, the Royal Society of Literature, and the Statistical Society of London. His influence, extending well over 150 years, was and is tremendous. It reaches from the East India Company to the Rockefeller Foundation, which has a capital fund of $500,000,000 and has recently stated that in order to prevent misery and hopelessness it will expand its support of research and "action programs in population dynamics and population stagnation."

Despite its elaborate presentation and later embellishments, the fundamental idea of Malthusianism can be stated very simply: there are too many people on the earth and they multiply too fast. Nature does not provide enough food for them all. Hence misery, vices, poverty, division into the haves and have-nots, violence, wars. Merely by checking the too great increase in population, we can check and abolish most of these calamities. Malthus recommended that the workers practice control of births as a remedy against social evils. What was new in his reasoning was that he explained economic phenomena like poverty and unemployment not from the field of economics but from biology—namely, from sexual life. This basic idea seemed convincing then, and it still seems to be convincing to many today.

According to Malthus, the population grows faster than the production of food. He states that the population grows in geometric progression (1, 2, 4, 8, 16, 32 . . .), while the food production increases only in an arithmetical series (1, 2, 3, 4, 5, 6 . . .). He enumerates the only factors which can counteract this discrepancy and can establish a necessary harmony between the number of people and the available means for their subsistence: moral restraint (by which he means sexual abstinence), limitation of births, pestilence, and war. The earth is always overpopulated, and therefore there is always misery and poverty. That is the eternal fate of mankind. Malthus concludes from this that practical steps have to be taken to decrease the surplus population. Instead of social-welfare measures to feed the supernumerary people, we should try to decrease and limit their number. As a matter of fact, as pointed out by Margaret Cole in her biography of Beatrice Webb, belief in "the bogy of population continually tending to outrun the means of subsistence" was a tremendous obstacle to progressive legislation in England. It was believed that any relief given to destitute persons would encourage them to breed at the expense of their industrious neighbors. Malthus denies that every man living on this earth has a right to an existence minimum. Nature, he quotes from a poem, bids the poor man to be gone. According to him, the remedy for existing social evils is not in a change of social conditions, but in reduction of the number of human beings.

The neo-Malthusians have brought the idea of the menace of overpopulation again into vogue, just as it was 150 years ago. A lot has been written on the subject in the past fifteen years—for example, William Vogt's *Road to Survival* (1948; summarized in the *Reader's Digest*) and E. Pendell's *Population on the Loose* (1951).

In all this literature, without exception, the basic principle of Malthus has remained unchanged. New surgical or chemical techniques may be discussed or new action programs outlined, but the fundamental idea is the same: natural-science factors are offered as solutions of social problems, biological laws are supposed to explain social phenomena, and natural causes are substituted for socioeconomic ones. If people live in social misery and poverty, it is mostly their own fault, because they lack the good sense not to multiply so fast.

Sometimes it is openly stated that biology should be substituted for politics. For example, Aldous Huxley writes that "beneath the political problems lie the problems of rocketing population" and that therefore political difficulties have to be attacked "on the biological front." This is pure Malthus. As opposed to this, a member of Parliament stated in the House of Commons that "the main political fact in the world today is hunger." This is literally true. It is a *political* fact and not a biological fact. Mass starvation is not made in bedchambers but in council chambers. Social and economic problems cannot be solved with biology. We are dealing here with a general law of political sociology: every reactionary political tendency of modern times—be it apartheid, Nazism, ultraconservative theory, Friedrich Hayek's *Road to Serfdom,* or Barry Goldwater's extremism—contains Malthusian elements.

The neo-Malthusians never cite the name of the best-known man who endorses the Malthusian point of view—Ebenezer Scrooge. Speaking of the poor, he said it would be best to "decrease the surplus population." One high point in the propaganda against propagation was a full-page advertisement in *The New York Times* in the early 1960's. It proclaims that the current "population explosion" is a sure prelude to disaster. It states that foreign-aid programs are frustrated and the heroic efforts of friendly governments minimized if the increase in population remains unchecked. It uses such phrases as the "runaway inflation of people," "unimpeded fertility," and "population crisis." The words "population explosion" occur no less than three times. It regards the "runaway population" as a "basic cause" and a threat to world peace. It demands population control. This manifesto against human multiplication was signed in touching harmony by pillars of the economic establishment (steel, oil, utilities, banks, advertising, and so on) on the one hand and of the intellectual establishment on the other (universities, newspapers, churches, foundations, book clubs, and so on). We find side by side in brotherly union the Standard Oil Company of New Jersey; Batten, Barton, Durstine & Osborne; Morgan Guaranty Trust Company; Gulf Oil Corporation; Republic Steel Corporation; and Jacques Barzun, Van Wyck Brooks, John Gunther, Fannie Hurst, and Archibald MacLeish. The military was represented too. Characteristically, the advertisement was illustrated with a large photograph of milling masses of darkskinned people. All the signers were white.

Is there a scientific basis for all this? Malthus took for granted that the causes of poverty and human misery are natural or even eternal and not social, transitory, or amenable to constructive social endeavor. Whatever his intention, he was not merely concerned with explaining poverty, but actually justified its existence. That is a crucial point in the critique of his ideas. He provided, in fact, a systematic argument in defense of the naturalness of human misery. According to him, an excessive number of people, an overgrowth of population, is something absolute. He diagnoses and measures it not in relation to social and economic conditions but with a simple biological yardstick: the plain formula, census versus food.

For Malthus and the neo-Malthusians, overpopulation means overcopulation. But a surplus population is never absolute. It is always relative to other factors of production, distribution, and social organization. It is relative also in respect to occupation, sex, and age. There may be a surplus population of workers, of unskilled laborers, of women or children, and so on. It is never, however,

an absolute overgrowth. It is not that there are categorically too
many people and that this explains economic conditions. The reverse is true. There are definite socioeconomic conditions that explain why at certain times and in certain places there are too many
people.

Questions of population are an international matter. There are
no absolutely supernumerary people. They are only relatively surplus and superfluous, having been made so by social, economic,
and political conditions. At present, less than one-third of the population of the earth has more than 80 percent of the income. Better
planned economy would do away with a lot of the problems of
planned parenthood. Abstract laws of population exist only for
plants and animals—and then only if human beings do not interfere constructively or destructively. Surplus populations of human
beings are not an abstract phenomenon dependent on nature, but
always represent very concrete social problems. Human beings do
not suffer from hunger or live in misery because there are too
many of them but because they do not possess anything which
would enable them to work and supply what they need. Nor have
they the money to buy the food that exists. If they become demoralized, it is always secondary and not due to nationality, race,
climate, or nature in general. It is not the quantity of the people
but the quality of their social environment, in the widest sense,
which explains their condition. People are not poor because they
are superfluous, they are superfluous because they are poor.

Neither Malthus nor the neo-Malthusians have ever been able
to give scientific proof or documentation for what is the cornerstone of their theory, namely, that the population has a permanent
inherent tendency to outgrow the available means of subsistence.
The accumulated facts and the scientific reasoning based on those
facts contradict their theory. It is not accidental that from totally
different points of view both Marx and Freud disagreed with him.

It has been estimated that around 1800, Europe had about 180,-
000,000 inhabitants. By about 1900, the number had increased to
450,000,000. They had a higher standard of living and were better
nourished and dressed than their great-grandparents. It is most
likely that if we want to carry out all the tasks of civilization that
lie ahead for mankind, the number of people will have to be

greater and not smaller. Nobody can set the limit beyond which scientifiic food production cannot go. Justus von Liebig (1803–1873), the first agricultural chemist, the scientist who first classified food into proteins, carbohydrates, and fats, and the first to introduce chemical fertilizers to agriculture, stated years ago that with the proper methods and practices the soil will be practically inexhaustible. Malthusianism says that the produce of the soil can *never* keep pace with the increase in population. It relies on a simple equation with only two factors: soil and population. It leaves out a third factor, science, which is specifically human. It neglects both the progress of science as such and the progress and practical application of the discoveries of science. Agriculture has made and is making tremendous advances: chemical fertilizers, pesticides, newer machines, reclamation, conservation, irrigation, reforestation, automation, and so on. What poor farmers need most are not antifertility measures in their beds but fertilizers for their fields. The resources of oceans have hardly been tapped. Fishing is still in the stage farming was when men used wooden plows. In the foreseeable future we can raise more food than we can consume. Taking an international point of view, we can say that it is not that people cannot find the means of subsistence, but rather that the means of subsistence cannot find them. For through social conditions, the means are kept from them. Exclusion from multiplication is a drastic step to make up for exclusion from the market.

It is obvious that families should not have more children than they can bring up decently. But mass birth-control measures are effective only if the living standards of the masses of underprivileged people are raised first. That is the sequence, not the other way around. People can begin to take an interest in regulating the size of their families only after they have been given a chance to acquire halfway decent food and shelter and a modicum of security and dignity.

If the enormous sums now being spent all over the world on war preparations were to go to depressed areas, hunger and poverty in its worst forms could be abolished. Even a relatively small percentage of these expenditures would greatly alleviate them. Who can imagine what would happen if the same amount of scientific ingenuity now spent on the means of mass destruction were to be applied to human betterment? The great nuclear physicist and mathematician Max Born is one of the few scientists in these fields who has occupied himself seriously and responsibly with our modern social problems. He recognizes the problem of overpopulation and points out that one-third of the world population has enough to eat, two-thirds do not; if one takes into account vitamins and similar factors, 85 percent suffer from some form of malnutrition. But Born rejects the neo-Malthusian theory according to which overpopulation is the most fundamental problem. On the contrary, he comes to the conclusion that violence and violence preparation —*i.e.,* war and superarmament—are the ultimate greatest and most dangerous plague.

Malthusian thinking implies a disparagement and debasing of human sexuality. Among some species of ants, large numbers suppress their sex instinct to solve their economic problems. They do that for the communal good. It is assumed that they achieve this by some particular mode of nutrition. We are not ants. Mankind should have and has learned better and less primitive methods for dealing with economic questions. Human sexuality is on a level totally different from that of animals. Malthus advised sexual abstinence for workers. The neo-Malthusians rely more on birth control and mass sterilization. Both prescribe food and lots of contraception as cures for the ills of the world. The way they speak about sex constitutes a dehumanization of sexuality. A large part of mankind, according to them, multiply frivolously and heedlessly. Speaking of the hard-pressed Puerto Rican immigrants in the United States, the Malthus-oriented social scientists and writers become almost indecent in a mixture of obscenity and righteousness. "Fertility" is a favorite word. They talk about "runaway fertility," "primitive fertility," "uncontrolled fertility." One would think they were talking about animal husbandry. When we read some of the detailed emotional and extravagant writings about alleged overpopulation, we cannot avoid noticing an almost morbid preoccupation with the sex life of others.

Malthusian tendencies have played a considerable role in psychiatry. The dean of American psychiatry, Professor Adolf Meyer of Johns Hopkins, advised that people should practice what he called "maximal spacing." By that he meant that there should be as infrequent sexual intercourse as possible. This amounted to a kind of hidden Malthusian antisexuality. Freud considered it one of his tasks to free the sex life of mankind from imposed or self-imposed harmful restrictions. He found in society a devaluation and disparagement of sexuality, a mixture of prudery and licentiousness. He specifically named Malthusianism and regarded it as a wrong path. We must make clear to ourselves Freud's anti-Malthusianism in order to understand the sociohistorical background of his sexual theories.

According to Malthus, it is nature which has decreed that a discrepancy is bound to exist between food production and population increase and that therefore only a privileged stratum can fully enjoy life. The others either are superfluous or become so. Who are these superfluous people? The poor and the foreign. It is interesting to note which groups the various Malthus-imbued writers mention. The philosophy professor who contributed a paper to the philosophical congress in Venice mentioned as examples of groups who "must control population" Japan, India, and China. William Vogt specifically mentions Indians and Chinese; we must stop sending them food to save the lives of 10,000,000 because what will happen otherwise is that in five years 50,000,000 will perish. *Time* magazine had a cover story on "That Population Explosion." The cover picture showed mothers and children of different races and nationalities. Two Negro women—one the largest and most conspicuous figure in the picture—were depicted with bared breasts. All the other women were decorously dressed. This not only shows the racial angle, but also implies a disrespect for colored people in American publications which is resented by many people all over the world. The "population explosion" advertisement in *The New York Times* whose signers constituted a *mariage de convenance* between industry and intelligentsia names as instances of "runaway populations" Asia, Africa, the Middle East, Latin America, India, and Pakistan.

This classification of people, for that is what it amounts to, is reminiscent of the Kaiser, who appealed to the peoples of Europe to "guard their holiest possessions" against the yellow peril. Who can assign to himself the right to call for a *numerus clausus* for the earth? Evidently those whom the British used to call the "better sort of people." In a recent report of the 1933 class of Wellesley College, it is stated with pride that the class has an offspring considerably larger than 1,200 grandchildren. No explosion here. It is a matter for congratulation.

The neo-Malthusian call for population control plainly represents a kind of discrimination. Although it is not always frankly stated, the supernumerary and surplus people whose reproduction we have to prevent are to be found among colonial, semicolonial, poorer, or underdeveloped countries and in nonwhite and dark-skinned races. Color and race are not mentioned, but are—even if not on the conscious level—clearly involved. "Millions of natives" are, in the words of Frantz Fanon, thought of as "breeding swarms."

Underneath all Malthusian writing and thinking lies hidden a suggestion of death and violence. This manifests itself in many different ways. However concealed under a cover of moralisms, the whole idea includes a depreciation and devaluation of human life. Death rates and birthrates are discussed in conjunction, with the same high-handedness. A high birthrate is an unmitigated evil and the sole cause of further evils. A high death rate is a boon. "One of the greatest national assets of Chile," writes a neo-Malthusian scientist, "perhaps its greatest asset, is its high death rate." Mass deaths as an asset is a dangerous idea. Yet another writer states: "The greatest tragedy that China could suffer, at the present time, would be a reduction in her death rate." These writers deplore the fact that despite malnutrition, despite the war and the Nazi massacres, populations have not decreased.

The very terms "population bomb" and the now generally accepted "population explosion" are not only indelicate but also have overtones of mass violence. Typical is a recent letter from a clergyman to *The New York Times* about overpopulation. The letter cites India and Latin America as examples and says: "The population explosion has one built-in evil . . . we cannot deliberately destroy people because there are too many [of them]." Is it an "evil" that we can't kill them?

It is a dehumanization to speak of the procreation of people as barnyard activity or rabbitlike behavior. The superfluous people, and especially their parents, are regarded as really guilty. The equation is simple: poverty is equal to superfluousness, super-fluousness is equal to a crime. The consequence is punishment. You may have the right to exist, but you lose the right to procreate. If someone in authority tells us that we have no right to procreate, it is only one step further for him to tell us we have no right to live. As William Hazlitt summarized the Malthusian theory: "The poor have no right to live any longer than the rich will let them." The overpopulation theory lends itself to abuse as justification for letting people die, for hidden violence.

Sometimes a tendency to violence crops up quite openly in Malthusian writing. At the time of Malthus, a pamphlet appeared anonymously which proposed "painless extinction." It advocated the organization of a special institution in which children of the poor were to be done away with. Every poor family was to be allowed an average of two and a half children; any others were to be "painlessly" killed. At the turn of the century a German Malthusian political economist, Alexander Tille, wrote that society may have to care for those who are incapable of working, but only on condition that they don't procreate. He stated that those who do not submit to these conditions should be left to perish without mercy.

A lot has been said about mass hunger as a possible cause of violence. It is apt to be forgotten that violence is one of the causes of hunger. Much of the poverty and social misery in under-developed countries is due not to excess sexual activity but to the results of excessive violence. The people do not reap enough harvests of food because they are still reaping the harvest of past violence against them. And the world as a whole spends much of its substance preparing the soil for new violence. As the sociologist Robert MacIver expressed it: "Man could have . . . had much better opportunities to develop his ingenuity for the improvement of his lot if it had not been for the endless raids and invasions, increasing in devastating efficiency as better weapons of destruction were devised."

The Malthus-oriented writers rationalize the existence of hidden violence. According to them, mass starvation and excessive mortality are due entirely to biological causes and therefore are practically inevitable unless these causes are removed. When there are too many people, they will of inexorable necessity *have* to suffer. In reality, what brought mass hunger into the arena of history was not overpopulation but colonial oppression and ruthless distribution of natural resources.

Controlling the size of a whole nation, although the avowed motive may be to bring about a better life, comes perilously close to forcible elimination. The theoreticians of the Nazi "population politics," like the German-Swiss psychiatrist Professor Ernst Ruedin, were steeped in Malthusianism. A recent communication to a West German magazine states that the menace of overpopulation shows how sensible and beneficial for all mankind Hitler's "population politics" could have been. It is strange how few people realize the close connections—psychological, social, and political—between the very term "population explosion" and the extermination of populations.

Historically, Malthusianism has from its very beginning "explained" war and seen beneficial results from it. According to Malthusian reasoning, wars do not come about through political, economic, and social circumstances. Their main cause is overpopulation. The signers of *The New York Times* advertisement state that the government could make "an enormous contribution to world peace" by meeting the population crisis. In other words, they regard overpopulation as a main cause of war. Influential scientists have unfortunately expressed the same idea. Dr. George Kistiakowsky of Harvard University, who was President Eisenhower's Special Assistant on Science, goes so far as to state: "In a population explosion, war is inevitable." Is that going to be the excuse?

The neo-Malthusians consider war an inevitable consequence of what they assert are "the controlling laws of nature." They have popularized the idea that sexual improvidence is what propels us into war. The uninhibited and uninhibitable satisfaction of the sexual instinct causes overpopulation and thereby war. In other words, nobody is responsible for war unless we shift the blame onto the shoulders of those who make too many babies and those who fail to provide the parents with enough contraceptives and sterilization operations. If we accept such propaganda, we are already absolving from guilt all those who would unleash the next world war. And we ourselves are relieved of all social responsibility. This attitude justifies the existence of war—and if we justify something, we help to bring it about.

Since war reduces the population, the neo-Malthusians cannot help seeing good features in it, according to their own theories. Whether or not they mean to, they supply elaborate apologetics for war. By their social pessimism they discourage real steps to bring about real peace. They become the psychological trailblazers of atomic war.

Neo-Malthusianism is a potential violence-producing factor especially in relation to "underdeveloped" countries. This very term was not in use before these countries awakened politically. It stresses for the first time their economic reality, namely, their industrial and agricultural underdevelopment. Western intellectuals who for ostensibly humanitarian reasons raise the cry "There are too many of you!" lack comprehension of what it is like to be a citizen of an underdeveloped country. For their Malthusianism implies that in these "overpopulated" regions further development is neither possible nor desirable and that the inhabitants will (or even should) continue their preindustrial attitudes. If their conditions of industrial production are regarded as unchangeable, no amount of birth control will bring basic help. The masses in these countries will eventually have no choice except the hidden violence from which they now suffer or the open violence to which they may be driven.

How frivolous and irrational these Malthusian explanations of violence are can be seen from the ease with which they have been completely refuted again recently by modern studies on strictly scientific grounds. Dr. A. C. Weerekoon demonstrated by his studies, presented in a paper before the Ceylon Association for the Advancement of Science in 1954, that Malthus' basic propositions about food production are entirely incorrect. He discussed animals, plants, and soil. According to him, Malthus' thesis is as wrong as it would be to speculate that the supply of oxygen will some day limit the further increase of man in the world. The director of the Food Research Institute of Stanford University, Dr. Karl Brandt, presented his findings at a symposium of the World Affairs Council of Northern California and the American Assembly of Columbia

University. He called Malthusianism an absurd oversimplification. Some of his points based on modern scientific data are: many other important factors are operative besides birthrate; reduction of the population might even make conditions worse; resources are not fixed entities in fixed geographical locations; world food production is outpacing population increase; modern agricultural methods can give any country all the food it needs; the United States is underpopulated and will have a higher standard of living when its population increases greatly; it is a false cliché that population pressure creates poverty; on-the-spot studies in India show that that country could produce enough food even if its population were more than doubled; there is a right to procreate based on human dignity; it is an "arrogant idea . . . that we can take other nations into a sort of socio-politico-economic and sex clinic and thereby solve urgent problems."

The population problem is of direct and crucial importance for a country like China. This example is indispensable and constructive because within its borders live more than a quarter of the world's children. The annual rate of population increase is 2 percent, or more than 10,000,000—certainly enough to arouse the death wishes of Malthusians. (The average annual increase in the Soviet Union between 1926 and 1939 was 1.31 percent.) The Chinese have had extensive experience with mass hunger and disease. Starvation was so fierce and widespread that in Shanghai, which used to be called the New York of China, 20,000 dead bodies of adults and children used to be picked up every year from the streets. In the province of Sinkiang, which is twice as big as France, there used to be for the whole population only fifteen trained physicians. The public-health authorities of present-day China have taken up the problem of overpopulation very seriously and according to the latest scientific knowledge. They are entirely opposed to Malthusianism. They do advocate planned parenthood for families on three grounds: the health of mothers, to improve the living standards, to help the upbringing and education of children. But they do not regard the relation between food production and rate of population growth as a basic problem. They calculate that China's territory, her resources, and the natural conditions there suffice for their population, considering the progress being made in production.

The main defects of the Malthusian theory can be summarized:

1. It views population growth abstractly as a process independent of more fundamental social developments.
2. It underestimates natural resources.
3. It underestimates the enormous existing and potential progress of science and its power to create means to influence nature, *e.g.,* atomic energy.
4. It is not neutral or socially progressive, but is intimately linked to a reactionary status quoism.
5. It is linked to racism and "leading power" claims and privileges.
6. It devaluates human life as such and debases human sexuality.
7. It prevents the recognition and remedy of basic social problems by substituting biological (sexual) for sociological reasoning for their solution.
8. It is incompatible with both modern scientific biology and social science.
9. It has served extensively as an excuse and justification for hidden violence, domestic and foreign, and also indirectly for overt violence.

Malthus' doctrine was produced and had wide acceptance around 1800. After the middle of the nineteenth century, it receded somewhat into the background. Bernard Shaw ridiculed the "cry of overpopulation." Now, more than 150 years later, it has moved out of the wings and into the center of the stage again. Why is it so enthusiastically received today after such a long interval? Considering how wrong it is, why was it accepted in the first place, and why is it acclaimed now?

The answer can be found only in a comparative study of the historical background of the two epochs. Whenever the status quo appears to be challenged by profound social and economic changes, theories are apt to be propounded in its defense. One type of theory seeks to disregard the social determinants of inequities and to look for their causes in nature. The Malthus doctrine is ideal for that purpose. That does not mean that everyone who has propounded this theory is aware of this. There is a difference between personal motives and social motives.

At the time of Malthus' dominance, the Industrial Revolution took place in England. The concentration of landed property set laborers free to work in industry. Machines were perfected and used more and more. Big industries flourished, and machines replaced human labor. The new processes of production made many people superfluous. It looked as if too many of them were being born. Ebenezer Scrooge thought so. The American Revolution, the influence of which on European thought is still so widely underestimated, and the subsequent French Revolution demonstrated the possibilities and practicality of social changes. The war of the European nations against revolutionary France needed theoretical justification. Under these circumstances, the Malthus doctrine was useful and fitted in with the hidden wishes of some sections of society. Here seemed to be an ideological bulwark against new social and political ideas.

We must take care not to be too schematic in the comparison between two historical epochs. But since neo-Malthusian writing is so similar in content to the earlier literature on the subject, the similarities in the sociohistorical background cannot be insignificant. We merely have to substitute for the new machines our modern automation, for the technological advances of the Industrial Revolution present-day atomic energy, for the concentration of landed property our agrarian problem with the increasing dispossession of small farmers, for the American and French revolutions the Russian and especially the Chinese revolution, for the war against Napoleonic France the "police action" wars in Asia and Africa, for the Chartist demands of British laborers the demands of underdeveloped colonial and half-colonial peoples. The conclusion is inevitable that the circumstances have a great resemblance to one another. Can the meaning be so very different? We live in an era which requires bold and peaceful adjustment to new conditions—technological, social, political. The Malthus myth obscures that path and prevents us from banning the specter of mass violence. Shelley in the preface to his poetic drama *Prometheus Unbound* said that he would rather be damned with Plato than go to heaven with Malthus. The danger is that in the near future, many people will not have a choice.

# CHAPTER SEVEN

# Alarm at Breakfast

## THE FUTURE OF WAR

SOCRATES: Then parts of foreign lands
will be covetously eyed by us, and ours
by them, if, like ourselves, they exceed
the limits of necessity, and give in to the
unlimited accumulation of wealth?
GLAUCON: That, Socrates, will be inevitable.
SOCRATES: And so we shall go to war,
Glaucon. Shall we not?
Most certainly, he replied.

—PLATO

Not that they die,
But that they die like sheep.
—VACHEL LINDSAY

THE next war, if and when it breaks out, will be an orgy of violence. It will be a catastrophe for countless men, women, and
children. The suffering of human beings and animals will be almost
unimaginable. At breakfast we learn from the newspapers or from
television about the latest weapons and the forecasts of the number
of casualties. We are truly alarmed. But how long does our concern last? We have to catch a subway, a bus, or a train and go
after what Shakespeare called our "self-affairs." And our solicitude
recedes.

Modern war is a highly specialized undertaking. We have scientists and engineers who devise ever-new weapons, biologists and
chemists with new methods of annihilation, military analysts, industrial experts for war production, political analysts, trained
diplomats who decide on the right time for war, experts on morale,
communication, and public relations. The waging of war is in the

hands of specialists, but the prevention of war is everybody's business.

Wars of different historical epochs have much in common, so we can speak abstractly of war in general. But not all wars are by any means alike. They differ greatly in cause, methods, and effects. The new character of the next world war cannot be summarized entirely by reference to the new atomic weapons, although they would play the largest part. Napalm and flamethrowers, currently used in smaller wars in Asia, brutally burn people to death. So even if the next world war should be what is officially called a "conventional" war, it would be fought with what are, strictly speaking, rather unconventional means. It would be naïve of us to assume that the war would really be "conventional" or "civilized."

Since we hear so much about the "population explosion," we might also ponder about the casualties explosion of modern war: in the Franco-Prussian War of 1870–1871, 215,000 dead; in the First World War, some 10,000,000 dead; in the Second World War, 55,000,000 dead (Ploetz). In the Thirty Years' War it took thirty years to kill more than 7,000,000 people. Now that can be done in less than thirty hours.

In the First World War many soldiers had private graves. In the Second World War most of them were in mass graves. In an atomic war the vast majority of the dead will have no graves at all. The Unknown Soldier will merge indistinguishably with the silicated landscape and the pulverized civilians.

An atomic world war will be the first civilians' war. It will deserve that name, despite the fact that civilians were killed in previous wars too. The names Coventry, London, Leningrad, Warsaw, Antwerp, Hamburg, Dresden, Tokyo, Hiroshima, Nagasaki tell part of the story. Killing noncombatants, including women and children, has become more and more a perfectly customary and established war practice. It is now part of our civilization, and there was and is extraordinarily little moral reaction against it from statesmen, political parties, churches, or writers. The range of our conscience has not expanded with the range of our missiles.

In the next big war, although they will not be announced as such, civilians will be the main target and will suffer the most casualties. Entire populations of a region are now the impersonal hostages. The very long-range rockets are chiefly countercity arms, good for the annihilation of places of habitation and industrial regions. According to the military experts, they hit a target with so little accuracy that their value against strictly military installations is limited. In a recent court case in London, when demonstrators against an air base to be used for modern warfare were on trial, a witness for the prosecution, an air commodore, testified that if circumstances demanded it he would press a button that he knew would annihilate millions of people. Whereupon one of the accused demonstrators said in court: "Murder, we all agree, is a grave capital offense. Yet Air Commodore M. has said that in certain circumstances he would murder millions of people. I cannot understand why he is not locked up." This demonstrator was evidently behind the times (or maybe he was ahead of them).

The question of killing civilians during actual warfare has a long history. It can be divided into three phases. Originally the unarmed inhabitants of an invaded country were treated like the armed combatants. This treatment varied at different times and places. Sometimes it was merciful, sometimes cruel. In the second phase, a distinction was made between the armed forces and the non-combatants. This came about very gradually, after a long struggle on the part of humane writers and statesmen. It was finally established that peaceful inhabitants, especially women and children, "should not be subject to violence." For example, the Military Code of King Gustavus Adolphus of 1621 specifically protected "aged people, men or women, maides or children, unless they first take arms against them." The English Military Code of Charles I contained similar provisions.

We are now in the third phase of this historical development. In effect, though not in pronouncement, the humaneness of the relatively recent past has been discarded. We are prepared, physically and morally, to kill in the next war, in a few hours or minutes, as many civilians, including women and children, as possible. It is sheer hypocrisy to deny that. The guardians of faith and morality have acquiesced in it, and we do not seem to have enough humane writers or statesmen to counteract it. According to American military law, a soldier or officer has to obey every order according to its terms, the only exception being "a command to do a thing wholly irregular and improper" (Winthrop, *Military Law and Precedents,* 1920). Suppose a man were to refuse to drop an atom bomb on a city where he knows it would kill many women and children, on the ground that it was "irregular and improper"? He would be told he was completely wrong; for in this third phase, to kill women and children is wholly regular and proper.

The third phase was ushered in at Guernica in April, 1937. The civilian population of this town in northern Spain was attacked by the "voluntary" Condor Legion of the Nazi Air Force with high-explosive and incendiary bombs. After three hours of bombardment the victims numbered 1,654 dead and 889 wounded. Guernica put the stamp on a century. Few of us realized it then; few of us realize it now. It signaled the eclipse of international decency. Symbolic of this is the career of an officer who participated in this terror raid, Heinz Trettner. He was promoted afterward and has been promoted ever since. He ordered the bombardment of Rotterdam. He was involved in the mass killing of Spaniards, Norwegians, Dutchmen, Greeks, and Italians. Shortly before his suicide, Hitler promoted Trettner to lieutenant general. Today General Trettner is high in the councils of NATO, a member of the NATO Military Commission, and chief of all German NATO armed land, sea, and air forces. Toward the end of 1964, he was responsible for what has been called the Trettner Plan—the demand for a belt of atomic mines on the German border. Guernica is more than a memory or a painting by Picasso.

A special case of war killing of noncombatants occurred in parts of Russia occupied by the German armies in World War II. Masses of people, not only Jews but the general population, were rounded up and deliberately killed. This was totally different from victimizing civilians by air bombing. The over-all master plan was to make room for eventual German settlers. Great efforts have been made—and very successfully—to make it appear that this was outside of the war as such, that only special Nazi formations like the SS were responsible for this slaughter, and that the army leadership which was in control of all these regions had nothing to do with this and disapproved of it. This is a very dangerous idea. It prevents us from understanding the modern devaluation of human life. One single episode can disprove this claim. Historians do not mention this scene; students of violence cannot omit it. On January 25, 1944, an assembly of German Army leaders from all fronts took place in Posen (Poznan). It was the biggest such meeting during the whole war. Two hundred and fifty generals and admirals were present. These men were highly trained and educated, they had been to universities and military colleges, had been attachés in foreign countries, and so on. A considerable proportion of them were aristocrats. The majority were not national socialists. Some of these generals have great influence now in NATO and eventually may have a say about the atom bomb. To this meeting, Himmler outlined the rationale of the extermination policy for the occupied Eastern European regions. No pretense was made of putting down any resistance movement. He stressed that the women and children had to be killed. Himmler's pet idea was the extermination of Jews and Slavs to prepare the ground for a greater German empire. At that time, masses of civilians, men, women, and children, had already been slaughtered. What was the reaction of those generals and admirals? They applauded enthusiastically. Only five abstained. This episode was a historic turning point. Genocide had come of age. Not to realize the significance of this for the future of war would be careless. It certainly is quite a progression since the famous Japanese general Nogi of the Russo-Japanese war of 1904–1905, after a bloody but victorious battle, said with tears in his eyes, "It has cost us both too dearly."

We associate the functions of the police with civilian law-breakers and the function of the army with military enemies. But in recent years, police thinking and military thinking have become intertwined. In some countries the constabulary use armored cars and machine guns. We can observe a militarization of the police and a policification of the army, to the point where an outright war like the Korean War is called a "police action." This is inevitably confusing to both our ethical and our political thinking. An extreme but instructive case is the Union of South Africa. In that country, police and army form practically a unit, in armaments and in organization. The Union spends more on preparation for civil war than on defense in a foreign war. In 1962 alone its expenses for jails, police, and army were greater than its expenditures for defense in the whole Second World War.

The question of war or peace is the overriding question of our time. We must try to see it, at least in its arithmetical form, in historical perspective. Historians claim that only 300 of the last 3,500 years of history were warless. It has been calculated that between 1500 B.C. and A.D. 1860 about 8,000 peace treaties were made. Many of them were meant to bring about permanent peace. But all told, each peace lasted on an average only two years. It has been estimated that the wars in the first half of the twentieth century took a toll of 150,000,000 lives.

Kant said that what we wrongly call peace treaties have been merely armistices. Instead of being easier, it seems to have become even harder in modern times to make a sensible and stable peace after a war. Whatever we may think of these unbalanced settlements politically—the Taiwan arrangement, the division of Germany and of Berlin, and the division of Korea and of Vietnam—they are not conducive to the prevention of war, but rather to its production.

Since there is no peace treaty, the present postwar period is a peaceless peace. The greatest danger of that is that it gives so many the feeling that there are problems which cannot be solved except by violence.

Nothing in history has ever been prepared more thoroughly, both materially and psychologically, than the next world war. In international life, just as in individual life, communication is the opposite of violence. The modern means of communication would permit us to exchange understanding on the largest scale. We could build bridges of goodwill between the nations, but we build walls of hostility instead. This has two aspects. On the one hand, people do not really learn to know one another, their local achievements, their problems, their traditions. The less they learn, the more likelihood there is of a clash. Nations collide without making contact. On the other hand, we continually stir up negative social emotions: contempt, suspicion, fear, and vilification. In this way, emotional preparedness for war is created.

Whether so intended or not, the psychological preparation for war begins with children. Through stories in comic books, on television, and in other media, they become first fascinated with the ferocity of war and warlike activities and then accustomed to them. The very word "war" has become for them a commonplace expression like a ride or a dance. Children learn to regard war as natural and not especially deplorable. I have found that many young people look at the Vietnam war films the same way they look at Westerns. For them, Lyndon Johnson has become "the fastest gun in the West."

Along with moral disarmament goes physical armament foisted on children by advertisements and commercials. In the mid-sixties there were business booms in military toys. The weekly newspaper *National Observer* quoted a toy store executive: "They really brainwash the kids. This year military toys are the big items—not just any gun, not just any bazooka, but the ones the kids have seen advertised on TV."

For older children, preteens and teenagers, their whole social value system has changed during the past fifteen or so years. They no longer stress the old civic and social values. For many of them the social ideal is a victorious war.

The psychological preparation of adults proceeds on the radio, in the press, on the screen, in the legislative forum, and by similar agencies. People all over the world have a deep desire and need for peace. They don't cherish slugging it out with anybody. But they are easily influenced in innumerable ways, not only on occasion, for a specific war, or against a special enemy, but to a warlike attitude in general. In recent years much material in the mass media, both news and entertainment, is so militarily tinged that it amounts to what we might call war commercials.

We underestimate how much normal minds can be manipulated. In order to make people war prone we don't have to play on their bad instincts; we can make use of their good, idealistic ones. The machinery of hate has been so perfected that it can be turned against any nation on earth, against inhabitants of outer space, or against the citizen of the dreamlands of the poets—Ruritania, Shangri-La, Poictesme, Orplid. All we need is the name of the country and we shall find experts to discover its faults.

We hear a lot about "psychopathic hate," "neurotic hate," "irrational hate," but little of the institutionally instilled spirit of cold brutality. An example is provided by a full-page illustrated advertisement in the trade magazine *Iron Age:* "According to legend the master armorers of Damascus tempered their world-famous swords by thrusting them red-hot into living Nubian slaves. It was rough on the slaves but it produced blades of unmatched strength and keenness."

War movies are a good objective index. Of most American war movies, *The New York Times* critic Bosley Crowther has said almost all that has to be said in one sentence: The movie producers "make war appear as a big adventure while pretending to execrate it." In West German movie theaters between 1951 and 1959, no less than 626 war and military movies were shown.

Newscasters pride themselves on not editorializing. But that is manifestly not possible, for the very selection and presentation of foreign news inevitably have peaceable or bellicose overtones. News is carefully sifted, and there is a struggle for survival of the news that is "fittest" to print. In the evening, as persistently as Mrs. Caudle but with less humor, news commentators are apt to give us Iron Curtain lectures. Often we are left in the position of Dr. Watson. Sherlock Holmes tells him many details, but he does not furnish the clues which would help Watson to fit them together and fully understand them. Sometimes propaganda is mixed in too. While the truth may make us free, the lie will make us fight.

In the over-all picture of foreign news, we are asked to acquiesce in things which we are not sufficiently informed about. On the one hand, there is incitement to aggressive feelings; on the other, we are conditioned to social passivity. It may happen that we shall become so passive that one day we shall wake up to find ourselves radioactive.

Militarism is the belief in the omnipotence of violence. Undoubtedly some nations are historically more militaristic than others. But even those nations which, like the United States, pride themselves on being unmilitaristic have employed military force more often than we are apt to realize. In 1890 the marines landed in Buenos Aires, in 1891 in Chile; in 1899 Cuba was occupied; in 1904 the navy went to the Dominican Republic; from 1906 to 1909 Cuba was occupied again; in 1910 the marines landed in

Nicaragua; in 1912 Cuba was again occupied, and the marines landed in Nicaragua and Honduras; in 1914 the marines landed in Haiti, troops moved into Mexico and occupied Vera Cruz; in 1915 the marines occupied towns in Haiti; in 1916 troops went to Mexico and the Dominican Republic; in 1917 Cuba was again occupied; in 1919 the marines landed in Honduras; in 1926 troops went to Nicaragua; in 1933 the marines landed again in Cuba. Right now, in 1966, two whole divisions of marines are in Vietnam.

This is the era of the automation of killing, but the availability of modern means of mass destruction is not in itself a direct factor leading to war. It is wrong to say that science has become the slave of war, although some scientists have. Scientific advances do not cause wars. But unfortunately war preparations have played and are still playing an important obstetrical function in the progress of scientific technology. The application of atomic energy would not have advanced so far and so fast if it had been entirely dependent on ordinary market calculation. What was merely a possibility became an early reality through military influences. This, of course, should not lead us to regard war for all time as a useful factor in the development of science and technology. On the contrary, it should stimulate us to adjust socioeconomic conditions to the unhindered growth of science and its application *without* war. We should not forget that centuries ago the Chinese invented gunpowder for peaceful purposes. It was only later misused for war. Surely there is a lesson here.

Science and politics meet head on in the field of violence prevention. The danger is that first-rate scientists place the means of mass destruction in the hands of second-rate politicians. Politicians have no hesitation about using scientists. But scientists, both in physics and in psychology, are afraid of dirtying their hands if they take up what they consider extraneous or at least secondary matters. For example, thermonuclear tests were carried out before nuclear fallout was adequately studied; strong insecticides were widely used without recognition of the possible serious consequences to both animals and man; detergents were elaborately advertised and marketed and widely used without adequate study of the dangers for sanitation. By leaving out the social connections, science fosters unscientific attitudes. The famous atomic scientist

Werner Heisenberg, in his book *Philosophical Problems of Nuclear Science,* says that politics represents nothing but a struggle of one set of illusions and misleading ideas against another set of illusions and equally misleading ideas; with this he contrasts pure natural science (by which he means chiefly physics), on which any world order must be based and by which alone right or wrong can be decided. This would mean, of course, that decisions would be made entirely by a highly and one-sidedly trained elite. Would we like to see the world run by some of the atomic scientists who helped to select two densely populated cities as targets for the atom bomb and who now play with the idea of preventive war?

The belief that the scientific attitude implies complete neutrality does only harm. The scientific intelligentsia has never been neutral, as has been apparent in any serious social and political upheaval. It may have wanted to be. A. V. Hill, the British neurophysiologist and Nobel Prize winner, was emphatic in claiming that the scientist should be detached and not tied "to particular social or economic theories." Later, however, disproving his theory in practice, he held an important government post which was not unconnected with "social or economic theories." The political independence of the scientist is an illusion. Knowledge is never unpolitical; ignorance is.

In any study of the violence of our time, we cannot discuss politics without science or science without politics. This can be illustrated by a historical episode. Niels Bohr, the great pioneer in atomic physics, appealed to Winston Churchill in an interview in London for efforts toward some kind of international control of atomic energy. The conversation lasted for half an hour. After Bohr had left, Churchill turned to his secretary and asked, "Did he talk about politics or physics?"

We are still living under the shadow of Hiroshima (in the post-violence phase). In Hiroshima the largest number of human beings was killed in the shortest time. It was an entirely new step in the methodology of mass killing. According to the mayor of the city, a total of 210,000 to 240,000 died. It has been estimated that almost every second person who stayed in the city at the time perished.

Was Hiroshima necessary? A clear answer has been given by

history: it was not. Former President Eisenhower was commander of Allied Armies in Europe and in a good position to have an over-all view of the progress of the war. He wrote in 1963 that Hiroshima was "completely unnecessary," that Japan was already defeated, that the bomb was no longer mandatory to save American lives, that at the time of the preparations for dropping the bomb it was his opinion that the United States should not introduce such weapons into war. Others have expressed similar opinions, among them Dr. Leo Szilard, one of the first to envisage the construction of atomic arms; General Douglas MacArthur; Lawrence L. Malis, who flew twenty-six B-29 missions over Japan.

Many factors entered into that fateful decision to drop atomic bombs over Hiroshima and Nagasaki. One of them was a lack of sufficient communication. The contact between the scientists, the military men, and the politicians was far from complete enough, in view of the gravity of the decision to be made. The President, the commander in chief, was not fully and directly informed of all the objections and suggestions. The existence and power of the atom bomb could have been demonstrated in different ways—without mass killing. The questions to be decided were: Should the bomb be dropped with warning or without warning? Should the warning consist in specifying a number of areas and warning the people there to leave? Should a technical demonstration be given first, and if so should it be in the United States—in a desert, for example— or in Japan—in the bay of Tokyo, for example? Before the bomb was used, should the terms of surrender be made public in detail to the Japanese and perhaps also to the American people? Should the responsibility be fully shared with the Allies? Should the bomb be dropped on an uninhabited area or an inhabited one? Should the target be a straight military object (*e.g.,* a naval installation) or a civilian area?

One failure of communication took place between the American and Japanese governments, a striking fact in view of modern proficiency in transmitting messages. The Japanese had made serious peace feelers in early July, 1945. On July 28, 1945, the Japanese prime minister, Susuki, answered the Potsdam peace proclamation of the Allies to the press. He said his government was following a policy of *mokusatsu*. This Japanese word can have two meanings.

One is "to ignore, to consider unworthy of attention"; the other meaning is "to get some distance from [it]." Susuki had meant the second. But the Japanese news agency Domei translated the word wrongly. So the American government acted on the false idea that the Potsdam peace proclamation would be ignored by the Japanese government. Susuki's reply is still officially referred to as having been "unworthy of public notice." Many people have found—and many more will find—a violent death as a consequence of this failure of communication.

We should not overlook the racial angle in the use of nuclear bombs. They were used twice, in Hiroshima and Nagasaki, against the Japanese; twice they were seriously considered, during the Korean War and before the fall of Dien Bien Phu in Vietnam. On all four occasions the victims were, or would have been, nonwhite. This was no accident. The Secretary General of the United Nations, U Thant, who has openly drawn attention to this racial factor, called it "a very important element." And one of the airmen involved in the bombing of Hiroshima said openly in a television interview, "We were dealing with Asiatics and not with people like ourselves." One of the best authorities on modern China, Edgar Snow, observed prophetically long before China produced an atom bomb that when this happened it would mean in Asian countries that a "colored" voice would have to be heard and that the white man's monopoly of terror would have to come to an end.

The question of responsibility for the atomic holocaust is difficult, but some facts are definitely known now. The military men were in favor of dropping the bomb first as a technical demonstration in the bay of Tokyo or—if it were used in earnest—on a military object. A number of scientists were for giving a warning first, in some form. There is a persistent myth, which many still believe, that the nuclear scientists besought the government not to use the atom bomb against the Japanese and that they were overridden by the government. In reality, the most influential scientists advocated and approved that the bomb be dropped on an inhabited civilian area—and without any warning. They actually helped to select the sites of Hiroshima and Nagasaki, which had been spared previously from incendiary bombs and were therefore a good field for evaluating the destruction. A very small panel of top scientists who were asked to weigh the objections of some of their colleagues stated: "We have no claim to special competence in solving the political, social, and military problems which are presented by the advent of atomic power." This is in essence the Eichmann argument; we do what we are asked to do, and what that may lead to is not our responsibility. As a matter of fact, these atomic scientists in selecting on the map the sites for the mass killing of civilians did even more than they had been asked as scientists to do and very definitely did engage in "political, social, and military" matters. After Hiroshima a top scientist of the project said that "this thing had to be done." We know today that it did *not* have to be done, certainly not in the way it was done. It was the demonstration both of the power of a new force and of our own readiness to use it without humanitarian considerations.

The future philosophy of ethics will have to take into account the discrepancy between highly specialized scientific training and human compassion. The scientist without mercy is an important image for the understanding of the violence of the twentieth century.

Hiroshima and Nagasaki opened a new epoch in history. There is no cause to be optimistic about the atom bomb; mushroom clouds have no silver lining.

In recent years a new literature with a large output has emerged. One of the points it discusses is which kind of thermonuclear war is a little better or a little worse than which other kind. The "little" is reckoned in millions of casualties. For example, it has been estimated that in a third world war 900,000,000 people will die. It may appear that all this writing about millions of dead makes war abhorrent. Not so: it has the opposite effect. It is a ghoulish game. The human dimension is missing. People get used to these mathematics of mass murder and forget that behind every figure in these enormous numbers there stands a real person—a man, a woman, or a child. The cultural anthropologist Geoffrey Gorer reports that "more than once I heard it stated that it would be worth sacrificing three-quarters of the population of the United States if thereby the whole population of the Soviet Union could be destroyed." Statesmen have become rather generous with human lives, in reckoning how many millions of dead we shall be able to afford. We talk glibly of the next war's casualties in terms of minutes and millions. It is a new kind of callousness. This utter emotional incomprehension of death is reminiscent of the story of the concert musician who played occasionally at funerals. Once after a funeral a man shook his hand enthusiastically and said, "That was so moving! Would you play at my funeral?" "I'd be glad to," replied the musician. "What would you like to hear?"

Many of the calculations about future casualties are arrived at with the aid of computers. Recently at Cambridge University in England, mathematicians fed all relevant information into an electronic computer to find out who would be the winner in a horse race. The electronic brain answered that the winner would be a horse. If only there were a computer which, after being fed all the information about hydrogen bombs, missiles, first and second strikes, deterrence, preventive war, and so on, when asked who will die would answer, "A human being."

One special variety of future war much discussed today is "accidental war." Some writers have gone so far as to say that accidental war is the most important issue confronting us today. It is of course within the realm of possibility that with such a highly complicated system of instruments of mass destruction, something may go mechanically wrong. But that does not relieve us of responsibility. It will not be the fault of the button. In the strictest sense, there can be no accidental war.

One of the greatest obstacles to the prevention of war is the widespread belief that war is an eternal prospect for mankind and that any attempt to abolish it is hopeless. An influential German writer, Ernst Juenger, one of whose war books has been translated into many languages (including English, French, Spanish, Rumanian, Polish), has expressed this tersely: "Those people who want to abolish war are just as ridiculous as the ascetic people who preach against intercourse."

Another obstacle is the idea that is so taken for granted today: if you want peace, prepare for war. *Si vis pacem, para bellum.* This goes back to Dio Chrysostomus, who wrote in the first century A.D. that the one who is best prepared for war has the greatest chance to live in peace. We have had a chance for almost 2,000 years to test this principle. It has never been true in all of history. Far more true is the African proverb "A newly sharpened sword marches by itself to the next village." If we want peace, we must prepare for *peace*.

According to a widely held illusion, war in our time is impossible and about to disappear by itself because modern weapons are so destructive. The same argument was used when hand grenades were perfected, when machine guns became widely used, when tanks became part of warfare. The inventor of dynamite, Alfred Nobel, wrote to Bertha von Suttner, whose novel *Down with Arms!* had a great vogue toward the end of the nineteenth century: "My factories are perhaps more likely to make an end to war than your [peace] congresses. On the day when two army corps can annihilate each other in a second, all civilized nations will probably shudder back from a war and dismiss their troops." In 1893 he wrote her again, announcing his Peace Prize. He intended that it be given every five years, altogether six times—"for if in thirty years reform of the present system has not been accomplished, reversion to barbarism will be inevitable."

The belief that modern weapons will destroy all mankind is dubious and is certainly not a sure deterrent of war. Already there are in some countries elaborate installations deep under the earth. They are secured against atomic radiations, they get fresh air through filter systems and uncontaminated water from special deep wells. They also have complete hospital facilities. That does not mean that any large-scale civil defense is possible in an atomic war. There is only one safe method of civil defense, and that is the prevention of war.

To expect that moral considerations about the number of casualties will prevent war is just wishful thinking. We underestimate the ruthlessness of some and the indifference of others. Wars will be made impossible not by the perfection of techniques of killing, but by improvement of the ways of living.

Pacifism as a movement isolates the war problem. It regards war as something absolute and assumes that we can abolish it without any really fundamental changes. That means not recognizing how intimately war is built into our political, social, and economic life. The problem of war and peace cannot be reduced to just the clash between two opponents. It has to be understood in the light of the long history of social development and its laws.

Pacifism is apt not to take up the objective conditions and to bypass the conflicts and real issues. Pacifists neglect the issues behind their good intentions; bellicists hide their bad intentions behind the issues.

In 1915, the second year of the First World War, the Swiss psychiatrist Auguste Forel published a pamphlet "The United States of the World." This was one of the first modern proposals for a world government. Forel suggested the organization of what he called a "supernational areopagus." The term and the idea go back to ancient Greece. The Areopagus was a high court which functioned as an independent inspection and control agency. The establishment of such a world government is often regarded as the immediate solution to the war problem. The difficulty is that a possibility which belongs to the distant future is projected into the present in an unrealistic way. The illusion that we can work directly now toward a world government detracts from efforts to pursue short-term tasks which are prerequisites for the larger goal. The path to a warless world leads over many intermediate stages which cannot be skipped or telescoped. One great hurdle is nationalism, which at the moment is worse than it ever was in history. World government can be based only on a world democracy. We are still a long way from the time when it could be said, in the words of the philosopher Ortega y Gasset, that "coexistence and society are equivalent terms." A grim joke is told in the corridors of the United Nations. By 1990, the story goes, a world government will be so strong that it can send a thousand planes with superhydrogen bombs to any part of the world to enforce peace.

Efforts toward disarmament are important because they are practical steps and not just pious hopes. Forty years ago, after the First World War, Thomas Mann wrote from Paris: "In the battle against war not much can be accomplished in the name of culture. Pacifism of today is a matter of the most practical reasoning." Any far-reaching measures of disarmament come up inevitably against underlying social and economic problems. Disarmament is not only an international but an intranational problem. The long-range task is not only of disarming but also of solving and settling social issues and conflicts.

Armaments play an enormous economic role. About half of our economy is in some way dependent on defense. When the summit meeting between Khrushchev and President Eisenhower failed, the financial section of *The New York Times* had a headline:

SUMMIT FAILURE A MARKET TONIC

Ninety per cent of the employees in the aircraft industry work solely on defense projects. Armaments have become the pilot sector of our economy. There is a division within this economy. Under present conditions, one sector is materially interested in war production and armaments. Another sector is more interested in world-wide trade. This division, never clearly spelled out, nevertheless exists and has wide political repercussions. To deal with it for the furthering of disarmament certainly requires what Thomas Mann termed the "most practical reasoning."

Physical disarmament alone is not enough; it must be coupled with psychological disarmament. We must try to dismantle the machinery of hate that exists in our whole communication and entertainment system. Vilification, the creation of suspicion, the denigration of whole nations—all these are weapons too, and ones that should be gradually reduced. Misguided men are as dangerous as guided missiles. A great deal could be done in creating and strengthening an atmosphere of peace and dispelling the smog of international hate that we are exposed to. To ask for psychological disarmament requires as much civil courage as to ask for reduction of physical arms. I have been more abused for advocating disarmament in the nursery than in atomic arsenals.

Can psychiatry prevent war? That claim is often made. Of course, it can help to unravel false rationalizations and to understand irrational attitudes. For example, Freud has described the symptom of denial. It consists in the fact that many neurotics deny to themselves the very existence of an unpleasant truth which they cannot face. In analogy to this, under very different circumstances, many not necessarily neurotic people deny the danger of an atomic war. According to them, it would be too horrible, we are too civilized, it would be suicidal, and so on. But to deny something does not abolish it.

War is not a psychiatric problem, and psychiatry cannot bear the main share of preventing war. The momentous problem of war and peace cannot be contained in or subsumed under the category of health versus disease. We cannot face up to the very real challenge of war if we confine ourselves to terms of personal pathology.

Nevertheless facile psychoanalytic-psychiatric explanations of war have been widely popularized. Freud observed that the root of individual neurosis goes back to early childhood. This has now been extended to furnish the cause of wars. We are told that the wish to fight wars is pathological; that the origin of wars can be traced to early infancy; that we need an outlet for natural aggressiveness, which will always be there; that it is feelings of inferiority, guilt, and fear which make people fight wars; that it all goes back to a parent who is either too stern or too weak or has similar failings. In a misuse of both the term and the idea, the unconscious is blamed for war. Such explanations have in common the fact that we cannot do anything about where the fault allegedly lies, and so we are relieved of all responsibility. The unconscious is a concept applied to scientific psychology, not a device to be used as a convenient and mysterious hiding place for national violence.

Sometimes persuasive psychiatric theories go hand in hand with reliance on and defense of mass violence. Dr. George B. Chisholm, who has held important posts in psychiatry and who has popularized the it's-all-neurotic theory of war, went so far as to advocate that psychopathology be taught to all children in primary and secondary schools. On the other hand, he said in a lecture that the "people who definitely do not want to fight any more wars must promise total annihilation to any nation which starts to fight and must be prepared immediately and ruthlessly to carry out that promise without parley or negotiation."

All purely psychiatric explanations of war are evasions. War is not an invention of neurotic individuals. It is not a psychological symptom, but the result of historical facts and events. The aggressive impulses of individuals do not conglomerate to make a war, nor can wars be understood in terms of individual intentions or character dispositions. The great danger is that economic and social forces may drive us to a war beyond any individual control. Without recognition of the social sources, the personal explanations remain fragmentary. Whatever conflicts of personalities may exist, it is the conflict of national interests that leads to war. The violent clashes of nations cannot be understood from the history of individuals without the history of the societies in which they live.

It is easy to give a psychological twist to historical events and to switch the emphasis from the social province to the private sphere. That means leaving out the concrete historical background, which is different for every war and every peace. The image of man that we start from is most important. If we say that the human being is and always will be violent (even if we use the embellishing term "aggressive"), we are giving in to civil and military violence. If atomic scientists are guilty of participating in the misuse of their discoveries, we psychiatrists are equally guilty, if not more so, when we use our theories to explain away the true nature of war and to furnish evasive generalizations for it.

For the first time in history it would be theoretically possible to build a world civilization. Scientific and technological advances and the perfection of communication have laid the foundation. Yet we are far from it. It is easy to say abstractly that in principle all war, all violence, and all force are wrong. To face concretely the historical and especially the economic conditions that lead up to wars is far more difficult. If peace movements are entirely negative or are based on fear, they cannot succeed; but just as it is possible to stir us up to hate, so it should be possible to stir us up to peaceableness and create a positive mentality of peace. That means getting away from the philosophy that the main goal is to get ahead of the others, personally, socially, nationally.

Any attempts at disarmament and arms bans are constructive, but they cannot solve the permanent problem of war. Wars do not come from the arms race; the arms race comes from the belief in war. To take away part of Mars' weapons is not enough. He has to be dethroned. Violence is a perversion of human relations, and war is its extreme, institutionalized form. This perversion is not inevitable and not due to innate instincts, as the it's-all-aggression theorists would have it. War is a historically developed and surmountable social phenomenon.

One year before the American Revolution the philosopher Kant wrote a little treatise on "Perpetual Peace." His ideas may seem somewhat removed from the realities we face today, but one sentence of his should be framed and hung in every high government office of every land:

On the day when war breaks out, the government should immediately and voluntarily relinquish its power, for it has demonstrated that it was not able to avert the very thing whose prevention was the whole sense of its office.

# CHAPTER EIGHT

# "*Looking at Potatoes from Below*"

## ADMINISTRATIVE MASS KILLINGS

> What kind of murder is it, which not only
> many suffer, but which also many com-
> mit?
> —DIETRICH GOLDSCHMIDT, Professor
> of Sociology, Berlin

THE administrative mass killings of the Nazi era constitute something new in the rich history of human violence. Even individuals
cannot be completely understood henceforth without a realization
of how easy it is for a civilized society to revert to a state of
brutality. No single deed or event of this period is entirely new.
But the total process is new. It manifests itself on different levels—
political, psychological, military, institutional, and economic. It is
a mixture of brutality, efficiency, and cynicism about human life.
From the concentration camp Flossenbürg in Bavaria, where
thousands of resistance fighters were killed, a guard wrote in a
letter to a friend that there was always room there for more people
"because from time to time some of them look at the potatoes
from below."

The methods by which the victims were killed, their numbers,
the deliberate inclusion of women and children, and the way it
was rationalized, accepted, defended, and perpetrated are all a
recent dimension of violence. We cannot visualize this from big
generalizations, but only from typical examples. In the neighborhood of the Serbian town of Kragujevac, partisans clashed with
a Nazi detachment. As a result, 6,000 inhabitants of the town
were later seized as hostages and killed. Among them was a whole

secondary school, of which the director, the teacher, and every single pupil were killed. Such acts were not committed, as is sometimes stated, by "outsiders of society." They were carried out by ordinary people and planned, ordered, and acknowledged by the highest authorities.

The mass killing in concentration camps cannot be subsumed under any of the old categories. It is not bestial, because even the most predatory animals do not exterminate their own species. It is not barbaric, because barbarians did not have such organized, planned, and advanced techniques for killing people and processing them into such commercial products as fertilizers. It is not medieval —it is indeed very twentieth century. It is not strictly a national matter, for the perpetrators had no difficulty in finding collaborators —even very active ones—in other countries. It is not a past, historical episode, because it is still largely unresolved legally, politically, psychologically and educationally. It is not a unique occurrence, because there is no certainty whatsoever that it will not be repeated when similar circumstances arise. It is not an unforeseeable natural catastrophe, because it was long foreshadowed. It is not the work of madmen, for many of the perpetrators and organizers led (both before and after the killings) normal, average bourgeois, working-class, professional, aristocratic, or intellectual lives. The term "genocide" covers only a part of it (although a very large one), because the earliest part was strictly political: Germans killing Germans. It was not a disorderly orgy of primitive violence but a mass action lasting years and carried out with pedantic orderliness.

A mass murderer used to be a man who killed maybe four or five or, say, even ten or fifteen people. Those were what are called the good old days. Now mass killing involves hundreds or thousands. These numbers are so large that we can hardly imagine them. It is also difficult to apply to them the categories of individual responsibility, guilt, being an accessory, punishment, and so on.

The people killed in concentration camps included political prisoners, Jews (the largest number), gypsies (the most completely exterminated group), Slavs, prisoners of war, and undesirable civilians. It has been estimated that 7,500,000 people were confined in concentration camps, of whom a bare 500,000 survived, many with serious mental and physical aftereffects. The number of Jews killed in concentration camps and outside is estimated at between 5,000,000 and 6,000,000.

By 1945 there were in Germany, Austria, and occupied countries more than a thousand concentration camps. Among them were:

Auschwitz (Oswiecim)

Belsen, near Hanover

Belzec, in Poland, the first big concentration camp where gas chambers were installed; about 600,000 victims died there

Birkenau, the poetically named camp (meaning "meadow of white birches") which was part of the Auschwitz complex

Buchenwald, near Weimar

Chelmo (Kulmhof)

Dachau, one of the earliest central camps

Dora, in Thuringia, part of the Buchenwald complex, where V-2 rockets were manufactured by slave labor and many died in the subterranean installations

Flossenbürg, in Bavaria, for political prisoners and others

Gross-Rosen

Hellerberg, near Dresden; nearly all its inmates were later killed in Auschwitz

Hohnstein, in Saxony, which was regarded as one of the worst

Janowska, in Poland

Maidanek, also in Poland, one of the largest annihilation camps

Mauthausen, in Austria

Natzweiler, in Alsace

Neuengamme, near Hamburg

Oranienburg, near Berlin, one of the earliest camps

Ravensbrück, in Brandenburg, a central death camp for women, where 92,000 women and children were killed

Sachsenhausen

Sobibor, in Poland

Theresienstadt (Terezin), in Czechoslovakia

Treblinka, in Poland

From Belzec, Sobibor, and Treblinka, the authorities, after deduction of all overhead and expenses for transportation, derived pure profits of $44,500,000, profits which were handled by the Reichsbank and the Ministry of Economics. (This sum included profits from the victims' possessions, clothes, gold teeth, hair, and so on.)

We are apt to think of concentration camps as enclosures with a few buildings surrounded by barbed-wire fences and located in isolated places. In reality there were barracks, many buildings, big industrial installations, factories, railway stations with regular railway services, ramps, roads, connections with nearby towns and villages, big warehouses for products from the corpses and the victims' belongings, installations for torture and killing, research institutes, distribution centers, gas ovens, crematory furnaces, human-bone-milling plants, well-appointed kennels for hundreds of police dogs, agricultural fields, gardens for the officials, and so on. Some of the bigger camps were in reality groups or systems of different camps. All this in the aggregate covered large territories and involved wide communications. These ramifications alone show the absurdity of the claim and belief that the population knew nothing about them. These camps were going concerns. Thousands of people in the camps and in the population had working contacts with them.

The methods used in these camps were varied. They included, among others, shooting, hanging, poisoning, torturing, beating to death, "extermination by labor" (*i.e.,* working to death), starvation, carbolic acid injections into the heart, burning alive, wounding and leaving to die in mass graves with others already dead, vivisection, stomping, drowning, electrocution, locking as a group in a bunker and throwing hand grenades into it, freezing either in icy water or from standing naked in snow, clubbing or kicking to death, and keeping people packed in upright position in a cell with only standing room till they died.

One aspect of the administrative mass murders was the inclusion of children. This fact has been generally soft-pedaled and is little mentioned. This is an omission which helps to obscure the whole picture of the violence of our time. It has been estimated that about 1,500,000 children were killed, ranging in age from infancy up. Many of them were asphyxiated in gas ovens. The expression generally used for this procedure was "chasing the children up the chimney." The child phase of the mass murders had three features. First, it was carried out with the greatest brutality. Second, it was not a matter of individual excesses (although that happened often too, especially for sexual reasons), but was part of the routine and a regular constituent of policy and strategy mapped out at the desks of highly placed officials. Third, it was not carried out only by the SS; ordinary people did it as well. Painful medical experiments that often led to death were also carried out on children by physicians.

We can best imagine the official attitude toward children in concentration camps from a scene that took place in Auschwitz. A young child walked straight through the camp. Around his neck was hung on a string a placard with his name on it in big letters. That was most unusual. Why was he wearing it? He was the son of the camp leader, Aumeier, on his way to visit his father, and if he had not worn such a sign he might have been snatched up on the spot and tossed into one of the gas ovens.

There are two kinds of violence. The first is violence accompanied by emotion: feelings of hate, sadism, sex, and other passions. The second variety has very little to do with the personal passions of men. It is impersonal and bureaucratic, and those who order, commission, and organize it as well as those who execute it have extremely little feeling for their victims, be it sympathy or hate. They are executioners or slaughterers. Among the Nazi killings were many examples of sadistic cruelty, but the bulk of these killings was on a different plane. It is difficult to grasp intellectually or emotionally the reality of these assembly-line executions. We must string together a whole list of adjectives to convey their nature: collective, bureaucratic, administrative, methodical, planned, calculated, organized, systematic, stereotyped, routine, efficient, impersonal, purposeful. As one survivor expressed it, it was "a fantastically well-organized, spick-and-span hell."

The roots of this callousness go back to the time before the Nazi regime. The twenties in Central Europe was not only the time of the Weimar Republic of Thomas Mann and the Bauhaus, but also very much the time of the rise of extreme reactionary groups, who made no secret of their intentions. The portents of this previolence phase were not recognized then and are not even fully recognized historically now. If we do not follow all the sources of the administrative mass murders, it means that these victims have not only suffered, they have suffered in vain. Odd Nansen, the son of the explorer and Nobel Peace Prize winner Fridtjof Nansen, was an inmate of the Sachsenhausen concentration camp. He described his experiences and observations and wrote: "The worst crime you can commit today against yourself and society is to forget what happened and sink back into indifference. It was the indifference of mankind that let it take place."

We should not regard the Nazi mass killings of civilians in isolation. Many extensive massacres and exterminations have occurred in the past: the Crusades (a million victims); the Massacre of St. Bartholomew's Day; the Inquisition (a quarter of a million); the burning of witches (at least 20,000); the subjection of colonies in South America (more than 15,000,000); the island of Haiti (14,000 survivors out of 1,000,000 inhabitants after thirty-five years of colonization); the extermination of the Indians in Argentina and Uruguay, the island of Mauritius (the work slaves died so fast that 1,200 had to be imported annually); Java (the Dutch East India Company extorted in twelve years $830,000,000 from the slave labor of 5,000,000 natives, untold numbers of whom perished); the Congo (of 30,000,000 inhabitants at the time of its colonial take-over, 8,500,000 were still alive in 1911); India (open violence such the Amritsar Massacre: during the dispersal of an assemblage, 379 were killed and 1,500 wounded, in an episode which had a lasting effect on Nehru's political development); the Indians in the United States (the great anthropologist Henry Lewis Morgan had the courage to denounce their vilification); Nanking (the massacre by the Japanese); the Hereros in Southwest Africa (40,000 men, women, and children were surrounded, driven to the desert, and left to die of hunger and thirst. Neither the German Parliament nor the traders or missionaries protested. Report of the German General Staff: the Hereros had ceased "to exist as an independent tribe." The General Staff today is the same institution with the same traditions. General Heusinger, former chief of the General Staff and presently chairman of the NATO Permanent Military Committee in Washington, used the expression "merciless hardness"); Armenians (1,500,000 were driven from the place they had cultivated for more than 2,000 years; many men, women, and children were massacred or left to perish in the desert); and so on and on.

These massacres have a number of features in common. They are not usually committed by the hotheaded anonymous groups or mobs which we like to accuse, but by cold-blooded ruling powers, for material advantages. They are characterized by a mixture of commercial and sadistic motives, by cruelty, by the vilification of victims regarded as subpeople and not really human, by the failure —or connivance—of what one might regard as restraining agencies and institutions. The history books tell us little about these events, although much can be learned from them. Viewed against this background, the Nazi holocaust appears as the historical intersection of past vilifications and unresolved violences.

What makes the Nazi administrative mass killings so outstanding is not their numbers, their efficiency, or their cruelty, but the fact that they occurred in an epoch when nobody thought it was humanly or socially possible. Therein lies their deepest lesson. If it was possible then, why not again? What has fundamentally changed? The curtain may have gone down—but only for the intermission. No social scientist or psychologist had predicted that near the mid-century some 8,000,000 nonparticipants in any war action would be deliberately killed. Is it not indicated for behavioral scientists to reexamine their perspective and to realize how closely violence is interwoven in the very fabric of our social life?

A strong economic lever promoted the mass violence. The material interestedness involved the state, the big corporations, and countless ordinary people who profited. Until February, 1945, the police and SS bureaucrat Himmler met frequently with his advisory circle of thirty to forty leading industrialists, bankers, and other members of the economic elite. A high-level order from the central office of the SS addressed to the commanders of all concentration camps said: "It is self-understood that the first thing to be considered is the hundred percent economic use of the inmates."

The commercialization of mass violence proceeded along five main lines:

1. Slave labor

2. Disposal of victims' property and personal belongings
3. Commercial utilization of human bodies
4. Supplying gas chambers and crematory furnaces as well as chemicals, for killing and disposing of bodies
5. Using victims as test objects for commercial products

## Slave Labor

Slave labor had a tremendous, still vastly underrated importance, both as a way of killing and as a method of making profits. It was a matter not only of lives but of ledgers as well. As a report to Himmler stated, the concentration camps had to be shaped from their "one-sided political form into an organization corresponding to the economic tasks." Protocols of conferences are extant in which Himmler and Goebbels agreed on the principle of "extermination by labor." The rationale of the procedure—and it *was* a rationale and not irrational sadism—was to give the inmates as little as possible to eat and to make them work until they died of exhaustion or (when they could not possibly work any more) to kill them. There was only a short step between exploitation and extermination. This treatment was to be applied on the largest scale to Jews, Russians, Poles, Czechs, gypsies, prisoners of war, German criminals and political prisoners. Lieutenant General Helmar Moser of the German Army, former military commander of the town of Lublin, expressed it to a court this way: "The doomed people in the camp were forced to perform extremely hard work beyond their strength and were urged on by brutal beatings." Or, as a Nazi official put it: "Those harnessed to the labor process work willingly on the basis of continuous fear of death." Among these slave laborers were many children under fifteen. They had to work under the same murderous conditions as the adults.

A common practice was to have weakened prisoners, "slow workers," exchanged for sturdier ones. The weak ones were disposed of. They were sent to a place with mass-killing equipment and were killed. This was part of the routine of the whole industrial procedure. A regular weekly report of I. G. Auschwitz (part of the dye trust I. G. Farben) for the period from February 8, 1943 on, states that the SS and the industry managers "agreed that all weak prisoners could be got rid of so that we have the guarantee of almost full working performance."

Slave labor was used in three main localities: in general concentration camps; in plants and factories organized and operated by private industrial firms near and in intimate collaboration with concentration camps; in plants away from the camps, like the I. G. Farben factory at Ludwigshafen. The revealing term "company camps" (*Firmenlager*) came into general usage.

Inmates had to work long hours—usually eleven hours—including Sundays and holidays. From 1933 to 1945 the expenses for the SS for one inmate averaged about ten cents a day. That included board, clothing, "supervision," housing. Inmates were rented out to private industry at the price of $1 a day or, for skilled workers, $1.50 a day. That made a huge profit for the SS, which, as is often overlooked, became a very big commercial undertaking itself and also piled up enormous profits for the private industrial corporations from the cheap labor.

Executives, engineers, and managers of the private industrial corporations knew, of course, of their labor supply, its source, the conditions of work, and the final fate of the exhausted laborers. Many of them inspected the scene. In Auschwitz they were shown the crematorium. Some complained of the "terrible smell" from the cremation furnaces. In camp Dora there was a special building with a large chimney which smoked almost constantly, where the bodies of the laborer-victims were cremated. Nobody who saw the inside of the camp could have missed this building and its purpose.

In one of the subcamps of the Buchenwald compound, which was operated directly by and for the big electrical company of Siemens, every six or eight weeks 500 inmates perished. But the camp's quota of 15,000 laborers was kept filled by replacements. According to the minutes of their meetings, the directors of the Siemens company over a period of several years discussed the progress of requisitioning this slave labor to replace the dead.

Even in private industrial plants employing slave labor, where there were no concentration-camp commanders and no SS, the firms assigned to themselves the right to work people to death and kill them with impunity. For example, the Leipzig concern Hasag maintained three plants in Poland. In all three there were barbed-wire-enclosed camps under the surveillance of the private civilian company guards. Inmates were tortured, bitten by dogs set on them, and even literally beaten to death. One of the plants had its own place of execution for laborers too starved or exhausted to work any more. Even pregnant women were executed there. The SS had nothing to do with this. It was private enterprise. Involved in this routine of mistreatment and murder, and tried in court after the war, were managers, masters, foremen, factory guards, and twenty-three directors of this private concern.

The revenue from slave labor was carefully computed. According to official documents, the average duration of a slave laborer's life was nine months. (In Auschwitz, according to testimony of SS physician Dr. Muench, it was six months.) Each item was carefully figured out: the daily income from renting out prisoners; from this was subtracted the cost of feeding them and the depreciation of their clothes; subtracted also were the costs of cremating them. Added to the gain was the rational utilization of the corpse: the gold from the teeth; the clothes in which they were arrested; their valuables and whatever money they may have had on them. Especially to be added were the proceeds from the commercial utilization of their bones and their ashes. Finally the total gain was calculated on an "average duration of life of nine months."

Some of the large industrial concerns had an insatiable demand for more and more cheap slave labor. The percentage of such labor in some industries was at times very great. For example, at one time fully one-half of the 200,000 workers employed by I. G. Farben were slave laborers. The branches of industry which employed this labor were very diverse: chemicals, rubber, armament, electrical equipment, china, granite and stone quarries, construction, mineral water, textiles, leather, building, and so on. Among the better-known names of firms employing this slave labor from concentration camps are Krupp, Siemens, AEG (General Electric Company), I. G. Farben, Volkswagen-Works, Messerschmitt, Junkers-Works, Heinkel, Argus-Works, Continental Rubber, Daimler-Benz, Shell (Floridsdorf, near Vienna), and Bavarian

Motor Works. Some commercial undertakings involved in slave labor are now closely connected with American capital, so that this period merges into our own economic system.

## Disposal of Property and Personal Belongings

A further source of considerable income was that from the disposal and utilization of the property of the victims who perished. Apart from the property confiscated, such as furniture, furnishings, and similar items from domiciles, this consisted of personal belongings such as clothes, jewelry, cameras, and so on. This added up to a vast amount of material, which in the aggregate represented huge sums of money. There were shoes of every description, for men, women, and children (in Maidanek 820,000 pairs of footwear, from babies' shoes to soldiers' boots, were found); underwear; thousands of spectacles; men's ties; women's belts; robes; watches; mountains of children's toys; nipples for babies' feeding bottles; scissors; suitcases; artificial limbs; and so on. All these articles were collected, carefully sorted, packed, stacked, and dispatched to central places. The commercial and financial phases were negotiated and handled by the civil servants in the Reichsbank and the Ministry of Economics.

## Utilization of Human Bodies

How human bodies were turned to profitable account forms a unique chapter in the history of violence. And it is not old history but contemporary history. Even in ancient times, what we call primitive people made graves for the dead; they did not utilize or barter parts of the bodies. That was left to the civilized barbarism of *our* time.

In the First World War, British Intelligence spread a false story that the Germans were making soap from corpses. It was left to the Second World War to make this a reality.

In Gdansk (Danzig) during the Second World War, a brick building was erected for a factory for a new branch of industry. Here methods were worked out for the utilization of human fat to make soap and human skin to make boots, briefcases, and bags. In the basement of the building there were large square concrete baths covered with zinc sheeting. Ten bodies were placed in carbolic acid solutions in each bath. Experts have established that among those who were shot, hanged or clubbed before being so treated, some still showed signs of life. In one room of the factory were big boilers in which the human soap was made. This was successful, and specimens of the soap (in pails) are still extant. The production of human leather did not progress so far and led only to semifinished articles of tanned human skin.

This industry was designed and organized by scientists and doctors. Even courses for production of human soap were given to other doctors from different concentration camps. Of course, such an industry was feasible only on the basis of a policy of mass extermination. The existence of this undertaking for the use of human raw material for soap factories and tanneries was no secret. Prominent people visited the place, including the rector of Danzig University, the Minister of Health, the Minister of National Education.

Gold teeth and fillings were taken out of the mouths of those who died or were killed in the concentration camps. No corpse could be burned without a stamp on the chest: "Inspected for gold fillings." This added up to thousands of pounds of gold.

Women's hair, and men's as well, was cut off, collected, and stored in sacks or barrels. Then it was sold, to be used for the production of felt hats, mattresses, and other felt products. A private felt factory in Roth near Nuremberg did a flourishing business of this kind.

The ashes of those cremated were utilized as fertilizer. That made a lot of fertilizer and represented a great economic asset. It was used on fields and in gardens. There were also special mills for the grinding of human bones. A very efficient mass-production bone-milling plant existed, for example, in the camp Chelmo, near Posen. Both ground bones and ashes were placed in large tin cans and shipped all over Germany for fertilizing the fields. Even a special method for using small human bones and ashes as fertilizer was worked out. It consisted of "a layer of human bones, a layer of human ashes, a layer of manure."

## Supplying Machinery for Extermination

The supplying of crematories, gas furnaces, and chemicals for killing and disposing of bodies became a lucrative business for large private concerns. No businessman seems to have had the slightest scruples about it. And with the introduction of gas ovens and big crematory furnaces, mass murder became industrialized. This is something new in the history of both violence and economics. Perfectly legitimate and highly regarded concerns took part in it. For example, a big electrical company, Siemens, devised and manufactured gas-chamber installations in which the murders were carried out. The company had a monopoly on gas-chamber electrical equipment. It introduced new and ingenious devices. Among them was a ventilating system by which gas could be drawn out and fresh gas blown in quickly. This made it possible to kill as many as 10,000 persons within a twenty-four-hour period.

Chemicals and poison gas, like Zyklon B gas (which gives off cyanide when exposed to the air), were manufactured for the purpose of mass killing in the camps by the big chemical concern I. G. Farben (the subsidiary firm Degesch). With these products, wholesale numbers of prisoners, including the spent slave laborers who worked in their own plants, were exterminated. In other words, you earn money by obtaining cheap prison laborers, and then you make more money by selling the means to kill them when they get exhausted.

Mass killing presented new technical problems. What to do with the corpses for instance? At first that seemed an unsolvable question. But it was solved by using the most modern equipment for burning garbage and refuse in a large city and transforming the bodies into usable products. In the city of Berlin it had been found that high temperatures—up to 1,400 degrees Centigrade—were needed to accomplish this. Exactly the same method was introduced in the concentration-camp crematory furnaces. In Maidanek, for example, temperatures of 1,500 degrees Centigrade were used. The crematorium there, a huge stone building with a big factory chimney, was the world's largest.

## *Use of Prisoners as Test Objects for Commercial Products*

Another economic gain from mass violence was the use of human beings as test objects for experiments with marketable pharmaceutical products and with chemical war weapons such as poison gas. A letter from an official of the I. G. Farben chemical trust to the Auschwitz concentration-camp administration is typical of the matter-of-fact use of human guinea pigs: "We have received the 150 women we asked for. Although extremely exhausted, they met our requirements. The tests were successful. All the subjects died. We are soon starting negotiations for another lot." Children were used in the same way. For example, six girl inmates aged eight to fourteen were infected with hepatitis to try out a new remedy for this disease. The name Murder, Inc., would have been more appropriate for the firms which supplied the installations and chemicals for the specific purpose of mass killing of civilians and disposal of their bodies than for the gangster syndicate which was responsible for a mere thousand murders.

Some of the cruel medical experiments on inmates to test new drugs did not originate in the heads of individual doctors, but were asked for and initiated by pharmaceutical firms. This combination of business, pharmacology, and violence is a significant sociological fact. There is, for example, the scene of the group of prisoners in the Sachsenhausen concentration camp marching—singing and whistling—under the influence of a new energy pill that was being tested for a pharmaceutical firm. They were marching like this to their death in the gas chamber.

These inhuman experiments are not a thing of the past. They are still taken for granted and commercially cited. One of the cruelest and most painful medical experiments in the Dachau camp was the immersion of inmates in ice-cold water. Some were given a drug; those in a control group were not. It was claimed that those who got the drug survived, while those who did not died. Now, two decades later, advertising specifically refers to these "cold water experiments" in promoting this same drug (which is, incidentally, of very doubtful value).

The cheap labor furnished by concentration-camp inmates was an enormous economic asset. We cannot do justice to these cruel facts psychoanalytically alone. Slave labor did not satisfy any deep aggressive instincts; it satisfied the stockholders. The historian J. Schmelzer, of the Martin Luther University in Halle-Wittenberg, made an interesting sociological study of the responsible officials of the I. G. Farben concern who were involved in the slave-labor period and what positions they hold today. The study shows how the action phase of this mass violence merges imperceptibly into the respectability of the postviolence phase. An interesting sidelight is the fact that Friedrich Vialon, a high Nazi official who had to do with the renting out of slave laborers to private industry, is today State Secretary in the ministry for aid to underdeveloped countries.

What happened to the firms who used slave labor? Many of them, or their successors, are doing fine. Their shares are sound financially, even if not morally. Some of the prominent men and concerns involved in these sources of labor today hold more concentrated economic power than ever. This means that in the postviolence phase, violence was not resolved but was rewarded.

The Krupp concern built places of production near such death camps as Auschwitz. In the places of production, thousands of inmates were worked half—or rather three-quarters—to death, then in the camps they were pushed the rest of the way. The number of Krupp forced laborers in the original factories and the camp plants comprised at least 75,000 civilians and 25,000 prisoners of war. Alfred Krupp, head of the firm, was sentenced to twelve years in jail for the use and abuse of slave labor. Long before his sentence was due to expire, after four years in a pleasant prison, he went free. His release was celebrated in the biggest hotel in town with a champagne breakfast. He gave a press conference for more than fifty press representatives at a flower-decorated table and was greeted like a national hero. Asked whether he would repent what he had done, he replied that he had not thought out philosophically the ramifications of his conduct. Judging by what has happened since, we have not either. Today, with an assist from the financial and political establishment of the United States, he is head of one of the largest individually owned industrial concerns in the world. In 1957 there was a great celebration of his fiftieth birthday. As of 1965 the Krupp group had net assets of more than a billion dollars and was entirely owned by Alfred Krupp. The company now produces twice as much steel as it did before World War II.

This is a twentieth-century success story—success for the perpetration of violence. For since the violence of slave labor worked so well, financially speaking, it is an endorsement and a direct incentive for the future. In a wider perspective the firms which profit from the apartheid conditions in South Africa play a role comparable to that of the industries in Germany which profited from slave labor directly. In a typical year (1962), American companies operating in South Africa made profits of $72,000,000. That is double the average revenue from American investments abroad (11.8 percent).

What was in the minds of those who participated in one way or another in the administrative mass murders? According to the federal bureau charged with the prosecution of Nazi crimes, 80,000 persons participated in the exterminations. Of course, some of them were abnormal, sadistic, hostility-ridden personalities who acted from uncontrolled primitive drives. But in view of the very large numbers of participants in these massacres, the problem of individual character recedes into the background. Only social psychology can help us to understand this collective behavior. Many of these persons not only were inhuman officials but were officially inhuman. At the one pole were those who carried out the deeds; at the other, those who may be called the desk murderers, the intellectual originators. In between were the middlemen of murder. In vain do we look for any number of colorful, eccentric personalities. Instead we find a large gray mass of functionaries, bureaucrats, and rank-and-file killers. Here were the policy makers, the diplomats who made the orders palatable for foreign consumption, men who gave the orders, the transmitters of the orders, the organizers and supervisors, the civil servants, the technical personnel, the legal experts, the physicians (present in every concentration camp and acting like anything but physicians), the clerks, the workers, the approving bystanders and spectators.

It has frequently been stated that the population as a whole just accepted the political directives and responded passively. Sociological analysis of the evidence from the first years of the regime, when the mass violence started, indicates that this is not true. The people did not take the avalanche of authoritarian violence without question. We can reconstruct a whole fever curve: puzzlement, indecisiveness, refusal, illusion, awakening, awareness of the closing in of the propaganda and the violence, insecurity, passive resistance, disappointment with the wrong prognostications of the liberal leaders, emptiness, anxiety, hope of help from other countries, helplessness, resignation, toleration, disappointment, indifference, submission, fascination with the new dynamic regime, adherence. During this period while the victims lost their freedom, many intellectuals lost their convictions.

The central fact that stands out from the study of the administrative mass murders is the power of incitement. It can corrode the thinking of the innocent. People, practically all people, can be incited to violence. They may not all carry it out themselves; they may only help from a distance and tolerate and thereby foster it. But it is a fallacy to assume that the majority of right-thinking people are immune to these mass influences and that only predisposed personalities succumb to them. Even the good man, as George Gissing wrote long ago, "becomes ready for any evil to which contagion prompts him." If we place all our emphasis on the unconscious, we neglect the role of conscious manipulation.

Effective incitement to violence does not proceed as simple, direct suggestion or exhortation. It always has to be combined, as Georges Sorel, a political theoretician of violence, has pointed out, with a "myth." One such suitable myth consists in the complete vilification of opponents. They are the ones toward whom heroic hardness is to be shown. Along with the myth that the life of other people has no value goes a tremendous, pleasant feeling of superiority. An SS man put it this way in his diary: "How superior we feel after each one of the Fuehrer's speeches!" If the potential opponents are regarded as subhuman, as subpeople, their complete destruction becomes morally permissible and even necessary. We underestimate the absolute cruelty that can be engendered in this way and only in this way.

The next step follows with a certain inevitability. For both the higher ranks—the planners—and the lower ranks—the doers—it became a habit to use violence for settling tasks and solving problems. This habit became more and more ingrained. When Abe Reles, one of the executioners of Murder, Inc., was asked by the District Attorney, "Did your conscience ever bother you?" he answered, "How did you feel when you tried your first law case?" The District Attorney replied that he was nervous but that later he got used to it. And Reles responded, "It's the same with murder. I got used to it."

CHAPTER NINE

# The Geranium in the Window

## THE "EUTHANASIA" MURDERS

> If the physician presumes to take into
> consideration in his work whether a life
> has value or not, the consequences are
> boundless and the physician becomes the
> most dangerous man in the state.
> —DR. CHRISTOPH HUFELAND
> (1762–1836)

IF we want to understand violence as a whole, we cannot leave any
of its major manifestations in a fog of half-knowledge. But this
is exactly what has happened with an unprecedented occurrence
of mass violence, the deliberate killing of large numbers of mental
patients, for which psychiatrists were directly responsible. To
both the general public and the psychiatric profession, the details
and the background are still imperfectly known. This is not only
a chapter in the history of violence; it is also a chapter in the
history of psychiatry. Silence does not wipe it out, minimizing
it does not expunge it. It must be faced. We must try to understand
and resolve it.

It should be kept in mind at the outset that it is a great achievement of psychiatry to have brought about the scientific and humane
treatment of mental patients after centuries of struggles against
great obstacles. In this progress, as is universally acknowledged,
German psychiatrists played a prominent part. And German public
psychiatric hospitals had been among the best and most humane
in the world.

In the latter part of 1939, four men, in the presence of a whole
group of physicians and an expert chemist, were purposely killed
(with carbon monoxide gas). They had done nothing wrong, had
caused no disturbance, and were trusting and cooperative. They

were ordinary mental patients of a state psychiatric hospital which was—or should have been—responsible for their welfare. This successful experiment led to the installation of gas chambers in a number of psychiatric hospitals (Grafeneck, Brandenburg, Hartheim, Sonnenstein, Hadamar, Bernburg).

Let us visualize a historical scene. Dr. Max de Crinis is professor of psychiatry at Berlin University and director of the psychiatric department of the Charité, one of the most famous hospitals of Europe. He is one of the top scientists and organizers of the mass destruction of mental patients. Dr. de Crinis visits the psychiatric institution Sonnenstein, near Dresden, to supervise the working of his organization. He wants to see how the plans are carried out. Sonnenstein is a state hospital with an old tradition of scientific psychiatry and humaneness. In the company of psychiatrists of the institution, Dr. de Crinis now inspects the latest installation, a shower-roomlike chamber. Through a small peephole in an adjoining room he watches twenty nude men being led into the chamber and the door closed. They are not disturbed patients, just quiet and cooperative ones. Carbon monoxide is released into the chamber. The men get weaker and weaker; they try frantically to breathe, totter, and finally drop down. Minutes later their suffering is over and they are all dead. This is a scene repeated many, many times throughout the program. A psychiatrist or staff physician turns on the gas, waits briefly, and then looks over the dead patients afterward, men, women, and children.

The mass killing of mental patients was a large project. It was organized as well as any modern community psychiatric project, and better than most. It began with a careful preparatory and planning stage. Then came the detailed working out of methods, the formation of agencies for transporting patients, their registration and similar tasks (there were three main agencies with impressive bureaucratic names), the installing of crematory furnaces at the psychiatric institutions, and finally the action. It all went like clockwork, the clock being the hourglass of death. The organization comprised a whole chain of mental hospitals and institutions, university professors of psychiatry, and directors and staff members of mental hospitals. Psychiatrists completely reversed their historical role and passed death sentences. It became a matter of routine. These psychiatrists, without coercion, acted not figuratively but literally in line with the slogan of one of the most notorious concentration-camp commanders, Koch, the husband of Ilse Koch: "There are no sick men in my camp. They are either well or dead."

The whole undertaking went by different designations: "help for the dying," "mercy deaths," "mercy killings," "destruction of life devoid of value," "mercy action"—or, more briefly, the "action." They all became fused in the sonorous and misleading term "euthanasia." Strangely enough—or perhaps not so strangely —the name has persisted. We hear and read of the "euthanasia program," "euthanasia experiments," "euthanasia campaign," "euthanasia action," "euthanasia trials." In reality, these mass killings had nothing whatever to do with euthanasia. These were not mercy deaths but merciless murders. It was the merciless destruction of helpless people by those who were supposed to help them. There was nothing individual about it; it was a systematic, planned, massive killing operation. The whole proceeding was characterized by the complete absence of any compassion, mercy, or pity for the individual. What a physician does or should do with a special individual patient under special circumstances had absolutely nothing to do with those mass exterminations.

The greatest mistake we can make is to assume or believe that there was a morally, medically, or socially legitimate program and that all that was wrong was merely the excesses. There were no excesses. Rarely has a civil social action been planned, organized, and carried through with such precision. It was not a "good" death, as the term "euthanasia" implies (from *eu*, "well," and *thanatos*, "death"), but a bad death; not a euthanasia but what may be called a dysthanasia. Often it took up to five minutes of suffocation and suffering before the patients died. If we minimize the cruelty involved (or believe those who minimize it), these patients are betrayed a second time. It was often a slow, terrible death for them. For example, a male nurse of one of the state mental hospitals described the routine he saw through the peephole of the gas chamber: "One after the other the patients sagged and finally fell all over each other." Others have reported that the dead gassed victims were found with their lips pushed outward, the tip of the tongue stuck out between them, clearly showing that they had been gasping for breath.

The false term "euthanasia" was used by those who planned, organized, and carried out the action, and it is still being used now by those who do not know, or do not want to know, what really happened.

The ancients meant by euthanasia the art and discipline of dying in peace and dignity. The only legitimate medicosocial extension of this meaning is *help* toward that end, with special emphasis on relief from pain and suffering. Euthanasia in this sense is the mitigation and relief of pain and suffering of the death agony by medication or other medical means. For the physician, that means a careful diagnosis, prognosis, and consequent action in relation to a special clinical state. As in any other medical procedures, this may involve a certain risk which requires the physician's best responsible judgment in the individual case. Whatever problems this may represent, they have no relation whatsoever to this massacre of mental patients. To confuse the two means to confuse humanity with inhumanity.

When Dr. Hans Hoff, professor of psychiatry at the University of Vienna, begins his introduction to the recent book *Euthanasia and Destruction of Life Devoid of Value* like this: "As long as there are incurable, suffering and painfully dying people, the problem of euthanasia will be open to discussion," he is adding to the confusion and concealment, as does the author of this whitewashing book. These victims were not dying, they were not in pain, they were not suffering, and most of them were not incurable.

From the very beginning—that is, before the outbreak of war and before any written expression by Hitler—it was officially known to leading professors of psychiatry and directors of mental hospitals that under the designation of "euthanasia" a program was about to be carried through by them and with their help to kill mental patients in the whole of Germany. The object was "the destruction of life devoid of value." That definition was flexible enough for a summary proceeding of extermination of patients.

The term "euthanasia" was deliberately used to conceal the actual purpose of the project. But there is also a real confusion about the term that reaches into many quarters. In the *American*

*College Dictionary,* for example, "euthanasia" is defined as "the putting of a person to death painlessly." That is not euthanasia; it is homicide. If you "put a person to death," that is, deliberately kill him, you are committing murder. If it is done painlessly, it is still murder. Many murders, just like suicides, are committed without inflicting pain. In similar fashion, a widely used recent dictionary of psychological and psychoanalytical terms defines "euthanasia" as "the practice of ending life painlessly." Criminology is familiar with cases of mass murderers who made it a practice to do just that. For example, the man who over a considerable period of time lured good-looking young boys into the woods and put them to sleep, a sleep from which they never woke up. They were found, partly undressed, with peaceful expressions on their faces. That was not euthanasia, however; it was mass murder. The fact that such confused and confusing definitions are given in standard dictionaries is another documentation of my thesis that violence is much more solidly and insidiously set in our social thinking than is generally believed.

Just as the designation has been left in ambiguity, so also has the number of the victims. We read about "thousands" or "tens of thousands" or "almost a hundred thousand." But how many were there? One would think that this fact would be indispensable for understanding not only the history of violence but even that of psychiatry and of modern civilization in general. Yet in none of the publications, books, or news reports of recent years is a more-or-less-correct figure given. It is characteristic that without exception all the figures that are mentioned are far below the reality. The individual psychiatric hospitals were not so squeamish about the number of patients put to death while the program lasted. For example, in 1941 the psychiatric institution Hadamar celebrated the cremation of the ten thousandth mental patient in a special ceremony. Psychiatrists, nurses, attendants, and secretaries all participated. Everybody received a bottle of beer for the occasion.

We can get an idea of the proportional numbers involved by studying some partial but exact statistics referring to a special locality. From 1939 to 1945 the number of patients in the psychiatric hospitals of Berlin dropped to one-fourth of the original total. As the cause of this drop the official statistics give "evacuations." That is a euphemistic expression for the fact that three-fourths of the patients were transported to other institutions and killed. Sometimes patients slated for murder were not sent directly to the hospitals that had the proper installations, but went first temporarily to so-called intermediate institutions. In 1938 the psychiatric institutions of the province of Brandenburg had 16,295 mental patients of the city of Berlin. In 1945 only 2,379 were left. Almost 14,000 were destroyed. In the institution Berlin-Buch, of 2,500 patients, 500 survived; in the hospital of Kaufbeuren in Bavaria, of 2,000 patients, 200 were left. Many institutions, even big ones, *i.e.,* in Berlin, in Silesia, in Baden, in Saxony, in Austria, were closed entirely because all the patients had been liquidated.

In the special killing institutions the turnover was fast. The psychiatric institution Grafeneck normally had 100 beds. Early in the "action," within thirty-three days 594 patients died (*i.e.,* were killed). A while later, within forty-seven days 2,019 inmates were written off. Eventually the crematorium of Grafeneck smoked incessantly.

In 1939 about 300,000 mental patients (according to some figures it was 320,000) were in psychiatric hospitals, institutions, or clinics. In 1946 their number was 40,000. It was discussed during the project that 300,000 hospital beds would be made available by getting rid of mental patients.

The most reliable estimates of the number of psychiatric patients killed are at least 275,000. We have to realize particularly that the largest proportion of them were not "incurable," as is often lightly stated. Even if "euthanasia" is defined, as it falsely is, as "the killing of incurable mentally diseased persons," that is not at all what happened. According to the best established psychiatric knowledge, about 50 percent of them either would have improved to such an extent that they could have been discharged and lived a social life outside a hospital or would have gotten completely well.

Another misconception widely credited is that these patients had hereditary diseases. Even publications completely condemning the "euthanasia" action fall into this error. However, in the largest number of patients the hereditary factor played either no role at all or only the slightest (and that not well established scientifically). The whole number comprises both curable and incurable conditions, psychopathic personalities, epileptics, encephalitics, neurological cases, mental defectives of both severe and mild degree, arteriosclerotics, deaf-mutes, patients with all kinds of nervous diseases, handicapped patients who had lost a limb in the First World War and were in a state hospital, "cripples" of every description, *et al.*

The indications became wider and wider and eventually included as criteria "superfluous people," the unfit, the unproductive, any "useless eaters," misfits, undesirables. The over-all picture is best understood as the identification and elimination of the weak.

A considerable percentage of the whole number were senile cases, including people who had no senile psychosis but were merely aged and infirm. Many of the old people included in the program were not in institutions but were living at home, in good health, with their families. A psychiatrist would go to these homes and give the aged people a cursory psychiatric examination. Of course, it is easy, if you confront a very old person with a lot of psychological questions, to make it appear that something is mentally wrong with him. The psychiatrist would then suggest that such people be placed under guardianship and sent to an institution for a while. From there they were quickly put into gas chambers. It is difficult to conceive that thousands of normal men and women would permit their parents or grandparents to be disposed of in this way without more protest, but that is what happened. As early as September, 1939, word had gotten about among the population in Berlin that inmates of homes for the aged had been exterminated and that it was planned to kill all aged invalids as quickly as possible.

During the first phase of the program, Jewish mental patients, old and young, were strictly spared and excluded. The reason given was that they did not deserve the "benefit" of psychiatric euthanasia. This lasted up to the second half of 1940. Eventually they were all rounded up, however, and by 1941, practically without exception, were exterminated.

Thousands of children were disposed of. A special agency existed for them, consisting of a commission of three experts: one a psychiatrist and director of a state hospital, the other two prominent pediatricians. The children came from psychiatric hospitals, institutions for mental defectives, children's homes, university pediatric clinics, children's hospitals, pediatricians, *et al*. They were killed in both psychiatric institutions and pediatric clinics. Especially in the latter a number of woman physicians were actively involved in the murders. Among these children were those with mental diseases, mental defectives—even those with only slightly retarded intelligence—handicapped children, children with neurological conditions, and mongoloid children (even with minimal mental defects). Also in this number were children in training schools or reformatories. Admission to such child-care institutions occurs often on a social indication and not for any intrinsic personality difficulties of the child. One physician who killed such training-school boys and girls with intravenous injections of morphia stated in court to explain his actions: "I see today that it was not right. . . . I was always told that the responsibility lies with the professors from Berlin."

The chief of the mental institution Hadamar was responsible for the murder of "over a thousand patients." He personally opened the containers of gas and watched through the peephole the death agonies of the patients, including children. He stated: "I was of course torn this way and that. It reassured me to learn what eminent scientists partook in the action: Professor Carl Schneider, Professor Heyde, Professor Nitsche." This, of course, is not an excuse either legally or morally, but it is a causal factor which has to be taken into account. And when Dr. Karl Brandt, the medical chief of the euthanasia project, defended himself for his leading role in the action, he stated that he had asked for the "most critical" evaluation of who was mentally incurable. And he added: "Were not the regular professors of the universities with the program? Who could there be who was better qualified than they?"

These statements that leading psychiatrists supplied the rationalization for these cruelties and took a responsible part in them are true. We must ask ourselves what was the prehistory, in the previolence phase, of their ideas. Historically there were tendencies in psychiatry (and not only in German psychiatry) to pronounce value judgments not only on individuals, on medical grounds, but on whole groups, on medicosociological grounds. What was (and still is) widely regarded as scientific writing prepared the way. Most influential was the book *The Release of the Destruction of Life Devoid of Value,* published in Leipzig in 1920. Its popularity is attested by the fact that two years later a second edition became necessary. The book advocated that the killing of "worthless people" be released from penalty and legally permitted. It was written by two prominent scientists, the jurist Karl Binding and the psychiatrist Alfred Hoche. The concept of "life devoid of value" or "life not worth living" was not a Nazi invention, as is often thought. It derives from this book.

Binding and Hoche speak of "absolutely worthless human beings"; they plead for "the killing of those who cannot be rescued and whose death is urgently necessary"; they refer to those who are below the level of beasts and who have "neither the will to live nor to die"; they write about those who are "mentally completely dead" and who "represent a foreign body in human society." It is noteworthy that among the arguments adduced for killing, the economic factor is stressed, namely, the cost of keeping these patients alive and caring for them. The psychiatrist author decries any show of sympathy in such cases, because it would be based on "erroneous thinking." The jurist author recognizes that errors in diagnosis and execution might be made. But he dismisses that like this: "Humanity loses so many members through error that one more or less really hardly makes any difference." In the beginning of the book we read about the feeling of "pity" for the patient. But in the bulk of the text the question of pity does not come up any more. It gets completely lost. Instead, both authors enlarge on the economic factor, the waste of money and labor in the care of the retarded. Both extol "heroism" and a "heroic attitude" which our time is supposed to have lost.

These ideas were expressed in 1920. Surely Hoche and Binding had not heard of Hitler at that time, nor did Hitler read this book. It is not without significance that at this time, when Hitler was just starting his career, the "life devoid of value" slogan was launched from a different source. Evidently there is such a thing as a spirit of the times which emanates from the depths of economic-historical processes.

This little book influenced—or at any rate crystallized—the thinking of a whole generation. Considering how violence-stimulating the ideas in it are, it is significant that both authors were eminent men who played a role as intellectual leaders in a special historical period. This illustrates the proposition that violence does not usually come from the uncontrolled instincts of the under-educated, but frequently is a rationalized policy from above. Hoche was professor of psychiatry and director of the psychiatric clinic at Freiburg from 1902 to 1934. He made valuable contributions to neuropsychiatry. In his clinic a number of eminent specialists were trained—for example, Dr. Robert Wartenberg, who later became one of the outstanding and most popular teachers of neurology in California. Hoche's sound views on classification of mental diseases had considerable influence on American psychiatry, especially through Adolf Meyer, professor of psychiatry at Johns Hopkins.

Wherever his work touched on the social field, however, he had illiberal tendencies. For example, in a series of monographs which he edited, he published and gave wide currency to a book which tried to prove women intellectually inferior to men. In his work on forensic psychiatry, he exhibited a punitive, legalistic attitude with regard to sexual deviations. He was a reactionary opponent of psychoanalysis, not recognizing even Freud's well-established clinical observations. He regarded his book on the destruction of "life devoid of value" as one of his "more important" works.

The other author, Karl Binding, was professor of jurisprudence at the University of Leipzig. He was the chief representative of the retribution theory in criminal law. He combatted the idea that the protection of society is the purpose of punishment and that the personality of the criminal has to be taken into account. He taught that for every criminal deed there has to be full retribution. His son Rudolf G. Binding was also a jurist, and a recognized poet as well. When Romain Rolland in 1933 warned against Nazi violence and pleaded for humaneness, Rudolf G. Binding answered in a "Letter to the World." He advocated fanaticism on the part of everybody and called for "fanatics big and small, down to the children."

Another intellectual stream that contributed to the final massacre of mental patients was the exaggeration of the influence of heredity on mental disorders. The chief representative of this trend was Ernst Ruedin. Ruedin was professor of psychiatry at the universities of Basel, in Switzerland, and Munich. Some of his studies on heredity, and those of his pupils and associates (like Eugen Kahn, who later became professor of psychiatry at Yale), were undoubtedly valuable. This was widely recognized. He participated in the First International Congress for Mental Hygiene in Washington, D.C. But it was he who supplied the "scientific" reasons according to which mass sterilizations of all kinds of physically and mentally handicapped people took place. He was the chief architect of the compulsory sterilization law of 1933. This law was so vigorously formulated and interpreted (by Ruedin in 1934) that, for example, any young man with a harmless phimosis was forced to be sterilized. The summary official explanation for this was that he would be "incapable of achieving extraordinary performances in sport, in life, in war, or in overcoming dangers." The results of enforced castrations in the period from 1933 to 1945 are still quoted in current psychiatric literature without any critique of their inhumanity.

The compulsory sterilization law was the forerunner of the mass killing of psychiatric patients, which was organized and carried out with Ruedin's full knowledge. He expressly warned psychiatrists against the "excessive compassion and love of one's neighbor characteristic of the past centuries."

Against this theoretical-intellectual background, mental patients were sacrificed in psychiatric institutions and in the name of psychiatry. From its very inception the "euthanasia" program was guided in all important matters, including concrete details, by psychiatrists. The administrative sector was handled by bureaucrats who dealt merely with executive, management, and formal questions such as transport of patients, cremation, notification of relatives, and so on. Even the false death certificates were signed by psychiatrists. The psychiatrists made the decisions. For these physicians, as the physical chemist Professor Robert Havemann expressed it, denouncing the "euthanasia" murders, "the patient is no longer a human being needing help, but merely an object whose value is measured according to whether his life or his destruction is more expedient for the nation. The physicians took over the function of judge over life and death. . . . They made themselves into infallible gods." How matter-of-factly they considered this role is illustrated by the replies of the veteran director of one of the biggest and formerly most well-administered psychiatric hospitals during an interrogation:

Q. To how many children have you applied euthanasia in your hospital?
A. I couldn't tell you exactly. . . .
Q. To how many have you done that? 200? 500? 1,000?
A. For God's sake, I really don't remember how many there were. I really don't know whether there were a hundred or more.
Q. Do you know when euthanasia was practiced on the last child in your hospital?
A. I don't know exactly. But Dr. ———— says that until a short time before the arrival of the Americans [the American Army], children were still subjected to euthanasia.
Q. For how long have you practiced the euthanasia of children?
A. After so much time, I can't remember the dates exactly.
Q. When did the extermination of these children stop?
A. The extermination of these children never stopped until the end. I never received an order [to stop it].
Q. To how many adults did you apply euthanasia in your institution?
A. I don't know any more.
Q. How many adults have you submitted to euthanasia in your institution?
A. That didn't happen in my institution. I contented myself with transferring the patients [to other institutions where they were killed].

It has been stated that the psychiatrists were merely following a law or were being forced to obey an order. Again and again we read—as if it were a historical fact—of Hitler's secret order to exterminate those suffering from severe mental defect or disease. Those who hold the one-man theory of history (sometimes called the great-man theory of history), according to which important developments, for good or evil, are to be explained by the wish and will of one individual person, favor the illusion that such an order was the entire cause of the extermination of psychiatric patients. According to this view, everything was fine until that order was given and became fine again when the order was revoked. The reality was very different. There was no law and no such order. The tragedy is that the psychiatrists did not have to have an order.

They acted on their own. They were not carrying out a death sentence pronounced by somebody else. They were the legislators who laid down the rules for deciding who was to die; they were the administrators who worked out the procedures, provided the patients and places, and decided the methods of killing; they pronounced a sentence of life or death in every individual case; they were the executioners who carried the sentences out or—without being coerced to do so—surrendered their patients to be killed in other institutions; they supervised and often watched the slow deaths.

The evidence is very clear on this. The psychiatrists did not have to work in these hospitals; they did so voluntarily, were able to resign if they wished, and could refuse to do special tasks. For example, the psychiatrist Dr. F. Hoelzel was asked by the psychiatric director of the mental institution Eglfing-Haar to head a children's division in which many handicapped and disturbed children were killed (right up to 1945). He refused in a pathetic letter saying that his "temperament was not suited to this task," that he was "too soft."

Hitler gave no order to kill mental patients indiscriminately. As late as mid-1940 (when thousands of patients had been killed in psychiatric institutions), Minister of Justice Guertner wrote to Minister Hans Lammers: "The Fuehrer has declined to enact a law [for putting mental patients to death]." There was no legal sanction for it. All we have is one note, not on official stationery but on Hitler's own private paper, written in October, 1939, and predated September 1, 1939. Meetings of psychiatrists working out the "euthanasia" program had taken place long before that. Hitler's note is addressed to Philipp Bouhler, chief of Hitler's chancellery, and to Dr. Karl Brandt, Hitler's personal physician at the time and Reich Commissioner for Health. (Bouhler committed suicide; Dr. Brandt was sentenced to death and executed.) The note reads as follows:

Reichleader Bouhler and
Dr. Med. Brandt

are responsibly commissioned to extend the authority of physicians, to be designated by name, so that a mercy

death may be granted to patients who according to human judgment are incurably ill according to the most critical evaluation of
the state of their disease.

(Signed) Adolf Hitler

To kill patients (Hitler does not speak of mental patients), even
if one were sure that they are incurable, is bad enough. But even
if his wish, as the note clearly expresses it, had been executed, the
number of victims would have been infinitely smaller and the whole
proceeding could not have been carried out in the way in which it
was carried out. Referring to this note, anyone could have refused
to do what was later actually done. The note does not give the
order to kill, but the *power* to kill. That is something very different. The physicians made use of this power extensively, ruthlessly, cruelly. The note is not a command but an assignment of
authority and responsibility to a particular group of persons,
namely, physicians, psychiatrists, and pediatricians. This assignment, far from ordering it, did not even give psychiatrists official
permission to do what they did on a grand scale, *i.e.,* kill all kinds
of people who were not at all incurable or even mentally ill, making no attempt even to examine them first. The assignment gives
to the psychiatrist the widest leeway for "human judgment" and a
"most critical evaluation." It certainly cannot be construed as an
order to kill people with no serious disease or with no disease at all.

Even if the note was not meant to be taken literally, it was a
formal concession to ethics and offered a loophole for contradiction or at least question. The psychiatrists in authority did not take
advantage of this. Instead they initiated the most extreme measures
and cloaked them in scientific terminology and academic respectability. No mental patients were killed without psychiatrists being
involved. Without the scientific rationalization which they supplied
from the very beginning and without their mobilization of their
own psychiatric hospitals and facilities, the whole proceeding could
not have taken the shape it did. They were responsible for their
own judgments, their own decisions, their own acts. It helps us
to understand the wide social ramifications of violence if we realize
that from the highest echelons down, the psychiatrists acted spontaneously, without being forced.

A court in Coblenz probed this question most carefully in the case of three hospital psychiatrists who were charged with "aid to murder in an indefinite number of cases": "They have taken this task upon themselves voluntarily, just as altogether the collaboration in the 'action' was voluntary throughout." This is borne out by a letter from Himmler, chief of the SS, in response to an inquiry by a high judge: "What happens in the place in question [a psychiatric institution] is carried out by a commission of physicians. . . . The SS furnish only help in vehicles, cars, etc. The medical specialist, expert and responsible, is the one who gives the orders." In this connection the statement of Dr. Hans Hefelmann, an agronomist who was a highly placed bureaucrat in the "euthanasia" program, is significant. He made it in the abortive "euthanasia" trial at Limburg in 1964: "No doctor was ever ordered to participate in the euthanasia program; they came of their own volition." Other evidence confirms this.

What psychiatrists did made even members of the Nazi Party weep. When patients were transferred from their regular institution to one where they were to be killed, they were usually told that it was only a regular normal transfer from one hospital to another or that it was a change to a better place. Sometimes a glimpse of the truth would become known to patients, and scenes worthy of Callot or Goya would follow. Here is such a (true) scene. In the sleepy little town of Absberg, two large autobuses (belonging to a central transport agency of the "euthanasia" program) are parked on the street near an institution where there are several hundred mental patients. Some time before, twenty-five patients had been fetched by such a bus. Of these twenty-five, twenty-four "died" and one woman patient returned. The other patients in the institution learned what had happened, as did the inhabitants of the town. As the patients leave the institution to enter the buses, they are afraid, they refuse and remonstrate. Force is used by the personnel, and each patient is shoved violently into a bus. A large group of bystanders has assembled. They are so moved that they break into tears. The whole operation is presided over by an experienced psychiatrist from the big state hospital Erlangen. Among those spectators who cried openly at this pitiful spectacle were—as

the official Nazi report states—"even members of the Nazi Party."
There is no mention anywhere that doctors had any tears in their
eyes.

To place causal responsibility on the physician does not in any
way diminish the responsibility of the high and low Nazi officials
and bureaucrats involved. But by the same token, placing full responsibility on these officials does not in the slightest diminish the
role of the psychiatrist in the slaughter. In order to get the proper
focus, we must think in terms of causal factors. If it takes two to
plan and commit deliberate murder, that does not mean that only
one is guilty. Even if the psychiatrists had been under orders,
which they were not, it is noteworthy that their complete mobilization for killing patients went as speedily and as smoothly as the
military mobilization of soldiers to fight the enemy.

Two "extenuating" circumstances, often claimed, have to be
seriously weighed. One is that the psychiatrists did not know; the
other is that very few were involved. In the very beginning, some
psychiatrists may not have known what happened to their patients
when they were transferred en masse in buses to other, unnamed
institutions. But it is preposterous to assume that this ignorance
could last after tens of thousands had been killed. The claim that
only a few psychiatrists were involved is equally invalid. The
lowest estimate is that there were "perhaps fifty" who participated.
Even if this were a correct number (which it is not), among them
were some of the most renowned and distinguished academic and
hospital figures. Actually, the extent of the operation makes it
inevitable that there were many more involved in Germany and in
Austria, perhaps three or four times that many (not to speak of the
many psychiatric nurses acting under the instructions of psychiatrists). Of course, the degree of participation varied. For example,
in the internationally famous hospital of Gütersloh, the director
and his staff did not "select" patients for annihilation. But they
delivered the patients, without resistance or protest, to the guards
and escorts who drove up for them in trucks. That is participating
in murder too.

In July, 1939, several months before Hitler's note was written,
a conference took place in Berlin in which the program to kill
mental patients in the whole of Germany was outlined in concrete,

final form. Present and ready to participate were the regular professors of psychiatry and chairmen of the departments of psychiatry of the leading universities and medical schools of Germany: Berlin, Heidelberg, Bonn, Würzburg. Historians of medicine and sociologists will have a lot of work to do to explain this. So far they have not stated the problem or even noted the fact. At a conference in Dresden in March, 1940, Professor de Crinis, of Berlin University, talked over the program with the chief psychiatrists of large public mental hospitals (state hospitals). The classification of mental disorders on which devoted physicians in all countries had worked for centuries was reduced to a simple formula: patients "not worthy to live" and patients "worthy to be helped." There was no opposition on the part of the physicians, every one of whom held a responsible position in the state-hospital system. Questions of ethics or the juridical aspects were not even mentioned. The only questions raised by the participants at the conference were how the project could be carried through most "practically and cheaply." For example, the transfer of patients from their original institution to one where they were to be killed was called "impractical" because it meant "wasting of gasoline." Mass graves, to be leveled later, were recommended as being an economical procedure.

For several years during the time of the program, psychiatrists held meetings every three months in Heidelberg under the chairmanship of the professor of psychiatry at the University of Heidelberg. At these conferences the ways to conduct the extermination action were studied, and suitable measures were suggested to assure its efficacy.

The whole project is a model of the most bureaucratic mass murder in history. It functioned as follows. In the preparatory meetings the chief psychiatric experts of the project worked out the criteria by which patients should be selected. Questionnaires were prepared with questions as to diagnosis, duration of stay in the institution, and so on. In October, 1939, the first questionnaires went out to state hospitals and other public and private institutions where mental patients, epileptics, the mentally retarded, and other handicapped persons were taken care of. Copies of each filled-out questionnaire were sent to four psychiatric experts, who indicated with a + or — their opinion about whether the patient was to live or die. (No expert gave an opinion on questionnaires filled out for patients in his own institution, but only on those of other institutions. Therefore he had no personal knowledge whatsoever of the patients.) This typical correspondence shows that the psychiatric experts worked very hard.

Letter from the "euthanasia" central office in Berlin to Member of the Commission of Experts, dated November 25, 1940:

Enclosed I am sending you 300 report sheets [questionnaires] from the institution Lüneburg with the request for your expert opinion.
(Signed)

Answering letter from the Member of the Commission of Experts to the central office in Berlin, dated November 29, 1940:

Enclosed I am sending you the 107th batch of report sheets, namely, 300 sheets complete with my expert opinion.
(Signed)

This rapid selection and certification of death candidates is not a record or by any means exceptional. The same expert formed his opinion on 2,190 questionnaires in two weeks and on 258 in two days.

The questionnaires with expert opinions indicated by the + or the — were then sent to a chief expert, who passed the final judgment. Beginning in January, 1940, the patients marked for death were transferred, directly or via intermediate stations, to the six psychiatric institutions in which gas chambers had been installed for the program. In these lethal institutions the patients were dealt with summarily and quickly, as this typical letter shows, from the social-welfare association Swabia to the director of the state hospital Kaufbeuren:

I have the honor to inform you that the female patients transferred from your hospital on November 8, 1940, all died in the month of November in the institutions Grafeneck, Bernburg, Sonnenstein, and Hartheim.
(Signed)

In some institutions, like Hartheim in Austria, things went so fast sometimes that it took only four hours from the time a patient was admitted till he left "through the chimney."

The backbone of the whole project was the experts. It was their decision which sealed the fate of every victim. Who were these men? That is the most remarkable part of the story—and the most important one for the future of violence and, I believe, of mankind. They were not nonentities or outsiders. Most of them had all the hallmarks of civic and scientific respectability. They were not Nazi puppets, but had made their careers and reputations as psychiatrists long before Hitler came to power. Among them were more than twelve full professors at universities. Most of their names read like a roster of prominent psychiatrists. They have made valuable contributions to scientific psychiatry. They are still quoted in international psychiatric literature, which testifies to their scientific stature. The bibliography of their papers, monographs, and books—not to mention their graduate and postgraduate lectures and their editorial work on leading psychiatric journals—would fill a whole brochure. We must make ourselves familiar with the caliber of these men if we want to comprehend the full meaning of this historical occurrence.

Dr. Max de Crinis was professor of psychiatry at the University of Berlin and director of the psychiatric department of the famous Charité Hospital. He was originally chief physician at the psychiatric clinic at the University of Graz. Those who knew him personally describe him as a "charming Austrian." He has many scientific studies to his credit, on alcoholism, epilepsy, war neuroses, pathology of the central nervous system (brain edema and brain swelling), etc. He was especially interested in the bodily concomitants of mental disorders—for instance, malfunction of the liver. Textbooks, including recent ones, refer to some of his scientific work as authoritative. In 1944, he published an interesting book on the somatic foundations of emotions which is still quoted in the scientific literature today. It is not easy to understand—but is important to know—how such a man could deliberately and personally, from his own department in the university hospital, send a thirteen-year-old boy afflicted with mongolism, with only minor mental impairment, to one of the murder institutions—the children's division of Goerden—to be killed. In 1945, when his car could not get through the Russian encirclement of Berlin, Dr. de

Crinis committed suicide with a government-supplied capsule of cyanide.

One of the most distinguished (and most unexpected) members of the team of experts which was the heart of the whole killing operation was Werner Villinger, who at the time was professor of psychiatry at the University of Breslau. Prior to that he was head of the department of child psychiatry at Tuebingen and then psychiatric director at Bethel, a world-famous institution for epileptics and mentally and physically disabled persons founded in 1867. From 1946 to 1956 he was professor of psychiatry at the University of Marburg. His clinical research on the outbreak of an acute psychosis after the commitment of a violent crime became well known. He wrote especially on the psychological and social difficulties of children and youths, on child guidance, group therapy, juvenile delinquency, and similar subjects. He has been decorated by the West German government. In 1950 he was invited to participate in the White House Conference on Children and Youth and did so.

His name alone, quite apart from his activity in it, gave a great boost to the "euthanasia" project. For his name suggested to others, especially younger psychiatrists, that there could be nothing wrong with the "action." It is difficult to understand how a man with concern for youths could not only consent to but actively participate in projects of killing them, but we may find some slight hints in his previous writings. Two years before Hitler came to power, Villinger advocated the sterilization of patients with hereditary diseases. Writing about the "limits of educability," he stated that "the deepest roots of what we call temperament and character are deep in the inherited constitution." Contrary to our modern point of view, he regarded the chances for the rehabilitation of juvenile delinquents with definite emotional difficulties as very poor.

During the preparation of the "euthanasia" trial in Limburg, Dr. Villinger was questioned by the prosecutor in three sessions. At about the same period, it became publicly known that he was implicated in the "euthanasia" murders in a leading, active role. He went to the mountains near Innsbruck and committed suicide. An attempt was made later to make this appear an accident, but there is no doubt about what happened.

To find Dr. Carl Schneider as a leading member of a wholesale murder project is also unexpected. For twelve years he was professor of psychiatry at the University of Heidelberg. As such he held the same important position as Emil Kraepelin a generation before. And Kraepelin was the founder of modern clinical psychiatry. In a recent textbook, Schneider's scientific work is referred to eleven times. In some of the most recent publications on the course of mental diseases and on the effect of tranquilizers, his clinical subdivisions are taken as a basis. He made clinical investigations of mental disorders in organic brain diseases and in pernicious anemia. He wrote on abnormal personalities in relation to diminished legal responsibility. Since experimental psychoses are currently much investigated, it is of interest that more than thirty years ago he induced an experimental psychosis in himself with mescaline. He described it in his monograph on hallucinations. One of his monographs deals with "The Treatment and Prevention of Mental Disorders." He studied epilepsy and expressed modern views about it, and his research on that subject is still quoted. He wrote two books on schizophrenia. The first, *The Psychology of Schizophrenia,* is considered a landmark of this type of clinical study. Originally more interested in subtle psychological analyses, he stressed more and more the hereditary factor.

Carl Schneider was very active in all phases of the program. He served as expert for the processing of death questionnaires, participated in the frequent conferences, and regularly instructed younger psychiatrists in the methods and procedures of the project. Perhaps the most extraordinary part of this story is that before going to Heidelberg, he, like Werner Villinger, had held the highly respected position of chief physician at the universally recognized institution Bethel. Ten years later, when he was professor at Heidelberg, he appeared with an SS commission at Bethel, went over the questionnaires, ordered the personnel to present patients to him, and personally selected the candidates for extermination. When, after the defeat of the Nazi regime, Dr. Schneider was to be put on trial, he committed suicide.

Another psychiatrist with an international reputation is Professor Paul Nitsche. He was successively director of several state hospitals, including the tradition-rich Sonnenstein in Saxony, which was the first psychiatric state hospital in Germany. In the authoritative *Handbook of Psychiatry* (1925–1932), he wrote the section on "Therapy of Mental Diseases," based on his own vast experience. He was one of the editors of the German *Journal for Mental Hygiene*. He wrote understandingly on modern psychotherapeutic measures in mental hospitals. He was interested in psychoses in prisoners (prison psychoses), and his book on the subject appeared in the best American monograph series on nervous and mental diseases. In the killing project he held a top position. He functioned as a representative of Dr. Brandt, the "leader" of the medical sector (as opposed to the strictly administrative bureau). He did his work of organizing and selecting death candidates so well that during the project he was advanced from expert to chief expert.

Nitsche presents perhaps the most remarkable psychological enigma. Colleagues of his who knew him well and who condemn him for his "euthanasia" work nevertheless say of him that he was "an exceptionally good psychiatrist, especially kind to his patients and concerned about them day and night." So can a false fanatical social orientation play havoc with a man's character. Here we come up against a contradiction which plays a great role in modern violence: the contrast in the same individual between the private, intimate, spontaneous personality and the corporate, public, official personality.

After the Nazi regime ended, Dr. Nitsche was tried in Dresden for the murder of mental patients and was sentenced to death. In 1947 he was executed.

Perhaps the greatest break with the humane traditions of psychiatry is connected with the name of Dr. Werner Heyde. Heyde was professor of psychiatry at the University of Würzburg and director of the psychiatric clinic there. Few places in the world can look back on such a long history of successful care of mental patients. The clinic grew out of a division of a general hospital where mental patients were admitted and kindly treated as early as the last decades of the sixteenth century. It is interesting that exactly contemporary with the extant case histories of this hospital are the descriptions by Cervantes in *Don Quixote* (first chapter of the second part) of the mental institution in Seville (around 1600).

Cervantes' stories of the inmates show that this institution (*casa de los locos*) was humanely administered. In other words, in two geographically widely separated and different localities, Seville and Würzburg, pioneer work was done that long ago in treating the mentally afflicted as human beings and as medical patients. It is certainly a problem for the historian of culture, as it is for the student of violence, that in the same place where mental patients were treated most humanely in 1583, they were doomed to be killed in 1940. In the later nineteenth and in the twentieth century, the Würzburg psychiatric clinic played a prominent role in scientific research. A number of outstanding psychiatrists got their training there. The first intelligence test was devised there in 1888. One of the earliest clinical observations and descriptions of what was later called schizophrenia came from that clinic.

Dr. Heyde's reputation as a scientic psychiatrist was excellent. He worked for several years in the clinic, became director of the out-patient department, and began his teaching there in 1932.

One of Heyde's predecessors as head of the Würzburg clinic, Conrad Rieger, who studied especially the history of psychiatry, wrote, almost prophetically, in his autobiography in 1929 (ten years before the start of the extermination program): "Whether it is deliberate or through negligence, it is wrong to kill human beings and to deprive them of care. On the contrary, we must care for them and protect them, well and humanely. This care and protection is needed in the same measure for the so-called curable and the so-called incurable." We do not know whether Heyde ever read this statement, which he so completely reversed. Heyde was a key figure in the program. When carbon monoxide was suggested as a method for killing, this proposal had to be submitted first to him for evaluation. He approved the method and directed the idea into the proper administrative channels for its practical realization. He was the head of one of the agencies of the project, the Reich Society for Mental Institutions (state hospitals). In his office the data from these institutions were collected and the last word pronounced about the patients to be sent to the special extermination hospitals. He played the leading role in the preparatory and organizing conferences (before Hitler's private note), helped in working out the questionnaires, functioned as chief expert, and selected the younger psychiatrists for the program and instructed them in their task.

From the beginning, he personally inspected the death institutions and the installation of the gas chambers, to make sure that everything functioned expeditiously. In addition, far from being told what to do, he gave lectures before high officials in the Nazi ministries to promote and explain the weeding out of those "not worthy to live." For example, on April 23, 1941, in the Department of Justice, he gave a lecture on "The Euthanasia Program" before high officials, judges, and prosecutors. The most important person present was the president of the highest court, the Reich Court, Judge Erwin Bumke. Bumke had been appointed to his office in 1929, during the democratic Weimar Republic. He raised no objection to the mass killing after this lecture, and the doom—the legal doom—of the mental patients was sealed. Psychiatry and law had met in the spirit of violence.

After the collapse of the Nazi regime, Heyde was arrested, but he escaped from custody. A warrant for his arrest ("Wanted for Murder . . ."), with his picture on it, was sent out. It said that he was probably working as a physician. For twelve years he lived a charmed existence under a different name. He was employed by a state insurance agency, again as chief expert. He did a great deal of work for courts. During this time his wife was receiving a widow's pension, and from money earned in his new career she bought a beautiful house on Lake Starnberg, near Munich. Many private persons—judges, prosecutors, physicians, university professors, and high state officials—knew his real identity. There was a certain solidarity in protecting this secret of violence. When his identity did come out, almost by accident, he surrendered to the authorities. His trial at Limburg was delayed for four years for preliminary investigation. He made another attempt to escape, which failed. When he was left unguarded in his cell five days before the trial was due to start, he committed suicide.

This trial, which would have been the most important "euthanasia" trial, delayed overlong, never took place. One day before Dr. Heyde's suicide, his codefendant, Dr. Friedrich Tillman, who from 1934 to 1945 was director of orphanages in Cologne and who has been called a "bookkeeper of death," jumped or was pushed from a tenth-story window. Another defendant, Dr. Gerhard Bohne, escaped from jail to South America. And the fourth defendant, Dr. Hefelmann, was declared not able to stand trial because of illness. The widely held belief that there was great pressure against this trial's taking place seems to be not without foundation.

Among other outstanding professors of psychiatry who were involved in the program were the following:

Dr. Berthold Kihn was the professor of psychiatry at the famous University of Jena, where Hegel, Fichte, Schiller, and Haeckel taught, where Karl Marx got his doctor's degree and the composer Schumann an honorary doctorate. He contributed chapters to several authoritative textbooks—for example, on neurosyphilis, on peripheral nerves, and on disorders of old age. He did research on the microscopic study of brain tissues. Kihn not only was busy making the death crosses on questionnaires, but also personally supervised the selection of patients for extermination in various institutions. He and Dr. Carl Schneider were among the charter members of one of the main project agencies.

Dr. Friedrich Mauz was professor of psychiatry at Koenigsberg from 1939 to 1945 and has held the same position at the University of Münster since 1953. A good deal of his scientific work became generally acknowledged: his studies on hysteria and epilepsy, with interesting clinical observations; on psychoses in juveniles; on the physical constitution in mental disorders. From him comes the term "schizophrenic catastrophe," for the most severe progressive types of the disease. In 1948 he participated as one of three official delegates from Germany at an international mental hygiene meeting in London. At that congress, the World Federation for Mental Health was founded, its purpose being the "furthering of good human relations."

Dr. Mauz excused himself later, without any condemnation of the "euthanasia" project, by saying that his invitation to a "euthanasia" conference in Berlin was "harmlessly formulated" and that as late as the autumn of 1940 (when tens of thousands of patients from all over Germany had been killed and whole hospitals closed because all the patients had been evacuated to death institutions), he, who held a responsible and administrative position in psychiatry, did not know anything about any "carrying through of the euthanasia program."

This list is far from complete.

In the whole "euthanasia" matter the universities, including the psychiatric and pediatric departments, wrapped themselves in silence. How easy it would have been (and riskless) to refuse, had anyone been so minded, is shown by the case of Gottfried Ewald, professor of psychiatry in Göttingen. He was invited to a conference at the central office in Berlin under the chairmanship of Heyde and was asked to join the program. He refused and left the conference. He remained unmolested and had no disadvantage on account of his complete refusal.

There is an interesting sidelight on his exceptional behavior. Among those whom the experts marked on the questionnaires or report sheets as "unworthy to live," and who were consequently killed, were veterans who had lost an arm or leg in the war. The records are clear about that. For example, among a group of male patients transferred from the state hospital Rottenmuenster to a death institution was one whose "euthanasia" questionnaire said: "Receives war pension. Handicapped for work through loss of an arm." Professor Ewald had lost his left arm in World War I and referred to it occasionally in his lectures. Maybe that made it easier for him to identify with the victims.

A young German psychiatrist of much lower rank, Dr. Theo Lang, made a serious attempt to stem the whole program. He was at that time in Germany and later became chief physician of the institution Herisau in Switzerland. On January 20, 1941, he obtained an interview with Dr. M. H. Goering at the German Institute for Psychological Research and Psychotherapy. His plan was to get Dr. Goering to sign a declaration against the extermination of mental patients. When he tried to tell Dr. Goering the whole story of the program, which at that time had been going on for more than a year, he found that Dr. Goering knew all about it and confirmed its truth. However, he refused to sign the declaration, and so nothing came of this *démarche*.

In taking this step—and for this reason his name should not be forgotten—Dr. Lang showed extraordinary courage. In going to Dr. Goering, he knew that he was approaching the very seats of

Nazi power, both political and psychiatric. Dr. Goering was a cousin of Marshal Hermann Goering, with whom he was in personal contact. And his close collaborator and coeditor on the Nazi-coordinated *Journal for Psychotherapy* for several years was Dr. C. G. Jung. Dr. Jung, in the words of the then State Secretary for Health, Dr. Conti, "represented German psychiatry under the Nazis." So Dr. Lang could not reach any higher with his plea for mercy and decency.

In addition to the professors of psychiatry, the experts included directors of large and well-known state hospitals from different parts of Germany, like Buch, near Berlin, and Eglfing, near Munich. They were also busy making the death crosses on the questionnaires and helping in other ways. These experts were not new appointees of the Nazi regime, but had had long and honorable careers. They were by no means products of Nazism, but were parallel phenomena. Their thinking was similar: the attacking of a social problem by violence. However well disguised by high-sounding terms like "eugenics" and "euthanasia," the problem was essentially economic and sociopolitical, namely, the cost of care for the temporarily "unproductive" and the prosperity and glory of the nation.

It is important to keep in mind that among those in responsible positions and most actively engaged in the killing were psychiatrists of ability. For example, Dr. Valentin Falthauser, director of a state hospital, was sentenced to three years in prison for practices that contributed to the death of three hundred hospital inmates. He was coauthor of an important book *Home Care in Psychiatry and Allied Fields,* which contains ideas which are still of great actuality for current community psychiatry.

The special agency for child "euthanasia," the Reich Commission for the Scientific Registration of Hereditary and Constitutional Severe Disorders, had as its most prominent expert Dr. Werner Catel, who was subsequently professor of pediatrics at the University of Kiel until the sixties. This was a commission of experts, psychiatric and pediatric, that decided—entirely on its own—which children should be killed as being mentally below par or handicapped or physically malformed. Dr. Catel still defends and advocates his type of "euthanasia" today—for instance, in his book *Borderline Situations of Life* (1962). It is a noteworthy fact for the recognition of the violence content of a democratic society that the head of a child-killing organization with thousands of victims should become the professor of pediatrics and head of a pediatric clinic at a renowned university.

The children slated for death were sent to special "children's divisions," first Goerden, then Eichberg, Idstein, Steinhof (near Vienna), and Eglfing. They were killed mostly by increasing doses of Luminal or other drugs either spoon-fed as medicine or mixed with their food. Their dying lasted for days, sometimes for weeks. In actual practice, the indications for killing eventually became wider and wider. Included were children who had "badly modeled ears," who were bed wetters, or who were perfectly healthy but designated as "difficult to educate." The children coming under the authority of the Reich Commission were originally mostly infants. The age was then increased from three years to seventeen years. Later, in 1944 and 1945, the work of the commission also included adults.

A further method of "child euthanasia" was deliberately and literally starving children to death in the "children's divisions." This happened to very many children. In most instances, these deaths were recorded as normal or natural deaths. But many people knew about the fact itself. As early as autumn 1939, a student of psychology, later a public-school teacher, Ludwig Lehner, was permitted with other visitors to go through the state hospital Eglfing-Haar. He went there as part of his studies in psychology. In the children's ward were some twenty-five half-starved children ranging in age from one to five years. The director of the institution, Dr. Pfannmueller, explained the routine. We don't do it, he said, with poisons or injections. "Our method is much simpler and more natural." With these words, the fat and smiling doctor lifted an emaciated, whimpering child from his little bed, holding him up like a dead rabbit. He went on to explain that food is not withdrawn all at once, but the rations are gradually decreased. "With this child," he added, "it will take another two or three days."

Surely this is a scene worse than Dante. But the punishment was anything but Dantesque. In 1948, Dr. Pfannmueller was specifically charged in court with having ordered the killing of at least 120 children and having killed some himself. It was testified that he had personally killed some of the children with injections. He was sentenced to six years in jail, of which he served two years. That makes about six days per killed child.

How great the professional moral confusion can become is evident from this sidelight. Professor Julius Hallervorden, a well-known neuropathologist, after whom a special brain disease is named (Hallervorden-Spatz disease), asked the central office of the program to send him the brains of "euthanasia" victims for his microscopic studies. While the victims were still alive, he gave instructions about how the brains should be removed, preserved, and shipped to him. Altogether he got from the psychiatric death institutions no less than six hundred brains of adults and children. It evidently did not occur to him, or to anybody else, that this of course involved him seriously in the whole proceeding. An American professor of psychiatry at a well-known medical school told a national magazine that there was no ethical problem involved here and that Dr. Hallervorden "merely took advantage of an opportunity."

By the middle of 1941, at least four of the death hospitals in Germany and Austria not only killed patients but became regular murder schools: Grafeneck, in Brandenburg; Hadamar, near Limburg; Sonnenstein, in Saxony; and Hartheim, near Linz. They gave a comprehensive course in lethal institutional psychiatry. Personnel were trained in the methods of assembly-line killing. They were taught the mass-killing techniques, "gassing," cremation, and so on. It was called basic training in "mercy killing." The "material" for all this training was mental hospital patients. On them the methods were tried out and tested before they were applied later to Jewish and other civilian populations of the occupied countries. Technical experience first gained with killing psychiatric patients was utilized later for the destruction of millions. The psychiatric murders came first. It is a revealing detail that a man named Gomerski, who was engaged in mass killing in the death camps of Sobibor and Treblinka, was nicknamed the Doctor because of his "euthanasia" training in the psychiatric hospital Hadamar.

The method of taking out gold fillings and gold teeth from victims was first tried, worked out, and routinely used on the mental-

hospital patients killed. Only after that was it practiced on concentration-camp inmates. The patients had to open their mouths
and a number was stamped on their chests. From this number the
personnel knew which patients had gold teeth, so that they could
be removed later. The first human-derived ingots of gold for the
Reichsbank were made from the gold from the mouths of these
mental patients. According to sworn testimony, several grams of
gold meant several thousand people killed. In Berlin there was a
special office, the Central Accounting Office, to keep track of the
proceeds from killed mental patients. How to take gold teeth from
the dead was taught as a special skill. For example, in the institution Hadamar, a man named Loeding had learned this "breaking of teeth," as it was called. Later he was transferred for this
purpose to the institution Eichberg. All this was done in the name
of euthanasia. Later it was applied to millions of people.

Toward the end of 1941 the gas chambers in the death institutions were dismantled, transported to the east, and there freshly
erected for their new tasks in concentration camps. Meanwhile the
killing of mental patients went on with other methods, with injections, for instance. "Only" a few thousand were now being killed
each month.

Some of the same psychiatrists who selected patients in hospitals went to concentration camps and selected death candidates
there. Himmler had the idea of having the inmates of these camps
examined "to comb out" those to be eliminated. He needed suitable physicians. So the central bureau of the "euthanasia" program
supplied him with "experienced psychiatrists." In practice, this
worked out as follows. In 1941 a commission of five went to the
concentration camp Dachau to select prisoners to be transferred to
Mauthausen to be killed. All five men were psychiatrists, and their
chief was a professor of psychiatry of the University of Berlin. As
they sat at tables put up between two barracks, the inmates had
to file past while the doctors looked at their records. The criteria
for selection were set by two chief experts in psychiatry. They
consisted in (*a*) ability to work and (*b*) political reports. Several
hundred of the so-selected prisoners were sent to Mauthausen and
destroyed there.

The director of the state hospital Eichberg, Dr. Fritz Mennecke, who went to concentration camps as expert to select death candidates, was asked in court about the two types of cases he had judged interchangeably, the mental patients on medical grounds and the camp prisoners on political grounds. "One cannot separate them," he answered. "They were not subdivided and neatly separated from each other."

The typical case of Dr. Adolf Wahlmann, psychiatrist at the state hospital Hadamar, shows how easy the change was for some psychiatrists from killing mental patients to killing foreign civilians. He was not a Nazi and not a sadist. He had had a good medical education in the universities of Giessen, Marburg, Erlangen, and Kiel and had worked for years in responsible psychiatric posts in different institutions. In the Hadamar institution, thousands of mental patients were killed. In 1944 shipments of Polish and Russian men, women, and children from other institutions and work camps in occupied territories were sent to Hadamar. They were killed by lethal injections which he prescribed, exactly as he had done before with mental patients.

There is a persistent myth about the whole "euthanasia" project which serves to ease the conscience of the civilized world. It is entirely false. According to this myth, Hitler stopped the program after about a year (when "only" some 70,000 patients had been killed) because of protests and pressure from the churches and the public. The "euthanasia" killing was *not* stopped. It went on until 1945, to the end of the Hitler regime—and in some places, *e.g.,* Bavaria, even a few days longer. There is no evidence that it was stopped; all the evidence is that it continued. It did not end; it merely changed its outer form. It did not even get less cruel but in many cases was more cruel. The killing was not done as before, in the form of conspicuous big actions, but was carried out in a more cautious form and at a slower pace. From 1941 on, instead of the gas chambers (which had been transferred), other methods were used. Without any formal procedure and without any norm, it was carried out by individual institutions and individual doctors. They selected, decided, and acted. The end effect was the same. The methods employed were deliberate withdrawal of food, poisoning, or in many cases a combination of both. The poisoning was done by injections of overdoses of drugs. Patients screaming from hunger were not unusual. If it got too bad, they were given injections which quieted them, made them apathetic, or killed them. This was called euthanasia too. "Euthanasia" by starvation. Such methods had the advantage of more discretion: patients who were destroyed in this way could be more easily counted as "natural deaths." It was the occupation by the Allied armies both in the north and in the south which freed the remaining patients from the psychiatrists.

Examples of continued general "mercy killings" after their alleged end in the summer of 1941 exist for every year thereafter, until 1945. At the end of 1942, at a conference of state officials and the directors of state hospitals, there was a discussion of the "excellent" method of making the "useless eaters" (*i.e.,* patients) die by "slow starvation." A hospital employee has reported that in 1940 she worked in one of the death-dealing hospitals; then she was transferred to another, where the patients were not killed with gas but with injections and overdoses of drugs; she worked there until 1943; she was sent to a third hospital, where the same procedures were used until the overthrow of the regime in 1945. The chief male nurse of one mental hospital described the progression. In 1940 the program started when mental patients were gassed to death and then burned. In 1941 the gassing was discontinued. Beginning in 1942 the patients were killed with lethal doses of morphine, scopolamine, Veronal, and chloral. In 1944 foreign slave laborers from the camp were also admitted to the hospital and killed in the same way. This account is entirely uncontested testimony and is typical for the whole project. In 1944 patients were still being transported from their hospitals to "special institutions" (to be killed) under the pretext that it was a regular routine transfer from one hospital to another.

With respect to children, the legend of the 1941 ending of "mercy deaths" does not have even a semblance of truth. The child-killing agency functioned openly and efficiently till the collapse of the regime in 1945. Nobody has claimed that it ended before. Under its auspices, the mass murder of children continued routinely all over Germany and Austria. In Vienna, for example— the golden Viennese heart notwithstanding—children were killed in the children's division of the famous institution Steinhof and the municipal children's institution Spiegelgrund until the end of the war. Professor I. A. Caruso, now well known for his book *Existential Psychology,* who as a young psychologist witnessed some of this himself, says of the Reich Commission that its "murderous activity" was "massive." It was also, as one writer put it, unbelievably cruel.

As for the Hitler "order" for the alleged termination of the project, no document existed, not even a private note as at the outset of the "action." What happened was that in the late summer of 1941 in his General Headquarters, in a conversation with his physician, Dr. Karl Brandt, Hitler asked for the "provisional cessation of the euthanasia action on a large scale." This was purely verbal and was not written. It was an organizational change. It was clearly foreshadowed in a previous statement by Gestapo chief Himmler that there were "faults in the practical procedures." (The killing with the gas installations was too conspicuous.) Soon after Hitler's talk with Dr. Brandt, the chief expert, Professor Heyde, made it very plain in a written communication that the change was merely a "technical matter." Indeed, the gas chambers were moved, but the killing in the mental institutions in Germany continued with other methods.

As for the resistance of the churches, the fact that the killing did continue shows that it was not so strong or so persistent as to be effective. It was not enough. Dr. Karl Brandt stated that it was Hitler's opinion (which proved right) that resistance to the "euthanasia" killings on the part of the churches would under the circumstances not play a great role. The efforts were sporadic, isolated, and fragmentary. At certain levels the attitude was for a long time so passive and ambiguous that a top bureaucrat in the mercy killings, Hans Hefelmann, could state truthfully in court in Limburg that it had been his understanding that the church "was willing to tolerate such killings [at the time] under certain conditions."

What clergymen did was sixfold. They first protested about the transfer and eventual killing of patients in institutions under their jurisdiction. They wrote to the government and submitted evidence. They protested against the project from the pulpit. In some, but not all, institutions where religious sisters worked as nurses, the clergy made the further work of the sisters dependent on the assurance that they did not *have* to "participate" in any way in any part of the project. They reported instances to local juridical authorities as punishable crimes. (This was of no effect, because all complaints relating to the "action" were forwarded to Berlin and disregarded.) Finally we know of at least one occasion when a prominent clergyman achieved a long personal interview with one of the officials of the program and pleaded with him. A highly respected pastor, Fritz von Bodelschwingh, the chief of the Bethel institution, invited Dr. Karl Brandt to visit Bethel. Dr. Brandt accepted and the two men conferred for three hours.

It was a memorable event. Dr. Karl Brandt was a complex personality. He knew Dr. Albert Schweitzer well, was impressed with his theory of "reverence for life" and interested in his philanthropic work. As a young doctor he had planned to work with him as an assistant in Lambaréné in Africa. The only reason why that did not come about was that Brandt was born in Alsace and the French would have called him up in Lambaréné for military service. We can speculate that his whole career might have been different—in fact, might have taken just the opposite direction—if social preparation for war and violence had not prevented it. From what Pastor Bodelschwingh related later of their talk, Dr. Brandt tried to explain that the "euthanasia" project was necessary to save the nation. Bodelschwingh's position was that nobody has the right to be inhuman to his fellowmen. It seems that as a result of this discussion the liquidation of the "not worthy to live" inmates of Bethel was at least postponed and it may have helped many to escape this fate.

On March 8, 1941, the Catholic bishop Clemens von Galen of Münster, in Westphalia, spoke from the pulpit against the "euthanasia" action. He said: "These unfortunate patients must die because according to the judgment of some doctor or the expert opinion of some commission they have become 'unworthy to live' and because according to these experts they belong to the category of 'unproductive' citizens. Who, then, from now on could still have confidence in a physician?" This sermon helped to inform the public further but it had no lasting effect. For it was only a one-shot condemnation, not followed up by the bishop, not reinforced by higher dignitaries of the church, and not backed by Rome. (Von

Galen died a Cardinal in 1946.) The forces of destruction and propaganda had become so entrenched that the public could no longer do anything about it anyhow.

Why, then, in 1941 was the program changed in methods, speed, and conspicuousness? From the historical context of events and opinions, it is abundantly clear why Hitler interfered. He was concerned, and rightly so, with military morale. Would the spirit of the troops hold out to see the war through? It was late summer of 1941. Soldiers were learning that at home Germans were killing Germans. They were afraid that the wounded with head injuries would be sent to the gas chambers—and this might well happen to them. So the gas chambers were conspicuously dismantled. Moreover, going home on leave they might find that a grandparent or other aged relative had disappeared. Morale became affected, so it was more or less officially given out that the program was stopped. In reality it continued, but less blatantly than before.

In June, 1945, the American Military Government, through its Public Health and Security officers, investigated the psychiatric institution Eglfing-Haar, on the outskirts of Munich. In this hospital, some 300 children, from six months to sixteen years old, and about 2,000 adult patients had been killed on a thoroughly organized basis. This went on until the American occupation. Some of the adult patients had not been killed in the place itself but had been sent to an institution at Linz for killing and cremation. There were, at the very minimum, thirty such hospitals in Germany with "special departments" for destroying patients.

In Eglfing-Haar, which had had an excellent reputation as a psychiatric hospital, there was a children's division with a capacity of about 150 children called the *Kinderhaus*. This division had a "special department" with twenty-five beds and cribs for the children about to be exterminated. In June, 1945, it was still occupied by twenty children. They were saved by the American Army. In the children's "special department" there was a small room. It was bare except for a small white-tiled table. At the window was a geranium plant which was always carefully watered. Four or five times a month a psychiatrist and a nurse took a child to this little room. A little while later they came out, alone.

The killing of children was carried out by different methods.

One was overdoses of Luminal given either by injection or as a powder sprinkled over food. Another method was injection of a drug called modiscope, a combination of morphine, dionine, and scopolamine. Some children were given iodine injections with the result that they died in convulsions. Among the victims were retarded children who could have been taught and have led well-adjusted lives. Some were emotionally disturbed children who could not play well with other children and were regarded as "antisocial." The brains of the murdered children were sent to a psychiatric research institution for scientific microscopic studies.

The killing of adults was done almost entirely by deliberate starvation. The patients were given only vegetables and water until they died. They never got bread or meat or anything else. In this "special department," until the American Military Government took over, no patient got any treatment whatsoever, mental or physical. If he cut himself, he was not bandaged and was allowed to bleed. The selection of the patients to be put into this "special department" was largely in the hands of the staff psychiatrists and was a matter of routine. One criterion for selection was the length of stay in the institution. The whole procedure was known to all the hospital personnel.

We are still in the postviolence phase of the "euthanasia" murders. That is perhaps one of the darkest spots of the story. For the whole action has been minimized and left in a cloud of obfuscation, concealment, and social forgetfulness. We read about errors where there really was precision, about excesses where there were regular procedures, about dictates where there was all too ready compliance, about "misunderstood humaneness" where there was routine inhumanity. This happens not only in popular literature, but also in the writings of leading professional men.

To some extent, the courts have contributed to the confusion, which in its turn breeds indifference. For what were identical or very similar crimes, the sentences were of the greatest imaginable variety. A very few of those involved were sentenced to death and either executed or given death sentences which were commuted to life imprisonment and then reduced further; many were pardoned; in a number of cases, the courts decided that there was no case and no occasion for a trial; many were acquitted or received relatively short jail sentences; most remained entirely unmolested by the law and continued their professional or academic careers.

In some instances, the courts have made general statements about the project which tend to minimize its wrongfulness. For example, a court in Munich decided that "the extermination of mental patients was not murder, but manslaughter." In this summary form, which has been quoted in newspapers and magazines, the statement might give some people the dangerous idea that killing one person may be murder, but killing many is just manslaughter.

The reasons the courts have given for leniency or acquittal are revealing:

A court in Cologne, in acquitting one of the physicians, spoke of the victims, the patients, as "burned-out human husks." In another court opinion, the patients are called "poor, miserable creatures."

The director of a psychiatric hospital which served as an "intermediate institution" had accepted patients and then sent them on to death institutions with full knowledge of their eventual fate. The court gave as one reason for his acquittal that his role "does not represent an acceleration of the process of destruction, but a delay, and therefore a gain of time [for the patients]."

The director of a state hospital was acquitted on the ground that the many patients in whose death he was instrumental would have perished anyhow.

In a number of cases, the courts acted as if to kill or not to kill was a metaphysical question, like "to be or not to be." They quote the "ethics of Plato and Seneca" or speak of a "tragic conflict of duties" (acquittal in both cases).

Classic is the judgment of a Frankfurt court about a psychiatrist who not only killed many patients—adults and children—personally, but also watched their death agonies through the peep window of the gas chambers. "We deal," said the court, "with a certain human weakness which does not as yet deserve moral condemnation."

In the same way, in the case of a pediatric clinic in Hamburg where many children were deliberately killed ruthlessly, a medical organization proclaimed that the "actions of the inculpated female and male physicians in the years from 1941 to 1943 under the circumstances obtaining at that time did not represent any serious moral transgressions." And a medical journal stated that no professional action was indicated (such as depriving the physicians of their right to practice or to work in hospitals) because after the murders "their work in their profession was beyond reproach."

There has been—and still is—a great reluctance to face the whole "euthanasia" project as what it really was. We are concerned that the truth may damage the image of psychiatry (and pediatrics). But is not the substance more important than the image? A successful effort has been made to hush the whole thing up, in a cloud of silence, distortion, abstract speculations about life and death, irrelevant discussions of the duties of the doctor, and wholly irrelevant misuse of the term "euthanasia." In a recent book by a physician, Professor de Crinis is praised as a "courageous and energetic physician." The book *Euthanasia and Destruction of Life Devoid of Value* (1965), by the present professor of forensic and social psychiatry at the University of Marburg, speaks of the "comparatively few [*sic*] mental patients" killed. (This book is highly recommended in a recent number of an American psychiatric journal.)

In 1950 the then director of the state hospital Bernburg wrote an article in a scientific psychiatric journal in celebration of the seventy-fifth anniversary of that institution's beginning. In Bernburg more than 60,000 people had been murdered, the psychiatric director during that time having been a willing tool of the "euthanasia" project. The anniversary article speaks three times of the "reputation of the institution" as if that were the main point and calls the period of the mass killing an "episode and a step backwards" comparable to the (unavoidable) disruption of the service in the First World War.

This is violence unresolved. The psychiatric profession, to the limited extent that it has spoken at all, claims that the "euthanasia" murders were "ordered" by the Nazis. The record shows that is not true. But even supposing it were true, can we accept the position that if a political party "orders" the psychiatric profession to murder most of its patients, it is justified in doing so?

A recent trial in Munich throws light on several aspects of both the action phase and the postviolence phase of the "euthanasia"

murders. What was established there was entirely typical. Tried
for participation in murder were fourteen nurses of the psychiatric
state hospital Obrawalde-Meseritz in which at least 8,000 mental
patients (including children) were killed. This killing went on
until 1945. The nurses gave lethal doses of drugs to the patients.
The staff psychiatrists, male and female, selected the patients who
were to be killed, prescribed the lethal doses, and ordered the killing. Once, in the beginning, when a nurse refused to give a
deadly dose of Veronal (barbital) to a woman patient, the female
chief psychiatrist gave her a "big bawling out." The defense of
the nurses was that "we had to bow to the orders of the physicians."
Routinely two or three patients were killed every day; in 1945
the number was increased to four a day. On the weekends there was
no killing; it was a matter of "never on Sunday." After the end
of the Nazi regime, most of the fourteen nurses continued in their
regular professional work in hospitals as before. Three were working as nurses in hospitals at the time of the trial. All fourteen were
acquitted. It was a triumph for the Goddess of Violence.

We are not dealing here with just the behavior of individual
practitioners or professors or with just an accident in the practice
of a science. What confront us are crucial problems in the relation
of science and medicine to society and politics, of the value of
human life versus national and social policy. We can learn what
Dr. Richard Madden, a physician and social historian of "fana-
ticisms," wrote a hundred years ago, that behind all the veneer
there is still "a great deal of savagery in the heart's core of
civilization."

CHAPTER TEN

# School for Violence

## MAYHEM IN THE MASS MEDIA

> ... we but teach
> Bloody instructions, which, being taught, return
> To plague the inventor.
> —SHAKESPEARE

To discuss violence without referring to mass media is as impossible as to discuss modern mass media without referring to violence. If somebody had said a generation ago that a school to teach the art and uses of violence would be established, no one would have believed him. He would have been told that those whose mandate is the mental welfare of children, the parents and the professionals, would prevent it. And yet this education for violence is precisely what has happened and is still happening: we teach violence to young people to an extent that has never been known before in history.

This has become possible through two circumstances. One, of course, consists in tremendous technological advances. The other is the fact that the effects of mass media on the young were not sufficiently recognized. It was a new dimension of the environmental influence on the child. That some ingredients might do and have done harm was as little suspected as it was with cigarette smoking until it was studied clinically.

Solution by violence is a great temptation; control of violence is a difficult task. That is why promotion of violence in all its forms and disguises is a threat to progress. For thousands of years mankind has striven to get away from it. All the wise men who have ever written and spoken about it, as Schopenhauer pointed out, have said more or less the same thing. But what happens is that we, at the height of power and prosperity, fill the minds of children with an endless stream of images of violence, often glamorous, always exciting. The youngest children are stimulated and encouraged to a primitive response of "hitting out." That, in the School for Violence, is the elementary lesson. Preschool children learn it. The TV program *The Three Stooges* is an ideal primer. The advanced course is the pursuit of happiness by violence.

That there is an inordinate amount of violence in the mass media is an indisputable fact. No other ingredient plays such a predominant role. If one wanted to list all possible varieties and methods of killing, torturing, or injuring people, no more complete source would be available than the modern mass media. Textbooks of forensic psychiatry and criminology are left far behind.

The modern child is exposed to a variety of mass media: radio, movies, television, comic books, magazines. Even bubble-gum cards (often ugly and violent) may be included. These media have fundamental differences in their manner of technical production and their distribution. They also have socially and aesthetically different values. So for most problems, each would have to be taken up separately. But as far as violence content and its effect are concerned, they may be considered together. At different ages and in varying degrees, many children, or the peer group with which they are in contact, may be exposed to all of them. There is also considerable overlapping, as when more and more movies are shown on television. A nonvisual medium like radio, although by no means violence-free, has least effect. Crime comic books are at the bottom, with very little aesthetic value and great impact on the youngest child. They have demonstrably influenced not only the taste of children but—being so successful in their formulas— also the television producers.

Comic books are the greatest publishing success in history. They were made possible by a special printing process. One edition is about 500,000 copies. (Comic books are to be distinguished from newspaper comic strips, which are very different. The comic-book industry encourages confusion of the two.) Millions of comic books are published every month. At one time, 100,000,000 comic books were published a month (not a year, but a *month*). No other publishing undertaking has ever approached this number. The vast majority of these comic books were not funny and animal comics (which adults assumed they were) but were *crime* comic books; that is to say, they dealt with crime and violence. Their settings may vary, but the substance is the same, whether depicted in the jungle, in the home, on the street, in an urban environment, in a Western setting, on the sea, in outer space, or wherever. Many war comics belong to the same category, with the crime and violence dressed up in patriotic disguise.

The wildest scenes are now not being published any more, although violence still abounds. But the older comic books are still around in large numbers—and in the hands of children—being sold and traded.

Killing is commonplace. In one story (not a whole comic book, but one story in it) there are, for example, thirty-seven killings. Brutality, torture, and sadism are featured. The connection between cruelty and sex is stressed in millions of comic books. Girls are flagellated even in a Western setting. Or in an Oriental setting the mysterious villain threatens the half-nude heroine: "I know that you shall love me and be loyal after you have taken a dozen or so lashes across your beautiful back." Just after she has undressed for bed, the "debutante of the year" is stabbed so that the blood runs across her breast. The killer is a girl who kills two other girls and plans to kill "half a dozen prominent women." Then, she says, "they'll know I mean business."

Killing is carried out usually by what, in analogy with modern military terminology, one might call conventional means: shooting, stabbing, clubbing, strangling, drowning, burning. The techniques of all these methods are very fully described. But unconventional nuclear means are also used. For example, radioactive dust is squirted on the markedly protruding breast of a girl. Special varieties of hurting and killing are often shown. One of these is deliberate injury to the eyes. This is so frequent and has induced so many children to try it out that my associates and I have classified it as the "eye motif."

Shooting policemen to the accompaniment of contemptuous remarks belongs to the comic-book repertory. The police officer asks the driver for his license. "It's a pleasure," says the driver, and shoots him: *Bang!* It seems strange that shooting a policeman is considered an especially serious crime and at the same time an especially suitable entertainment for children. The public was astonished when in recent race riots, youngsters attacked the police. We have been teaching them for years that is the thing to do. It is part of the advanced course.

When those who carry out content analyses of crime comics record conventional methods of murder, the industry and its defenders reply that this is part of life and that children should learn about it. When they refer to particularly outlandish ways of homicide, the reply is that these are just wild fantasies which every child knows cannot be true and real—like the slaying of the dragon in the fairy tale. One such cruel method is to drag a person to death by tying him to an automobile and then driving off. Crime comics call it "erasing faces." Millions of children have read about that. It is a visual object lesson of a particularly cruel and exciting method of killing. When I pointed out that this is described and illustrated in many comic books (and illustrated it in my book *Seduction of the Innocent*), I was told that this was only fantasy and never really occurs. Students of criminology and of pathology know better. Such an idea should not be planted in the minds of young children; but adults should know that it has happened, and how and where it can happen. In the beginning of the Fascist regime in Italy, a workman, the secretary of the metalworkers' union in Turin, was dragged behind a truck in just this way, and his unrecognizable body was left in the street. In Sikeston, Missouri, a young Negro millworker, accused of attempting to attack a white woman, was tied by the feet to an automobile. Then the car sped at seventy miles an hour through the streets of the Negro section of the city and the man was dragged to his death. A pretty Negro girl, Gloria La Verne Floyd aged nine, was lassoed and dragged behind a car by white youths in Jackson, Mississippi. She received multiple injuries. (This case even reached the *Congressional Record* of 1963.)

How carefully the violence is calculated to go to the limits of what parents might stand for is proved by the instructions given to those who write the text and draw the pictures. For instance, a "Note to Writers and Artists" from the editor of one of the biggest comic-book publishers has a list of taboos, *i.e.,* things to be avoided. The memorandum shows clearly that these comics are directed to children (which is frequently denied by apologists for the comics). The editor writes that if the list is followed, the product "will not offend the mothers and fathers of our readers." What are these taboos? Item No. 7: "We must not roast anybody alive." Item No. 12: "We must not chop limbs off characters."

In addition to the depiction of violence, there are auxiliary characteristics which reinforce the lesson. Race prejudice is all-pervasive. The clean-cut, tall, white, Arrow-collar Nordic is contrasted with all others, who are inferior, criminals, or menaces. Negroes are depicted as slaves, savages, or fit subjects to be hanged. Indians, Mexicans, Mediterranean people are downgraded. Oriental people are shown as ugly, brutal, and threatening, even as subhuman. This is a veritable hate literature. Even before children can think for themselves, they are taught to hate. It is an automatic hate. Those interested in civil rights have neglected this long racist indoctrination of children.

In addition, the tools of violence in play and real action have been displayed for many years in a profusian of alluring advertisements. Until recently there were advertisements for real guns. That is the postgraduate course.

When *Seduction of the Innocent* appeared in the middle fifties, it started a grass-roots social reaction. For the first time, a series of reproductions of typical illustrations from crime comic books were called to the attention of parents, behavioral scientists, and other adults unassociated with the trade. Some of the stories crime comics contained were also recounted. Many people learned for the first time what was in these "funny" books. Scientific clinical evidence was also given of the effects of crime-comic reading. A change occurred. Murder in comic books decreased, and so did the number of crime-comic-book publishers. Within a few years after the publication of *Seduction of the Innocent,* twenty-four out of twenty-nine crime-comic-book publishers went out of business. But it was only a partial victory. The damage that had been done is still with us. We now meet some of the child comic-book readers as parents of the "battered child" or in similar roles. Moreover, very many of the old comic books are still around at reduced prices. It is true that straight crime *titles* (not stories) have decreased and are not displayed on the cover any more. (One is tempted to say they have gone undercover.) And murder stories in realistic urban settings have become less frequent. Now the setting is more apt to be science fictional, with superman and superwoman types and interplanetary, outer-space, superhuman creatures. The motives are the same: revenge, money, lust for power, destruction. Westerns have changed least and are as brutal as ever. Girls' necklines have been raised, but sadistic women in tight-fitting garments abound, as hateful and destructive as ever. Crime and violence still reign supreme, though often in disguise.

Comic books are regarded by many as "trivia," not worth mentioning or studying. The investors' journals think differently. They point out the huge profits in the business, counted in millions. According to Richard Lemon, writing in the *Saturday Evening Post* in December, 1964, the comic-book industry takes in about $100,000,000 a year. Now that the public has again become less aware, comic books have been having an upswing, with both violence and profits rising. Crime may not pay, but violence sells.

The complacency of parents has made this possible. They have been lulled into the belief that everything is now all right. Perhaps this is the most important aspect of the comic-book question. For if we follow the extent of this complacency, we find that underestimation of the atmosphere of violence penetrates the most unexpected social institutions. The National Congress of Parents and Teachers has officially praised the "high standards of comic books." This was at about the same time that an experienced magazine editor, Jerome Ellison, wrote that on examining comic books in a country general store, he found "a grisly display of blood-letting, mass killing . . . rampant sadism, and all piously labelled 'Approved by the Comics Code Authority.' " And the president of the Comics Magazine Association of America, which administers this code, was invited to address the White House Conference on Children and Youth! Of course, this was invaluable publicity for the crime comic books. Where can the imaginative, susceptible child count on uncompromising and unqualified protection?

Television should really not be mentioned in the same breath as comic books. Comic books are cheap, shoddy, anonymous. Children spend their good money for bad paper, bad English, and, more often than not, bad drawings. Comic-book readers are apt to rely on the pictures for the meaning of what they see, and a habitual comic-book reader is often a nonreader of noncomic books. Comic books have a generally antieducational influence. This makes children so conditioned even more defenseless against the temptation of television violence. We teach computers to think, nowadays, and children *not* to think. Many children have a real imagination for science. Comic books deflect that gift into the lowest forms of science fiction. Yet this is not generally realized or acknowledged. For example, a chairman of the New York State Youth Commission stated at an awards luncheon: "If there is to be a cultural renaissance to keep in step with that of science, it might well be based on the comic books." This was said in the year in which the Russians launched the first Sputnik.

Television represents one of the greatest technological advances and is an entirely new, potent method of communication. Unfortunately, as it is presently used, it does have something in common with crime comic books: the devotion to violence. In the School for Violence, television represents the classical course. Many of the movies being shown increasingly on the TV screen also have a lot of violence in them and so merge with the over-all picture.

We must make clear to ourselves what mass audience means in terms of television. Suppose a murder is shown on the stage in a theater in a large metropolitan city and is shown on the TV screen. In order to reach an audience as big as television provides in one single evening, the play would have to run in the theater to full houses for half a century. (This is one answer to people who excuse violence on television by saying that good drama may have violence too.) The quantity of violence on the screen is staggering. In one week, mostly in children's viewing time, one station showed 334 completed or attempted killings. Promotion spots showed over and over again eight murders within sixty-second periods (sometimes it was only thirty seconds and four murders). The future historians of our civilization cannot afford to ignore such items. The different channels in one large city showed in one week 7,887 acts of violence and 1,087 threats of violence (such as "I'll

break your legs!"). Not counting war pictures, there were in one
week 895 completed or attempted homicides. One single episode
of a well-known Western series whose title, at least, is based on
a famous novel by Owen Wister, showed to millions of children
on Christmas night twenty-one violent acts. Thirteen of them were
killings, five were fights, and three were assaults. When this novel
came out originally, President Theodore Roosevelt objected to a
violent scene in it. This series is incomparably more violent, but
nobody seems to object at all, which is surely a sign of the times.
Programs featuring violence constitute more than half of prime
viewing time in the evening on two major networks. An average
American youth may, between the ages of five and fourteen, see
on the screen the violent destruction of more than 12,000 people.
In half an hour on the screen a child may witness more violence
than the average adult now experiences in a lifetime. According to
the official British *Report of the Committee on Broadcasting
(Pilkington Report),* scenes of physical violence are an almost in-
variable ingredient of all American importations (other than comedy and musical shows).

Apart from the numbers, it is equally necessary to look at this
in the round and consider how the violence is committed. The
portrayal is always vivid. All varieties of injury or killing occur:
the deliberately cruel, the gruesome, the mad, the fanatic, the
sneaky, the passionate, the sadistic, the clearly sexual, and so on.
Most prevalent is the casual, matter-of-fact, kill-as-you-go violence.
It is all made very simple for the young (and the not-so-young)
minds. The man is in the way, he disagrees with you, he is of the
opposite faction, you want his property, he has wronged you—so
of course you kill him. What alternatives are there? A new program is announced with this slogan: "Sometimes Killing Is the
Only Answer."

In a very good grass-roots survey by the Philadelphia Home and
School Association, about 1,000 parents were asked about their
six months' observation of the screen. Their reaction to TV was
favorable except for the rising trend of violence. One parent stated:
"Killing is becoming a commonplace, everyday occurrence. The
youngsters seem completely insensitive to murder." Another de-
cribed the trend like this: "The killings used to take place off

camera. That was bad enough. But now we see the whole gory process."

Violence on the screen is depicted as a method of life. Few arguments or conflicts on TV are settled without a fight. Never, literally never, is it taught in this School for Violence that violence in itself is something reprehensible. There is no such course. Most Westerns live entirely on violence. The patriotic, historic, or geographic disguise makes it appear that murder in this setting is different. But homicide on horseback is the same as homicide on foot, in a car, or in a spaceship. The alleged historical authenticity of some Westerns is merely a smoke screen. The stories are not of violence for history's sake, but of history for violence's sake.

Wherever possible, vivid violence is introduced. Shakespeare only suggests the terror that follows Macbeth's ascent to the throne. In the screen version, you see men hanged from trees. In the show about the historical Jesse James, you see him as he begins to shoot down twenty-six young, unarmed prisoners. Even the friendly *Lassie* series offers violence in considerable doses. Ever-new motives for violence are dug up: a beautiful young girl in one of the usually good series has the desire to see men killed over her and satisfies that desire until she is finally killed herself. In one of the medical series, the psychiatrist as "therapy" punches a man in the jaw.

Nobody can understand the violence in the world of today if he does not know what we put and permit on the airwaves. We are hypocritically surprised when young people in slums fight the police. On the screen, as in the preparatory course in comic books, the sport of killing policemen flourishes. Television too has the scene (shown Saturday afternoon at six-thirty, for example) of the policeman asking for a license and being promptly shot and killed. A policeman is shot twice in the back, and you are shown his blood in a close-up. Police brutality is also graphically displayed. While two of his men hold a prisoner, Elliot Ness, the hero-detective of the series *The Untouchables,* hits him in the face.

Children appear on the screen as instigators of violence as well as killers and victims of killers. The little boy reproaches the old sheriff for not shooting an outlaw: "Isn't there anything you can do," he asks, "even if you aren't young?" So the ex-sheriff thus exhorted does shoot the man. A little girl is shown being lured and killed by a "monster" in human form. Race and national prejudice is common and is even used as a prop for plots. In a historical film often shown, the particular cruelty of a man is explained at the end by the fact that he had "Indian blood" in him—a lesson not in history, but in prejudice.

Sometimes the brutality is extreme. People are kicked in the face; a man is beaten and thrown alive into a garbage can to die; a man is suspended by his feet with his head over a fire until he dies; another man is suspended by his hands with his feet over a fire ("I'll kill you *my* way, slow-like," says his tormentor); in one episode of a well-known series, a lawyer's tongue is cut out, then the knife is brandished in a pretty girl's face, with the threat that the same thing will happen to her and nobody will kiss her any more. This is followed by a singing commercial about a brand of milk: "Today's Brand Milk Pours Like Cream." Whatever qualities the milk may have, it was certainly not the milk of human kindness.

Scenes of what may be called sneering sadism are typical, in which the torturer or murderer expresses cynical contempt for his victim while hurting him. Children have learned to love that. For example, while one man lies on the ground with an arrow in his chest, a second man says, "Don't worry, it won't hurt much longer," and pushes the arrow deeper into his chest and kills him. I have heard children call such remarks "cute." The School has evidently not taught them that violence is *never* cute.

The "eye motif" is also prevalent on the screen. During a fight, a man throws mud in another man's face, aiming for his eyes; a lighted match is thrown into a man's eyes and face; a man is blinded by acid thrown in his face; molten lead is thrown into a man's eyes; in an outer-space program, a girl squirts a chemical straight into a man's eyes and face—he screams out in pain and falls down; "Do exactly what I tell you," the strong-arm man says to the man he is beating. "The chances are you won't lose more than one eye"; and so on *ad nauseam*. One device consists in using a bullwhip to injure an eye. In one show a prisoner's eye is put out with such a whip; in another an observer comments on a man wielding such a whip, "He can pick a man's eye out with that whip as easy as picking a grape!"

While injury to the eyes is blatantly represented, injury to genitals is only suggested—but it is not forgotten. A man heats the rowel of a spur over a flame and runs it over the middle of another man's body from the neck down, to the accompaniment of shrieks and groans from the tortured victim. The man with the spur says, "They say no one ever got further than the belly before he got results."

Monster shows, sometimes in a pseudoscientific setting of outer space, are frequent screen fare. The monsters serve as a convenient disguise for violence. They have been given a moral carte blanche to get away with all sorts of black deeds that ordinary humans might not so easily be permitted. The monster programs combine the cult of violence with the cult of ugliness which we foist on children. Some of these "horror shows" might be better named "cruelty shows." In them, contempt for human life goes hand in hand with contempt for beauty. The moral confusion that is presented to youths is shown by the behavior of censors and producers. A scene where an animal approached another animal with mating intent was cut out by the censors, while scenes where a human being was tortured and killed by another human being were given a clean bill of health. And a producer of horror films said with pride over the radio, "Our pictures are absolutely clean. The monster might abduct the young bride, but only to kill her." "Only" is the significant word here.

A good example of the mass media's presentation of violence to the young is the screen history of Jack the Ripper. It is a sign of the times that from all the crimes in the world these most sadistic ones were selected. Five young women are stabbed and killed in the film. There are close-ups of the knife blade and the faces of the victims. When this sex-murder film was shown in some movie houses, the younger set was regaled in addition with a cartoon show. The program was announced over the radio and in newspapers like this:

COME ALL KIDDIES!! CARTOON SHOW FOLLOWED BY JACK THE RIPPER

Recently, *Jack the Ripper* was shown on television eight times in one week, at times particularly available to children and young people. On Saturday it was shown at noon, immediately after a program specifically addressed to children. On Sunday it was shown twice in the time between 11:30 A.M and 3:30 P.M. The different showings were followed by a promotion spot showing the killing of four police officers. This is the intensive course.

What are the effects of all this mass-media mayhem? The harmful effects are still doubted or denied by some. Among writers on the subject, we must distinguish two psychological types of experts. The fundamental driving power of some of them is centered in the living human being, the child. The basic interest of others, consciously or unconsciously, is influenced by a leaning toward the mass-media industry. We may call the first group of writers child-directed (CD) and the second group industry-directed (ID). The influence of the ID's is far-reaching. Among the officially approved books in the special library in the White House in Washington is the book *The Effects of Mass Communication,* written by an ID expert. Supposing the President of the United States or one of his aides wishes to inform himself on this subject and consults this book. What information does it give him? The author reaches the conclusion that "nothing is known about the relationship, if any, between the incidence of violence in media programs and the likelihood that it will produce effects." And he amplifies this: "Absolutely nothing is known regarding the relative potential of varying amounts of stimuli." This book, published as a volume in a series on Communication Research, was sent out free to professional people as promotional material by a leading television network (which also financed the study). We can only hope that the information which the President of the United States receives about atomic violence is a little better chosen, more scientific, and less biased than that about children.

The economic specific gravity of the mass-media industries in our society is so great that investigators and writers are influenced, whether they realize it or not, to veer toward apologetic views. As a result, much research—or, rather, pseudoresearch—by ID experts has misled the public. Even UNESCO has fallen into this trap. In its pamphlet on the "Effects of Television on Children and Adolescents," we find all the old cliché-alibis minimizing the harm done by mass-media violence. The pamphlet claims to present an inclusive survey of research results but departs from scientific custom by completely omitting contrary findings in American and European scientific journals. The editor, in a previous, similarly evasive book, *Television in the Lives of Our Children,* had asked the reader to eradicate from his thinking the "stereotype of the Big Media and the little Me." But this is far from being a wrong stereotype; the contrast between the immensely powerful mass media and the individual family *and child* is one of the most essential facts of our social existence. Many films and TV recordings are exported to underdeveloped nations, their violence content being especially harmful for children with less educational and recreational opportunities. This is, so to say, the correspondence course of the School for Violence.

The influence of television is much more potent than that of comic books. But in any contemporary study of the effects of mass-media violence and brutality, comic books must be included. It is a kind of snobbishness, an indication of estrangement from the masses, that in studies of mass-communication effects, comic books are so often left out. Evidently a large part of the solid intelligentsia does not know how poor people live. Many youthful members of the TV audience have been conditioned by comic books. Even if they have not read or looked at them themselves, many of them have been influenced by others who have. Whatever is shown on television is shown in the context of an approved medium, an acknowledged great modern means of communication. The relationship of TV to comic books is like that of flowers to weeds. For research purposes, comic books have the great advantage that we can speak to the same child one or two years later with the same comic books available that came up in the original interviews. With television and movies this is not possible.

Three methods have been used to study mass-media effects: the questionnaire method, the experimental method, and the clinical method,. The first two, the questionnaire and the experimental methods, give only partial and often highly misleading results. They disregard the clinical examination of actual cases, thus leaving out what is truly human in the child. From their results, the real, concrete child as he exists in our society does not emerge.

Within narrow limits, both the experimental and the questionnaire methods can provide useful hints, but they cannot provide the backbone of valid conclusions in this field. The third method, the clinical one, is the only one that can give valid, lifelike results.

In the questionnaire method, children are given a list of questions to answer. Their answers are then compared with those of a control group and statistically evaluated. This method *sounds* objective and is, in fact, regarded by many as an objective, sociological approach. In reality, however, it is very subjective, rigid, and based on arbitrary presuppositions. The questionnaire-answer method is sometimes disguised by such euphemistic terms as "semistructured interview." Even if they mean to, children cannot tell you whether or how much they have been influenced. These children are not examined. It is assumed that what is not in the questions is irrelevant. Subjecting a child to such a set of formal questions is very different from—in fact, almost the opposite of—a clinical examination. The whole child is not considered, his spontaneity is not taken into account, his concrete life situation is neglected. No statistical refinement can overcome the errors and ambiguities contained in the original data. Strictly comparable control groups do not exist in this intricate field because there are too many variable factors. The statistical–control-group method of the physical sciences has been inappropriately applied to emotional and mental phenomena. Nobody has proved statistically with control groups, for instance, what the effects are of coveting your neighbor's wife.

In the experimental method, a film with violent scenes is exposed and the reactions of the subjects are tested by various devices and recorded. At best, the results of this technique for measuring "aggressive" attitudes are fragmentary and superficial. These artificially set up experiments are similar to animal experiments, but they are not adequate because children are not rats. Moreover, the immediate effects after seeing a show are relatively unimportant compared with the significant long-range consequences. We neglect the difference between animals and men if we underestimate the fact that children have imagination. The experimental situation is unlifelike and does not mirror or reproduce real life.

The many human potentialities cannot be reduced to simple experimental terms. The human part gets lost. What we want to study is the meeting of two settings: the world of make-believe of the mass media and the world of the child's real environment. That is not a mechanical encounter. Between the images of television and the effects on a child in the audience is the profound personal reaction of that particular child.

The only method that permits us to arrive at carefully developed, valid results is the clinical method, which permits us to study the whole child and not just one facet. Nothing can replace concrete clinical analyses of actual significant cases. Clinical study means thorough examination and observation, follow-up studies over a considerable period, analysis of early conditioning, study of physique and of social situation. Playroom observation is helpful with young children, group sessions with adolescents and teenagers. Psychological tests are an important adjunct; *e.g.,* the mosaic test, which shows ego organization, or the Duess test, which in young children is valuable for analysis of the family and social relationships. The clinical approach is not content with a cross section through a subject's life at a given moment. It aims at a longitudinal view of his life, at an understanding of psychological processes. You cannot question or interview a child as if he were a job applicant. You must gain his confidence and show him that you are really interested.

Most important is an open-mindedness for the finding of any harmful factors, however inconspicuous. Wrong psychological presuppositions prevent us from seeing things in their proper perspective. False theories lead not only to wrong conclusions but to wrong observations. For example, in publications from the Gesell Institute at Yale University are these statements: "Many perfectly normal children at some ages of childhood, particularly around 7–8 years of age, experience a spontaneous and apparently uninduced love for blood, murder and torture." And: "Normal school-age children often have an addiction to violence which . . . surpasses anything they will see in print." And again, in another place: "Relish for death and destruction appears to be just plain natural for many children." In considering theories like this, we go far beyond the narrow problem of mass-media effects. We face a widespread attitude which regards such curses of mankind as violence and torture as natural.

By clinical analysis, we can disentangle the various elements that enter into a person's thinking and behavior. We can trace the connections between different events, thoughts, and actions and follow the subtle conditioning that molds minds. While adults are by no means immune, it is the immature minds of children and adolescents that are most vulnerable to all kinds of untoward influences. This is most clearly known from brain pathology. The disease epidemic encephalitis attacks both adults and children, but it is mostly in children that it causes definite psychological symptoms.

It was with the clinical method that I discovered and demonstrated for the first time that the excessive radiation of children's minds with violent images by the mass media is a definite harmful influence. It meant taking seriously what seemed to be a triviality. But it was a new dimension in medical psychology, just as the equally trivial-seeming cigarettes as a factor in malignancy and special drugs as a factor in malformations were a new dimension in physical pathology.

The profusion of mass-media violence has potentially an adverse effect on children's lives. It is lamentable that one first has to prove that. My conclusions are based specifically on the clinical study of three hundred cases in large mental-hygiene clinics and in private practice. The cases include both poorer and well-to-do youths. Many of them were not patients, but relatives (sons, daughters, brothers, sisters) of patients. The younger the child, the more he is exposed; but no age group is invulnerable. Children with emotional, intellectual, or social handicaps are more apt to be affected in certain directions. But there is no clinical evidence that the healthy, well-adjusted, and lovingly brought-up child is immune. On the contrary, according to the principle *corrupto optimi pessima*—the corruption of the best is the worst—the influence on the character development of some of these children and adolescents is especially deplorable. Overlooking the mass-media factor is as unscientific as overstressing it. For example, through the neglect of mass-media influences, many false diagnoses of childhood schizophrenia have been made, especially in underprivileged and culturally deprived children. Mass-media violence does not produce psychological effects simply or mechanically. Like other environmental factors, it impinges on a living human being in whom pliable and controlling forces contend. Many a child well adjusted to the social values inculcated by comic books and television has been called *mal*adjusted.

Children have absorbed and are absorbing from the mass media the idealization of violence. Not the association of violence with hate and hostility, but the association of violence with that which is good and just—that is the most harmful ingredient. We present to children a model figure to emulate and a model method to follow. The model figure is the victorious man of violence. The model method is the employment of violent means. The hero's reasoning is usually only a gimmick; his violent action is very real. The child who sits down to view one of the ubiquitous Westerns or similar stories can be sure of two things: there will be foul play somewhere, and it will be solved by violence. The ideal is not the pursuit of happiness, but the happiness of pursuit. That is their introduction to life. It is an entirely false and dangerous conception. This stock of images fastens itself on the subconscious of children's minds and is used by them almost automatically to interpret situations in real life. No wonder so many come to stumble over it later in one form or another! They have learned to think in terms of violence. That is not easy to undo with reeducation or psychotherapy.

The idealization works in two areas: the glamour of the violent act and the glorification of the man of ready violence. Hero worship, which is a natural phenomenon, becomes violence worship. Typical is the reply of a twelve-year-old boy who was asked what he liked best in the adventure and Western stories. His reply: "The shooting and the beating. The heroes!" That is the lesson, and it has been learned. Identification with a heroic figure is one of the great means of education, but when the hero is one who overcomes all obstacles through sheer brute strength, it becomes miseducation.

The influence of mass-media violence varies with different age groups, personality types, and social circumstances. But the most important underlying effect, distilled from my examinations and observations, can be summed up concisely: the blunting of sensitivity. Many young people have become hardened. That is a clinical fact. We are bringing up, and have brought up, a generation not of ugly Americans but of *hard* Americans. If we want that—and it may be that there are some who do—we are doing an excellent job. As Dostoevski wrote: "The best man in the world can become insensitive from habit." Our children have been conditioned to an acceptance of violence as no civilized nation has ever been before. How? That is very simple. You crowd the minds of the young with violent images—continuously, relentlessly, in every context and costume. It begins in the nursery when we arm children physically and disarm them morally. We teach them that violence is fun. We have silently passed an amendment to the Sixth Commandment: "Thou shalt not kill, but it is perfectly all right for you to enjoy watching other people do it."

The desensitization manifests itself on different levels. Children have an inborn capacity for sympathy. But that sympathy has to be cultivated. This is one of the most delicate points in the educational process. And it is this point that the mass media trample on. Even before the natural feelings of compassion have a chance to develop, the fascination of overpowering and hurting others is displayed in endless profusion. Before the soil is prepared for sympathy, the seeds of sadism are planted. The clinical result is that feeling for the suffering of others is interfered with. These youngsters show a coarsening of responses and an unfeeling attitude. Their indifference to acts of brutality on the screen and in life is not a simple, elementary quality consisting merely in an absence of emotion. I have studied children who were profoundly blasé about death and human suffering, yet showed spontaneously the most generous and altruistic impulses. While some adults winced, seven-year-old children watched the murder of Lee Harvey Oswald by Jack Ruby with unruffled equanimity. They had seen quick, remorseless killings so often! Hurting other people is the natural thing. They had learned in the School for Violence that the victim is not an individual but a "bad guy," a criminal, an outcast, an enemy, a radically inferior person. He is not a person but a target. The comic-book-brought-up and teledirected children do not feel with Walt Whitman any more that

> I do not ask the wounded person how he feels,
> I myself become the wounded person.

They have been conditioned to identify not with the victim but with the one who lands the blow.

In older children, teenagers, and young adults, the blunting of sensitivity can lead to a false image of human relationships. They develop what may be called an I-don't-want-to-be-involved attitude, a social indifference. Instead of the principle of "creative cooperation" that H. G. Wells used to talk about, they think in terms of destructive competition, of winning and losing instead of right and wrong. They are guided by the power instinct and by the feeling that cruelty is all right if it is successful. Once they have become so unfeeling by habit, these young people miss a lot of the minor excitements that come from ordinary human relationships. This emotional emptiness may drive them to extravagant acts, especially to violent ones. All this is of course not caused or furthered by mass media alone. However, the fact that there are so many other influences working in a similar vein does not make the mass-media factor less potent but more so. Whatever the seeds of sadism may be, we certainly fertilize the ground for them to grow in.

I know of few methods for hurting, torturing, or killing people that have not been displayed to young people in the mass media. For many years, men have been trying to abolish physical torture as a legal method for obtaining confessions. Montaigne's writing and the French Revolution were milestones in this endeavor. Now young people have been conditioned by the mass media to believe that beating and torturing are legitimate to make people tell the whereabouts of the opponent or to reveal where the loot is. They consider it a sophisticated and manly method for getting at the truth. This psychological effect is a combination of the idealization of violence and the blunting of sensitivity. In one study, 78 percent of schoolchildren felt that it is "O.K. for the Lone Ranger and Hopalong Cassidy to beat up outlaws to make them confess."

These are our future citizens, our law-enforcement officers, voters, and soldiers.

In addition to the methods, almost all the motives—especially the baser ones—that may lead to violence are represented in the mass media. Every form of hate is espoused as a vehicle for a plot and as an excuse for introducing brutality. A typical example is revenge. For a long time, mankind has striven to do away with individual revenge. In the phrase of Francis Bacon, in his essay "Of Revenge," we have tried "to weed it out" by law. In the mass media it is a stock motive. Many young people have learned to take hate and revenge for granted. They have absorbed the idea that individual revenge is natural, necessary, and heroic. An elaborate TV show in a well-known series has the title "The Sweet Taste of Vengeance." This describes well the spirit of innumerable comic-book and television stories.

In a number of instances recently, victims have been robbed, beaten, stabbed, raped, or killed while bystanders and witnesses watched without attempting to help or to call the police. The first such case widely publicized was that of a young woman in New York, Catherine Genovese, who was stabbed to death literally under the eyes of some thirty-eight witnesses over a period of about half an hour's time. A lot has been written about such cases, and many reasons have been adduced for this callous behavior. One important factor has not been pointed out. These noninterventionists had seen in the mass media so many vivid portrayals of revenge that their behavior was affected by it: if a man is discharged from jail, of course he forthwith devotes all his energy to killing or injuring a judge, a witness, or anybody else whom he holds responsible for his arrest. If you help the law, the lawbreaker will get you. So don't get involved. That is the lesson. We should not be so surprised at the predictable behavior of the graduates.

Superman plays a special role, just as the superman concept did for the youth of pre-Nazi Germany. He is Jack London's "overman," in contrast to the "herd" of the great mass of the people. The Superman idea is unhealthy both psychologically and socially. In the minds of immature adolescents, he does not, as his promoters claim, represent a do-gooder who can fly through the air, but has very different connotations.

Superman has a double impact, appearing both in crime comic books and on television. He is in millions of copies of seven different comic books. On TV he is in 104 episodes which are rerun regularly. The series began a decade ago. For 1966 we are promised a new Superman in full color. The profits of Superman enterprises are good for adults, especially since the price of the comic books was raised from ten cents to twelve. There are 2,500 shareholders.

The mass-media Superman is the symbol of power, force, and violence. The rationalization is that he imposes punishment. Children have gotten the idea that there are three classes of people. First, Superman and the other Superman figures, like Batman. They are at the top and determine the course of events. Second, the ordinary people, who are merely bystanders and onlookers. That is us. And third, an endless chain of villains, scoundrels, inferiors, enemies, spies, criminals, traitors, dissenters, opponents, bad guys, subversives. Superman continually needs new persons of this sort so that he can assert himself in action. Superman, like Oswald, can choose all by himself who the proper adversary is. He is above all democratic law. In the child's mind, the image of a hostile world is created. "I pay more attention now," a healthy twelve-year-old boy described it. "I keep myself always ready. Everywhere I go I think of enemies."

Superman is also above the laws of physics. For a former generation, Captain Nemo of Jules Verne's *Twenty Thousand Leagues Under the Sea,* which predicted the submarine, represented the invincible spirit of science which overcomes all obstacles. He is replaced now by Superman, who represents superstition and has caused children to "fly" from high places to injury and death.

Superman is the embodiment of racial superiority, race pride, race prejudice. He explicitly belongs to a "super race." No dark-skinned or dark-complexioned or not-so-tall-or-so-full-chested youngster, whoever he is or whatever he achieves, can measure up to the white Superman. To the people of the East and of Africa, whose feelings we ignore, the Superman whom we teach to our children has become the symbol of the arrogance of the West.

President Eisenhower once told a news conference that in the United States "we are raised in the tradition of no supermen." It is true we have tried to banish supermen from politics, but we let them rule supreme in childhood entertainment. Nietzsche expected the superman from the future; Hitler installed him in the present; Freud projected him to the earliest beginnings of human history. The mass-media industry has put him in the nursery. We teach the young that they must delegate their individual responsibilities to a superior strong being who will take care of law and order because the community is incapable or unwilling to do it. It is a fertile soil for the juvenile violence we see around us. Among delinquency- and trouble-prone youngsters, an inordinate number of Superman devotees is to be found. It is not necessarily a direct, conscious imitation, but is rather a half-conscious underlying attitude. The public-service pages in the Superman comic books teaching civic virtues do not affect children; they merely misguide parents.

The mass media mediate lessons and impulses. Most of the impulses remain latent and do not lead to overt actions. What are induced are dispositions and tendencies. Sometimes clinical study permits us to predict the danger of future violent acts. But so many combinations of psychological and social factors may enter into violent acts, both in juveniles and in adults, that often we cannot

> look into the seeds of time
> and say which grain will grow and which will not.

Midway between dispositions and fantasies on the one hand and real violent acts on the other is children's play. When children play sex, we are alarmed; when they play killing, we are not. In fact, we provide them with the weapons. If a visitor from Mars were to inspect our crime comic books and crime and Western television shows he would conclude that on earth intercourse is forbidden and killing is taught. In the last decade and a half, children's play has become more violent. From the nature of the play it is demonstrable that this is partly due to the influence of the mass media. What used to be playful fighting now is apt to be hitting and choking for real. Boys used to play "fresh" with girls in a bantering manner. Now not infrequently they play roughly, "tie them up," and really hurt them. Many children act out TV and comic-book stories in playroom observation and therapy. For example, a nine-year-old boy played the criminal and "gunned down" the other children, calling some of them enemies, others policemen. Finally he said, "Now, here comes the good guy, like on television—they always have one. He kills the criminal. This is the end of the story."

The effect on mental attitudes is the most important, even if a less dramatic, consequence of mass-media violence on individual and social health. In addition, the saturation with violent stories is a contributing causal factor to some overt violent acts. Two sets of facts are indisputable. First, in real life, more violent acts are committed by younger people, an increase not explained by the growth of population. Second, there is an inordinate amount of violence and cruelty in the mass media to which many millions of young people are exposed. To assume that these two sets of facts have nothing to do with each other and that they are purely coincidental is both frivolous and unscientific. The connection is never mechanical. We have to decide in the individual case by clinical judgment whether and to what extent the mass-media factor plays a role. Sometimes it is the whole atmosphere of violence exuded by the media which conditions immature minds to react with violence. In a department store a little boy approached Santa Claus and gave him a vicious kick in the shins saying, "Here, that's for last year!" That particular scene wasn't one the boy had seen on the screen, but he had seen enough beating and kicking of every variety. Other boys in my case material push little kids out of a swing, which they also have not seen in mass media; it is their translation of more mature forms of brutality which they *have* seen there.

The idea of violence may attach itself to feelings of kindness. A gentle boy of twelve was devoted to his dog and took very good care of him. One day the dog was inadvertently run over. The boy walked up to the driver and said very seriously, "If that dog dies, I'll kill you." Like many other children, he had seen so much supposedly justified killing on the screen that a threat like this occurred to him naturally, like a reflex.

Even children who are naturally sensitive and fundamentally nonhostile may become indurated to callousness by the overexposure to what Morris Ernst has called the "gospel of violence." They have become used to images of injury and violent death. They have learned from the media that to take pity on somebody is a sign of weakness. The stereotyped world of brutal force has become their frame of reference. That has limited their horizon and given them a distorted perspective. On the one hand, mass media have a specific appeal to the conscious thinking of people. On the other, they provide a climate, a social opinion, a norm. They have already established a tradition of violence.

Violent acts, both mild and serious, may be the result of very different psychological processes. In an equally great variety of ways, the mass-media factor may be connected with these processes. At one extreme it may merely tip the scales at the last moment. Only a slight impetus may be needed to translate ideas into actions. At the other extreme it may be a prime incitement and incentive. Usually the effect lies between: crime and violence shows arouse an appetite for violence, reinforce it when it is present, show a method to carry it out, teach the best way to get away with it, stimulate the connection between cruelty and sex (sadism), blur the child's awareness of its wrongness. That is the curriculum of the School for Violence.

Why *is* there so much violence in the mass media? That is a question not to be shirked. Is it merely accidental? Can we dismiss it as merely a symptom of the times?

There are three main reasons. First, violence is exciting. It is an effective attention-getting device. You know the story of the man who said he could persuade a mule to do anything—by first whacking him over the head to get his attention. We have become somewhat like that mule. Violence onstage is an easy way to arouse interest, win an audience, and hold it. To keep the interest up, more and more violence is needed. In the words of a film critic, the appeal of violence "is calculated as coldly as if it were money— which indeed it is."

Second, mass-media violence is a reflection of a part of our social reality. There are people who half-consciously believe that violence is a good method for solving problems. They may not intend it explicitly in the individual case, but they tolerate it because they think the violent are the strong and will win. The imagination of some statesmen does not seem to reach much further. They want to send the marines as quickly as Superman flies out the window.

Third, the excessive display of violence exists against the background of a whole system of defense arguments, alibis, and rationalizations. The same or very similar reasons are repeated over and over again with the resounding voice of conviction. One or the other continually crops up in newspapers, magazines, books or scientific papers, publicity releases, radio and TV discussions, PTA meetings, practically all the books on mass-media effects, government brochures, articles about juvenile delinquency, mental-hygiene pamphlets, and so on.

What makes these arguments and others like them so important is that they not only amount to an acceptance of violence in advance, but are applied also to other social evils, such as poverty, slums, racism, alcoholism, and so on. They are comforting assumptions and evasions which tend to relieve us of responsibility. It is necessary to take a good look at them.

It is variously claimed:

*That the emotionally healthy and well-adjusted child from a harmonious family is not harmed*—as if we could be sure of such a blanket immunity against the suggestive and seductive influences to which millions of children are exposed. The healthiest child from the most harmonious family may have some weak points that are not readily apparent. Every normal child is immature and therefore susceptible to harmful influences.

*That it is all up to the family to shield the child*—as if we were still living on farms and in the preelectronic age. It is fashionable to blame parents, especially mothers, for any kind of maladjustment of their offspring. In this way, all the outside influences are disregarded—those which come to the child over the parents' heads and over which the family has little control. Parents have been so brainwashed into a belief in their own guilt that it is hard to reverse it. John Ruskin wrote long ago: "If good fathers and mothers always had as good children, the world would soon be angelic." To put all the emphasis on the family means to bypass the community, the society which conditions the family.

*That the mass media merely give the public, and the children, what they want.* If you tie a goat to a post, he will eat the grass that he can reach. That does not mean that he prefers it. Clinical child psychiatry cannot agree with Dr. Spock when he writes in his book on baby and child care: "The people who write and draw [the comic books] are only turning out what they have found that children want most," and, "When children show a universal craving for something, whether it's comics or candy or jazz, we have got to assume that it has a positive, constructive value for them." Children did not call for crime and horror comic books, for murder, blood, and torture. It was foisted upon them. A decade ago, horror comic books were forbidden in England. Does that mean that English children now do not get what they "want most"? It is also a fallacy when he adds that "the child must first go through a period of blood and thunder adventure." When will we learn what Goethe's mother knew so long ago, that we *don't* need blood in the nursery? A network executive, as quoted in the magazine *Television Age,* has explained very clearly how you can *make* an appetite for special programs: "You make it just as you make an appetite for violence. You make an appetite for violence by selling violence."

How misleading this children-want-violence argument is can be seen from a comparison of present research results with investigations carried out earlier. More than thirty years ago Dr. Edgar Dale reported the answers given by children from nine to thirteen to the question "What do you dislike most in motion pictures?" The following replies are typical:

"I don't like to see people killed. Killing makes you too excited."
"Bloody pictures make me sick—show you how to kill."
"Killing makes you have bad habits."
"Shooting and killing bad. Hate to see people suffer."
"It looks awful to see people killed."

Evidently children did *not* always "want most" to see people killed. We have instilled in them the habits of violence and insensibility.

Those who claim that the adult public merely gets the brutality and violence that it wants can point to a real expert as their witness. Hitler said: "Why should one talk a lot about brutality and get indignant about tortures? The masses want this. They want something that makes them shudder with horror."

*That violence is part of human life and that you have to teach children to cope with reality.* We can teach a child that—unfortunately—there still is violence in the world without overloading his imagination with violent images. You can tell a child where babies come from without showing him.

The blood and brutality in the mass media are not realism but pseudorealism. It leaves out the continuity of experience, both individual and social.

*That seeing a lot of murder and torture in the mass media will prevent Junior in real life from hitting his little brother or from resenting his mother's urging to do his homework.* This is called "getting rid of pent-up aggressions vicariously." If I were asked to give an example of brainwashing successfully carried out on a great number of educated people, I would cite the prevalence of this theory. It has become the magic formula to explain—and excuse—violence.

This formula appears in many forms and variations: violent stories provide children with a natural, harmless outlet for their innate aggressiveness; the screen gives normal children relief from their pent-up aggressions which cannot be discharged in real life; children get a vicarious outlet for their latent hostility by looking at violent pictures; watching violent shows helps children get rid of their frustrations; guilt-free expression of their hostile feelings is afforded; children's hostility can be siphoned off by looking at violent programs; watching violent shows gives children an outlet in fantasy for aggression which otherwise might express itself in reality; an abundance of gunplay relieves the child's latent hostility; the mass media provide a safety valve for children's aggressiveness; and so on and on. All these are formulations taken from professional and lay publications. This is the monotonous cult of the cliché.

This outlet theory is not only overdone; it is false. It is pseudoscientific dogma. There is no shred of clinical evidence for it. In reality the programs do not provide a catharsis for children's feelings. On the contrary, the children are overexcited without being given adequate release. Delinquent behavior is not prevented but promoted. Far from providing an innocuous outlet, the brutal and sadistic stories of the mass media stimulate, overstimulate, and lead natural drives into unhealthy channels. For example, the brutal mishandling of girls leads to sadistic masturbatory daydreams.

Mass-media producers and toy-gun and war-toy manufacturers have made ample use of this fallacious defense argument. For instance, one toy manufacturer has made a statement as false as it is frightening to parents, namely, that denying children war toys "can turn young boys, without outlets for their aggressiveness and destructive urges, into homosexuals." Thus can the old catharsis theory be distorted and put to good commercial use—at the expense of the well-being of children.

For this healthy-outlet—getting-rid-of-aggression theory, Aristotle and Freud are sometimes invoked. There is no justification in either case. Aristotle in his *Poetics* wrote about purification (*katharsis*) through pity (*eleos*) and fear (*phobos*) in tragedies presented in the Greek theater. According to Goethe, Aristotle was referring not to the spectator but to the characters in the play. However that may be, the quality of the classical tragedies was very different from the violence hackwork of the mass media. And Greek children did not go to the theater for several hours every day. What's more, violence was *never* shown onstage in the Greek theater, and Aristotle actually advocated that children should be excluded by law from many plays.

Present-day overstimulation of children with violent stories did not exist in Freud's time. (Crime comic books started the year he died.) He would have been horrified at the current mass-media violence being declared harmless—or even good!—for children. He advocated relieving repressed emotions through analysis of their causes and understanding of the circumstances through which they arose.

The stereotyped getting-rid-of-aggression theory is not only bad for children; it has dangerous political consequences. In 1940 a well-known American psychoanalyst, Dr. Gregory Zilboorg, stated: "We should do nothing about the Nazis, because they have to live out their aggressions."

*That there is no proved relationship between pictures and the printed word on the one hand and human behavior on the other.* Nothing contradicts this except the history of mankind. There are very few truly human relationships which are better established, although it may be difficult to prove statistically.

*That critique of mass-media violence may lead to censorship and interfere with civil liberties.* Social control for the protection of children has nothing to do with censorship for adults. Children have the right to grow up healthy and uncorrupted. The battle for civil liberties should not be fought on the backs of children. Those who fight for freedom of expression would be in a stronger position if they conceded that outspoken sadism should be withheld from children.

The argument that control of what is advertised and exposed to children would interfere with civil liberties has no historical foundation. Civil liberties are not guaranteed but are vilified if under their protection children are harmed. It has never happened in the history of the world that regulations to protect children—be they with regard to child labor, food, drink, arms, sex, publications, entertainment, or plastic toys—have played any role whatsoever in the abridgment of political or civil liberties for adults. Where freedom has fallen, it has come about in totally different ways.

*That, at any rate, only a few children are affected.* It all depends on what value we place on human life. We do not know what small seeds may have been sown that may come to fruit in unfavorable circumstances arising much later. If the mass media seduce only one child each year to unfeeling, violent attitudes, and this child influences yearly only one other child, who in turn affects only one other, there would be in twenty years 1,048,575 violence-prone people. The mass-media audience is so large that what their apologists call very few may be actually a very large number indeed. In 1952 only the very small proportion of 0.024 percent per 100,000 died in automobile accidents. Applied to the whole population of the United States, that means that 37,794 people lost their lives.

*That only the predisposed, maladjusted, emotionally disturbed, abnormal, insecure, immature, unstable, already aggressive, neurotic, or predisposed child is affected.* Such a preclassification into rigid categories, vulnerable and invulnerable, is not possible. There is no evidence that only previously disturbed children followed the

Pied Piper of Hamelin. Sometimes this theory is put like this: violence will not hurt the child if the child is psychologically healthy. My clinical researches do not bear this out. It is not only the abnormal and maladjusted child who can learn—and be seduced. Every sex offender knows that. Healthy and well-adjusted children are not inaccessible. They learn, they are sympathetic and interested, they can be taught the bad as well as the good. The School for Violence is an integrated school. It teaches all children.

We cannot start out with the bias of such a preclassification, especially one that in practice is so liable to be influenced by race prejudice, class prejudice, and intellectual-elite prejudice. The mass media affect in various degrees and various ways what the French psychologists call *l'individu moyen,* the average individual. If a child is adversely affected, there is no reason for claiming right away that "there must have been something wrong with him before." Freud in his very first publication on a psychological subject stressed the fact that "the majority of healthy persons" are subject to the influence of suggestion.

To say that only the allegedly "predisposed" child is affected is a lame excuse. What this predisposition consists in is left entirely undefined. These children are never concretely, clinically described. All children are impressionable. It is a kind of intellectual violence, and entirely inhuman, to divide children—without examining them—into two groups: the predisposed, who are assumed to be vulnerable, and the well-adjusted, who are supposed to be immune. The real child and his problems get lost.

The dogma that harm can come only to the predisposed child leads to a contradictory and irresponsible attitude on the part of adults. The argument goes like this: constructive programs on TV are praised for giving children constructive ideas; at the same time, it is denied that destructive scenes give children destructive ideas. Healthy, normal children are not supposed to be affected by screen fare. And for unhealthy, abnormal children it is not supposed to matter, because if they were not influenced by the screen, they would be influenced by something else. An extreme version of this view, often expressed, is that a child must have some mental disorder before he can be adversely affected by mass media. We are certainly deceiving ourselves if we think that our social conditions, our education, and our entertainment are so good that only emotionally disturbed children can get into trouble!

*That violence is also in classical literature and in fairy tales.* This means confusing violence for plot's sake with plots for violence's sake. There is a great difference. In good literature, violence is characterized as a calamity, a tragic error, an aberration. Often it is no more than an exclamation after a stirring exposition of dramatic, emotional, and moral conflicts. Death itself is depicted movingly. In many mass-media stories, violence is a device of common living and a routine commonplace.

Fairy tales are on a totally different psychological and aesthetic level. No child expects a pumpkin to turn into a getaway car. For years crime comic books had advertisements for guns and switchblade knives, but Grimm's fairy tales never carried advertisements for crossbows. Fairy tales do not exist in such numbers as the endless mass-media violence stories. And, of course, children spend incomparably less time with them. "In the movies," an eleven-year-old boy told me, "they hit the girl in the face. On TV they shoot her. In horror shows they choke her."

"What about fairy tales?" I asked him.

"Oh, in the fairy tales they don't get killed. They live happily forever after. I don't read fairy tales because I like to look at the hopped-up stuff."

The fact that so many responsible people equate crime and horror stories in mass media with fairy tales is a sign of a confusion and complacency about violence. To say that crime comics and fairy tales are the same because there is violence in both is like saying the institutions of marriage and of brothels are the same because in both there is sexual intercourse. Fairy tales are not arbitrarily concocted, but often embody some popular folk wisdom. They are unreal on a narrative level, but real on a constructive, ethical level. In fairy tales the people play a role in social life. They are fishermen or farmers or millers or parents or children or grandparents. In comic books they do not have any social ties. Fairy tales deal with the fates of people; crime comics have only action, and that mostly violent action. Of course, there are also horrors in some fairy tales, and they are certainly not suitable for young children. Rousseau called these *"leçons d'inhumanité."* But even they do not stimulate imitation in the everyday world so different from fairyland. The moral of many fairy tales is an integral part of the story. In the mass-media story, if there is a moral, it gets completely lost in the general effect of the action. What remain are images, and it is with these that we have saturated children's minds.

*That children are so resilient that they can take it.* Why should they have to? The child's psyche is not resilient, but plastic and pliable. Any long continued influence on a child is either educational or miseducational, never neutral.

*That good always triumphs in the end and that therefore the effect can be only salutary.* The deep impression made on children (and many adults) by individual exciting scenes is not blotted out by the end. How many adults remember the end and the resolution of *Macbeth, Hamlet, War and Peace, Faust, Native Son,* or *Swan Lake?* In most mass-media stories, if the killer is conquered at the end, it is merely the violent continuation of a violent plot. The ending in violence makes the criminal a hero because he has been fighting against hopeless odds and dies in glory for his convictions. The sadistic suggestion is retained, the lip service at the very end is forgotten. Younger children do not comprehend the moral; older ones sense its insincerity.

What generally happens psychologically is this: the sadistic stories arouse strong emotions, which in their turn lead to half-automatic reactions. The purely intellectual moral ending cannot prevail against these strong emotions and their effects. The endless repetition of these emotional-sadistic stories finally completely nullifies any possible effect of moral-rational endings. The question is not what "moral" the mass-media editor or producer claims is drawn, but what the child picks up from the story. You cannot teach morals in a context of violence. The nonviolent moral is lost in the violent detail.

Here is an eleven-year-old girl's typical description of a TV program:

They threaten to kill, to betray. A good man knocks an old man down, they kidnap a girl, the men have guns. Two men are tied, there's a lady captive. They bring money as ransom, but they threaten to kill them anyhow. Two men kick one man with their heels. The criminals shoot each other. A bad Indian captures the lady and uses her as a shield—holds a knife on her. One man is shot. The sergeant kills the Indian by breaking his neck and choking him with an underarm grip.

Such descriptions indicate that children do *not* learn from these shows that "good guys win over bad guys"; rather, they learn that violence is exciting—and, since we allow so much of it to be shown to them, that it is probably a pretty good thing. (A child accustomed to such a rich diet of murders and other violence on the screen may have trouble understanding why his minor transgressions, such as slugging his little sister, call for any punishment.)

What some children do absorb from screen violence is that all life is a fight, that gentle persuasion is never successful—and is sissy anyhow. In spy stories and shows, the ingenious and intrepid spy appears to youths often as more attractive than the representative of the law. A little boy, when asked what he wanted to be when he grew up, answered, "I want to be a security risk!"

In many mass-media stories, the "good guys" are not so different from the "bad guys." The dignity of the individual is violated by both. The winning heroes are often vigilante types. It is generally accepted that in the end, good triumphs over evil. That is how we allow ourselves to be lulled into unconcern. Content analysis shows that in some of the most exciting stories, just the opposite happens. One TV story: A man kills his wife by hitting her over the head with an iron poker. He makes an ingenious defense and goes completely free. At the story's end, he is happily tending the roses in his garden, glad to be rid of his nagging wife, who did not like roses. This is a real school lesson both in method and in morals. There are whole comic books in which every single story ends with the triumph of evil, with a perfect crime unpunished and actually glorified. In one comic-book story a man commits a murder and at the end of the story goes scot-free. He triumphs because an innocent man is so beaten in a police station that he confesses to a crime he did not commit.

*That any trouble does not come from the media but is determined by what the child brings to them.* As the man said when his dog killed a rabbit, it was the rabbit that started the fight. We cannot rigidly separate what is in the child and what is in the environment. There is a subtle interaction between them. Physicists studying a bridge know that because of the interaction of the "free vibrations" (from the structure of the bridge) and the "forced vibrations" (induced from outside), even a relatively small load may be dangerous under certain circumstances.

*That mass media cannot really* cause *any harm, but merely trigger it.* The word "triggering" as a substitute for "causing" is fashionable but loaded. It is as if a man who shot somebody to death would say, "I did not cause his death, I merely pulled the trigger." In mental life there is no mechanical, automatic causation. Stimuli that set things in motion or reinforce them or continue them merge with one another.

A similarly evasive and even more fashionable term is "basic." It comes in many versions and is used in every conceivable context. Mass media cannot touch the "basic personality structure"; they cannot be a "basic cause" or a "basic traumatic factor"; they cannot influence "basic processes" or "basic reactions"; the "basically normal child" is not affected; whatever causes trouble is "deeper and more basic." Such a term as "basic" in this connection is purely subjective and pretentious. It means whatever a writer wishes it to mean. This is not where science can begin, but where it ends. Eighty percent of the mortality in the United States is accounted for by three conditions: cardiovascular diseases, cancer, accidents. In none of them do we know the "basic" cause, but in all of them we know a great deal about contributing and conditioning factors. It is this knowledge which enables us to treat and prevent. In the same way, in medical psychology, attention must be paid not only to the search for "basic" causes, which in human behavior are elusive anyhow, but to any conditioning and contributing factors—physical, psychological, and environmental-social.

Another glibly applied term is "aggression." It is often used as an innocuous-sounding substitute for "violence." It is also used to mean a cause of violence—or again something different from violence. Freud regarded "aggression" originally as sadism, that is, as a part of sexuality. Later he used it interchangeably with "destruction." Currently, "aggression" is a fashionable term applied in an ambiguous way to mean something constructive or destructive or neutral. Frequently it includes—and conceals—the intent and fact of naked violence. Abstract discussions of aggression have little value. Any big psychological generalization with the term "aggression" is apt not to explain but to becloud the issue.

*That only contact with significant real persons in the child's life influences him, while pictures and printed words do not.* The great success of the many printed advertisements and television commercials directed at children would indicate that they have considerable effect. This is well known to the "significant real persons" who have to pay for the advertised products.

*That when children say that they saw something in the mass media, they are making it up just as an excuse.* This implies complete misunderstanding of the clinical examination. The careful clinician does not suggest anything to a child by leading questions, nor does he accept anything at its face value. Among the many children examined by my associates and myself, what's more, no child has ever volunteered the statement about mass media as an excuse for anything he had done. Typical is the case of a seven-year-old boy who set fires. He said nothing about either comic books or television, but when asked what he saw on a Rorschach plate during a test, he began a long stream of talk about monsters who cause explosions and set fires.

*That so many factors enter into a child's development that we cannot gauge the effect of any single one.* This would mean that scientific study of human behavior is not possible and that the status quo is inscrutable.

The only-one-factor argument comes sometimes in the form of "Mass media violence is only one little thing" in a child's life. The answer is that it is just many "little things" which determine a child's development.

*That children are not affected by mass-media violence because they know that it is only make-believe and not really true.* Suppose you showed on television a bed and a man and a woman doing something they should not be doing on TV. Would you let your small child watch that and say, "Oh, she knows that is just make-believe"? In sex we realize this is suggestive and exciting. But when it comes to violence, we are blinded.

Quite apart from the fact that it is not always easy for children to distinguish between what is fantasy and what reality, this argument comes from a misunderstanding of how propaganda works, for children as well as adults. Propaganda is based not on reason and truth but on emotion.

The argument that the violence on the screen is not real but only enacted by actors is an old one. It was answered by Shakespeare in *A Midsummer Night's Dream:*

STARVELING: I believe we must leave the killing out, when all is done.
BOTTOM: Not a whit! I have a device to make all well. Write me a prologue; and let the prologue seem to say, we will do no harm with our swords and that Pyramus is not killed indeed; and . . . that I Pyramus am not Pyramus, but Bottom the weaver.

*That the character of a child has "jelled" at the age of seven (others say at five or three) and that later influences are therefore negligible.* This, like some of the other arguments, is misunderstood and misapplied Freud. As Alexander Pope wrote: "So by false learning is good sense defaced." Of course, early infantile experiences play a role. But they do not determine the future course of a person mechanically and fatalistically. To say, as often has been said, that mass media cannot do harm unless the parent-child relationships had been disturbed in the first place is unscientific both for practical purposes and in theory. What Freud said about outside influences was that up to the age of sixteen or seventeen, children were "still in the formative period . . . and ought not to be exposed to perverse influences." And in one of his last writings, he stated about the causes of disturbed behavior that in addition to early childhood experiences, "we must not forget to include the influence of civilization."

*That to see a relationship between mass media and behavior means using mass media as a scapegoat for social problems.* The modern mass media in their present state *are* a social problem.

# CHAPTER ELEVEN

# The Jungle of Legal Insanity

## PSYCHIATRY, LAW, AND VIOLENT CRIME

One's heart ought to be shown in the
enforcement of law—not in its relaxation.
—JOHN RUSKIN

A MURDER is committed. Almost immediately in any civilized society—in fact, that is a measure of its civilization—it is realized
that in this postviolence phase, the deed has to be in some way
resolved. If not, it or something like it will be repeated. For centuries upon centuries, mankind has labored to work out a legal
machinery to deal with violent crime. Even though it may lag
behind social development and sometimes be slanted in a conflict-
ridden society, the criminal law nevertheless represents a collective
moral judgment. If a man violates this judgment, he faces not
angry men, as in former times, but impersonal law. The rationale
of this legal procedure is the protection of society while fully
protecting the rights of the individual. This represents a delicate
institution which speaks (or should speak) to the community in
clear and unmistakable terms.

Now, in certain cases, psychiatry steps in, a defense of legal
insanity is interposed, and the whole ordinary legal process is
suspended. This is a very serious step. It goes to the heart of the
law, the question of guilt or lack of guilt. In 1846, in one of the
first American cases in which an insanity plea based on scientific
psychiatry was made, William Seward, later Secretary of State in
Lincoln's Cabinet, stated: "When true, the plea of insanity is of
all pleas the most perfect and complete defense that can be of-

fered in any human tribunal." His psychiatric expert was Dr. Amariah Bingham, the first editor of the *American Journal of Psychiatry,* then called the *American Journal of Insanity.*

The relation between psychiatry, law, and violent crime is perhaps the most sensitive and revealing indicator of a society's attitude to violence. It raises problems of science, of law, and of democracy.

The key concept of the criminal law is responsibility; the key concept of forensic (medicolegal) psychiatry is disease. However these concepts may be defined or criticized, up to now no civilized society has been able to do without them. Maybe that will be different in the distant future, but we are still far removed from that. It is not a question of any abstract principle of freedom of the will or the lack thereof. What is involved is the scientific clinical determination of severe pathological affliction which affects responsibility from the psychiatric point of view. The man who commits a violent crime on the basis of a severe mental disease cannot be measured with the usual yardsticks applicable to the normal. Nor are the interests of society served if he is treated with the same corrective measures instead of with medical-psychiatric ones.

There are of course offenders who, as the District Court of Appeals of California expressed it in a recent opinion (1964), are "simultaneously a correctional and a medical psychiatric problem, yet not altogether one or the other." These cases require the most advanced jurisprudence on the one hand, the most up-to-date psychiatry on the other, and the closest collaboration between the two. Drug addicts who commit violent crimes are an example.

The full collaboration of psychiatry and the law could be a great safeguard against violent crime. But at present it does not work out that way, and the promise is not yet fulfilled. Psychiatry should be used as a help and not as an evasion. Violence prevention in this whole field is grossly deficient. There would not be so much discussion about legal responsibility if there were more agreement about what is social responsibility. The fault does not lie with any legal theory, any one school of psychiatry, or any special persons, but with a general complacency about violence.

Nobody, whether lawyer, psychiatrist, or layman, would claim that the interaction between psychiatry and criminal law in our society is either clear or satisfactory. The difference between what the books say and what actually happens is striking. Legal cases with an insanity angle are the weakest link in American justice and one of the most vulnerable spots in the armor of society against violence.

At present the whole practical issue of psychiatry and law in cases of violence is a jungle. In this jungle are big trees of tradition difficult to uproot and casting a dark shadow over everything. There are poisonous plants of prejudice and brightly colored flowers of newfangled and captivating ideas without fruit. Underneath is a swamp of apathy.

In no other area of the administration of justice is there so much injustice, so much confusion, and so much flouting of scientific and moral principles on a large scale. A defendant with a mental disease of the very kind and degree for which laws of legal insanity have been made may be declared normal and sentenced to the electric chair or to life imprisonment without parole. This is, of course, a serious matter. For to put an insane person to death is like burning witches. Judge Van Voorhis of the New York State Court of Appeals has compared it with "euthanasia" murders.

Albert Fish was a mass sex murderer of children. He suffered from a severe, chronic paranoid psychosis with religious and other delusions. Yet he was executed. Over the years, I have discussed him with many psychiatrists and members of the legal profession. None of them had the slightest doubt that he was mentally severely diseased and legally insane. Executing him did the community no good. On the contrary, it did a great deal of harm, because the real problem in the case was how it was possible that this sick man not only for years but for decades could continue his fearful career, although he was often in the hands of the authorities, both legal and psychiatric. Killing him was considered a final solution. What should have been done was to use this case for an overhauling of the haphazard procedures which are still costing the lives of children like four-year-old Edith Kiecorius. (Her sixty-year-old rapist-murderer had assaulted his own young daughter, had been twice in psychiatric hospitals, and been twice arrested for violent behavior.)

On the other hand, a defendant in a murder case in whom nobody ever saw any signs of abnormality before his arrest may be declared insane, spend some time in an institution, and then be completely free without any parole or other supervision. If he ever commits another murder, his lawyers can point to his previous insanity record—and every prosecutor knows that *de facto* he cannot be convicted of first-degree murder. He has acquired a psychiatric hunting license to kill.

Martin Lavin was a professional gunman with a record of more than twenty arrests for serious felonies. After one particularly flagrant and cold-blooded murder, he engineered an insanity defense and got himself committed to an institution. When he was discharged after a year, he resumed his former career. In the course of it, he killed Sergeant Kilpatrick of the New York police force. Kilpatrick was wounded in a gun battle, and as he was lying in the street, Lavin stood over him and deliberately killed him with two shots in the back. At that time, the Bar Association of New York issued a stern warning and asked for reforms. But nothing affecting the real issues was done, and similar cases continue to occur.

An insanity defense often gets off to a wrong start from the very beginning. A violent crime is committed, and the lawyer feels he has no valid defense, "therefore" he pleads insanity. This is a very poor reason. The only justification for such a plea is not that there is no other defense but that there are reasons to suspect a genuine, serious mental disorder. The abuse of the insanity defense has led to what may be called the alibi of abnormality. Instability is not insanity, maladjustment not psychosis, a partial explanation not a total excuse.

The fact that underprivileged persons often cannot obtain a competent psychiatric defense has backfired against everyone—including the privileged. It has undermined the sense of justice in the population, endangered the security of society, and interfered with the civil liberties of the individual. For the privileged have to live with the underprivileged, normal and abnormal. The lesson to be learned from a murder case with an insanity angle is important for society. Only by understanding what has happened and why it has happened can we prevent what may happen in the future. An essential point is that the violent crimes committed by persons with severe mental disease could nearly always have been prevented long before.

Neurotics often make for themselves false conscious reasons for their inappropriate behavior. Societies may act in a similar way. It seems that every abuse has its apologists. In the field of the medicolegal handling of violent crime, a number of sweeping generalizations are widely propounded and credited. It is of the utmost importance to analyze them in detail, for they tend to perpetuate violence rather than counteract it. The writings with these generalizations are usually abstract discussions about freedom of the will, about what goes on in the (unconscious) mind of a judge, about the alleged inadequacy of the jury, about punishing without punishment, about faulty legal definitions, about psychiatrists belonging to the wrong school, and so on. Conspicuous is the absence of case material. Some books are entirely without concrete cases; others refer to inadequately studied cases. One typical book which is widely recommended as a "comprehensive" study contains only one clinical case—and that is one which the author never saw. Instead of establishing the observable facts and then arriving at theories, many writers on the subject theorize first and leave out the facts. Some of these generalizations are very contradictory. They are a reflection and therefore an indication of deeper-lying social disorders. That is what makes it so necessary to take them up.

According to the most far-reaching and most harmful generalization, whatever may be wrong with legal-insanity cases is all the fault of the juries. Eliminate the juries in these cases, we are told, leave the important decisions to psychiatric experts, and all will be well. This drive against juries paves the way for uncertainty and insecurity about violence and cannot be resisted too strongly.

Condemnation of juries is never backed up by cases in which the way the psychiatric facts were put before the jury are sufficiently scrutinized. Charles Starkweather, a youth of nineteen, killed eleven innocent people in a mad murder rampage. There is no doubt about his severe abnormality. Following a jury trial, he was executed. At the trial the psychiatric experts for the defense—despite repeated prodding—failed to give any psychiatric diagnosis, thereby dooming the defendant. So it is certainly not the jury which can be justly criticized. Of this type of testimony, the U.S. District Court of the District of Columbia ruled in 1962: "A physician's statement that a person is sick, without indicating the nature of the ailment, is worthy of but scant consideration." Shortly before Starkweather's execution, a grass-roots letter was published in the "Public Pulse" section of the Omaha *World-Herald*. It read: "If Charles Starkweather were the son of a rich family he would not be sitting in Death Row today."

Blaming juries takes many forms. We read in writings by psychiatrists and also jurists of the "jurors' confusion"; of "the twelve bewildered laymen"; of the "ancient institution" of the jury, with "its secret, esoteric process of decision-making"; of the lay jury being "individualistic and not without a considerable element of irrationality"; of the jury as a "manifestation of the mass mind" and therefore "fickle"; and so on.

Whether a person is so seriously affected (however psychiatrically defined) that he is not legally responsible (however legally defined) is an issue of *fact* and is therefore within the province of the jury. It is often stated that psychiatric testimony is "too complex" for the jury to make proper use of. This contention has been answered by Judge David L. Bazelon, Chief Judge of the U.S. Court of Appeals of the District of Columbia. He wrote: "We trust juries to believe or disbelieve all other aspects of the accused's defense, why should we think them any less reliable in this area— especially as it is one in which they have the benefit of expert psychiatric evidence?"

A specific case in which the jurors have been widely blamed is the Albert Fish case, one of the most important modern cases in which an insane man (according to any legal or medical definition) was executed. It has been stated—for example, in a book on forensic psychiatry—that the jurors did not pay heed to the psychiatric testimony but took account only of their own sense of indignation. But in that case, psychiatrists for the prosecution testified not only that Fish was legally sane but that he did not suffer from any mental disorder at all. What happened in that case was that a psychotic man who had tortured and killed many children had been admitted several times to psychiatric hospitals and each time was discharged after the most negligent and negligible examination and without any social history being taken. The public was aroused over the murders, and the authorities needed to have him declared normal. It is only against this social background that this miscarriage of justice becomes understandable. I discussed this case with several members of the jury. What prompted their decision was their—not unjustified—fear that Fish might be released again to commit further crimes.

Naturally jurors are influenced by the social environment in which they live. But the experts are not immune against these influences either. By and large, the members of a jury do not go by abstract theories, either legal or psychiatric. They want the expert to explain his opinion and the facts it is based on, in simple terms, and to establish the existence or absence of a serious disease with a beginning, a course, and a probable outcome. That is what sane or insane means to them. And that is exactly what it scientifically means. Fundamentally they are concerned with the questions: Could the violent crime have been prevented? Can it be prevented in the future?

Abolishing or restricting juries in cases of violent crime with a question of legal insanity is often regarded as representing a humanitarian attitude. Actually it works out as the opposite. It tends toward the rule of an authoritarian expert elite. It is antidemocratic. The jury system does not exist, as a prominent psychoanalyst wrote recently, because it "fulfills an unconscious magic need of the people." It is a hard-won democratic right which has an important function in the social process. Historically, juries were immune from the tyranny of the state; later they had to maintain themselves against the tyranny of judges. Now there is a danger of a tyranny of experts. The jury has been called by Lord Patrick Devlin, author of the book *Trial by Jury,* "the lamp that shows that freedom lives." And De Tocqueville, in his famous treatise on democracy in America, said that the jury "has saved English freedom in past times and may be expected to maintain American liberties also." If we want to prevent violence, we do not need less democracy but more.

Another generalization that has proved a great obstacle to constructive measures is the assertion that an intrinsic conflict exists between scientific psychiatry and the law. The myth is perpetuated (thus encouraging a bias in reality) that the two professions represent alien and antagonistic viewpoints which clash head on. This is sometimes described—rather frivolously, considering the seriousness of violent crime—as a tug-of-war. A difficulty or even a breakdown of communication between psychiatrists and lawyers has been claimed to exist. While psychiatrists have said that the lawyers are backward, the lawyers feel that some psychiatrists are forward. However, the claim that the legal and psychiatric professions do not understand each other is superficial and without any real basis. Indeed, I have seen prosecutors and their psychiatrists who understood one another only too well.

In reality, for many years court proceedings in cases with a psychiatric angle have taken place in which the procedure was strictly legal, humane, and scrupulously scientific. This was on the basis that violent crime is not merely a psychiatric problem and that psychiatry is only one tool among others.

The collaboration of law and psychiatry is greatly hampered by general statements to the effect that the law is social and psychiatry is individual. This sounds like a pithy slogan and is often used in arguments, but the argument doesn't hold water. There is no intrinsic conflict between our duty to the individual sufferer and our task to protect society. Any good district attorney represents *all* the people, including the accused. Nor is the assumption correct that psychiatry represents only the individual and not society's interests as well. If I testify in a murder case for the defendant whom I have examined, I am helping not only that individual but also society, which cannot possibly protect itself if it treats the sick and the well with the same methods.

It is an anarchistic notion to make an absolute of the differences between the personal and the social. The current exaggerated contrast and separation between individual and society is not a permanent part of human life. In a well-ordered society the interests of individual and society are identical.

Much has been made of the assertion that psychiatrists deal with the unconscious, while the law deals with conscious acts. This is not only an oversimplification but a distortion. Psychiatry does not deal only with the unconscious, and the law no more excludes the unconscious than it does X rays, electroencephalograms, or barely visible viruses. The study of the unconscious is an extension of the conscious. The one does not abolish the other, just as atomic physics and Einstein have not abolished classical physics and Newton. The law does object to the frequent purely speculative use of general psychiatric concepts. What it insists on is that the working of the unconscious be *demonstrated*. Freud himself insisted that distinguishing unconscious from other factors represents "a stock-taking of the facts of our observation." The main trouble is that dynamic psychiatry of the type which pays attention to unconscious factors is usually not available to underprivileged defendants.

A classic example of when unconscious features could have and should have been presented to the court is the Leonski case. Eddie Leonski was a twenty-four-year-old soldier who was stationed with the U.S. Army in Australia during the Second World War. He was born in New Jersey and worked as a grocery clerk in the Bronx before he entered the army. Within a period of two weeks, he killed three Australian women in Melbourne by strangling them. An army medical board composed of two physicians and a psychiatrist pronounced him technically and legally sane. The court regarded him as a "fiend," deplored the blot he cast on the service, and sentenced him to death. He was executed by hanging.

In reality, Leonski cast no blot on the army. No sane American soldier would act like that. This should and could have been established. There was no apparent motive or any provocation. The victims were not sexually molested, and nothing was stolen from them. Leonski made a full confession. Such a case can be understood and properly resolved only by considering unconscious motivation, which the defendant himself does not know or understand. Leonski was surprised that he had committed murder. "Fancy," he said in jail, "my being a murderer!" The law, once it admits psychiatric testimony, gives enough scope to psychological evidence about morbid phenomena, including the unconscious. But the court in this case (as in so many others) did not have a complete psychiatric picture laid before it.

Leonski was without doubt mentally deranged. His mother had been a patient in a mental hospital fourteen years before, and his older brother was in a New York state hospital at the time of the crimes, suffering from a chronic psychosis. He was a gentle, mild-

mannered young man. His sister said that as a little boy "he was
so good he used to scare me." Eddie was completely dependent on
his mother and was considered a mama's boy. The mother image
dominated his whole life. He could not free himself from it. That
his three victims were all women considerably older than he was
is psychiatrically most significant. The deeds constituted a symbolic matricide. The murders were repeated because each individual act was psychologically incomplete. He could not resolve his
unbearable conflict because its very nature eluded his consciousness and was therefore not accessible to his reason. He unconsciously linked the voices of his victims with his mother. Of one
woman he recalled, "She had a fascinating, lovely voice." Of
another he said, "I remember the woman singing. She seemed to
be singing just for me alone." Thus does the infant feel that his
mother's voice is just for him. The fact that Leonski drank on the
nights of the murders does not mean that the drinking caused the
killings—although it undoubtedly facilitated them—but that the
drinking itself was a symptom of the underlying mental disease.
The whole psychological explosion occurred in a period of deprivation when he was away from home and separated from his
mother—but not from her dominating image. The psychosis from
which he suffered, technically known as catathymic crisis, consists
in delusional thinking with the patient being driven to a violent
deed without a rational conscious motive, with the act having a
symbolic meaning and the victim not counting as a person but
as part of an overpowering image. Leonski's thinking was psy-
chotically disordered on the basis of unconscious processes. If
properly established, the law accepts this as interfering with full
responsibility.

Another example of this type of case was a woman of forty-two,
with two grown-up children, who shot and killed her husband.
She had married for the first time, at the early age of fifteen, a
much older man who was a friend of her father. This marriage
was very happy but rested on the morbid psychological foundation of a childlike dependence on a father substitute or father
image. When her first husband died, she married again, but her
new husband abused her. He threatened her with a revolver,
which he even took to bed with him. He tried to drive her to sui-

cide. She stood these and other abuses for fifteen years, like a child whose duty it is to obey. On the night of the murder, she tried to kill herself before her husband's eyes. He goaded her on to do so. At the last moment, her instinct of self-preservation asserted itself, and she shot him. Following my psychiatric testimony, which referred in detail to the psychological processes, including unconscious ones, operative in her mind, the jury acquitted her on the ground of insanity, and the judge remanded her to one of my clinics for out-patient treatment by psychotherapy.

One generalization which is a great obstacle to constructive handling of violent crime is the idea that murder is a disease. We read that violent crime is "always caused by sickness," that anybody doing violence to another person must be insane, deranged, irrational. This sounds modern and enlightened. However, it is ancient and primitive. The prehistoric Greeks thought that murder was so fearful that a murderer must be mad in the first place or have been driven to madness by the Erinyes. As George Thomson described this old belief: "He was mad to do it; and if he regains his sanity, the shock of realization drives him mad again." We have since seen more of murder and learned more about madness.

One sophisticated form of the view that a murderer must be sick is that he is neurotic and that his deed is caused by adverse infantile experiences. This is often expressed in an increasing body of literature, both fiction and nonfiction (the distinction is not always clear). In movies and on television, we often have not good guys and bad guys, but good guys and neurotics. The idea has exerted a tremendous influence not only on the lay public but also on the legal profession. Even judges have publicly commended Robert Lindner's *Rebel Without a Cause* as a "deep" study of crime. Yet this book is actually science fiction—psychological science fiction, if you will—in which the psychologist let his fancy have free rein and the subject told the psychologist what he wanted to hear. That this imaginative, unscientific book has been taken so seriously has done a lot of harm.

That violent crime is due to a neurosis is a comforting thought, for under this theory no one is really responsible. The roots are traced to early childhood. In reality, we have no well-studied clinical cases in which a single event in a person's infancy, or even a series of events in childhood, explained why he committed murder.

The it's-all-due-to-early-childhood exaggeration is often used to cover up social defaults. The killing of Edith Kiecorius could have been prevented by proper sociopsychiatric measures. Yet it was left as an event about which we could do nothing and from which we can learn nothing. As a prominent columnist expressed it, it was "monstrous and absurd in a meaningless void." The state psychiatrist in the hospital where Edith's murderer had been previously confined declared after the murder that the murderer "may have been an unconscious sex deviate . . . all sex deviation goes back to early childhood influences." Can that by the remotest stretch of imagination explain or help us to understand what happened? Still more important, the early-infantile dogma makes it appear that we cannot predict violent crime. Clinical psychiatry is advanced enough that we often can.

The whole idea that murder is a disease may sound extremely liberal. But it is the liberalism of the uninformed and therefore illiberal. It is not only ineffective; it is actually harmful. Cruelty and disease are not the same. The claim of the murder-is-a-disease school, that every killer has a serious emotional disorder, is not valid in any strict scientific sense. It diffuses the meaning of "emotional disorder" to such an extent that no concrete meaning remains. The reasoning amounts to no more than: a man commits a murder because he has an emotional disorder—or he has an emotional disorder because he commits murder. For scientific thinking, we need the background of individual normality in criminology and psychiatry just as we do in medicine. If we exculpate cold-blooded, scheming murderers, we deprive those who are genuinely mentally ill of the psychiatric testimony which they should have. It is an obsolete idea to say that there is no real difference between "normal" and "abnormal."

Nothing is more misleading in this field than the notion that there are only fleeting transitions between mental health and mental disease and that the boundaries will always remain hazy and indeterminable. It is true that we always look for the understandable in that which seems irrational, and we use the abnormal to learn about the normal. But whatever transitions exist, disease is not the same as health. Suffering is not a part of normal human life. That is the affirmation of modern science.

Confusion perpetuates violence. It creates confusion to propagate the idea, taken from psychological theories of neuroses, that murderers are always prompted by unconscious guilt feelings and "actually crave punishment." That may be true of a few very special cases, but it is a tremendous exaggeration if applied in general or even to a majority. The word "guilt" is often loosely used in forensic psychiatric literature. We may read about a murderer motivated by "unconscious guilt." No clear distinction is made between guilt, which is an objective fact; guilt feeling, which is an entirely subjective phenomenon; and guilt complex, which refers to repressed unconscious mental processes.

Widespread misuse is made of the term "compulsion" too. We hear and read about "compulsive murderers." Yet there is no such thing as a compulsive murderer. The term "compulsion" should in this connection be used only in its definite meaning in modern psychopathology, as part of an obsessive-compulsive neurosis. In this condition, as Pierre Janet, Freud, and Stekel have stated, and as shown by my own clinical observations, *murder is never committed*. There is not one single case in the literature where a person with obsessive-compulsive neurosis committed murder. This condition is actually a protection against murderous impulses. That fact is important for understanding the structure of the violent act in normal and abnormal people.

While some assume that the individual pathological condition supposed to make people murderers is caused by early infantile experiences, others accuse heredity. (In effect, the two are not so different, both ruling out social factors.) The crime-is-disease school is responsible for a renewed belief in inborn tendencies to violent crime. A great role in its propagation has been played by a book with the revealing title *Crime as Destiny,* by Professor Johannes Lange. The book is based on a study of twins. It claims to prove the overwhelming role of heredity in causing crime. Analysis of the data and the original material, however, shows that the study proves nothing of the kind and that its conclusions are without foundation. The idea of crime as an inherited pathological condition has proved highly persuasive. Even so good and progressive a biologist as J. B. S. Haldane gave this misleading book extravagant praise and wrote that "posterity will regard it as the most important book of the century."

Murder is a social phenomenon. Clinical psychiatry can cover only part of it. Psychoanalysis, being a part of psychiatry, can cover even less, however important its insights may be. On the average, almost five policemen in the United States are shot to death each month by people they are trying to arrest. Individual psychology cannot fully explain that. From 1958 to 1965 the crime rate increased five times as fast as the population, and that includes a considerable proportion of violent crime. Purely psychopathological theories put this on a very different and false level and would provide not an explanation but an evasion of the problem. As Marx discerned long ago, if crime increases more rapidly than the population, the flaw must be in society.

Prevention of violent crime demands that we differentiate between the man who has a severe mental disease and could not prevent his crime and the man who could. The well and the sick cannot be treated in the same way, either before the event or after. Responsibility is not a legal fiction but a fact. All the talk about abolishing the concept of responsibility and replacing it with clinical terms leaves out that fact pointed out by Lord Langford in *The Idea of Punishment,* that we cannot bypass this concept "while retaining anything like our existing legal system."

It is an illusion to believe that in our time, only madmen will commit murder or other violent crimes. Human life in our society is anything but sacrosanct. In some future state of society, healthy people will not commit violence because they will have no motives for it and because they have acquired deeply ingrained habits against it. That certainly does not describe our era. Wanton violence is still rampant in both our life and our literature. It is a cornerstone of my thesis that our wish to rid society of violence can never be realized if we assume that society to be better than in fact it is. By pretending that every murderer falls into the category of mental pathology, we deprive the genuinely sick of proper consideration and we deprive the community of protection. Psychiatry has a most useful scientific function, but it must perform it strictly and consciously in the social and historical framework.

Frequently when the unsatisfactory handling of problems of legal insanity is discussed, exclusive emphasis is placed on the battle of psychiatric experts in court. Although much more may be wrong in a given case, it is all apt to be summed up as if the only trouble were the disagreement between psychiatrists. The assumption is that if that could be abolished, then everything would be all right. But the battle of experts is not a cause but merely a symptom. Of course, it is an unedifying spectacle to see in a murder case the psychiatric experts on opposing sides expressing opposing views while those on the same side agree completely. In addition, some psychiatrists claim that what they have to say is too esoteric to be criticized by the layman. Often such opinions are given without any real clinical basis.

However, trials with opposing psychiatric testimony are relatively rare. They seem frequent because they are apt to receive so much publicity. Moreover, there are perfectly legitimate disagreements, just as there are in other fields. A prosecuting lawyer will tell the court that he can prove that the accused deliberately killed somebody, while the defense lawyer will say with the same assurance and certainty that he has proof that the accused was not even there. The U.S. Supreme Court, after many lawyers and courts have worked on a case for months or years, will be split five to four, but nobody will suggest that for that reason the court should be abolished. Of course, psychiatry is a science; but it is not a science in which we can measure with an exact yardstick, as Justice Felix Frankfurter pointed out in discussing my psychiatric studies on the psychological harm of school segregation in the 1954 U.S. Supreme Court hearings before the integration ruling was passed. There is a body of psychiatric knowledge on which all competent psychiatrists can agree, but this area is surrounded by a wider field where differences of opinion are all too frequent. Of course, there are also differences of opinion betwen psychiatrists in court which are based on anything but scientific grounds.

As it actually works out in practical life, agreement against a background of bureaucratic indifference may be more deadly than disagreement. In some of the "sexual psychopath" laws, agreeing psychiatrists, without any contrary opinion being offered, can recommend that a person—even before conviction—be committed to an institution for an indefinite period. Such laws have failed, especially with regard to the protection of society against violent crime. The fault for the unsatisfactory state of affairs does not lie so much with the partisan experts who disagree as with the appointed and institutionalized experts who agree. The latter wield greater and greater power.

The Ezra Pound case is a classic example of the dangerous abuse of psychiatry which can exist even when psychiatrists are unanimous. This misguided poet presented a vexing problem to the authorities. He had propagandized over the Axis radio against the United States and democracy and had incited to violence. He was even worse than Lord Haw-Haw. Transcripts and witnesses established that. It was considered awkward to prosecute a prominent poet. The problem could have been solved democratically by the proper use of clemency. Instead, recourse was had to a dubious psychiatry. In no important case, to my knowledge, has a scientifically more inadequate report been made than the joint report of four psychiatrists in the Pound case. (The full report is published and analyzed in my study "The Road to Rapallo.") It declared him "insane." No clinical diagnosis was made. Instead the report used the ambiguous term "paranoid state." One of the psychiatrists declared that one reason for the determination of insanity was Pound's belief in "fantastic" economic ideas. He evidently did not take into consideration that the Nobel Prize winner T. S. Eliot had the same "fantastic" economic ideas. Now, years after Pound's discharge from the mental institution to which he had been sent, it is clear that he neither was nor is "insane" in any sense of the term. It was an abuse of scientific psychiatry in the service of sociopolitical expediency. What we need to realize is that what was done with Pound to shield him can just as easily be done with somebody else to discredit him.

One remarkable feature of the Pound case is that the unanimity of the experts was followed by unanimity of public opinion. The prevailing attitude has been summed up by a critic: "The man Pound has been judged and found to be insane by the United

States Government, so that problem is not our concern." Editorially and historically, Pound had become overnight the "insane poet." Writers spoke of his "madness," his "senile dementia," his "ravings of an insane man," his "insanity." With such facile ways out, one cannot prevent violence or incitement to violence.

To eliminate the "battle of experts," a very simple remedy is often suggested. The proposal is that wherever the question of sanity is raised, a board or a committee or a commission of psychiatrists should make the decisions called for at different stages of the proceedings. It is this board which would decide the prisoner's fate. Actually there is no evidence whatsoever that such a committee would be any less arbitrary and partisan than conscientious individual psychiatrists. It is a purely formal, unrealistic solution which does not touch the social factors that lead to the battle of experts. Who will appoint the members of this impartial committee, and how will they be selected? All the chances are that these experts will be the very ones who now are most responsible for the things which we should like to remedy. The collective lack of responsibility of a committee would interfere with the allottable responsibility of individual experts. An accused person would stand defenseless and without redress before a medical committee which is really not medical, a court which is not really a court, a jury which is not really a jury. This would be not only detrimental to the proper settling of murder cases but would strike at the heart of democracy itself. It would be a dangerous step toward the exclusive jurisdiction of psychiatry and the creation of a self-perpetuating psychobureaucracy. The boards would in all probability be representative of the local academic and political establishments. Clarence Darrow, who had a lot of experience in this field, said long ago that the installation of such powerful boards would interfere with civil liberties and ultimately with the safety of the public.

How far such an appointed commission may be removed from the common man is shown by the criminologically important Irwin case. Robert Irwin was an impecunious sculptor who suffered from an insidious chronic psychosis with the unshakable delusion that his sex instinct prevented him from his artistic fulfillment. In circuitous but traceable ways, this delusion drove him to seek escape in violence, against himself and against others. He wanted to put himself "under pressure." He attempted to emasculate himself to "bottle up" his artistic energies and was treated in a hospital for the wound he inflicted on his penis. Within a period of four and a half years, he presented himself no less than ten times to medical agencies to ask for psychiatric help. Three times he was committed to state hospitals as psychotic. After his third discharge from a state hospital, he killed three people: his former landlady and her daughter, both of whom had befriended him, and a lodger whom he had never met. The case aroused a great deal of public interest, and a special commission was appointed, composed of two neuropsychiatrists and a lawyer. They declared Irwin sane, fit for trial, and implicitly fit for execution. He barely escaped the electric chair and was sentenced to 139 years in prison. A few days after arriving in Sing Sing, he was carefully examined by a psychiatrist and declared psychotic. As a result, he was sent to an institution for the criminally insane. He has been there now for many years, and there is no doubt of the diagnosis of severe psychosis. The question of sending him back to jail as a sane criminal never even came up. In this classic case, a committee made a demonstrably wrong decision, although all the facts were accessible to them.

Present conditions in the application of forensic psychiatry being as unsatisfactory as they are, it is natural that a convenient scapegoat was sought. It had to be one as formal and as far removed as possible from current social conditions. It was found in the legal definition of insanity used in most American states and in England, the McNaughton rule. (The name McNaughton is spelled and misspelled in sixteen different ways, which is symbolic of the confusion which surrounds this law.) Psychiatrists, jurists, and diverse writers vie with one another to denounce this definition as not scientific, hopelessly inadequate, and doing more harm than good. The determination with which all the ills of the psychiatry-law situation are blamed on a definition reminds one of the businessman who, on coming home from a trip, found his wife on the living-room sofa in a compromising situation with a man. He decided to remedy the situation. So he got rid of the sofa. It is claimed that if there were only a better definition of insanity, all would be well. This sweeping over-all denunciation does tremendous harm to the effective and democratic settling and prevention of violent crimes. It is a false explanation of what is wrong and therefore perpetuates the existing ills. The current exclusive emphasis on the definition is socially wrong because it tends to obscure all the other factors that enter into the situation. No definition is self-administering. The fault does not lie with definitions but with facts. It is not enough to change words; what have to be changed are things.

The arguments used in condemnation of the definition sound persuasive and have misled many. It is necessary therefore to examine them in detail, just like everything else that, however indirectly, bolsters the prevalence of violence in our society. Discussions of the insanity rule and its application are so important because they focus and illuminate the whole problem of psychiatry, law, and violent crime.

According to the McNaughton rule, "to establish a defence on the ground of insanity, it must be clearly proved that, at the time of the committing of the act, the party accused was labouring under such a defect of reason, from disease of the mind, as not to know the nature and quality of the act he was doing, or, if he did know it, that he did not know he was doing what was wrong."

Of course, the McNaughton rule has it faults. So have other legal definitions of behavior, such as the distinctions between first-degree homicide, second-degree homicide, and manslaughter, and the definitions of the crimes of fraud, of adulterating food, or of treason. Jurists agree that they are not perfect either. Whatever is difficult with the McNaughton definition of legal insanity is difficult with all the corresponding rules of legal insanity used in all the other countries, despite the differences in form of these laws. This is true also of the law of the Soviet Union which tries to overcome these difficulties by combining the medical and juridical criteria of responsibility and which has a similarity to the Durham rule proposed by Judge Bazelon. They all aim to circumscribe the possibility that a mental disease impairs legal responsibility. The difficulty is to make psychiatric findings legally meaningful. The law deals with what should be and what should not be; it uses norms and authoritative standards. Psychiatry deals with what is and what is not and

uses scientific criteria to determine what is clinically significant.
The task is to translate psychiatric evidence into legal evidence,
clinical thinking into normative thinking.

It is true that judges sometimes interpret the rule too narrowly.
But other judges have kept up with the times and given excellent
charges to the jury. Unfortunately these have not been collected
and published. Most important—but much neglected—is the
liberal version formulated by Judge Cordozo, who stressed the
"relation to the mental health and true capacity of the criminal."

The McNaughton rule has opened avenues of defense and has
preserved many lives. For that reason alone, it should not be
totally rejected. It is a legal safeguard, not complete but potentially effective, against abuses of psychiatry and false insanity pleas.
Many other things should come first before a change in the definition can do any good whatsoever. Definitions do not initiate progress; they are the result of progress in real life.

The McNaughton rule was pronounced in England in 1843.
McNaughton was an insane man who shot the private secretary
of the Home Secretary, mistaking him for the Home Secretary
himself. He was found not guilty on the ground of insanity. Subsequently a panel of judges formulated the main issues of legal insanity. Its opinions constitute what is now called the McNaughton
rule. The most often repeated argument against it is that it is too
old and therefore of no use now. I heard the New York State
Commissioner of Mental Hygiene tell a legislative committee that
the McNaughton rule is an obsolete "antique" and that in 1843
no scientific psychiatry worth talking about existed. This is a widespread erroneous belief which the history of psychiatry does not
bear out.

The accumulation of clinical observations beginning long before
1843 helped psychiatry and the law to collaborate long ago, and
(contrary to some recent glib opinions) they have done so often
and well ever since. In 1844 three of the most important scientific
psychiatric journals began publication: the *Annales Médico-Psy-
chologiques,* in France; the *American Journal of Insanity,* in the
United States; and the *Allgemeine Zeitschrift für Psychiatrie,* in
Germany. The first modern textbook of psychiatry appeared in
1845. It contains basic and still valuable material. When William

H. Seward was preparing his insanity defense, he read several scientific psychiatric books, English, French, and American. Delirium tremens was well described, with case histories and clear differentiation from other forms of delirium, in 1813. The term and the description of kleptomania go back to 1838, syphilophobia to 1848, chronic alcoholism to 1851. The word and definition of "kindergarten," so important for psychiatric child guidance, date back to 1840. We pride ourselves on the modern individualization in psychiatry. But the first book devoted to a single psychiatric case (with still valid observations) was published in 1810 by John Haslam. And in the very year of the McNaughton rule a scientific paper appeared by the psychiatrist Griesinger "On Mental Reflex Reactions" which is an important direct forerunner of the most modern psychiatric conceptions.

In a book published in 1817, also by the psychiatrist John Haslam, *Medical Jurisprudence as It Relates to Insanity,* we can find truly modern ideas. For example, the psychiatrist "is not to palm on the court the trash of medical hypothesis as the apology for crime"; "the physician should not come into court merely to give his opinion—he should be prepared to explain it and able to afford the reasons which influenced his decision." This book also states: "It is sufficient for the medical practitioner to know that [the defendant's] mind is deranged, and that such state of insanity will be sufficient to account for the irregularity of his actions, and that in a sound mind the same conduct would be deemed criminal." This is almost the same as the recent Durham rule.

Of course, we know more today, but these examples are all part of the scientific foundation. They bear out that what was expressed in 1843 need not be discarded because it is old.

An editorial comment in the *Journal of the American Medical Association* stated recently: "The McNaghten rule bears little relationship to the data of modern psychology." We could say in the same way about the American Constitution that it bears little direct relationship to the data of modern physics. In fact the Constitution makes no reference at all to television, atomic energy, outer space, jets, or lasers. Yet that does not make it out of date or make it necessary to change it with each major scientific discovery. Similarly, we do not need new legal rules for the new scientific methods like psychoanalysis. The results of the new methods can be fully applied under the old rules. It is unhistorical to think that what is old is necessarily obsolete and what is new is necessarily beneficial. True, one generation builds on the previous one. But social achievements may be lost too. The time of the McNaughton rule was an era of progressing democracy and heightening social consciousness. Some of its humanism and social understanding seems to have gotten lost later on. In England this uneven development can be traced clearly. The Lunacy Act of 1845, practically contemporary with the McNaughton rule, was an enlightened step forward in the social understanding of mental disease. Compared with it, the Lunacy Act of 1890 was a retrogression. The Mental Health Act of 1959 is again a great step forward, with new aspirations and a rediscovery of humanitarian ideas.

One of the major objections to the McNaughton rule is the statement that knowledge of right and wrong is outside of psychiatry, that it is a moralistic problem. This entails misunderstanding of jurisprudence as well as of psychiatry. If it were merely a question of right and wrong no psychiatrist would ever have been called to a courtroom. The courts and judges can decide that question for themselves. In fact, that is what they are there for. Suppose a man passes a red light, kills somebody, and tells the court that he did not know it was wrong to pass the red light. Certainly the court will not call a psychiatrist to say whether the man knew right from wrong. He will be punished so that he will learn it. Writers, psychiatrists, and jurists again and again refer to the McNaughton rule as the "right and wrong test." But it is nothing of the kind. No judge is interested in having a psychiatrist tell him what is the court's own business. What the court in a given case may want to learn is whether a defendant suffers from a mental disease which in turn interferes with his capacities, *e.g.,* to have knowledge of right and wrong. That is something totally different. The McNaughton rule is not the "right and wrong test," but a mental-disease test. That constituted the advance over other laws, and that explains the rule's value.

In other words, whatever opinion a psychiatrist expresses about a crime must first of all be based on a strictly medical determination. The fact that the McNaughton rule is a mental-disease test is of the greatest importance practically. Forensic psychiatry often explains its failures by the assertion that the law does not permit it to put its best foot forward and prevents the presentation of modern scientific knowledge. That is a weak excuse. Often, especially in the case of poor, friendless, or racially discriminated defendants—and that is a considerable proportion of the persons charged with violent crime—these data have not been properly ascertained in the first place. In one large psychiatric clinic attached to a high court, the time allotted by psychiatric (not legal) routine for the examination of criminals, including murderers, was one-half hour, with return visits not permitted.

In none of the classic examples of miscarriages of justice in insanity cases, like Fish, Leonski, Irwin, Starkweather, Lavin, and Ezra Pound, did the limitations of the McNaughton rule have anything to do with the outcome of the case. Very different factors were at work. If the law permits—or rather demands—that a psychiatric opinion be based on the scientific determination of a mental disease, every step and method that led to such clinical diagnosis can be presented in court, provided it is not what lawyers call hearsay evidence. The psychiatrist must have obtained it himself or it must have been presented as factual evidence in the court. This is a fair—in fact, necessary—condition. I have presented in testimony and in reports findings obtained with the most modern methods: the Rorschach and mosaic tests, electroencephalographic findings, psychoanalytic study of the inner-life history, electrical skin-response tests. Even a cross-examination of the psychiatrist under the McNaughton rule, if it is not frivolous, is an aid to the establishment of the truth and a democratic safeguard.

The frequent claim that the law prevents the psychiatrist from bringing modern scientific knowledge into court is contradicted not only by the law itself but also by the explicit interpretation given by the courts. In the case of a man who killed his wife, the Mississippi State Supreme Court ruled in 1963: "Where the defense is insanity the door is thrown wide open for the admission of evidence; every act of the party's life is relevant to the issue and admissible in evidence . . . the court should be very liberal in allowing the introduction of any and all evidence which tends to show the sanity or insanity of the accused." If a defendant in a violent crime has an experienced criminal lawyer to defend him—which is frequently not the case—the psychiatrist will have no difficulty presenting all relevant scientific data to the court. The Supreme Court of Illinois said in a murder case in September, 1953: "Where sanity is the subject of inquiry, broad boundaries of relevance are the rule. . . . This has come to be in part because of our lack of full knowledge of the many and varied forms of mental incapacity, their causes and their manifestations, and in part because . . . any circumstance in the life of the subject of the inquiry tends, in some degree at least, to prove either sanity or insanity . . . in determining insanity it is not feasible to limit the evidence to strictly contemporaneous observations of the subject, and the remoteness in time of an adjudication or an examination or of other evidence of insanity goes to the weight of the evidence rather than its competence." What more leeway can a psychiatrist ask for, under any legal rule?

The Federal Court of Appeals, Tenth Circuit, stated in 1963, in a case of attempted murder with an explosive, that the law "allows the behavioral scientists full freedom to put their professional findings and conclusions before the court and jury." The Court of Appeals of New York ruled in a murder case in 1952 that it is "essential that the jury should be informed as to the facts on which the expert based his conclusions. . . . If he rests his answers on facts and knowledge he has acquired himself, he must impart them to the jury." And the official rules of evidence (*American Jur. Evidence*) quoted by the Colorado State Supreme Court in a murder case in 1963 states: "Considerable latitude is allowed by the courts in admitting evidence which has a tendency to throw light on the mental condition of the defendant at the time of the commission of the crime, provided the proof tends to prove or disprove the issue involved. Every act of the defendant's life relevant to the issue is admissible in evidence when the sanity of the defendant is involved, to go into an inquiry concerning the mental condition of the defendant both before and after the commission of the act, provided the inquiry bears such relation to the person's condition of mind at the time of the crime as to be worthy of consideration in respect thereto." How often does it happen that psychiatrists are fully prepared to avail themselves of this opportunity in cases of violent crime?

The objection that the question concerning knowledge of right and wrong is unscientific and "nonmedical" is contradicted by the facts of psychiatry. The problem of knowing right and wrong comes up and has to be faced in patients in whom no question of legal insanity is involved. Wrong is not wrong because it is forbidden; it is forbidden because it is wrong. It is really primitive to think that modern psychopathology can dispense with that part of man's development that has to do with other people. One of its essential points is not to hurt anybody. The sense of right and wrong may be disturbed in many ways by objective social influence or by disease. As psychotherapists, we must pay serious attention to it, whether we call it ideal ego, superego, or conscience. Knowledge of right and wrong is not a mechanical knowledge of the same type as knowing that two plus two equals four. It involves the deepest layers of the personality and the highest functions of the human mind. That is why the inclusion of knowledge of right and wrong in the rule is not incongruous. It refers to a delicate part of the human mind that can easily be disordered. That is not moralistic but scientific. In the Rorschach test, individuals with good intelligence may show unreliable and inconsistent judgment in certain areas. There may be an absence of guiding principles and an indifference to standards of social behavior. Superficial conventionality may provide what is really only a pseudocontrol. If we translate this into a real-life situation, it would involve an inability to discern right from wrong.

If a psychotic person commits a violent crime, the clinical findings are all-important. For example, the diagnosis of general paresis (dementia paralytica) can be objectively established by psychiatric, neurological, serological, and psychological test findings. A person suffering from this brain disease, whatever answers he may give to a district attorney about what is forbidden, does not know the difference between right and wrong in the sense of the McNaughton rule. If his brain has been so seriously affected, he is not able to view and master the entire situation. I consider this a paradigm of all reasoning about legal insanity. It is the more important because with modern methods, some of these patients can be completely cured. This can also be established by objective methods, and they are then to be regarded as fully responsible. Vagueness is not inherent in psychiatry, though it sometimes is in psychiatrists.

If a person suffers from definite unshakable delusions, that is not an isolated symptom leaving his ethical orientation untouched. He does not have a free survey of the world because of his mental disease. He may be operating under a standard of morality all his own. The question is not whether he knew what is right in the abstract, but whether he thought that the act was right for him and right for him at the time. For example, if a psychotic person like Albert Fish has the delusion that his killing of a child is divinely sanctioned as a human sacrifice and that if it were not all right an angel would have stopped him, then because of his disease he does not know, in the sense of the McNaughton rule, that the act is wrong. That is the law, and that is psychiatry. It is up to us to see that the one is followed and the other practiced.

The question "Does the defendant know right from wrong?" (or, "Does he know the nature and quality of the act?") addressed to the psychiatrist divides itself into three phases:

1. Does he know right from wrong? That requires a conclusion.
2. Does he have the *capacity* to know right from wrong? That requires an evaluation.
3. Does he have the biological and psychological *foundation* to have the capacity to know right from wrong? That requires the definite demonstration of facts—namely, the symptoms of a disease and the diagnosis of a disease process.

If a person suffers from general paresis or a severe form of schizophrenia or a pronounced degree of mental deficiency or a clear catathymic crisis, he does not have the foundation to have the capacity to have the knowledge to know right from wrong in the sense of the statute. This is the extent and the limitation of psychiatric testimony. It applies equally to all other modern definitions of legal insanity.

Other criticisms of the McNaughton rule, emanating from desks rather than from clinical study or social life as it really is, are also without practical merit at present. With considerable monotony, writings on criminology and forensic psychiatry repeat that the rule provides purely intellectual criteria and "ignores completely the importance of emotional factors." Or it is deplored that the law fails "to measure emotional deviations." These objections do not take into account modern psychopathological views. The distinction between right and wrong is *not* a purely intellectual performance, but affects the whole personality and has definite and important emotional components. It is a kind of knowledge which, to use Cardinal Newman's term, is not merely "notional," but has to be really felt. So the rule inherently does include emotion and affect.

Every severe mental disease inevitably affects the emotional life of the person. The law allows the psychiatrist today all the proof of the diagnosis and degree of a mental disease before the court. According to scientific psychiatry, that includes necessarily the emotional part of the personality. If the law singles out one criterion for its own purposes, that does not mean that the psychiatrist has to seal off that aspect from the rest of the affected personality. A mental symptom is not something self-contained that is either added to or subtracted from an otherwise normal mind. It is a sign of a disordered mental life. No person can suffer just from delusions, hallucinations, or a severe memory defect and be otherwise perfectly intact mentally. The emphasis of the McNaughton rule is on the concept "mental disease." That opens the door wide for the utilization of psychiatric knowledge. We have no legal definitions of different diseases, but only medical-psychiatric ones. The law can ask the psychiatrist to express an opinion about the effects of a cold; it cannot express in legal terms what a cold is. That is the hurdle between psychiatry and law that has to be cleared. No definition of legal insanity can just abolish it.

Not only the absence of specific reference to emotion has been criticized in the law, but also the absence of reference to volition. We are told that a person may know all that the law postulates and still cannot conform his actions to his knowledge. It sounds like a compelling argument. However, it leaves out the modern theory of learning and adaptation. As the psychologist Gardner Murphy expresses it, "To adapt, one must act." In the clinical psychiatric view, knowledge and practice cannot be rigidly and mechanically separated, especially not in a severely disordered person. They are interconnected. In epidemic encephalitis, a brain disease attacking chiefly juveniles, the main symptom may be a disorder of volition. The patients with postencephalitic behavior disorder cannot control their impulses sufficiently. They are driven to overactivity which may lead them to destructive actions. Even cases of murder have been observed. But this disorder of impulse control and volition also is not isolated. It affects the whole personality, including ethical understanding and insight. The essence of the law is that a person is considered not responsible if, because of disease, he cannot act as a free agent. In the words of a leading legal scholar, Professor G. O. W. Mueller, "the power to control one's behavior should be regarded as an ingredient of rational action, not as something additional."

If a person is mentally so ill that he cannot prevent himself from murdering somebody, then the highest function of the personality, the discernment of right and wrong, is also affected. Full knowledge and understanding of an ethical issue in relation to oneself includes a volitional element. So the rule needs no special addition about volition. In those jurisdictions where a clause has been added about inability to make one's actions conform to legal and ethical requirements (which in essence is no more than a restatement of the irresistible-impulse doctrine), it has not proved of advantage in practice. "To conform one's conduct" has been suggested as an addition to the original formula. It is as if we found it necessary to amend the command "Thou shalt not covet thy neighbor's wife" to read "Thou shalt not covet thy neighbor's wife and shalt conform thy conduct to not coveting her."

But, ask critics of the McNaughton rule, does not the rule imply a rigid, either-or attitude? They claim that psychiatry can never express an opinion that a man is *either* responsible *or* not responsible, healthy or sick, and that there is only a continuous gradation of various shades of gray. But the difference between normal and abnormal, sanity and psychosis, is not purely quantitative; it is primarily a qualitative difference. We can clinically demonstrate and document it. Only by recognizing these qualitative distinctions can psychiatry be fully integrated into social action.

Diminished responsibility, although not usually formulated specifically in so many words in the law, is in actual practice constantly in use in criminal legal procedures. A criminal because of mitigating circumstances, of which a mental and emotional disorder short of insanity is one, may be permitted to make a plea to a lesser crime. This concept of diminished responsibility, although the term may not be applied, is in use much more often than the McNaughton rule. That is another reason why the McNaughton rule is not a suitable scapegoat for the deficiences in the legal handling of violent crime.

Those who demand that the McNaughton rule be abolished overlook the fact that it is not an absolute axiom, but is a guiding line that is elastic and can be extended in the different courts. Naturally the law has drawbacks. That is due not to the wording of the rule but to the very nature of the object matter and the socio-historical conditions under which it has to operate. Eventually, as society develops, it should and could be changed, but not in isolation all by itself. Attempting mere reformulations now without taking account of the social context is misleading. The time is not ripe for fundamental changes in the terminology of the law. Before real progress can be accomplished, serious obstacles to reform in the general social setting will have to be overcome. As long as the present-day conflicts and contradictions of our society continue in their current forms, laws like this will exist. Being has to come before wording, reform before formulation.

None of the present shortcomings is remedied by any of the proposed changes. Commenting on recent proposals, an editorial in *The New York Times* says: "We are finally beginning to realize that when we say 'insane' what we really mean is 'mentally ill.'" That was covered by the original rule of 1843.

Typical is the new law that was enacted in New York in 1965. It introduces the phrase "substantial capacity"—as if that were any better than just plain "capacity." For "to know" it substitutes "to know and to appreciate." That is no clarification. "To know" in the rule evidently does not refer to a superficial, elementary impression; it means real knowing and does not need any further tautological addition. According to modern understanding, the term "to know" should be meant here in the widest possible sense. As the Spanish philosopher Ortega y Gasset expressed it, "To know is to know what to hold oneself to" *(Saber es saber a que atenerse)*. This has also been aptly translated as "To know is to know how to act."

Instead of the "nature and quality of the act," the recent New York law says the "nature and consequence." This despite the fact that in the original formula, knowledge of the nature and quality of the act of course implicitly includes the consequences. If you know the nature of the act of pulling the trigger of a gun, you know the consequences if somebody is hit by your bullet. These utterly insignificant verbal changes were made without any adequate new clinical studies of actual cases. Similar modifications, also without fresh clinical research, were announced in 1966 by the U.S. Court of Appeals for the Second Circuit (embracing New York, Connecticut, and Vermont). Such patchwork on the McNaughton rules does not solve any of the concrete problems. This decision of a high court is partly based on a widespread misconception about clinical psychiatry. It states that "from the perspective of psychiatry . . . gradations are inevitable." But scientifically there are qualitative distinctions. For example, a person either has general paresis (dementia paralytica) or not. He cannot suffer from a gradation in between, just as a woman cannot be a little pregnant. Our general orientation should come from the clear cases, not the unclear ones.

Two alternatives to the McNaughton rule have been much written about. The irresistible-impulse doctrine, according to Dean Roscoe Pound, was developed largely as a method by which a jury might let off an offender who was guilty of the act but with whom the community sympathized. That more or less circumscribes its usefulness.

The Durham rule, suggested by Judge David Bazelon, is a serious attempt to replace the McNaughton rule which has led to fruitful discussions. This test requires that the plea of legal insanity must be based on the demonstration that the crime was the "product" of a mental disease. But this global formulation does not guide the jury sufficiently as to the degree of mental disease and gives too much leeway to the partisan or bureaucratic expert.

Why have the McNaughton rules lasted so long? Sir Norwood

East, an experienced forensic psychiatrist, has given a clear answer: "The rules are retained because no one has improved upon them in a manner which leaves the issue clear to the jury." And the basic issue, in my clinical-legal experience, is this: Does the person *have the capacity to act as a free agent with knowledge of the relevant facts, or is he prevented by disease?*

In the handling of abnormal persons who commit violent acts, the discrepancy is too great between what the books and journals say and what really happens. "We must make sure," in the words of Senator Dodd of the U.S. Senate Judiciary Committee, "that we do not attack the law when the deficiency may be elsewhere." The fact is that there are many violence-prone persons who are allowed by the authorities to drift in a social twilight between crime and disease. The deficiencies manifest themselves mainly in three areas:

1. Procedures
2. Within jurisprudence
3. Within psychiatry

## Procedures

In the late fifties a young man walked one night into a still-open delicatessen store. When the clerk turned his back to get the two items requested, he was shot three times and fell mortally wounded, crying out, "I am dying! I am dying!" The young man replied, "You are dead!" He took money from the till and departed. A few days later he entered a diner, shot the counterman in the head, again took what money he could find, and left. Only two nights later he entered still another diner, ordered fried eggs, then followed the waitress into the kitchen, tied her hand and foot, shot her in the head, took the money from the cash register, and drove away. The case was soon solved, for he told a companion from whom he bought a gun after the first two murders that he had killed two people. This companion told the police, and the twenty-seven-year-old murderer was arrested. He confessed at once.

Such behavior seems like lightning out of a clear sky to the public who hears of it first over radio or from the papers. But that is hardly ever the case. The victims, it is true, had no warning. But the community had ample warning before these events happened. Frank Bloeth was obviously a sick man who seriously needed care. He talked about killing as he would about swatting mosquitoes. "I would have killed more," he remarked, "but I ran out of ammunition." As a teenager he strangled some nine cats because he did not like the way they acted. He also killed a dog. As a young man he broke into an apartment and struck a woman on the head with a claw hammer. On another occasion he burglarized a house and stabbed a man. Once after a minor automobile accident, he assaulted the other motorist. He tried forcibly to rape a girl whom he had taken to a deserted place in his car. He threatened people with his revolver. Yet in revealing contrast to all this, he was a devoted husband and an exceptionally attentive and gentle father to his nine-month-old daughter. "I wouldn't shoot my wife, my mother, or my daughter," he said. But these were apparently the only exceptions he would make.

What procedures did society apply to him, and how were they coordinated? Bloeth had a taste of practically all of them. He was in children's courts, was sent several times to reformatories, was in jail, on parole, on probation. He was given suspended sentences; a short jail sentence, which he apparently never served; was examined for army service and rejected because of his behavior. He underwent eight different psychiatric examinations in clinics, institutions, and psychiatric hospitals. He never received proper psychotherapy. (That might well have prevented the later murders.) He got psychiatry without psychiatry. And instead of being coordinated, all the different procedures were applied in isolation, some of them contradicting one another. If a man is so often in the hands of the authorities and under the care of psychiatrists in hospitals and clinics and then commits a violent act, is not his responsibility diminished and our responsibility increased?

This is a typical example of the lack of integration of psychiatric, legal, penal, and administrative agencies in the previolence phase. It is paralleled by what happens in the postviolence phase, when defendants are shuttled back and forth among psychiatric city (or county) hospitals, institutions for the criminally insane, and jails, only to be released later without treatment or supervision. Recently I saw a man who had been implicated in the murder of a policeman. He had just been released after many years in an institution for the criminally insane. He was dressed in an ill-fitting suit, had absolutely no money, had no relatives or friends, had no training, felt bewildered by ordinary social life, and, of course, had not seen a girl for years and was sexually and socially confused. If he should commit a violent crime for sexual or monetary reasons, we have no right to be astonished.

Clarification of procedures and rules is greatly needed. It is, for instance, not clear—and is decided differently in different courts of the same jurisdiction—whether at different stages of the proceedings, the court has the power to commit an offender to a public hospital for observation even if either the defense counsel or the district attorney objects. Few lawyers can know what rights their clients have under such circumstances. Sometimes the district attorney, immediately upon the accused's arrest for murder, has the prisoner examined by psychiatrists whose opinions unfortunately can often be predicted. The procedures with regard to the right to psychiatric examination by an independent expert vary greatly and for no discernible compelling reason. Sometimes, especially in cases with much publicity, judges permit the defense to have a private psychiatrist, to be paid by the state; in other cases, they refuse it.

Great unclearness reigns about the questions whether, when, and under what circumstances psychiatric testimony aside from the assertion of insanity is admissible. Judges in the same court may make diametrically different decisions about this. But testimony about a defendant's mental condition may be most significant for a jury, even if it does not spell legal insanity. In two murder cases (that of the Trenton Six and the case of John Pfeffer), I have been permitted to testify about a prisoner's state of mind at the time of a confession and to express an opinion as to whether the confession was voluntary. (In both cases, it was not.) In other instances, such testimony was ruled inadmissible.

With regard to the medical-psychiatric methods admissible in criminal cases, there is considerable uncertainty. The American

Law Institute advocates that "any method may be employed which is accepted by the medical profession for the examination of those thought to be suffering from mental disease." But from my experience in psychiatric prison wards and court clinics, I side with those who object to the use in this field of some methods which may be useful in other medical practice, such as narcoanalysis (so-called truth serum), the "lie detector," and hypnosis. Whatever value they may have in civil practice, in the forensic field these methods are too unreliable and come too close to a third degree.

## Jurisprudence

Quite apart from the problems of collaboration with psychiatry, there are difficulties within the administration of criminal law as far as violent crime is concerned. According to the American Bar Association, of the some 300,000 persons charged with serious crimes in the state courts every year, at least half cannot afford to engage a lawyer in their defense. The statement that court-appointed lawyers are as effective as privately engaged ones is as true as that in our social setting a psychiatrist in a public clinic is the same as a privately engaged one. I have known devoted public practitioners in both professions; but as between public and private facilities, time, opportunity, and standing are vastly different.

In addition, the best efforts of the law in general are directed much more to civil than to criminal cases. The Chief Judge of the U.S. Court of Appeals for the circuit embracing New York, Connecticut, and Vermont, J. Edward Lumbard, expressed this very clearly recently: "There has never been a time when our bar and our bench were better trained and more expert in civil matters— yet never a time when the level of professional effort in the criminal courts was at a lower ebb."

By and large, the legal profession has at present an open mind with regard to psychiatry. But two extreme attitudes disturb that picture. Some archconservative jurists think that all psychiatry is unreliable and that psychiatrists can only guess. At the other pole are jurists who act as if a psychiatrist were looking over their shoulder. They are apt to accept some of the most speculative psychiatric claims and are afraid that otherwise they may not be considered sophisticated enough.

The most serious and far-reaching legal deficiency is the handling of psychiatric-legal cases without any determination of legal insanity according to strict criteria. This covers really the vast majority of such cases. Only one-half of 1 percent of the inmates in the New York State Institution for the Criminally Insane at Matteawan are there after being found "not guilty by reason of insanity." In other words, most cases were settled (or not settled, to be more precise) without any legal-insanity ruling.

In New York City, 90 to 95 percent of psychiatric-legal cases are handled through the code of criminal procedure in the pretrial action (without the McNaughton rule coming up at all). What the psychiatrist is asked to determine is formulated somewhat differently in different jurisdictions: Can the defendant understand the charges against him? Can he assist in his defense? Is he fit to plead? Is he capable of advising and assisting his counsel? Is he able to stand trial? Can he comprehend his position? Can he intelligently consult with counsel? Can he plan his own defense? Is he competent to understand the charges against him? Can he confer with counsel? These formulas may have a legitimate use in a number of cases, but their routine use is very detrimental to the settling of violent crime. The result is that many cases are not handled scientifically but administratively, not democratically but bureaucratically. The whole procedure lends itself to an assembly-line psychiatry—which, indeed, is widely practiced. The mistake in handling such cases starts right at the beginning. The defendants are sent to an institution, and any real decision is indefinitely postponed, often for years. As a result, many of these cases are never fully cleared up. The question of responsibility at the time of the crime and later should be decided right away. Theoretically these persons come to trial later, when they have recovered. That does happen in some cases. But many are never settled properly, for, understandably, many district attorneys and courts are not eager to try a man after a long stay in a mental hospital (during which time evidence and witnesses may have disappeared).

## Psychiatry

In the field of forensic psychiatry, there is a dearth of scientifically well-studied clinical cases with careful follow-up studies. This has affected both practice and theory. Sometimes too much reliance is put on an isolated test or laboratory finding, such as the electroencephalogram, which is never the whole diagnosis but merely an aid to clinical diagnosis. Such unclinical thinking is an obstacle to the constructive use of forensic psychiatry.

Especially in the important field of borderline conditions, a great unclearness reigns at present. For example, on one page of the official *Diagnostic and Statistical Manual: Mental Disorders,* which is binding for all clinic and hospital psychiatrists, the psychiatrist is supposed to be able to distinguish these diagnostic terms: "sociopathic," "antisocial," "dyssocial," "pseudosocial," "asocial." This is clearly a terminology of confusion. It is not a scientific way to aid the safety of the community. The much-used and ill-defined term "sociopathic personality" is an unclear, unfortunate term and lends itself to much bias. A poor sociopathic personality is sociopathic; a rich sociopathic personality is rich.

The term "antisocial" is often used indiscriminately in psychopathological diagnoses. "Now, in simple terms," a judge said to a psychiatrist in court, "antisocial personality—doesn't that mean he is a crook?" A typical case is a seriously abnormal and obviously not responsible young man who had killed his common-law wife. He was diagnosed by a psychiatrist as "beyond any doubt a psychopathic personality with amoral and antisocial traits." It was not accidental, but indicative of subtle prejudice, that this man was a Negro. He was convicted of murder in the first degree.

Also in the *Diagnostic and Statistical Manual* there appears the official diagnosis "Antisocial reaction with psychotic reaction." This awkward and unclinical label, replacing the previous diagnostic term "Psychosis with psychopathic personality," is an example of the misuse of "antisocial." It is supposed to cover a condition which is so frequent that more than a quarter of the inmates of the New York State Institution for the Criminally Insane at Matteawan fall under it. Yet this newfangled term, which was also introduced by fiat without any new clinical research, is highly misleading. The psychiatrist may be in court trying to explain that a certain violent act was the manifestation of a mental disease and not an antisocial act—and find himself restricted by this official designation.

Another much-used new diagnostic term is both evidence and cause of much confusion: "passive-aggressive personality." Though it may sound impressive, it is imprecise. In the official *Diagnostic and Statistical Manual* it has no less than three subdivisions, the third having again two subdivisions of its own! Nobody can possibly make these diagnoses with any degree of clearness. In practice, this leads to dangerous absurdity. For example, a man entered a house where two girls, aged nine and twelve, were asleep alone. He struck them both with a sledgehammer. One died. The other he took unconscious in his car, raped her, and dropped her, still living, into a drainage ditch, where she drowned. A defense psychiatrist testified that the diagnosis was "passive-aggressive personality, aggressive type" and that the accused did not intend to strike, kill, or sexually molest these victims. He was supposed to have indicated that under hypnosis. The psychiatrist defined "passive-aggressive personality" as one who "tends to be irritable, short-tempered, at times given to temper tantrums. He tends sometimes to harbor resentments to a pathological degree." The enormity of the crime disappears under these superficial, almost flippant-sounding explanations. If this were the best that psychiatry can do in such a crime, it would have no business in a courtroom and would be no help in either the understanding or the prevention of wanton violence. Evidently in the official delineation and classification of these borderline conditions, a far-reaching reform is necessary which must be based on the best traditions of clinical research.

A subject that has been left in considerable twilight in forensic psychiatry is that of simulation of major mental disease. We have not a single scientific psychiatric treatise about it based on modern methods. This is the more noteworthy since there are not many murder trials with an insanity defense in which some juror, district attorney, judge, lawyer, or spectator in the courtroom does not have a fleeting doubt about whether the mental disease may be faked or put on.

Such suspicions have done great harm in the case of genuinely diseased persons who have been sent to jail or even executed. On the other hand, the unclearness in which the whole subject is left has made it easier for cunning criminals to deceive.

A number of facile generalizations abound. One is that simulation, especially successful simulation, is exceedingly rare. Another is that "pure malingering" or "hundred percent malingerers" hardly exist. The idea is that if a man wants to make believe that he is insane, there must have been something very pathological in him in the first place. This is more a literary idea than a scientific one. Leonid Andreev, in his short story "Thought" (also translated as "A Dilemma"), has described a case where a murderer very cleverly simulates insanity but later is as divided in his own mind about it as the four psychiatrists who testify at his trial. To assume that every malingerer of mental disease must have something wrong with him anyhow betrays a lack of understanding of the criminal mind. Simulation is imposture. The key word for its understanding is the word "deliberate." A criminal facing severe punishment grasps at every straw. The simulation of a psychosis is especially important in crimes of violence for which the defendant faces the death penalty or a long jail term. Simulation in a murder case is a desperate deception.

Psychopathological and psychoanalytic generalizations about the "average simulator" do not correspond to life. Simulators have learned. Often a fellow prisoner, especially one who himself has been under psychiatric observation in a hospital, tells a man in jail how to behave so as to be sent to a psychiatric ward and how to act when he gets there. Sometimes a successful simulator instructs others even to the extent that he supplies the replies that should be given on intelligence or Rorschach tests.

Over the years in my research on the subject, I have collected a large number of cases of simulation, like that of Martin Lavin, including some in which follow-up studies of ten or more years proved the diagnosis. The diagnosis of simulation, or absence of simulation, is not always easy. It requires not only a careful examination, including a variety of modern tests, but, in addition to this cross section, a longitudinal study of the person's life. For scientific studies, it is particularly important to carry out follow-up studies, to see whether there was any genuine abnormality later on. When psychiatrists who have had contact with many criminals say flatly that they have never seen a successful simulator, that indicates just what is wrong. For simulation of a psychosis in order to evade punishment is at present not rare.

Collaboration of law and psychiatry does not require relaxation of due process by the law or of close scientific thinking by psychiatry. The more detailed and painstaking the psychiatric examination and the more clear-cut the diagnosis, the more possible will it be to fit clinical findings and judgment into legal categories required in a particular court. The psychiatrist should function not as an opinion pronouncer but as a fact finder. He elicits, evaluates, and presents information which otherwise would remain unconsidered. To throw at the court a vast generalization, such as that people act from motives of which they may not be conscious, is not enough. Recently a young man in Nebraska killed three persons, two men and a woman, during a bank robbery. A defense psychiatrist testified that he "had an uncontrollable impulse to kill that came from deep within his unconscious." If such a statement is not connected with concrete, verifiable facts, it only makes the jungle of legal insanity more impenetrable. It is necessary to unearth facts and connections between facts from which such an inference could be drawn. Only in this way can we explain and demonstrate the short circuits in the minds of people with genuine mental disease.

A distinction must be made between psychiatric expert opinions and full scientific investigations of the causes of violent crime. A part of the causes and conditions that lead to violence can be understood from the data and reasoning of psychopathology. But the category health-or-disease cannot cover the whole field. It shows a lack of understanding of violence as well as of psychiatry to think that psychiatry alone can be the whole answer. To explain human behavior without psychology is futile; to explain it with psychology alone means to be evasive of the social context. Even if a murderer is psychotic, his deed is not completely explained by his insanity— the social medium has a lot to do with it. In political murders, that is important. Whatever the mental condition of Oswald may have been, the social atmosphere of hate and violence enters into the total picture. That is the greatest challenge to violence prevention today.

CHAPTER TWELVE

# "Tired of Home, Sick of School, and Bored with Life"

## THE RISE OF JUVENILE VIOLENCE

Our children will be our judges.
—FRIEDRICH FROEBEL
(who organized the first
kindergarten)

A BOY of thirteen was walking home from school in a suburban area. A short distance from the house, a car roared up and several boys jumped out. They attacked and beat him unmercifully. Then they jumped back into the car and roared away. Their victim was taken to the hospital with severe facial lacerations and concussion of the brain. He did not know his attackers and had never seen them before.

A boy of nine and his seven-year-old sister were going home from church one evening. They were approached and stopped by a boy of nine and his eight-year-old girl companion. Each child in the holdup couple pressed a knife against the throat of his victim and demanded all his money.

A fourteen-year-old boy entered a small grocery store early one evening. He asked the woman who ran the store for a candy bar and offered her a dollar bill. When she reached for it, he flipped open a switchblade knife, held it at her throat, and said, "This is a holdup!" When he was asked about this later, he replied with utter sincerity, "I am tired of home, sick of school, and bored with life."

These are recent samples of the juvenile violence of our time. Here is an area where the Goddess of Violence, whom we have installed to rule, exerts her most insidious and entrapping influence: she makes the children officiate at her services. Juvenile violence is added to that of their elders.

It is necessary to distinguish between ordinary delinquency and acts of violence. Almost two decades ago, observing the trend during my clinical work, I predicted that more and more brutal violence would be committed by younger and younger age groups. This was met with disbelief. Today it is common knowledge among those dealing professionally with these problems. Even the police look for children in some murder cases, when formerly they would not have dreamed of doing so.

The present-day social significance of the famous Leopold-Loeb case is that while in those days it was unheard of for an eighteen-year-old boy to commit such a murder, in contemporary America murder by much younger youths has become commonplace. Clarence Darrow, a keen observer of the social scene, built his defense of Leopold and Loeb on their youth, and it was on that alone, not the flimsy psychiatric evidence, that the judge spared them the extreme penalty. In 1962 in New York City alone, there were twenty-nine youths under sixteen who committed murder. The youngest was a boy of eight, who murdered a little girl of four after sexually abusing her. Murder committed by children under fourteen is not a rarity. Today it is not uncommon to see deliberate murder committed by children of twelve or thirteen or even younger. Children of eight or nine are found torturing one another or committing serious acts of sadism. Childhood murders have become so frequent that they no longer make headlines, while nonlethal but nonetheless serious injuries by children are often not even reported. Many such cases (even serious ones) do not get into statistics. One reason is that they are hushed up, especially when the youths involved belong to more affluent social strata.

One can, of course, close one's eyes to the trend of increasing and ever more brutal youthful violence. Everyone is familiar with the cliché that juvenile violence has always been with us, that it has always been the same, that kids were always wild and destructive, that the newspapers now report it more and overestimate it, and so on. The only kernel of truth in all this is that juvenile gang warfare is greatly exaggerated in relation to other forms of violent delinquency. In reality, the trend of increase is very significant. A boy who commits one of these serious acts today has to be considered far less "sick" or individually disturbed than would have been the case twenty-five years ago.

This is the point where psychiatry has to be supplemented by psychiatric sociology. We have to consider the whole cultural atmosphere of violence in which American children are growing up today. In this connection, it is noteworthy also that in European countries, murders by children under fourteen are extremely rare. In both incidence and gravity, violent crimes by children and juveniles are very much fewer in London than in New York, Chicago, or other major U.S. cities. The child psychiatrist Dr. Lauretta Bender has pointed out that one of the warning signals in cases of child murders between five and fifteen was excessive fire setting. We may note that serious forms of fire setting also are less frequent in Europe.

Statistics of violent crime go back a long time. One of the earliest modern compilations was made by Henry Fielding, whose novel *Tom Jones* exposed hypocrisy and brutality. He was not only a writer but also a lawyer and city magistrate in London. In 1753, when there was a particularly great rise in violent crimes in London, he set up an office of criminal records which survives today in Scotland Yard. Statistics of crime are notoriously hard to use, but carefully used they give us valuable hints. In the early 1960's almost one-tenth of all murders were committed by youths under eighteen, as were almost one-fifth of all forcible rapes. This is a considerable increase over previous years and a more rapid increase than the population growth in the age group of ten to seventeen. In some states, no fingerprints are taken of youths under the age of sixteen and no record is kept of the nature of their offense. They may be adjudged delinquent without the court record supplying and classifying the delinquent act. So the verdict "juvenile delinquency" may cover anything from minor transgressions to murder. This is one of the points which illustrates well the difficulty of our society in dealing with the problem juridically, administratively, and correctionally. We have no national statistics about the number of children under fourteen who commit murder. We know that the number is considerable. Even murder by boys eleven years old is not unheard of any more.

For any understanding and action, it is necessary to distinguish between child and adolescent. Actually this line may be clearer than the one between adolescence and maturity.

That juvenile offenders have to be treated differently by society from adult offenders has been recognized for a long time. In 1841 Judge Matthew Davenport Hill introduced in Birmingham, England, suspended sentences for juveniles on a large scale. He combined this with what we would now call social-service measures. The results were very good. After thirteen years, four-fifths of the youths had not become recidivists. Despite this long history, the age at which a person is to be regarded as a juvenile in the juridical sense varies greatly and is fixed arbitrarily in different jurisdictions. The problem has been found most vexing in serious acts of violence. The differences in different countries with regard to the age limit of legal responsibility are impressive and revealing. The age varies from twenty, eighteen (in twenty-one American states), seventeen, sixteen to twelve. In 1965 the Assembly of the state of New Jersey passed a bill that would make it possible for a child of seven to be tried for murder.

The problem of violence committed by youths has changed from what it was twenty or twenty-five years ago. These qualitative changes are important. General books on juvenile delinquency are usually far behind and do not describe concretely what actually happens. If we do not know what these youths are doing, there is not much use in speculating about why they do it or how we can prevent it. The fact is that not only have violent acts become more frequent and carried out by ever younger children, they have become more brutal, more cruel, more ferocious. That is true even of murders. "Rooftop murders," in which boys of fifteen or sixteen throw younger girls from the roof of tall buildings, are not uncommon any more in forensic psychiatric practice.

Vandalism has become more extensive and more heedless of injury or even death to victims. In New York City, vandalism in the city schools causes damage of $5,000,000 a year, including 187,000 broken windowpanes. An eyewitness, a teacher, described what is

done to cars in some sections of New York: "The children attack
an automobile—literally *attack* it, as locusts attack a field. They
climb on top of it, get inside, and by combined cooperative effort
shake and tug until they leave it a wreck." Stripping the tires from
the car to sell them is a by-product. In California, boys of fifteen de-
railed a train by ingenious interference with the signaling system.
Eleven passengers were injured. The explanation the boys gave was
that they "wanted some excitement." Similar attempts were made in
other places. In New York a car plunged into the river, with the
result that eleven persons drowned. It was found that in different
parts of the city, youths had smashed red warning signals in
waterfront dead-end streets. When the city replaced these signs after
this accident, many were destroyed again, indicating the callousness about human life in the young vandals. Some juvenile violence
is tinged with alcohol, which is an important feature. When the
studio of Andrew Wyeth, one of the most renowned modern American painters, was vandalized and wrecked by youths, beer bottles
were strewn all over the place. The painter said later, "I don't
think that this act of vandalism was directed at me personally. It
was just an act of violence of some young people getting together."
It was a typical violent, impersonal "togetherness." Even in pros-
perous suburbs, children as young as eight have committed serious
acts of vandalism.

Random sniping has recently assumed almost epidemic character in different parts of the country. Often by sheer luck it has
had no serious results, but often it has. In New York an eleven-
year-old boy was wounded by a sixteen-year-old one who was
practicing target shooting from his family's fifth-floor apartment.
A twenty-six-year-old secretary was shot and killed by a bullet
from a .22-caliber rifle as she sat combing her hair in front of a
vanity in her furnished room. She had come to New York from
a small town only two months before, "to see what living in a big
city is like." Previously there had been complaints of shots being
fired at trains. The police picked up eleven rifles from youths in
the neighborhood. Indicating the atmosphere of fear these acts
create, the adults on the street are keeping the blinds drawn in
their rear windows. A sixteen-year-old student set up a sniper's nest
in a football stadium and fired some fifteen shots from a rifle into

a group of young girls doing gymnastics. After parties, boys have been riding up and down streets shooting at innocent bystanders. And innocent bystanders, including women, have been injured that way.

There have been many cases where boys fifteen and under have accidentally shot other boys. Most of these cases are genuine mishaps; but in some of them, closer study reveals that the accidents were not so accidental. An entirely new feature is the wanton shooting of animals in rural sections of the country. Boys go out at night to shoot at cows and calves in the fields, killing them or sometimes letting them lie there wounded.

A special form of wild shooting is directed at passing trains and automobiles, sometimes by boys as young as thirteen or fourteen. At midday on a crack train en route from Washington to New York, a bullet fired through the window struck a passenger in the head. He was a married man, father of a child. He was seriously wounded. On Long Island in New York, a two-mile stretch of a six-lane expressway running through a wooded area had to be closed for several hours because the cars were being fired at. Two drivers were wounded, and six cars, including a school bus, were hit. Two boys aged fourteen and fifteen were arrested. They had shot with a .22-caliber rifle "at anything that moved." Some children use BB guns in a similar way.

Incidents of stone throwing at trains and automobiles are increasing. A woman of sixty was killed by a stone that shattered the window of the train she was traveling in. Two schoolboys in their early teens were held responsible. Even after their arrest, stone throwing at commuter trains in the region continued, with windows being broken. One driver on a turnpike was struck and lost his right eye. Spring weather brings on an increase in stone throwing at trains. In one month recently, along an eight-mile stretch of one railway line, twenty-six trains were stoned. In different regions there have been many injuries to passengers and trainmen. In one incident, four juveniles were arrested for breaking eleven windows in one train. The vice-president of one line stated that the policy was to discourage rock throwing by not talking about it publicly. The use of railway policemen with walkie-talkies on the trains and along the right-of-way shows that this is not a minor problem. The reaction of the public is revealing. Many commuters have taken to pulling down the window shades as a shield. This is like a wartime blackout.

One form not mentioned in the delinquency books is so frequent that a few years ago I gave it a name suggested to me by a ten-year-old boy: the "overpass game." Two or three boys get together and lie in wait on an overpass or a bridge. When a vehicle or a ship passes under them, they throw down stones or rocks or pieces of metal pipe or bottles. Both adults and children have been injured or even killed by this practice. Recently a thirty-three-year-old driver sustained a neck fracture and was killed when a concrete slab from an overpass smashed through his windshield and struck him. Three youths were seen on the overpass at the time it happened. Characteristically, after that there was a veritable epidemic of motorists being stoned. Often drivers literally didn't know what hit them. For example, a medical student heard what sounded to him like a gong and saw a flash of light as he passed under an overpass. He could barely pull to the side of the street. Semiconscious, he was taken to a hospital by a passing driver who picked him up. This driver had seen two little boys drop a piece of pipe which had struck the student on the head. A thirteen-year-old boy was arrested recently for throwing stones from an overpass. One stone had smashed a car's windshield. Other cars have been heavily damaged. One sixteen-month-old baby was injured so badly that he had to be hospitalized. Stones and bricks have been thrown several times onto boats on sight-seeing trips around Manhattan. On at least one occasion, both adults and children on the ship were injured. A twelve-year-old girl suffered cuts on the head and had to be taken to the hospital. The boat line sent police a schedule indicating when their boats passed under the bridge and requested that police guards be assigned to the bridges. Somehow all these precautions do not sound like peacetime.

Automobiles are being used by minors as instruments of aggression, both as a prank and seriously. Recently, a twenty-year-old admitted that he had deliberately run down with his car a college student who was on his way to an ice-cream parlor with a group of teenagers. The student was knocked down and died. A businessman was walking his little dog when a car with "two

young kids" came by very close and tried to hit them. The man
tried to grab the door handle to pull out one of the youngsters, but
they stepped on the gas and drove off quickly. Then there are the
youths who try to run down Negro children when they are waiting
for school buses. (I am referring to observations made in the
North.) Others merely drive through rain puddles on the road so
as to splash bystanders. What the lawyers call involuntary (vehicular) manslaughter is sometimes on closer study voluntary murder.
Perhaps the most serious forms of this are attacks on policemen,
now so prevalent in various ways. Typical is the action of a
sixteen-year-old speeder. A policeman stopped him by forcing him
to the curb. Then the officer alighted to question the boy—and the
boy suddenly started up his motor and ran over the officer, breaking
both his legs. Some youngsters play games with human lives by
driving directly into an oncoming car in order to frighten the
other driver. The trick is to dodge the other car at the very last
moment. Some deadly accidents have happened this way. Another
sport indicative of disregard for life is the deliberate running down
of animals on the road—cats, dogs, groundhogs, pheasants.

Physical attacks against teachers in school, some of them serious,
are a new feature of child behavior. Knives and improvised weapons have been used. For example, a thirteen-year-old boy attacked
a teacher with a penknife. A sixteen-year-old boy fought two
teachers. The average age of these attackers is thirteen to fifteen;
some are even younger, others older. Every day in New York City
a teacher is beaten by a pupil. In five school days recently, fifteen
assaults against teachers took place. As a *New York Times* editorial put it: "Teachers can hardly be expected to carry arms." The
authorities play down the extent of this violence in the schools,
saying that only a small fraction of students is involved. The attacks on teachers are related to the violence of pupils against one
another. Policemen have been placed in schools, and not only in
slum areas. Even in suburban neighborhoods it has been found
necessary to have police on guard—even at high-school dances.

The change of pattern in a common form of delinquency, the
snatching of pocketbooks, is typical of the new brutality. Formerly
it was a more or less nonviolent act. The boy snatched the pocketbook and ran away as fast as he could. Now it is often carried out

with violent means. The perpetrators are getting younger too. I have examined boys of twelve who engaged in the practice, profitably. And the acts are getting more brutal all the time. Knives are displayed as a threat—or used; women are mugged or severely hit over the head from behind; sometimes water pistols are used to squirt substances into the victim's eyes. More and more frequently, utterly gratuitous brutality has become part of the act— even when there is no resistance. Here are three recent examples. A young woman was held up on a city street. She threw the boys her pocketbook, but she was severely beaten and kicked anyhow. An old lady was attacked on her way to church by a youth who took her purse. In the process, he grabbed her from behind, dragged her along, and, still holding her arms, smashed her to the ground. Both her upper arms were fractured. A woman of frail build was waiting for a bus in mid-Manhattan. A youth seized her bag and threw her to the ground with such force that she sustained a serious fracture of the pelvis which kept her in the hospital for six months.

The change in the direction of more violence has been even greater in girls than in boys. The Goddess of Violence ensnares not only male youths but also female ones. For instance, a taxi driver was held up during the daytime. Two boys and two girls, all about seventeen years old, had boarded his cab. They threatened him and took all his money. Then, just for good measure, one girl hit him over the head with her shoe and broke his glasses. In New York State, according to its Division for Youth, girls' injury-to-the-person cases used to be so few that they were not even separately listed in statistics but were placed under the general diversified rubric "other." By 1959 no less than 10 percent of all injury-to-the-person cases were girls' cases. Chief Justice Ben Cooper of the Special Sessions Court in New York City has stated that up to about 1950, cases of girls committing assaults with weapons were rarely seen. But then the picture changed and there were many of them. Young girls of twelve, thirteen, or fourteen not only commit violent acts now, like attacking a teacher, mugging or assaulting elderly women to snatch their purses, and so on; they also commit murder. Recently a girl of ten threw her seven-month-old stepsister from a fourth-floor window because she "didn't like the baby." A fourteen-year-old girl shot and killed a boy of nine because he teased her brother. Another fourteen-year-old girl took a .22-caliber pistol out of her loose-leaf notebook in class and killed a sixteen-year-old boy.

There is also an increase and an intensification in the sexual violent acts of youths and children. Sex murders by the fourteen-and-under age group are now a reality. Not long ago a thirteen-year-old boy raped and killed a six-year-old girl by banging a rock down on her head several times. When her almost nude body was found, it was in such a condition that the veteran policemen were appalled. The teachers of this boy described him as a perfect gentlemen at all times and "one of the nicest boys in the school." This murder took place in a suburban area. The boy's parents had remarked some time before how glad they were that they lived in a neighborhood where it was so safe, instead of being in the city. Another thirteen-year-old boy who was a boy scout and active in youth groups raped a three-year-old girl and stabbed her to death. Such youthful cases are no longer unusual.

When disturbed in their sex play by adults, some youths have been known to act with great ferocity. A boy of fifteen was playing with a thirteen-year-old girl in a clump of bushes in a city park. When a sixty-five-year-old man heard giggles and made some re-mark, the boy attacked him, beat him to the ground, and jumped on his head several times. The man died from a skull fracture and multiple injuries.

Murder is of course an extreme event. To every one of these cases correspond innumerable cases of minor brutalities. Children as young as ten, eleven, or twelve have tormented younger ones, tied them to trees, beaten them, burned their feet, sprinkled pepper into their eyes, branded them, and so on. Part of all this is just brutal play; a not insignificant part has sexual-sadistic overtones.

Among adolescents the brutalization in sex play is related to the relatively recent increases in nonviolent forms of sexual aggressive-ness and bravado. Exhibitionism is an example. In psychiatric lit-erature, only adult exhibitionism is described. Psychiatrists have distinguished two types. In one, the men are neurotically driven to exhibit themselves in front of women but do not commit any other transgression. In the second form, exhibition is only one symptom, and the men are apt to commit other, even violent, antisocial acts.

To these two adult forms, we must now add a third, adolescent exhibitionism. Young boys of an age that permits an erection at all have exhibited themselves on a dare or as an attack on very young girls. The boys have even given it a name; they call it "flag-waving." A more contemptuously aggressive and not sexual act is a game played by the younger sets of teenagers. Three or four boys wait on some bank next to a lonely road. and expose their bare behinds to passing motorists, either men or women. They call this "mooning." It is a game of defiance.

Juvenile violence is a direct reflection of adult life. Its prevention is so difficult not because the individuals are psychologically so disturbed but because the whole phenomenon is so deeply anchored in our social life. We cannot rely on the often-invoked formula that maybe in the normal child who commits a violent act, flaws in society play a role, while in the abnormal child the causes are all individually determined. Even in the most disturbed juvenile the distant causes come from the social environment. The attitude toward violence within adult society is what makes the violence of children possible.

Every society has the juvenile violence it creates. The causes lie for the most part not in the youths themselves but it the environment we have created for them. They want to establish their identity in their own personal way, and we have placed them in a world in which the greatest attention they get is as consumers. They want to be individuals, and we make them a tiny entity among millions. They want a modicum of safety; we present them with the spectacle of a frightening world. They want to learn; we put them in overcrowded classes and schools. They seek adventure, and we don't provide it except with the crudest murder and war toys. They wish for amusement, and we give them unrewarding—but for us remunerative—stereotyped comic-book and screen fare. The adolescents want to confide their health worries, but we have dismissed the family doctor and offer them advertisements and commercials of phony patent remedies. And so on. The real question is why there are not more violent juveniles. Children are not more violence prone than the society they live in.

Blaming all violent delinquency on the individual family, which is now so fashionable, is a good way to avoid the wider social implications. Those who wish to lay the whole burden on the family have evidently not spent much time conversing with parents whose children have perpetrated violence. Almost uniformly these parents describe how unable they were to shield their children from the extrafamilial influences on the street, in the schools, in publications, in entertainment. The parents are just making excuses, you say. Maybe it is those social scientists who blame everything on the family who are making excuses.

A number of times, young gang chiefs have conferred with me in the clinic. They had trouble with rival gangs and wanted to avoid bloodshed. They explained that adults were no help, and they could not talk openly with anybody—teachers, guidance counselors, truant officers, parents, clergymen, policemen. Society offered no lever. What adults did provide were all the weapons the gang members needed to be fully armed for the next fracas. The only remedy a gang chief had was to negotiate with the rival gang chief "from a position of strength"—just like his adult "betters."

Sometimes a very self-righteous person will proclaim that he too was exposed in childhood to all kinds of bad, aggression-promoting influences, but that on him they had no negative effects whatever. When we look at him more closely, we often find a typical ruthlessly aggressive individual making his way to success by stepping on those who are in his way. He was figuratively stomping as the delinquents factually do.

The occurrence of juvenile violence is not simply a matter of mechanical causation. At different ages and in different circumstances, a variety of factors enter. Some factors lead only to thought, others to acts, still others facilitate the transition from attitudes to action. For every youth committing a violent act, there are many who only think about it. There is no single X factor to explain why one influence leads to overt action while another affects only attitude. Always a constellation of psychological and social factors, interacting with one another, determines the result. Only on that basis can we predict.

When a child commits a violent act, the reason is not always— as is so widely assumed—that he feels hate and hostility, that he has an impulse to appropriate something, to hurt somebody, or to get even with someone, and so on. Often the main operative cause is a general intellectual, moral, or sexual confusion about legitimate pleasures, adventure, and social identity. He may have learned false ideas of authority and of possession from his environment. A little boy was walking in the park with his grandmother. As they went along, he asked her to jump over a low railing beside the path, and she was obliging and did so. Then the boy asked her to jump back and then back again. A passerby reproached him for making an old lady jump. The boy looked at him, arms akimbo, and stated firmly, "This is *my* grandmother, and I can make her jump as much as I want to!"

We often read and hear about "meaningless violence" among youths. But violence is never meaningless or senseless. Using such terms merely denotes that we have not decoded the signals—including the warning signals long before the violent act.

Of course, at different periods different motivations are operative. At the present time, three factors are important, but are very much underestimated with respect to their influence on young people's violence: the specific economic factor, race prejudice and atomic fear.

While thrill seeking, which at a certain age merges with sexual sadism, is well recognized, the economic factor is overlooked or glossed over. Even in young children, simple material gain, the elimination of an obstacle to material advantage, plays a role. This is true not only for the buffeted children of the poor but for the affluent youth of the suburbs. Robberies, with and without violence, which are attributed to thrill seeking are perpetrated by adolescents chiefly for the purpose of buying something they want or implementing their allowances. The classic example is the extortion racket. Boys of twelve have threatened younger children of nine or ten, forcing them to hand over regularly part of their lunch money or weekly allowance if they don't want to get hurt. Victims who did not comply have been severely beaten, stabbed with knives, or otherwise tormented. This extortion racket among children is no longer unusual. Often the young victims are afraid to tell about it for fear of reprisals—just like the victims of adult gangsters.

A second much-underestimated factor is race prejudice. This is deliberately evaded or minimized by the authorities. In case after case of group or gang violence among young people, official hand-outs state "no racial tensions involved at all" or "the fight had no racial overtones" or was "not a racial incident." When we study these cases, however, we find just the opposite, namely, that these group fights and battles have as their real basis race conflicts, prejudices, and antagonisms absorbed by these youths from the adult social climate.

What may be called "swimming-pool murders" are typical. In New York some time ago, within a period of two months two took place. The circumstances were almost identical: a gang of white boys regarded a public swimming pool as "their" pool and did not permit Negroes or Puerto Ricans to use it—so a young teenager was killed, another wounded; in each group, the youngest boy was just fifteen. Corresponding to such murders, there are innumerable fights and near-fights for similar reasons, corresponding to patterns of adult neighborhood and school discrimination and segregation. This angle is played down even in books that should concern themselves with the subject. For example, in a book based on children in Washington, D.C., *Delinquents, Their Families and the Community,* we read about a school where "the ratio of whites to non-whites was generally similar to that of the schools and the neighborhood. The neighborhood, however, had a higher concentration of non-whites than the total city." It would have been simpler and more scientific to call a segregated school a segregated school.

The third factor that is not given its due and which may be the most important at the present time is atomic fear. Juvenile violence is related to the threat of international violence. Of course, this is not a direct mechanical relationship. There are many intermediate links. Most affected are young predraft teenagers, but even much younger children are affected in some ways by the psychological fallout.

The possibility of atomic war has made the life of the younger generation more uncertain than that of any previous generation. We expect young people to accept the world as they find it and as we have made it for them. That includes the fact that they may be incinerated at any moment that adults (or seniles) decide to do it. While we are complacent about a war of intervention, juveniles are anxious about the intervention of war. Some four-fifths of the world's wealth is being expended at present on armaments. Is it really so astonishing if a little boy uses a gun? Our trigger-happy youths have to live among missile-happy adults. Among the tangled motives of young people, this has to be explored and taken into account.

Some of the recent violent group, club, and gang activities of sixteen-, seventeen- or eighteen-year-olds, consisting in excessive vandalism and especially brutal and sadistic acts, have a particular kind of bravado. Teenagers in different urban regions have secret clubrooms where they go through rituals of initiation, courts, sex orgies, and all kinds of brutalities. One incident of "hazing" was called by a judge who had to deal with it "sadistic, barbaric, and immoral." The ordinary explanations, Freudian or otherwise, are not enough. In vaguely conscious, unformulated ways, youths who engage in these outbursts of group violence are afraid of death and atomic annihilation. A sense of futility impels them. Their acts, during which they get "high and excited," are implicitly a triumph of the fact of life over the thought of death. During the excess, the threat of death is forgotten. In some ways, this is reminiscent of some of the ancient Greek mysteries which had a similar foundation.

Drug addiction among juveniles plays an increasing role. To get money for the drugs, some youths engage in violent acts which they otherwise would not do. One of these is the extortion racket with threats of violence. Even in junior high schools, "dope pushers" make their rounds. Pupils and teachers know that, but are afraid to do something about it lest there be violent reprisals. A drug definitely related to violent tendencies, LSD, has recently come into wide use among youths, including college and high-school students. Under its influence, a ready emergence of violent impulses and even actual homicidal and suicidal attempts have occurred. Strict legal control of the manufacture, sale, or possession of this drug is essential to prevent its illicit use.

Nobody can fully understand violent behavior in the contemporary child, from minor infractions to downright murder, who does not take into account the visual mass-media factor. The profusion of mass-media violence and sadism is so great that you can no more put all the blame, scientifically speaking, on the individual child than you can blame a plant for its susceptibility to a blight affecting a whole garden. That mass-media brutality has a potential negative effect on children's thoughts and feelings is now more and more acknowledged, owing to clinical studies and countless observations and experiences of parents. But it is still widely believed that such an effect can exist only on a child's thoughts and not on his acts. It is the intellectual fashion to postulate a complete contrast between what is called "general juvenile culture" or subculture, which is socially conditioned, and specific violent delinquency which comes from the child. But we cannot make such a sharp distinction between influence on attitude and influence on overt activity. Is it reasonable to assume that potentially harmful things influence only what a child thinks and not what he does?

Juvenile violence is learned behavior. That does not mean a simple mechanism of stimulus and response. What goes on in the child's mind is that different factors cause currents and cross-currents which augment, modify, or even reverse one another. The outcome may be a thought, a fantasy, or an act. In this way a minimal factor may have a maximum effect, and vice versa. Harmless or constructive inclinations, such as love of adventure, may be deflected into destructive channels.

The lure of brutal mass-media heroics may become so overpowering that it overrides the influence of significant persons in the child's life. In his study of the teenage mass murderer Charles Starkweather, Professor J. M. Reinhardt writes: "For him the only places where 'real' characters emerged were on the television screen and in comic books." Especially in young teenagers the image of the world that some of our mass-media stories conjure up is one where death counts for nothing and women for little. As a poet has expressed it:

> Cattle are there to be herded,
> Girls are there to be slept with,
> Men are there to be killed!

The two crucial points in the influence of mass-media violence on the immature mind are: first, the mobilization of latent imitative tendencies so that the depicted method is copied; second, and even more important, as a result of exposure to violent scenes, the resolution to carry out one's own deed may ripen. One boy who had beaten a girl told me that he had had daydreams of doing this for a long time. When he saw a girl being beaten on the screen, the idea of actually carrying out his daydreams came to him for the first time.

In recent years I have had to examine a number of adolescents and postadolescents charged with homicide. Among them were cases which aroused general interest because of either the age of the accused or the type of crime: the boy who killed the baby-sitter and the baby in Massachusetts; the boy who was charged with shooting the "model boy" on the streets of New York City (described in *The Circle of Guilt*); the high-school boy on Long Island who killed a fellow student with a shotgun in the school washroom; the Bible-carrying "model boy" who strangled to death a fifteen-year-old girl in New Jersey; the youth who shot a hotel employee during a robbery; the youth who was the leader of one group of young torturers and "thrill killers" in Brooklyn; the youth who was an associate of the youth who killed both his parents with poisoned champagne cocktails in New York to get their money.

The circumstances, background, motivation, and most other factors were very different in each case. But in each of them I found—and in several instances said so under oath—that the visual mass media (television, movies, and crime comic books and similar publications), though not decisive or fundamental, played a contributing part in the final tragedy. They did not start the fire but they added fuel to it.

Murders by children connected with a mass-media factor keep on occurring. A boy of eight sexually abused a four-year-old girl and strangled her to death with a clothesline. Neighbors described him as "a normal, very nice boy from a wonderful family." Young as he was, he already had a real Superman complex. Other children called him The Boss. He used to talk about Bat Masterson and tell "stories about Batman and the people from other planets." The charge against him: "juvenile delinquency—homicide."

When a reporter went to the Bronx to investigate the case after it was first announced, he found a little girl about five years old singing in the street:

He killed her, he killed her,
He took a rope and killed her.

And a boy of twelve asked him, "Will he get the electric chair? It was just like *Naked City*—all those cops around here! Will they burn him?" Can we afford to disregard these children's reactions?

A method of wanton brutality often shown on television (where I have monitored it in children's viewing time) is to knock a person down from behind and then as he lies there to kick him in the face. This is exactly what happened to a man in one of the larger subway stations in New York. He was slugged from behind by a group of youths and while on the ground, semiconscious, was vehemently kicked in the face.

Kick-killing a man while he is on the ground was a crime-comic-book device seen by multitudes of children. It now occurs also in life. In Brooklyn two boys, aged sixteen and seventeen, got annoyed at a man, the father of four children, because he was humming as he passed them. They knocked him down and kicked him to death.

A fourteen-year-old boy who committed an armed robbery copied his elaborate method of operation from television programs. At a lonely railroad station, wearing a handkerchief over his face, he pointed his rifle at a man who was waiting for a train. He took the man's wallet and ordered him to the ladies' room and locked him in. He had prepared the padlock beforehand. He remained up to date, learning from the media. Some time later he got into trouble when he used a very dangerous trick on another boy in the gymnasium. He had learned this trick from the super-violent movie *Goldfinger,* based on Ian Fleming's James Bond story. This boy was described by those who knew him as generally very friendly and considerate.

An eleven-year-old boy strangled a four-year-old girl to death with a string, pressing her face into the dirt. He had become fascinated with all the strangling scenes he had seen on television and had first tried it out on some cats and kittens. He had no feelings of hostility against this girl and also had no sexual intentions.

A teenage boy stabbed a fourteen-year-old girl to death. He

had watched many murder scenes on television. Whatever other hidden motives he may have had, he expressed one of them like this: "I wanted to see in reality the terrified expression on the face of a murder victim at her last moment."

An eleven-year-old country boy, his mind crowded with the scenes from the war pictures and Westerns which he liked to watch, waylaid a rural mail carrier. He raised the flag on a mailbox to do this. When the postman stopped, the boy shot him to death with a .22-caliber rifle, took money from the cashbox, and used the mail in the car to set the vehicle on fire. He was a normal boy with better than average grades.

A boy of fourteen tied up a little boy of seven in a way which he said he had often seen in comic books. Then he killed his victim with a hatchet.

Many more such children's cases of shooting, stabbing, stoning, burning, and so on, related to the visual mass media, result not in death but more frequently in major or minor injuries. How the media violence factor works in the immature mind can best be understood in analogy with findings of the new science of neuro-cybernetics. It is not the total environment that affects the child, although we read that so often, but only certain parts of it which enter his "action field." These signals reach the child's brain and have two different categories of effect. The first does not lead directly to any response in overt action. It is merely a preparatory accumulation of stimuli which determines attitudes. It may be called the attitude factor. The second type of effect, on the other hand, has a definite "trigger" result: it initiates action. This may be called the action factor. But this trigger effect can take place only if it has been preceded by a situation created by the sum of preparatory signals or stimuli. The end result of violent behavior is always a synthesis of the two.

An instructive example of the influence of printed illustrated material on the immature mind is the case of the so-called Brooklyn Thrill Killers, a group of four boys, aged fifteen to seventeen. They had tormented girls by whipping them with bullwhips on their bare legs. They burned, beat, whipped, and tortured men whom they attacked, mostly in parks. They were finally arrested after killing a young Negro whom they had found sleeping on a park bench. They dragged him away, burned, hit, beat, and tortured him, then kicked him—still alive—from a pier into the East River, where he drowned. This was not a Southern lynching by adults, but a Northern lynching by boys.

These youths were steeped in a publication called *Nights of Horror,* of which sixteen successive issues had appeared. All these publications describe in detail the same material: how to obtain the greatest sadistic sexual pleasure by torture. Every conceivable form of hurting people is described: beating, whipping, burning, hanging, violating, stabbing, branding, and so on. It is a veritable manual of how to become a sadistic sex criminal. In fact, the youths used this as a textbook, which they followed and imitated. For instance, they forced the victim to kiss his tormentor's feet.

Studying this series was not the only or even the main cause of these acts. But it was definitely a potent contributing factor. It fanned the flames. In my psychiatric report on the leader of the group, I stated that when individual responsibility is assessed medicolegally, the influence of such readily available literature on immature minds must be taken into account. The psychodynamics of young boys who carry out such sadistic violence is only partly explained by preexisting psychosexual dispositions. The other part is seduction, learned thrill seeking, conditioning, and imitation. (*Nights of Horror* was later banned by a decision of the New York State Supreme Court, upheld by the U.S. Supreme Court in Washington.)

The reaction of the community to the rise of juvenile violence is an important part of the whole picture. From what happens in the postviolence phase, we can learn something about the social conditions and attitudes in which the violence developed in the first place. The failure of the remedies illuminates the cause.

It is an understatement to say that the reaction of society is inexpedient. The results are around us. For one thing, there is a high violence and vindictiveness potential in the adult community. Two different metropolitan newspapers with large circulations at different times printed these two typical letters. The first said:

Take the ten worst juvenile delinquents arrested during the week and over a national television hookup tie them to posts, pull down their pants and beat their bare behinds until they scream for mercy.

Tying a child to a post and beating him sounds more like many current delinquent acts than like a remedy. The second letter advocates:

For stealing shave the punks' heads and cut off their fingers. For murder beat them unmercifully, send them to the hospital to recuperate for a week, then hang them on television.

These letters indicate the violence-weighted atmosphere in which some of these children grow up. That responsible editors of mass-circulation newspapers print such letters, thus conveying their sentiments to millions of readers, is surely a sign of the times.

Even the judicial mind sometimes goes to extremes. When a thirteen-year-old seventh grader in Kentucky was convicted of robbery with a pistol, the judge sentenced him "to spend the rest of his natural life at hard labor."

Some people hold the fatalistic view that juvenile violence is an inevitable occurrence and will always be with us. They regard some concrete measures as hopeless endeavors at the start. For example, recent statistical studies claim that social casework therapy makes no difference. This type of nihilistic conclusion is a roadblock in the treatment of violent delinquents and makes the efforts of the many devoted workers in this field much harder.

Cases of juvenile violence are often handled by a number of different agencies in anything but a systematic way. Youths may be shuttled back and forth among psychiatric hospitals, courts, agencies like Youth House, state and city clinics, reformatories, institutions for mental defectives, and so on. Recently a boy of seventeen was arrested and charged with two murders of women and ten sexual attacks. At the time of his arrest, he was out on bail from the New York State Supreme Court on a charge of rape. He had been previously convicted of arson and attempted rape and had been in Children's Court, Youth House, a psychiatric hospital, an institution for mental defectives, a state mental-hygiene clinic. This is a typical career. There was insufficient communication between some of these agencies, or he would not have been released on bail on such a serious charge. Commenting on this lack of communication between responsible agencies, a judge stated: "A crime of this kind does challenge our thinking, and we must turn the whole thing over in our minds." Evidently a little more than that is necessary.

While our adult crimes of violence are often well reported in the press—sometimes more accurately than in official documents—juvenile violence is often neglected or unreliably presented. For example, in the case of the seventeen-year-old Puerto Rican boy who was charged with killing a "model boy" on the street, the newspapers and newscasters created the legend of a dangerous, wild youth belonging to a minority group who was preying on innocent boys. This legend was without any basis. Relying on official handouts, heavily slanted for the prosecution of the boy and damaging to his case, the news media stated with certainty that he had been arrested before, that he carried the gun, that he was the chief of the gang, that he started the fight, that he had bad records in school, that the victim was not with a gang. I studied this case carefully—and *all* these details were untrue. If we do not know what happened, we cannot evaluate the causes. Nor did the news media later correct these wrong, stereotyped bits of misinformation. The truth does not always get equal time.

How unserious and superficial society's approach to juvenile violence is, in comparison with preparations for building a bridge, for example, can be seen from the "prediction tables" now widely in use. Large sums have been spent by foundations on their application, and Chief Justice Earl Warren of the U.S. Supreme Court wrote an introduction to the book *Predicting Delinquency and Crime* (1959), which first published them. These "predictions" as to whether a child will become delinquent or not are made by relying on five simple factors, such as "cohesiveness of the family" or "affection of the father" (or mother), which are then arbitrarily rated. It has been claimed that these scales "can serve as a Geiger counter to spot potential delinquents." Would it were so simple! Actually they overstress the isolated family situation and depend too much on subjective evaluations. They open the door to prejudgment and prejudice. Practically, they have achieved nothing "for determining the kind of correctional and therapeutic action" of which Justice Warren speaks in his introduction. The claims that the predictions have been validated by follow-up studies are not conclusive and do not alter the weakness of the basic premises.

It is presumptuous and dangerous to fixate in the preschool age the path a child will take in future. These facile methods for the early identification of predelinquents remind one of the toothache powders that used to be sold at country fairs: they would prevent the toothache provided they were taken half an hour before the toothache started. What makes this type of prediction so socially harmful is that it interferes with rational and constructive methods of prevention. Such a static, predetermined view of human behavior is a part of the previolence phase of further juvenile violence.

A similar, even more serious social miscarriage was the repeated announcements by an official New York City youth agency. They stated that research had "definitely shown" that 75 percent of all juvenile delinquency—as well as other social troubles, such as alcoholism, divorce, poverty, and so on—occurred in 20,000 families which had been "identified" by the agency. These families represented less than 1 percent of the city's family population. It was officially stated that these 20,000 families had been "pinpointed" and that a "comprehensive index" of the whole group was being prepared. This "hard core" group of "crime-breeding families" was officially designated "as being the source of New York City's delinquency problem." These families were described as "highly resistive to help from any source" and "tending to resist referral" to social agencies. In other words, it was officially presented as an established scientific fact that three-fourths of all delinquency in New York City comes from a small group of poor families whom we can identify beforehand. Later this conclusion was extended to the whole nation. The New York City Youth Commissioner told the 7,000 delegates of the White House Conference on Children and Youth that this relatively small number of "demoralized" families produced the overwhelming majority of New York's delinquents and that there is "every reason to believe that this ratio applies throughout the nation."

That this prejudicial story was universally accepted unchallenged indicates a mixture of complacence and credulity. Pediatric, psychiatric, and sociological publications regarded this "research" as authoritative. All the news media united in spreading the news, which one national newsmagazine called "surprising." Books on delinquency state that "these multiproblem or hard-core families" are to be seen as the main targets of all delinquency prevention. One New York State Supreme Court judge stated publicly that serious juvenile crime was due to these selected families: "How are you going to straighten out all these families? They are the hard-core families that you can do precious little with." Judges, in sentencing youths for violent acts, have stated: "You belong to a hard-core group, the group from which delinquency stems." Negroes, Puerto Ricans, and other minorities are often the butt of such a point of view.

What was the basis of all this? A myth had been created. Public relations had replaced public responsibility. These 20,000 families do not exist. Such a group is speculation. No "index" was ever prepared, because the story that these families had been "identified" had no basis in fact. A survey of 150 families had been made. As is routine in every good social agency or clinic, they were cleared through the Social Service Exchange (SSE), which lists for its members the names of other social agencies to which a client is known. These families were known to five or more agencies, sometimes to as many as fifteen. This sample was projected to the whole city ("75 percent of delinquency from less than 1 percent of the family population") and then by an even more daring leap to the whole nation ("the same ratio"). The youth agency called this "the isolation of the problem," and an estimate was presented as an established fact. As for the "great resistance of such families to outside help," one can look at that from a different angle. In my different clinics, I have had contact with many welfare services. If a family is known to as many as fifteen agencies, it does not speak for the efficiency of those agencies. It does not mean that the families are at fault, but that the members of the family got a runaround from agency to agency and then were turned into statistics. There are in Harlem alone 539 social agencies operating. A social caseworker, Elizabeth Wood, expressed it very well when she spoke of "families who represent the consolidated failures of social agencies." Often what happens is not that the families do not want help, but that the bureaucratic setup causes all kinds of delays and frustrations. Arbitrary orders from above sometimes wreck the usefulness of an agency.

The Juvenile Aid Bureau of the Police Department of New York City did constructive work helping children and their parents, as I found over the years in my clinics. An essential part of their program was that all officers, male and female, were in plain clothes and never in uniform. It was an authoritative approach without authoritarianism. The great importance of this has been pointed out by Sir Charles Martin, who headed the model Juvenile Liaison Officers Scheme in Liverpool, one of the most successful juvenile-delinquency agencies in the world, now copied by about twenty cities in England. Suddenly the Juvenile Aid Bureau officers were ordered back into uniform, and as a result many families were deprived of this efficient help. As uniformed members of the police department, the officers could not possibly achieve the same results as they had before.

The myth of the "20,000 families" does not die easily. It is such a convenient scapegoat to blame the ills of society on, juvenile violence included. In the past the famous family studies of the Jukes and the Kallikaks were used in a similar way. They served as models to provide general explanations of the way all kinds of social evils, such as crime or poverty, arise. Countless college students have been taught that these studies are valid. Yet they are no more than legends or scientific romances. Serious critics, like the British psychiatrists Henderson and Gillespie, the president of the New York State Prison Association, and the writer Samuel Hopkins Adams, have exposed these studies and pointed out that they are based on the flimsiest of hearsay evidence, that they are "pure folklore" and belong not to sociology but to mythology. Nevertheless the Jukes and Kallikaks survive in classrooms and in sociological, psychiatric, and general literature. Two recent publications, one sociological, the other psychiatric, refer to the Kallikak family in identical words. So the story of the 20,000 families will also have a chance to continue for a long time. If we want to prevent violence, we must work our way through a lot of myths.

Juvenile violence raises the whole problem of punishment in general with particular insistence, practically and philosophically.

If punishment does not have a well-defined, verifiable purpose, it is pure revenge. If the community just lets off steam, it is doing precisely what so many delinquents have done in the first place. On the other hand, there are people who reject the whole concept of legal punishment for violent juveniles. It is quite true that in the distant future, punishment as we know it will not exist any longer, and historians will condemn our time for using it. But the real condemnation will not be that legal punishment was used, but that we lived in a society which made it necessary. It is not a question of the relationship of law to morality but of the relationship of both law and morality to underlying conditions.

The suggestion is often made that parents should be severely punished for the vandalism and violent behavior or delinquencies of their children. These proposals overlook two things. First, these parents are already punished by what has happened; they need help, not retribution. Secondly, these juveniles may have the strongest emotional ties with their parents, even with parents who may be at fault. So punishing the parent does not help the child but hurts him emotionally and only adds to the confusion.

The punishment meted out for juvenile violence is often erratic. That is in large part due to the phenomenon itself, for which our institutions and agencies are not traditionally prepared and equipped. If the verdict on a child is "juvenile delinquency—murder," that is in itself self-contradictory. It is like labeling a dish "slightly overcooked—poison." For what are minor, nonviolent offenses, youths are often sentenced to a reformatory, where they may have to stay much longer than an adult would for a similar offense. When this is questioned, the excuse is made that the punishment is "treatment" and that the youth will receive some psychotherapy in the institution. This is often a mirage, for the psychotherapy is usually nonexistent or at best perfunctory. Once I asked a domestic-relations court judge why so many children are committed to reformatories in cases where I found it both inexpedient and unfair. The judge replied, not without considerable self-satisfaction, that children are taken from their family environment and committed by the court whenever the conditions in the home are not good. That certainly covers a lot of children, especially if the families live in the ghettos of our cities. It places

these children in double jeopardy. First they and their families are
discriminated against, a fact which creates bad home conditions.
Then these conditions are cited as justification for confining the
children in reformatories.

Legal discrimination is especially likely to affect Negro children.
Few of these cases become known. Some years ago in North
Carolina, a boy of seven and a boy of nine were sentenced to
fourteen years in a reformatory. What had happened? These
children had been playing with other children, and in the course
of their play a little white girl, aged seven, recognized the nine-
year-old boy, whose mother had worked in the girl's home. She
kissed him on the cheek. Both boys were promptly arrested and
charged with rape. Their parents didn't know where they were,
because the police did not notify them for several days. Eventually
a judge held a "separate but equal" hearing. In the morning, he
heard the mother of the little white girl; in the afternoon, the
mothers of the two Negro boys. It was only through protest demonstrations in London, Paris, Rome, and Rotterdam that American newspapers became cognizant of the case, and after less than
half a year, as a result of all the publicity, the children were
released. One French paper headlined the case:

INTERNÉS POUR UN BAISER!

Significantly it often occurs that sexual and property transgressions are regarded as more serious and more punishable than
violent acts. Recently in an affluent suburban area a teenager
drove his car as close as possible to three young schoolchildren
who were walking along the road. The game was to try to frighten
them and then dodge at the last moment, missing them by as few
inches as possible. At the third try, he hit one of the little boys,
knocking him down and causing lacerations and bruises. Without
stopping to find out how badly his victim was injured, he drove
off as fast as possible. For this violent play with human lives plus
the hit-and-run offense, the judge pronounced sentence: a fine
of $36. Maybe the boy thought the fun was worth it. Some teen-
agers spend that much on entertainment of other kinds. He certainly
was not given a chance to learn better.

During a hazing, two high-school seniors injured a fourteen-year-old pupil so seriously that he had to be hospitalized with internal injuries. The judge called the hazing actions "sadistic, barbaric, and immoral." For a legalistic technicality, the charges were dismissed, and the boys got no punishment at all. *The New York Times* commented on this and similar cases: "The confusion in an adolescent's mind after he gets off scot-free on such a technicality is . . . a serious matter, Young, unsophisticated minds may readily conclude that sadism and barbarism . . . are not really punishable." This is precisely what happens. The Goddess of Violence usurps the place of Themis, the Goddess of Law.

That the victims are apt to be neglected and violence not regarded with sufficient seriousness is well described in *The Young Life* by Leo Townsend, a novel evidently based on life. An eighteen-year-old youth with a group of other boys rapes a fourteen-year-old girl, holding a knife at her throat during the proceedings to prevent her from crying out. He is acquitted. Later he kills a woman. The public, including a psychiatrist, minimizes his responsibility. His guilt is explained away by the use of dubious modern psychology. At the same time, the author describes how much of the boy's bent to violence was contributed by society and how the seeds of sadism ripened in him. What goes on in the mind of a boy brought up on crime comic books and lurid stories as he watches sadistic movies?

He took great interest in the details. He liked particularly the ones where they did the women in and often he sat through it all over again so he could study the way it was done. They didn't half make them funny these days, too, you had to laugh. And after all, what did they think you were? What did they show them for and work you up like that if they were going to make a fuss about it afterwards? Everyone liked it really, only they hadn't all got the guts to do it. But they liked other people to do it. It was in the air.

The confusion of the boy is matched by that of those who handle his case.

A few decades ago a Chinese warlord, after conquering a city, would arrest ten inhabitants at random on the street and execute them. Some Juvenile Court judges seem to play Chinese warlord. They are interested in setting an example, but not in studying either the offense or the offender. They fight violent delinquents, but not violence and not delinquency.

Punishment of juveniles as well as adults can have a constructive effect only if it is a clear communication to the perpetrator and to the community covering five factors:

1. The protection of society. For a considerable period now, New Yorkers have found that they cannot ride safely on the subways or walk in the parks. The same is true of other cities.
2. Reeducation of the delinquent. The main problem here is that in a violence-saturated society, it may be necessary also to reeducate the reeducators.
3. Condemnation of the crime.
4. Making the public aware of the facts of the violence. If a community does not know what types of violence are possible and going on within its framework, it cannot defend itself.
5. Elucidation of the causes. The process of law includes this, although it may not be so stated expressly. For example, the establishment of mitigating circumstances points to contributing causal factors the youth is not responsible for. If it is a matter of guilt, it can never be placed solely on the immature youth.

These five factors are all closely interwoven.

Juvenile violence is not inevitable, nor does its treatment and prevention present insuperable difficulties. But the extent of the phenomenon has to be recognized. What these young people need is not complicated: a simple understanding of their problems as they see them; a clear and unmistakable condemnation of violence; an easing of social pressures not only on the family level but also on a wider sociological level; protection against unhealthy environmental influences. This plain bread we do not give them. Instead we talk about cake—or rather research about cake. Large sums of money are being spent by government agencies and by foundations on this research, which is rich in graphs and poor in results, while essential requirements are neglected. The violent child is a corrupted child. That does not mean that he is emotionally ill or that he will become a criminal. But it does mean that something has interfered with his normal, healthy development. Such a child needs help, protection, and reeducation.

There are two opposing views about the proper approach to the problem. According to one view, we must wait till we know the basic causes, the "basic processes operative in delinquency," as a recent book on delinquency expresses it. Nobody has ever demonstrated what these "basic processes" are. According to the other view, which I advocate, we have to deal with the known features rather than with speculative aspects.

Therapy and prevention are closely related. These youths need easily available, no-nonsense, down-to-earth guidance and psychotherapy. Problem children are not children who are problems, but children who have problems. One of the obstacles to arranging proper treatment is the current well-nigh ineradicable fallacy that a child "needs to act out his resentments" and "work off his hostilities." At a recent psychiatric meeting, it was stated that the desire to join a juvenile gang goes back to the seventh month of life. That is both way back and way out. As a matter of fact, if a child does feel resentment, he should be helped *not* to act it out but to understand it and overcome it. "Hostilities" do not have to be worked off; they should be worked out.

Of course, we cannot straighten out the minds of young people without also straightening out their lives. The task is to trace the personal and social roots. We seek to lessen the pathological feedback from the person and from society. Many youths from childhood on have been conditioned to the thrill of violence and destruction. So we face the paradoxical fact that they may need help to resist the temptation to adjust too much to the world we have created for them. These children did not choose violence. Violence chose them.

The over-all lesson seems to be that we are not only our brother's keeper, we are also the keeper of our brother's children.

# CHAPTER THIRTEEN

# Don't We Need Violence?

The victory of violence
Seems complete. But is the battle ended?
—BERTOLT BRECHT

The people in all these towns, they are
frightened and sometimes murderous, just
because in one way or another they're
crying in the dark.
—ARMINIA EVANS in GEORGE
LEIGHTON's *Five Cities*

## The Death Penalty

*Be certain what you do, sir, lest your justice
Prove violence.*
—SHAKESPEARE

THE idea that it is necessary to kill a human being as legal punishment for certain deeds seems to have a tremendous hold on people. Kant, who was an early and courageous advocate of "eternal peace" and whose moral categorical imperative greatly influenced philosophical ethics, was adamant in his absolute demand for capital punishment. He wrote in his *Treatise on the Metaphysical Elements of Jurisprudence*: "Even if a civil society with all its members unanimously dissolved itself (for example, a people living on an island would decide to separate and disperse all over the world) the last murderer in the jail would have to be executed first, so that everybody gets what his deeds deserve." The gentle and kindly Vicar of Wakefield expresses the same opinion: "In cases of murder . . . it is the duty of us all, from the law of self-defense, to cut off that man who has shown a disregard for the life of another."

The history of the death penalty is a long one. It probably started, as Sir James Frazer has conjectured, not as punishment but as exorcism. It was a way of cleansing the scene after a homicide, as if the murder were an infection affecting the whole community. The ghost of the victim not only haunted the murderer but threatened everybody. The blood of the murderer was shed as a human sacrifice. It was a purification, not a punishment. But by imperceptible stages, this ritual became an execution. Society no longer exorcises a ghost, but it exacts a penalty for an injury. A religious rite becomes criminal justice. In his ideal "State," Plato advocated the death penalty for slaves for not reporting the offense of another.

According to Professor G. O. W. Mueller, in the thirty-four years prior to 1964, 3,833 murderers, rapists, robbers, kidnappers, burglars, insane persons, "probably innocent persons," and others were executed in the United States. The largest number of executions, 364, occurred in Georgia. No Southern state is among those with no executions.

Alternatives to capital punishment are widely discussed. Mueller calls the present state one of "confused sophistication." In our era, perhaps the strongest impetus for the demand to retain the death penalty forever comes from a hidden, unacknowledged social motive. It is kept in reserve as a potent legal instrument against opponents of the political and socioeconomic setup. This motivation breaks through in such cases as that of Sacco and Vanzetti. The types of crimes for which the death penalty is invoked have more or less constantly dwindled in civilized countries. In 1870 in England, 240 offenses were punishable by death. They included fishing in the wrong stream and prostitution. In 1716 a girl of eleven was hanged for witchcraft, and as late as 1831 a boy of nine for arson. This seems far away. But in sixteen states of the United States, it is still at least legally possible to execute children as young as seven. In our era, in 1944, a boy of fourteen (of course a Negro) was electrocuted in South Carolina, charged with homicide.

The line between political murder and the death penalty is not always very sharply drawn. The Russian purge trials of people later "rehabilitated" are an example. In Nazi Germany between

1933 and 1945, after official verdicts of the death sentence, some 13,000 were executed. One clergyman stated recently that he had accompanied more than a thousand of them to their execution. Many Negroes sentenced to death and executed belong to the history of political murders rather than to the case material of jurisprudence.

The trend of civilization is undoubtedly toward restriction and eventual abolition of the death penalty. I am convinced that capital punishment should be, can be, and will be abolished. The main questions are when and how. In our society, as Warden Lewis E. Lawes of Sing Sing used to point out, capital punishment is applied mostly to the underprivileged and friendless. But to get rid of it is not so simple a matter as it seems. What is apt to happen under present circumstances is in a wider perspective more an adjournment than a lasting abolition. For if you abrogate capital punishment and do not change the conditions that lead to violence, it can always be reinstated. Ten American states have abolished capital punishment and reintroduced it. Chile gave it up and then introduced it again. Soviet Russia has prohibited it three times and restored it three times.

Evidently we cannot really abolish official legal killing by the government without doing more than that. We cannot isolate the problem of legal killing from the general problems of violence. We cannot take it out of the sociohistorical context. Abolition entails a fundamental change, and that cannot be achieved in the long run by leaving everything else basically as it is. It is like the question of war. We cannot abolish war pacifistically without removing or changing the underlying conditions that lead up to it. In the same way, we cannot work successfully against the death penalty without at the same time trying to bring about conditions so that it will disappear. The real problem is the reduction and abolition of murder and violence.

The question of the deterrent effect of the death penalty is often discussed, and all kinds of statistics have been adduced both pro and con. But these statistics usually deal with circumstances that are not strictly comparable in time and place. Many variable and not immediately apparent factors enter, like composition of the population in different states with regard to age, rural or urban location, occupation, social and economic differences, industrial problems, stages of increased general law enforcement, and publicity about crime waves. There are totally different kinds of murders and murderers, and we cannot generalize about what does or does not deter them as a whole. Moreover, a valid, reliable statistical study could not restrict itself to actual murders, but would have to include felonious wounding, robbery with violence, violent holdups, and cases of near-murder.

During a debate in which Clarence Darrow spoke against capital punishment, he had to defend himself against this argument: In the twenties in Montreal, many armed holdups occurred. The driver of a bank collecting car was shot to death. Subsequently six criminals were condemned to death, and four of them were hanged. For years afterward, there were no further holdups in the city. Evidently in that time and place, the penalty acted as a deterrent, at least to the extent that criminal elements avoided the city. But Darrow knew many instances which proved the opposite.

It is often stated with great confidence that statistics prove that capital punishment has no deterrent value. In essence, that is like saying that if you threaten someone with death, it has no effect on him whatsoever and the instinct of self-preservation does not exist. In the depth of the Depression, I examined quite a number of young holdup men in the Psychiatric Clinic of the Court of General Sessions (now Supreme Court) in New York. They thought that a holdup was the most clean-cut crime. They told me that they needed the money just to live. They didn't want to go to Times Square to stand in line for a bowl of soup from a public soup kitchen. They felt that it was beneath them and too sneaky to steal, embezzle, or forge checks. To confront a man in a store with a gun and ask for money seemed to them, rightly or wrongly, a more dignified crime. They did not commit murder, although when caught that might have helped them to escape arrest. One strong reason for *not* firing their guns was the death penalty. Who can know whether for every murder committed there are not at least a hundred people deterred from committing murder?

Those who claim that the death penalty has no deterrent effect whatsoever leave out its use as a terror method, both in peace, where this purpose is not openly acknowledged, and in war, where it is almost routine. This denial of the deterrent effect of capital punishment is part of the general underestimation of the fearful efficacy of violence. Many have wondered why at Stalingrad the German common soldiers despite terrible deprivations and suffering, held out to the last moment, although their situation was clearly hopeless. At least part of the explanation is the death penalty. In one sector in one week, 362 soldiers were executed for cowardice, being AWOL, desertion, and stealing food.

But the question of deterrence is not a fundamental criterion. Capital punishment has to be abolished eventually, not because it does not deter but because on principle it is inhuman, uncivilized, socially indecent and morally wrong. It is also inexpedient practically for the time when a truly nonviolent world is being built. We are still far from that, and any opposition to the death penalty must be coupled with a far more determined and extensive struggle against the many forms which violence takes in our society. If locally the death penalty is given up without that, and for wrong reasons (*e.g.* that it does not deter), this abrogation will be ill-founded and cannot last.

The abolition of capital punishment is a long-range, twofold task, against the penalty itself and the conditions which maintain it. With the sway of the Goddess of Violence in our society, one generation will not be able to accomplish this. But a lot in addition to legislation could be accomplished now in the way of humanization. For example, it is often said that the community "cries out" for the death penalty. When that happens, I have nearly always found that this sentiment has been whipped up to make people demand it. In the case of Caryl Chessman, who was charged with attacks on women, newspapers as well as national-opinion journals and newsmagazines reported that a seventeen-year-old girl became insane because of sexual attack by him. However, a very competent psychiatrist, a consultant to the Superior Court of Los Angeles, stated that he had examined her and that very definitely her psychosis had nothing whatever to do with any sexual attack.

Proscription of the death penalty for the insane applies also to cases of severe mental deficiency. In 1964, however, the United

States Court of Appeals, Third District, affirmed a death sentence of a mental defective accused of murder. The court stated that "the imposition, in a first degree murder case, of a death penalty on a mental defective . . . is not per se violative of the Fourteenth Amendment's proscription of cruel and inhuman punishment." Forward-looking members of the legal and psychiatric professions find it hard to accept this. The very definition of murder in the first degree by law rules out a bona fide mental defective, because psychiatrically he does not have the capacity "to act from a deliberate and premeditated design." Other courts have decided differently. A twenty-two-year-old girl whom I examined and testified for was charged with murder, having killed her two brothers, aged fourteen and twenty-one, by giving them poison. The court spared her the death penalty and committed her to an institution for the criminally insane. There had been—as there usually are—warning signals long before which had been disregarded.

Capital punishment is particularly cruel when the law plays with the life of a prisoner, much like a cat playing with a mouse. Mrs. Ethel Rosenberg was sent to the death house at Sing Sing while her husband, also sentenced to death, was kept in the federal jail in New York City. This separation, without any chance to speak to him, proved an enormous strain on her. It brought her to the verge of a prison psychosis. Only after psychiatric expert testimony was given in court to that effect was her husband also removed to Sing Sing. About two weeks before the execution, a high federal official told her, on behalf of another high federal official, that if she would cooperate and talk she would not be executed. That two otherwise respected federal government officials should lend themselves to a you-talk-or-we-will-kill-you maneuver is understandable only if we realize how deeply violence as a method is entrenched in our society. When the young mother was electrocuted, her two boys (then aged three and ten) were greatly affected, especially the older one. He was so crushed that it required prolonged psychotherapy to restore him to emotional balance. We have closed-season hunting laws for animals while they bring up their young. This principle should be extended to humans.

Caryl Chessman was in California's death row for eleven years and eleven months before he was executed. Edgar Labat, convicted of assisting in a rape, has been in Lousiana's death row now for more than twelve years. The legal case has gone on for fourteen years. His appeals have led to the U.S. Supreme Court four times. He has had nine stays of execution. Denying one of his petitions, a U.S. District Judge said: "This case seems to have no ending." That is Labat's feeling too. While waiting for reprieve or execution, he wrote poems like this:

> Living at the river's edge,
> When will they drive that final wedge?
> Will justice ever look my way?
> And when it does, what will it say?

## The Instrument of Nonviolent Resistance

The most provocative challenge to the belief that great historical changes cannot be achieved without bloodshed is the nonviolence movement. Wars, civil wars, and more or less violent revolutions have been part of most if not all really fundamental sociohistorical changes in the past. What is the position of the nonviolence movement? Has it raised extravagant hopes? What is the social frame of reference in which to assess it?

A young man was called before an investigating committee. It was no roundabout or Kafkaesque affair. The chairman, with a stern air, asked right off, "Do you believe in the overthrow of the government by force and violence?" The young man paused for a moment looking a little puzzled, evidently thinking it over. Then he answered quietly, "And how would you do it?"

This was no ordinary gag, but a statement of a very serious problem that has plagued mankind for a long time. People have been reproached for using violence at all, for using it too soon or too late or under wrong circumstances, and for not using it and submitting to tyranny, oppression, and mass deaths. Do we ever believe in force and violence? Did Abraham Lincoln? We cannot evade that question by saying that at present, under any and all circumstances, collective and political violence is always wrong when every history book teaches us that in the past it was not so. Thomas Paine, one of the most important champions of democratic rights wrote: "What we now see in the world, from the revolutions of America and France, is . . . a system of principles as universal as truth." Could this under any circumstances have been achieved in any other way? How individual political terrorists, much as we condemn them, have been confronted with this problem has been best described by the revolutionary Boris Savinkov (V. Ropshin) in fictional form in his novel *What Never Happened.* One of his terrorist heroes is verily haunted wherever he goes by the question "Can violence be justified, and if so, what is its justification?"

The whole problem of collective violence for sociopolitical ends is much more difficult than it appears on the surface, morally, politically, and legally. For instance, a high court, the New York State Appellate Division, declared in 1963 that "abstract advocacy" of the "forcible overthrow of the government" is not illegal.

The belief in the necessity of social violence is deeply entrenched in our society, although it is usually not openly expressed. In the latter part of the nineteenth century, the economist and philosopher Eugen Duehring developed the so-called violence theory, according to which violence is the fundamental moving force of history and all other factors, such as economic ones, are always secondary. All political power for Duehring is essentially military power. Violence is the guiding line in the historical process. Although Friedrich Engels refuted these ideas in detail, the conception of the primacy of military power in history as well as for future policies has had a lasting influence, even among those who have never read Duehring. Elements of the violence theory can be discerned in the utterances of leaders of the contemporary American military-industrial complex.

A similarly great but also mostly subterranean influence was exerted by Georges Sorel with his book *Reflections on Violence.* Sorel, originally a civil engineer, was an erudite but sometimes unclear writer. What is decisive in politics, according to him, is not intelligence and rationality but instinct and energy. He wrote with enthusiasm about the uses of violence. He played with violence despite his learnedness—or, one might say, with the aid of it. His idea that only a "myth" could move masses into action was more poetical than realistic. He himself spoke of his philosophy as an "apology for violence." In essence, what he advocated was what may be called drawing-room fascism. In fact, he imbued Mussolini with the idea of social violence as the central guiding line in theory and practice. The elevation of violence from an expedient to a principle really goes back to him.

We bar our road to understanding—and curbing—both individual and collective violence if we do not make clear to ourselves how much of it is inherent in the very society in which we live. When we "pacify" (which means make peaceful) other nations, we shoot. When we maintain the order under which we live, we often do the same. According to the *Amsterdam News,* in New York City the police killed ninety-five people in 1964. That means that the police were responsible for roughly one-sixth of the violent deaths in the city.

The reasons and motives for collective violence are as manifold as for individual deeds. One factor is the disorder of communication. In the language of cybernetics, one might speak of a failure of "feedbacks" from the ruled to the rulers, from those who suffer to those who could help. It has happened again and again that only violence, "propaganda by the deed," was able to break through the indifference of the public and draw attention to insufferable conditions. The violence of the Mau Mau played a role in the introduction of improved conditions in Kenya, for example.

One of the chief reasons for collective violence is the snail's pace of reform measures and social advances, both domestically and internationally. The Supreme Court orders desegregation in schools; it is carried out with relentless slowness. During the world crisis in 1931, there were some 30,000,000 unemployed. From this fact alone, we could have projected the violence of the next two decades. "What is at stake is to create such a life situation for all men that each one can develop his human nature freely, that he can live with his neighbor in a truly human relationship and not have to be afraid of violence shattering his life situation." That might have been said by President Kennedy, but it was said by Friedrich Engels 120 years before.

Considering the amount and extent of violence-maintained oppression in the world, it would seem that under specific circumstances, collective violence is a social necessity. However, this necessity is not an absolute one; it is a historical one. We have to overcome not only war and violence as such, but the necessity for war and violence. We have not yet reached that stage of civilization where this will not exist any more. The belief in the omnipotence of violence is a reactionary idea. But we deceive ourselves if we do not realize that, in the words of Milton, there are still occasions for

> . . . just men long oppressed . . .
> To quell the mighty of the earth, the oppressor,
> The brute and boisterous force of violent men.

The only justification for ever using violence is in order to abolish violence. Our perspective must be the ultimate goal—far distant as it seems—where no violence is necessary any longer. Before we reach that stage, we have to face the fact that there are situations in which violence may be the lesser evil. But we are apt to remember only that it is *lesser* and forget that it is evil.

It is against this background that nonviolent resistance has to be seen. Although it has come into general consciousness only recently with the civil-rights movement, it has a long history.

The father of nonviolence and passive resistance as a political weapon was Étienne de la Boétie who seems to have been given no credit for it. In the vast literature on nonviolence his name is never mentioned. He was a friend of Montaigne, whose opinions he influenced, and he died more than four hundred years ago, in 1563. But his treatise *Discours sur la Servitude Volontaire* is perhaps more pertinent today than some of the recent academic books on political science. It was almost forgotten until it was made known again by the philosopher and social reformer Félicité Lamennais (d. 1854).

The *Discours* is written in a simple, natural style. La Boétie discerned rightly that long-standing submissiveness to oppression "indicates indifference rather than cowardice." He wrote eloquently of the victory of "freedom over greed." As a determined enemy of violence, he taught that a great deal could be accomplished by strictly nonviolent resistance to oppression. He advocated what is now called passive resistance. His treatise is the first to urge nonviolent methods. It is a theoretical book. The general point of view is that laws have to be obeyed but that an oppressor can be gotten rid of without physical fighting. "Just don't support him!" La Boétie advises. "The country need not take anything from him, but it should not give him anything." From his knowledge of history, especially ancient history, he points out that tyrants are really weak. Because of their cruelty and injustice, they cannot have friends. When two of them get together, "they are not friends, but accomplices." *("Ils ne sont pas amys, mais ils sont complices.")* He was not for civil disobedience, but advocated nonviolent passive resistance within the law. He specifies: "If one does not give the tyrants anything any more and no longer obeys them, without violence, they will stand there uncovered and really amount to nothing any more." What is needed is a refusal, an action which is not only legitimate but a duty.

Just as La Boétie evidently reacted to the tyrannical absolutism and the bloody wars of his time, so Thoreau was influenced by his moral disapproval of two features of his time: slavery and the Mexican War. (It is interesting that in Congress, Abraham Lincoln voted against the declaration of this war.) And as La Boétie advised nonviolent resistance to an unjust government by "not obeying," so Thoreau elaborated a theory of civil disobedience to the government if it engages in unjust actions. A few years before, Dickens had coined the phrase "guilty governments." Among other things, Thoreau advised nopayment of taxes, not in general but only if the money was used for actions or institutions (like slavery) which he regarded as iniquitous. He felt that acts of civil disobedience would lead to a "bloodless revolution." However, Thoreau was not absolutely opposed to the use of social violence under all political circumstances. "Suppose," he asked, "blood should flow. Is there not a sort of bloodshed when the conscience is wounded?"

Thoreau greatly influenced Gandhi, and his conscientious civil disobedience became a guide for the Gandhian passive-resistance movement in India. There is also a certain similarity between both men's attitude toward authorities whom they did not wish to acknowledge. When a tax gatherer asked Thoreau what he should do, he answered: "If you really wish to do anything, resign your office." Gandhi, arrested for civil disobedience, told the judge:

"The only course open to you as a judge is to resign your position, or to inflict upon me the severest penalty."

Gandhi was the first to apply ancient Indian principles of non-violence in the sphere of politics. When, in 1919, special laws were proposed giving the authorities "emergency powers," he made a proclamation, a vow, in which he said that these laws are "unjust, subversive of the principles of freedom and justice, destructive of the elementary rights of individuals . . . we affirm solemnly that in case these projects become law . . . we shall refuse civically to obey these laws . . . and we affirm in addition that in this struggle we shall faithfully follow the truth and shall abstain from violence against lives, persons, and property."

The essence of the whole program was *ahimsa,* that is, non-violence. *Ahimsa,* Gandhi said, means "sacrifice," and sacrifice indeed it was. Ananda Coomaraswamy, the eminent Orientalist, wrote in 1945: "Today it is officially admitted that since the beginning of the present war British soldiers have repeatedly fired on unarmed crowds, flogging is a common punishment for political offenses, and thousands of elected representatives and other 'political offenders' (most of them committed to the employment of only 'nonviolent' means) have been long in prison without charge or trial, and no man knows when he may not be arrested and detained incommunicado in the same way."

Indian activities based on the principles of nonviolent resistance were much wider in scope than is often assumed. They included: domestic spinning on primitive looms, which amounted to a boycott of the British textile industry and gave the Indian peasant an income during the winter (between 1914 and 1923, the imports of British cloth to India declined by more than half); abolition of "untouchability," which included struggle against the division into sects and races (Gandhi affirmed what he called "the absolute identity of human nature"; this principle still has great significance here and now, because so much of current cross-cultural psychological research hides under the mantle of scientific objectivity a good deal of condescension); refusal to work or cooperate with the government in public offices, schools, and universities; refusal to pay taxes; strikes, political street demonstrations, picketing; and refusal to give evidence before a court or a commission which excluded Indians from bench or rostrum.

The nature and extent of these activities varied greatly over the years. Sometimes they were intensified. At other times, in the light of repression and the suffering of his followers, there was compromise, retreat, and provisional giving up of a policy, *e.g.,* noncooperation.

Gandhi's whole sociopolitical life was devoted to *ahimsa.* But he could be very outspoken about the application of violence. For example, he said: "I would prefer India liberated itself by violence rather than remain a slave chained to the violence of its rulers." And during the Second World War, in 1942, he warned that unless Britain granted independence to India, discontented elements would welcome a Japanese invasion. That is as if nowadays Dr. Martin Luther King were to warn the United States government that unless full equality is granted to Negroes, discontented elements will welcome an invasion by a foreign power.

Gandhi was also very outspoken about armaments. He told an interviewer: "Cannons only increase the number of cannons." Translated for our time this would say: "Atom bombs only increase the number of atom bombs."

Was Gandhi successful? Undoubtedly his movement played a large part in the liberation of India, more indirectly than in direct ways. His theories also played a role in the independence movements in other countries—for example, Ireland and, between 1950 and 1952, Ghana. But there are voices which, in the light of India's later development, are very critical of Gandhi's influence. His teaching has been criticized for encouraging an attitude of renunciation of modern needs and a regression to the simple life of a precapitalistic epoch. A recent uncommonly perceptive visitor, the Indian novelist V. S. Naipaul, writes about Gandhi: "No Indian attitude escapes him, no Indian problem; he looks down to the roots of the static, decayed society. And the picture of India which comes out of his writings and exhortations over more than thirty years still holds; this is the measure of his failure." Has Gandhi perhaps brought to India liberation without real liberty?

Among the sources of Gandhi's passive-resistance doctrine and civil-disobedience movement, a prominent place belongs to Tolstoi. His influence exerted itself in two ways. Gandhi had read Tolstoi's social-ethical books, some of them as early as 1894, and had accepted their main ideas. He quotes Tolstoi again and again in his writings. In addition, more specifically, he was acquainted with Tolstoi's views on India. In 1908 Tolstoi had written an important article dealing with India's problems. He pointed out that by violence, hundreds of millions of Indians were held in subjugation by a relatively small number of English people. He advised nonviolent resistance.

Tolstoi has given the classic answer to the standard question which all the advocates of nonviolence have to face: What would you do if a rape or murder were attempted in your presence? Tolstoi was asked this question by William Jennings Bryan. He replied: "Having lived seventy-five years, I have never, except in discussion, encountered that fantastic brigand who before my eyes desired to kill or violate a child . . . but the world, groaning under violence, lies before everyone's eyes. . . . The strife which can liberate men from violence is not a strife with the fantastic brigand but with all those actual brigands who practice violence over men."

Tolstoi was a great no-sayer. That is why he defended principles like those of the great abolitionist William Lloyd Garrison. He would have had little sympathy with the "deliberate speed"-ers of our time. His condemnation of national and international defaults was more uncompromising than that of any contemporary American muckraker. He disliked those who said "yes, but." He said "no." He had no patience with those liberals, now so flourishing, who are too liberal to draw conclusions. On the whole, however, Tolstoi was less successful in advocating nonviolence than he was in relentlessly exposing the violence of his—and our—time. For instance, in his pamphlet "I Cannot Remain Silent," he says: "One speaks and writes nowadays about executions, hangings, murders, and bombs as one formerly spoke of the weather."

Considering that Tolstoi advocated peace and nonviolence, it is significant what obstacles the distribution of his ideas had to face well into our time. His last book, *The Law of Love and the Law of Violence,* had to wait forty years before an English translation was published. Perhaps it was considered subversive—which, of course, it is. In the book, Tolstoi points out how some of our cherished institutions are based on coercion and violence. Among other things, he advocates no more taxes for harmful purposes, no more dissipation of human forces for war, no more fear of bombs. During the American occupation of Japan after World War II, Japanese translations of Tolstoi were heavily censored. From his treatise *What Must We Do?*, which had been published more than half a century and two world wars before, sentences and whole paragraphs were deleted by the occupying authorities.

Tolstoi was extraordinarily well read in the literature of both the West and the East. He was influenced, or confirmed in his ideas, by the Chinese philosopher Lao-tse and his teachings. Lao-tse did not directly advocate any nonviolent-resistance campaign, but he was one of the most outspoken critics of human violence of all time. Some of his statements deserve to be remembered:

> Where warriors have stayed, thistles and thorns grow.
> The big armies are followed by evil times.
> The competent wants decision and no more,
>
> .   .   .   .   .   .   .   .   .   .   .   .
>
> Decision far removed from violence.
>
> Weapons are tools that bring misfortune,
> Not tools for the enlightened.
> Only when he cannot do otherwise does he use them.
> Quiet and peace are for him the highest.
> He is victorious, but he doesn't enjoy it.
> He who would enjoy it would enjoy the murder of men.
>
> To kill men in large numbers, one should deplore with
>   tears of compassion.
>
> He who has won a victory in battle should act as at a
>   funeral service.

It is evidently traditions like this that made G. Lowes Dickinson, who was a lecturer in political science at Cambridge University, write in 1914: "The Chinese are alone among nations of the earth in detesting violence." And he adds in another place: "This attitude [belief in the power of reason and persuasion] does not exclude the use of violence, but I feel sure that it limits it far more than it has ever been limited in Europe. . . . And the one theory the West is teaching them is the absurdity of this attitude. Well, one day it is the West that will repent, because China has learned the lesson too well."

It is significant that Tolstoi, Gandhi, and Lao-tse had a general attitude in common, a liking for the simple life and a dislike for modern technological advances. Tolstoi extolled the life of the peasants. For Gandhi the home spinning wheel was more than a symbol or a means for a boycott. It was an effort to simplify life. Lao-tse looked back to a primitive agrarian collectivism. Their doubt of scientific technology is especially interesting in view of the fact that, in our atomic era, the image of technique and the image of killing have become so closely associated. This tendency to a certain primitivism and to a return to a simple life helps us to understand the three teachings. But it also means a certain limitation in present-day applicability.

The nonviolent-resistance movement in the Gold Coast (now Ghana) began in 1949. Kwame Nkrumah designates his conceptions as "philosophical consciencism" (*Consciencism,* 1964). He was greatly influenced by Gandhi. After the achievement of political independence for Ghana in 1957, Nkrumah gave special credit to Gandhi. He said: "After I had studied Gandhi's tactic for months and observed carefully its successes, I came to the conclusion that it might probably be a solution of the colonial problems, provided it was supported and carried out by a strong political organization." Like Gandhi (with his Congress Party), he combined nonviolent resistance with the parliamentary process (with his Convention People's Party). He sees three components in present-day African society, contradictory but forming a dynamic unity: the traditional African way of life, the Islamic traditions in Africa, and the influence of Christian traditions and Western European culture. Of these the last was the most violent in Africa.

Nkrumah called his nonviolent-resistance movement "positive action." The tools for the struggle were political propaganda, newspapers, campaigns for popular enlightenment, strikes, boycott, and refusal of any cooperation.

The current nonviolent civil-rights movement in the United States has drawn the attention of the world more than any nonviolent movement in the past. This may be partly due to the expansion of modern means of communication. A more important reason is the international repercussions. Much more than we realize, the present civil-rights movement is regarded almost as a test case of what years ago Rabindranath Tagore called "the moral prestige in Asia" of "the upholder[s] of Western race supremacy." To this we must add: and also in Africa.

There are different kinds of nonviolence, just as there are different kinds of violence. Dr. Martin Luther King learned about nonviolent resistance first from reading Thoreau and was greatly influenced by him and by Gandhi. Gandhi was in fact one of the driving forces in his practice and strategy. In his book *Stride Toward Freedom,* he mentions Gandhi five times on one page.

Dr. King speaks of his movement as applying "nonviolent creative techniques." In a world of violent destructive techniques, this is a considerable undertaking. The essence of the method of nonviolent direct action as applied by him and the other leaders of the civil-rights movement is collective refusal. This is not a "yes, but" or a "yes, if" but a clear-cut "no" in the sense of Thoreau, Tolstoi, Gandhi, and Nkrumah. It began in 1955 as a year-long boycott on the part of the Negro community of Montgomery, Alabama, against segregation on public buses. The bus strike ended in victory. It was a fundamental lesson. The elementary improvement of letting people use public conveyances without discomfort and humiliation was brought about not by Southern liberals, responsible citizens, writers, professional men, or clergymen, but by the people themselves—and without the use of violence. The national struggle has taken different forms and included different activities. As outlined by Dr. King, they are distribution of leaflets, mass boycott, sit-down protests, sit-ins, refusal to pay fines or bail for unjust arrests, mass marches, mass meetings, prayer pilgrimages, rallies, and, of course, publications.

The civil-rights movement has been seriously criticized. This criticism has come from both the right and the left. This fact is nothing characteristic of the movement itself. In periods of transition such as the one we are living in now, to be attacked from the right and the left is a typical phenomenon.

From the right, the criticism has been made that the demonstrations and sit-ins disturb and disrupt the ordinary life of the community. But the lives of those who do the demonstrating have for a long time been disturbed much more seriously. From the left, it has been said that the people suffering from injustice should be told that to achieve a real change, violence is necessary and that collective violence, not necessarily committed but at least threatened, would have accomplished much more. A common mistake is to confuse violence with action and nonviolence with passivity or inaction. Nonviolence on the part of intellectuals often hides nonaction. There is a difference between nonviolence as a literary fact and as an actual procedure. It is not merely something negative, but is a positive technique representing a special kind of militancy. Participating in a street rally is totally different from the liberal gesture of writing a letter to the newspapers or to one's congressman or lending one's name to a declamatory advertisement.

Nonviolent resistance means nonobedience. And we do well to remember the British scientist and novelist C. P. Snow's conclusion from history that far more violent, cruel acts "have been committed in the name of obedience than have ever been committed in the name of rebellion." The spirit of revolt is not the same as the spirit of violence. The IWW was a "rebellious" group whose name is often associated with violence in the public mind. They rebelled against having to work twelve to fourteen hours a day, but they did not believe in murder. As their secretary stated in 1965, "The IWW never believed in violence." He explained that "the bosses hired thugs," which was responsible for much of the later violence.

It is too early to assess conclusively the over-all practical achievements of the civil-rights passive-resistance movement, considerable as they are. An outstanding fact not to be overlooked—or excused—is the slowness of the reforms, *e.g.*, school desegregation in both North and South. One thing that the demonstrations have shown is that there is something to demonstrate about. It may be asked: Is that still necessary? It certainly is. In the summer of 1965, Oscar Handlin, director of the Harvard Center for the Study of the History of Liberty in America, wrote in *The New York Times Book Review* about our "inability to answer basic factual questions." And his first question was: "Does the absence of racial balance in schools and housing itself produce a sense of inferiority and create disadvantages for the minority?" Before we can answer this question, we must decode it into simpler terms: "absence of racial balance in schools" means segregation; "absence of racial balance in housing" means slums and shacks; "disadvantages for the minority" means humiliation and degradation for Negroes and Puerto Ricans. It is this simple truth that the civil-rights demonstrators are demonstrating about. That is what Gandhi spoke of in his engagement in *satyagraha,* "defense of truth." And Tolstoi knew that the truth is opposed by those who "wish that everything stays as it was and is."

The greatest achievement of the civil-rights movement is that it has restored the dignity of indignation. This will last for a long time. What is so important about the organized nonviolent activities is that they represent a collective experience. They also provide an effective antidote against fear, the very emotion which is one of the causes of impulsive violence. In this way, an underground is created, not in the sense of the police-minded, but an underground of decency such as Tolstoi created and addressed in his social writings.

The civil-rights movement has served as what one might call a social truth serum. It reveals that beneath the surface there is a layer of violence in the community. It shows up the inherent violence, latent and not so latent, of the racist system against which it is used. The brutal ways in which harmless marches and demonstrations have been met draws attention to the readiness with which violence is threatened and used by the authorities. They talk so much of the "man in the street," but they are rather rough in keeping him off the street. Of all the many different clashes in North and South, one of the least spectacular but most revealing occurred in New York in 1965. For it indicated the wide ramifications and interconnectedness of racism and violence, nationally and internationally. About six hundred students and young people from different organizations protested before a big bank near Wall Street against the bank's multimillion-dollar loan to the Union of South Africa with its infamous apartheid policy. As policemen put a Negro demonstrator in a police van, voices from among the bystanders shouted, "Kill him! Kill him!" The loan itself, as well as the reactions of these bystanders, is part of the previolence phase of the continuing violence under apartheid.

The advocacy of nonviolent direct action is an important instrument for human progress. In our present sociopolitical circumstances, this form of social disapproval fulfills a function as one of the supports of democracy. It seems that civil disobedience has become necessary to obtain civil rights. It is noteworthy that, at least partially, a certain confluence between civil-rights and antiwar movements has developed. The *mouvement d'action nonviolente* in France against the Algerian war was an example of passive antiwar resistance. The underlying affinity between civil-rights and antiwar nonviolent activities consists in the fact that both are directed against violence. For the conditions in which Negroes have lived for so long have in the last analysis been maintained by violence. Selma and Saigon are not so far from each other.

The movement can be judged only in its historical framework. It has neither established nor is it based on any eternal principles. It cannot give any absolute answers. The specific historical conditions were very different for La Boétie, Thoreau, Tolstoi, Gandhi, Nkrumah, and Martin Luther King. That does not mean that we should disregard these other historical circumstances, events, and writings but, on the contrary, that we can learn from their successes and failures and the reasons for them. To apply Gandhism straight to the present-day United States would be as fallacious as to ignore it completely.

The passive-resistance movement in its different forms has a role to play on the road to the abolition of violence. But this role is historically determined and limited. It is naïve and may even be harmful to regard it as a panacea. This would indeed be a simple world if the advocacy and practice of nonviolence alone would suffice to abolish violence in the long run, but to believe this means to minimize the overwhelming problem of violence.

Nonviolence is only a part of antiviolence. To say that all violence is evil and thereby attempt to exorcise it is not enough. The Goddess of Violence can be dethroned; she cannot be ignored.

The danger is that we may regard passive resistance as an absolute and evade the concrete questions that an ugly reality poses for us. In this way, the antidote may be as bad as the poison. In an emergency it may be all right, but not as a complete cure. It may usher in a symptom-free period and prevent the organism from becoming strong enough to get rid of the poison. In other words, making a universal fetish out of nonviolence may perpetuate potential violence. It may mislead people and lull them into the belief that the age of violence is already past. It is we who are wrong when we are astonished at the mass violence of the twentieth century. Violence is not something that we have overcome but is very much a part of the reality of this century.

A prominent psychiatrist wrote recently: "The success of nonviolent resistance depends on its power to undermine the will of the oppressor, and there is no reason to think that a tyrant's henchmen . . . would be personally immune to this type of pressure." Unfortunately, history, especially recent history, does not bear this out. Would it have helped the people in Auschwitz, in Hadamar, or in Guernica if they had marched in peaceful demonstrations? Long ago, La Boétie wrote of a tyrant's henchmen that they are accomplices in his cruelty, share in the plunder, are promoted in rank, and so on. Elevating nonviolence, in our time, to a universal principle may give the oppressor the assurance that he can practice violence with impunity. Should not the German people have made attempts before World War II—as many of them wanted to do—to resist Hitler with arms? Should not the Republicans in Spain—as many did—have opposed Franco in the civil war? The real task is, of course, to prevent tyrannies. Historically, as Lincoln Steffens pointed out, democracy is not always the method to achieve democracy.

The great question before mankind is: Can we abolish violence without violence? The problem is not philosophically abstract man against abstract violence; it is man against man. Violence is a matter of the relations between people. It will be a long and hard struggle to banish it. Eventually, I believe, this can and will be accomplished. The story writer Vladimir Korolenko, a courageous opponent of violence, described the ultimate goal like this: "Violence and oppression will disappear, the nations will come together in festivals of brotherhood, and never again will human blood be shed by human hands."

## CHAPTER FOURTEEN

# Blood and Oil

## THE ROLE OF ART AND LITERATURE

We had fed the heart on fantasies,
The heart's grown brutal from the fare.
—WILLIAM BUTLER YEATS

GUERNICA was painted twice, first in blood by Hitler, then in oil by Picasso. Is there a relationship between violence and the arts?

For any discussion of over-all aesthetic theory, it would be necessary to differentiate among the different forms of art, such as novels, paintings, plays, music, poetry, literary nonfiction, reportage, movies, and so on. But looking at art with an admittedly one-sided focus—namely, its relation to violence—permits one for at least a considerable part of the way to abstract from the differences.

The great mathematician Gaspard Monge, who laid the basis for the graphic methods used in mechanical engineering, spent nearly all his time at his work. Once friends of his wanted to provide him with an interruption and a treat and took him to the Paris opera, where Mozart's *Don Giovanni* was being played. He listened for three hours without saying a word. When the last curtain went down, he turned to his friends and asked, *"Eh bien, qu'est-ce que ça prouve?"* ("Well, what does that prove?") Evidently there are different ways of looking at art, different expectations, and different effects.

Why should we examine critically the representation of violence in art? There are more important questions in art than violence and more important questions in violence than its artistic repre-

sentation. Can we not leave individual violence to the criminologists, lawyers, legislators, psychiatrists, and the collective-military
violence to the politicians and the social and political scientists?
In other words, why drag in images when we have to deal with
acts? The answer is that we have learned from the clinic and
from history that violence in fiction and violence in fact are not
totally separate worlds. Sparks may fly from one to the other.

The question that must concern us is not so much what role
art has played in the history of violence. There can be no doubt
that great art has been a factor in making this world more civilized, and that includes, of course, making it less violent. But
there is also another side to the ledger. The Goddess of Violence
has had and still has a considerable hold on art in its different
varieties, especially on literature. This suggests once more that
violence cannot be explained as a deep, eternal instinct, but is
entrenched in the social environment that we have created for
ourselves and has become institutionalized. S. I. Hayakawa has expressed it this way: "If others prove troublesome—other individuals, other tribes, other nations—the thing to do is to strike them
down, clobber them, crush them, kill them. The human race has
institutionalized this form of behavior, hallowed it in poetry . . .
fiction and drama." Throughout the years, even artists of excellence
in their respective fields have not been sufficiently aware of their
responsibility in this area and have helped to train us to an acceptance of violence.

The artist may have an incalculable influence even outside his
own country. In the early thirties, the widely acclaimed novelist,
critic, and painter Wyndham Lewis wrote a series of literary essays
for a British magazine. They came out in England as a book
with the title *Hitler,* and the book was also published in Germany.
Its essence was the statement that "the Hitlerist dream is full of
an immanent classical serenity." Hitler is represented as heralding
the "Golden Age." Lewis writes: "I, as an artist, plump for the
Golden Age!" This book, appearing at a crucial time, had a
devastating effect on young German intellectuals.

In the previolent phase, individual and collective, civilian and
military, the heroization of the violent man plays a large role,
especially in our time. Mike Hammer and James Bond, subliterary

creations, have their counterparts in much more sophisticated literature. In the postviolence phase, after periods of tyranny, massacres, or war, the writers have an obligation to the victims, to enlighten us about the human truth—the more so if that truth was so strangled before that the contemporary writers could not express it. History relies on the survivors; art should make up for the silence of the victims. Who would claim that the victims of the era of the Second World War—civilians and military alike, men, women, and children—have been adequately celebrated in art, and literature? Visits to art galleries, libraries, modern museums, theaters, and movie houses are more likely to give us the impression that they have been forgotten.

The role of art in the action phase is best illustrated by the instance of war. War, Hayakawa writes, "is a culturally sanctioned institution. . . . It requires neither originality nor reflection to prepare for war as a way to attempting to remove a threat." Art and literature have contributed to this automatic and stereotyped way of thinking about war. During a war writers often show not less but more fanaticism than other people. If wars were won by hate, they would have contributed to many victories. They have often excelled in the vilification of the opponents. This is important because their productions, as artistic creations, have a much longer life than the speeches of politicians. Long after the wars have ended, they may contribute to continuing vilification of other people, other beliefs, other nations, other races—and thus are continually paving the way for more violence.

Two contrasting attitudes exist in the action phase of war, as shown—to select two great writers as examples—by Thomas Mann and Bernard Shaw. Thomas Mann was a consummate artist and later became one of the literary champions of democracy. Early in World War I, carried away by nationalism and the war spirit, he published a book on Frederick the Great. It was a real hate maker. He created a highly embellished legend of the Prussian king not compatible with the historical facts and very apt to inflame the young. The book, which contains some vilifying racist terms, also contains such statements as "democracy and militarism do not exclude each other"; "Germany's whole virtue and beauty unfolds only in war"; "the cathedral of Rheims has nothing whatever to do with civilization. It is . . . a flower of fanaticism and superstition"; "Germany recognized in the war the bringer of the Third Reich." And he wrote about the war: "If only this war would last another seven years, so that the moral blessing of this heroic era may be preserved for a long time to come." This particular wish was not fulfilled, but another war soon after made up for it. Mann later changed his mind; but his book, well written and persuasive, is still read and quoted some fifty years later—now when we are in the previolence phase of the next war.

A contrasting response of art to the action phase of violence is shown by Bernard Shaw. At the same time that Thomas Mann began his war writings, namely, at the very beginning of World War I, Shaw sent a poem to a newspaper:

> So we lay down the pen,
> So we forbear the building of the rhyme,
> And bid our hearts be steel, for times and a time.
> Till ends the strife, and then,
> When the peaceful age is verily begun,
> God grant that we may do the things undone.

This was not only a difference between two men or two artists; it was a difference in orientation.

The arts are an important constructive factor in the struggle for a world without violence. It is not merely a question of whether the arts *can* help; the struggle cannot possibly be won without them. In assigning this additional social role to the arts, one is faced immediately with the reproach that one is underestimating the sublimity of art. But is it not better to underestimate art than to underestimate people? It depends on the urgency of the task. We live in a time which—despite much lip service to the contrary—is characterized by a persistent contempt for life. Large-scale remediable and preventable suffering, directly or indirectly caused by violence, is a main threat nowadays. The prevalence of murder and violent acts, the renewal of torture, the reign of racism, which inevitably leads to violence, the readiness to use aerial bombing, and the perfection of atomic arms and rockets—all are part of the general picture. We stand at a crossroad just as our ancestors did tens of thousands of years ago. At that time, political inventions made the very primitive combats obsolete. What we face now is the opposite. Our technology advances threaten to make our political inventions obsolete.

"Art," in the words of Sir John Pratt, "is in a sense an aspect of the social, economic and political developments of the time." It reflects a given stage in history. At different times, art has had a different meaning and varying aesthetic tasks: technical perfection, beauty, adaptation to the new media, realistic representation, abstraction, humanization, experimentation, popularization, elevation, and so on and on. At some seasons of history and in some localities, one gains precedence over the other. It is a matter of emphasis. We should not, of course, get our proportions and priorities mixed. At present, some emphasis should be given— not exclusively, of course—to the problems of violence. They do not concern only politics, science, sociology, psychology, or philosophy, but also the arts.

In the last analysis, all great art is an expression which promotes a fuller and more intense life, a more zestful life, a more beautiful life, a more elevated life, and—in our present era—a more peaceable life. In fundamental life questions, art is not and cannot be neutral. There is no iron wall separating truthfulness and tendentiousness. Truthfulness about violence includes tendentiousness, for the real artist is against it. Even if it finds no expression in a special work of art, he cannot be aloof in the conflict between destruction and decency. Whether he knows it or not, he is influenced. In our time the truth is always controversial. In future times this may be very different. Contrary to what some of the spokesmen for the mass-entertainment industries want to tell us, a large audience—unless it has been corrupted—desires more from art and literature than entertainment and escape. I have found this out by studying how people's lives are influenced. Truman Capote, watching a theater audience, expressed it like this: "Is there nothing in their faces but the desire to be amused? . . . As the lights sink, as the curtain rolls up, watch, you can see it on their faces. . . . It says: tell us truth, give us an answer, give us something which is not a smoke ring, but an emblem against our time."

If we believe that art has no social function, we deprive ourselves of one of the best weapons against the reign of violence. It is the artist who can reduce events and whole epochs of terror and suffering to proportions that we can comprehend. He creates images which enable us to participate emotionally and therefore to understand better. This does not imply that the artist has to be more socially than artistically conscious. Harmonizing both, his task in our time requires a wider orientation which can fully recognize the reality of violence and the violence of our reality.

This may be regarded as a too utilitarian view of art. But the great artists have not felt that way. They were not afraid that their work would be used for the public good; rather did they fear that it would *not* be used. Art is a power. If in a given society it is not, we should scrutinize why it is not and under what special circumstances. The art-for-art's-sake doctrine which derives from Edgar Allan Poe's poem "for the poem's sake" had an important role to play in freeing art and literature from the shackles of outside interference. It proclaimed the autonomy of art. But this has become so exaggerated that it distorts the function of art. That function cannot always be the same in different historical epochs.

In general, in the words of a modern philosopher of aesthetics, Susanne Langer, "we learn feeling from seeing it expressed in art . . . our ideas of the world are formed by the influence of images." And here is a place for some consideration of the problems of violence. Robert Louis Stevenson, speaking of his own development, wrote that fictional works "clarify the lessons of life." We are receiving today many life lessons from violence; they certainly need clarifying.

One fact stands out: there is at present an inordinate amount of cultivation of detailed brutality, sadism, and violence in the literary arts. One justification frequently offered for the abundance of violence in the arts is that it is in accordance with the spirit of the times—which indeed it is. But art is not merely something passive and negative; it can be a positive force which can help to overcome the spirit of the time. In the same vein, a professor of psychology tells us that it is "obvious that murder is a necessity in fiction because it is a fact of experience." The false and misleading word here is "necessity." At most it can be a provisional, restricted, temporary, and local expedient. That murder is a "fact of experience" is a misfortune. The necessity is not to depict it, but to overcome it. Fiction can help toward that end.

We are often told that for any dramatic effect in literature, violence is indispensable, that it is an essential part of all drama. That disregards a lot of good dramas. One can adduce Ibsen, Shaw, Molière, Bjørnson, Strindberg, Chekhov, O'Neill, plays from Henry James's stories, Pirandello, Galsworthy, Lorca, and many others. The classical plays of India shun violence entirely. Advocates of the indispensability of violence in art refer again and again to ancient Greek plays. But this example indicates just the opposite of what they are trying to prove. In the thirty-two Greek tragedies that we know, not one single person is killed onstage, nor is one single violent act committed in the sight of the audience. As a matter of fact, the Greeks invented special devices to keep violence off the stage: a messenger reports about an act; an actor behind closed doors cries out (*e.g.,* the cry of Clytemnestra); an actor standing by an open door tells what he sees inside a room; a dead body is carried across the stage in a ceremony. What is particularly interesting about this is that some modern writers of plays, novels, movies, and TV plays do exactly the opposite: they invent almost any conceivable device and method not to *conceal* but to *introduce* violence and provide occasions for showing it in detail.

The prevalence of violence and sadism in the arts is defended also by appeal to the aesthetic principle of realism. Realism, we are often told, demands that we give full artistic sway to violence in all its forms and under all circumstances where it can and does occur "for real." Dickens certainly was a realist who did not shun the darker sides of life, but there is remarkably little physical brutality in his many novels. The problem of realism is the problem of reality. It depends on what matters to us—the stock exchange, the civil-rights stirrings, or any of the multiple other aspects of our social and biological reality. For the scholastic philosophers of the Middle Ages, reality was God, the *ens realissimum*.

The façade of our present "reality" may conceal from us essential phenomena. Freud's reality principle is too much of an abstraction, for it does not say what kind of reality. He does not distinguish between a good one and a bad one. As used in psychological literature, the term "reality," as the social scientist Lawrence K. Frank has pointed out, "may imply a wide range of assumptions." We cannot always know what reality is for us, but—much more modestly—we can know what infringes upon us, what is wrong and cruel, and what exists that we can do something about: violence, for instance. Heinrich Heine said that nobody has made clear what love is; but what a good thrashing is, everybody knows. The most "real" aspect of reality is that it changes, that it changes us, and that we change it. Art not only reveals to us beauty that we did not see or feel before; it also helps us to cast off what had been taken for granted as reality—for example, violence. If the argument of realism is invoked as justification for sadistic art, the answer is that art is a factor not only for apperceiving reality, but also for changing it.

The principle that physical violence is needed in literature has, upon analysis, more serious implications than merely aesthetic ones. Going more deeply into the psychological background, it becomes evident that those who uphold the principle so wholeheartedly are implying, either consciously or unconsciously, that we need violence not only in representation but in fact, not only in art but in life. Sometimes this has been stated explicitly. The poet Emilio Marinetti, in his *Futurismo e Fascismo,* proclaimed the *"necessità della violenza"* in literature and in politics. And more recently, the literary critic Eric Bentley, speaking of violence in literature, said that "without violence there would be nothing *in the world* [my italics] but goodness." In other words, he not only defends violence in literature; he takes for granted its existence in real life. Should not art help us to get over our everyday habit of taking for granted things which we should overcome?

In one of the Aesopian fables, a trumpeter is captured in battle by the enemy. He asks his captors to set him free because he is not carrying any weapons—just a trumpet. They refuse, saying, "You do not fight yourself, but you stir others up to do it." Most artists and writers would deny that such a story has any bearing on their work, either in war or in peace. But looking at art historically as a social phenomenon, it is possible in certain instances and epochs to distinguish two tendencies: antiviolence and pro-violence tendencies. Fascist art is for violence. It propagates it and tries to justify it. That does not represent anything entirely new, but is a continuation and exaggeration of various preexisting trends.

Of course, one cannot, except in the most extreme and outspoken cases, divide and classify works of art into two such large categories. But the trends and tendencies exist. In our violence-ridden time, it would be remarkable if they did not. There has never been a reign of violence where there has not also been, openly or disguised, a reign of the ideas of violence.

Both art and literature participate in the development and progress of a people. They express and reflect not only the social forces but, intentionally or not, its hopes, fears, and best desires. Violence, even if it is not an actual theme, enters into the larger plots of life and literature. If it is represented as a decisive and necessary life process, it is being perpetuated; the tendency, however far beneath the surface, is pro-violence. If violence is viewed genuinely in the long perspective, this contributes to its restriction and eventual abolition. The tendency then is antiviolence. Of course, such a distinction cannot be made schematically. It indicates directions, as can be seen from the study of concrete examples.

## Antiviolence Tendencies

The Spanish painter Francisco Goya represented the suffering caused by violence in a scope and manner equaled by no other artist before him. The one closest to him was Jacques Callot (d. 1635), who in his series of etchings *The Miseries of War* depicted scenes of the Thirty Years' War. Goya did not give any specific messages or do any preaching. He put social content into dynamic form. He showed the truth of violence—artistic, psychological, social, and political. Among his paintings are such scenes as processions of flagellants, summary mass executions, meetings of the Spanish Inquisition. In his series of etchings *Los Desastres de la Guerra,* first published in 1863, he created in artistic form a powerful social critique of war. He depicted scenes from the

Napoleonic wars of conquest in Spain. It does not take much imagination to translate this suffering into that caused by atomic bombs, napalm, or other modern weapons.

Three other artists, from different countries and creating in very different styles, may be cited to exemplify antiviolence tendencies (not to be confused with abstract pacifist tendencies) with regard to war. The Russian painter Vasili Vereshchagin showed the face of war in many paintings. His *Apotheosis of War* has a huge pyramid composed entirely of skulls in a desolate landscape, with ravens hovering over it or perched on skulls. Honoré Daumier, the French painter, dealt with war in some of his best lithographs. One is titled *War and Peace Play the Game Europe.* It shows two female figures, one representing war, the other peace, playing a game of shuttlecock. The shuttlecock they are tossing back and forth is Europe. In another beautiful lithograph, Daumier drew Europe as a woman precariously balanced on a big round bomb about to explode. These lithographs are high points of graphic art and of critique of violence. The Flemish artist Frans Masereel showed both the horrors and the social mechanisms of violence. In one picture, we see a soldier dying in agony in a barbed-wire entanglement. Another represents a marionette theater, with marionettes on strings slaying one another. The hands which move the strings are just indicated.

In the widest sense, antiviolence tendencies do not imply that violent subjects are represented. Violence is disorder. Abstract painters like Mondrian or Lissitzky reveal to us the elements of general principles of order of an implicitly social character. From this point of view, their art has a social antiviolent content.

In literature the tragedy of violence and war can be conveyed without depicting horrors and suffering. A classic example is a poem by the Japanese poet Matsuo Basho (d. 1694), who visited a battlefield:

> The green of the summer,
> That is all that is left
> Of the dreams of dead warriors.

It would be wrong to assume that all great literature is in the service of antiviolence. But in practically all great literature, there is evidence of strong antiviolence tendencies. Homer's *Iliad* is a poem of war. Yet its whole tenor is essentially against war. That is not usually pointed out in classrooms, but scrutiny of the text from this point of view leaves no doubt. Subtle emphasis throughout is on the "countless woes" brought on by war. Scenes relating to the world of peace are presented poetically. In a typical pathetic scene, Hector, going off to battle, takes leave of his wife and infant son. In contrast, all the scenes of fighting and its results are given starkly and without any embellishment. From reading the *Iliad,* one is hardly conscious of whether the author is a Greek or a Trojan. He deplores the suffering of all, the devastation, the deaths of young men. In Homer's description, what prolongs and enlarges the war is not the warriors but the ruling gods and their rivalries. He did not know the term "escalation," but he knew the fact. To him the destruction of a city like Troy was a great tragedy. We in the era of rockets seem to have lost that sense.

Another epic, the *Ramayana* of the Hindus, is not unlike the *Iliad.* In its barest outline it is an account of the abduction and recovery of a bride. Its spirit is one of purity and antiviolence. Significantly, the *Ramayana* was a favorite of Gandhi's. For him it was so much more than just literature that he often referred to it as authoritative, especially in the troubled political times in the forties.

In keeping with his times and with the plots that he, so to say, inherited, Shakespeare did not shun violence. It has been computed that he presented fifty-two violent deaths onstage and sixty-four behind the scenes. These deeds do not occur for themselves, but are entirely subordinate to the plots. Antiviolence tendencies in Shakespeare's plays are strong, although they also are not usually emphasized in the classrooms. There is an interesting progression from the *Iliad* to Shakespeare. In the *Iliad* the warriors are not driven by passion; they act as if obeying a blind external force, the *fatum* decreed for them by the whims of the gods. In the Shakespearean tragedy, individual passions rule—love, jealousy, ambition, greed, desire for revenge, pride. It is a humanization. One aspect of this is that in the psychological plot, individual guilt, atonement, and retribution play a predominant role. As William H. Honan expressed it: "What violence Shakespeare displayed on the stage was dramatically overshadowed by the retribution which followed—a far cry from the manner in which cowboys are left heaped about the television screen." In accordance with Elizabethan conventions, Shakespeare indicated guilt feelings, fears, and retribution with ghosts, spirits, and visions. Gordon Craig has pointed out the importance of these apparitions in the staging of the plays. According to him, in such plays as *Macbeth, Hamlet, Richard III,* or *Julius Caesar,* "they are integral, not extraneous, parts of the drama." Shakespeare clearly deplored the violence attending the succession of one reigning sovereign by another. If his historical plays are seen the way they should be played or read, their cry is: "Can't we change the government from one dynasty to another without killing?" An antiviolence tendency can also be seen in the fact that Shakespeare, more than any other writer, described the evils of absolute monarchy. "Shakespeare's Histories," wrote the young Ezra Pound, "give away the show of absolute monarchy. They are the greatest indictment ever written." Shakespeare knew about the relation of power to violence, as in Isabella's speech in *Measure for Measure:*

> . . . man, proud man,
> Drest in a little brief authority.

*Othello* is a strong antiviolence play. It shows how lies lead to violence, an insight needed today more than ever before.

Perhaps the greatest modern novel dealing with the subject of violence is Richard Wright's *Native Son.* It illustrates the paradox of art, that fiction, a story, may be the best instrument for telling the truth about certain things. It is a book well known in many countries. The story is about murder in the heart, but it is traced to murderous institutions. Wright describes for us what one may call the condition of violence. He explores the outermost limits and elucidates points where violence becomes almost inevitable. The violence of *Native Son* grows out of situations where nothing else is possible. *Native Son* enlightens those who do the oppressing deliberately or unwittingly about what the psychological results of their actions are. But the most important antiviolence tendency is contained in another facet of the novel. Wright's hero, Bigger

Thomas, is completely entangled in the direction of violence. But he also struggles to transcend and go beyond it. Wright sees the violence and he sees further. He depicts with the greatest fidelity a sociohistorical situation in which violence becomes a psychological necessity. He achieves universality by showing at the same time the necessity of rising above violence.

One modern problem of violence is greatly neglected in scientific psychological and sociological literature: the question of collective violent resistance against oppression. Is it always wrong? Under what circumstances and with what timing may it become a necessity? If such questions are not faced realistically, nonviolent resistance becomes an absolute and remains abstract. The whole subject is brought to sharpest focus in the novel *Revolt of the Holy Ones,* by the Austrian writer Ernst Sommer (d. 1955). The scene of this novel is geographically far away from that of *Native Son,* but the human problems of violence transcend all boundaries. The action takes place in Poland in a Nazi slave-labor camp for five hundred especially skilled Jewish workers. The demands for productivity are constantly increased, and those who can't keep it up are eventually killed in one way or another. Although their names are not mentioned, the book is like a dialogue with Tolstoi or Gandhi. Some inmates want to fight, others are against it. The opponents of an armed uprising say that the moral law teaches patience and is valid for all times. "Even prophets and teachers of the law who preach violence have erred," says their spokesman. . . . "I am against violence." The man who advocates armed resistance replies, "You imagine that there is only one message, once and for all time. But every time has its own message." The inmates wait for the last moment and revolt only when they realize that all is lost. The book makes clear the limitations of nonviolence in the most extreme situation. In this way it helps to put antiviolence on a more realistic and concrete basis. Although the story takes place in a specific place and with specific people, its meaning applies in many different parts of the world and under other historical circumstances. Thus, in a way, Sommer's book anticipates Dr. Frantz Fanon's advocacy of violence for the native people of completely oppressed nations. For both say that when institutions are created where all justice, mercy, and persuasion end, violence is a natural consequence. Nonviolence as a principle can exist only if it recognizes this contingency.

The infectiousness of violence is a phenomenon which has to be taken into account for any comprehensive antiviolence endeavors. It has been better recognized and described by writers than by behavioral scientists. A good example is the excellent story "The Martyrdom of the House," by Alex Comfort. The story does not deal specifically with murder or physical injury to people, but is about vandalism. Extreme vandalism is psychologically an equivalent to violence to the person. The two phenomena have the closest connection with each other, and the mechanisms of their occurrence overlap to a considerable extent. In "The Martyrdom of the House," five soldiers, during a hopeless retreat characterized by many hardships, find themselves in a lonely country house which has been deserted by its inhabitants, who were apparently a young married couple. They are ordinary soldiers who have led peaceful civilian lives. One was a punctilious railway inspector, another an artistically inclined student of architecture. One of them finds a woman's clothes and uses them as blankets when lying down to sleep. While he is drinking from a fine china cup, one of them accidentally drops it. They all laugh. Then somebody deliberately tosses a plate into the fireplace—and in a crescendo of infectious destructiveness, they tear up and break everything and demolish the house. They "killed the pretty things" in all the different rooms.

On several occasions I have examined teenagers who had committed very serious vandalism. They described the same sequence, in almost the same words—how one youth imitated the other and the contagion spread. The narrator of "The Martyrdom of the House" ends his story by saying, "It is the only time I ever killed—even in battle." The story spells out no message, but it has a powerful antiviolence impact.

The modern manifestations of violence have created special artistic problems. How convey their real nature, their influences, the depth of their cruelty? When we read the *Inferno* of Dante's *Divine Comedy* today, we cannot help but feel that in comparison with the secret mass cruelty that we know about, Dante's imagina-

tion was comparatively moderate. In the Inferno the guilty ones
are punished. And in addition to the Inferno, there are the Pur-
gatorio and the Paradiso. Can you imagine a Dante wandering
through Auschwitz, Hiroshima, or a napalm-strafed Vietnamese
village? In the history of violence and cruelty, the Dantesque has
been followed by the Kafkaesque.

The classic writer on antiviolence in relation to modern experience is Franz Kafka. That of course does not sum up his
work, but it is one important aspect of it. The Kafka literature,
with its great variety of interpretations, now comprises about 5,000
books and articles. It is significant, not to say ominous, how they
neglect the antiviolence tendency. Kafka not only described the
inner conflicts of the individual, as is so widely described; he also
invented an artistic technique for recording the cruelties around us.
It is hard to agree with the critic Georg Lukács that the basic
motif of Kafka's writings is anxiety, panic, despair, and feelings of
powerlessness. Kafka foresaw what was coming. His vision was
prevision. And prevision is part of prevention. His imagination is
deeply rooted in reality. "Today," as Alex Comfort observed, "he
could equally well be writing documentaries." That is a profoundly true remark, telling us more about Kafka and about
aesthetic expression than many of the 5,000 interpretations.

Shakespeare represented in dramatic form the violence of passion. Not one of Kafka's figures would qualify as a Shakespearean
hero. Kafka recognized that the typical violence of our age is not
something which can be localized in the individual passions deep
down in the human heart. He saw its presence in routine proceedings and in the castles of our power structures. According to
him, the violences are in the institutions which we have built ourselves and which have become mysterious because we have let
them grow and have not learned to control them. More than any
other author of his time, he implicitly prophesied the violence that
would come unless something was done about it. Kafka foreshadowed the impersonal brutality of modern society, the almost automatic, self-reproducing bureaucracy of violence. He stressed its
anonymity.

Antiviolence can be discerned not only in Kafka's work but also
in his life. The biographers usually do not mention these facts.

Before the First World War, as a youth, he participated in anti-
militaristic and antiwar passive-resistance demonstrations. The
police eventually stopped them—*tout comme chez nous*. He was
also present at a meeting in Prague protesting the execution in
Spain of the famous Francisco Ferrer, the founder of liberal experimental schools in a number of Spanish cities. (New York City had
an experimental school named after Francisco Ferrer, at which Will
Durant taught as a young man.) The Spanish government did not
approve of these schools, but it found no way to prosecute Ferrer
for them. So it accused him of a political conspiracy, and he was
executed in 1909. The charges were later admitted to have been
false. There is an obvious connection, which has never been pointed
out, between Kafka's hero K. in *The Trial* and the Ferrer case.

Kafka was also at a mass meeting of protest against the execution of a harmless French shoemaker's helper, Liabeauf. Liabeauf
had been wrongly denounced by the secret police and as a result
was expelled from Paris. He returned and shot a policeman. His
execution for that aroused a storm of protest in Paris, and thousands demonstrated against the police near the prison La Santé.
The protest meeting in Prague was raided by the police, Kafka
was arrested, taken to the police station, and had to pay a fine.
These data seem to me more important than many of the speculations offered about his fantasy life.

That Kafka in his artistic vision described things that are both
special and true can be seen from the fact that, again and again,
when writers want to convey a variety of cruelty, they refer to
him. For example, William Bradford Huie, in his *Three Lives for
Mississippi,* speaking of the impersonal discussions that led to the
"police-assisted" murder of James Chaney in Mississippi in 1964,
succeeds in imparting to us the whole atmosphere by saying that
Kafka "would have appreciated" them.

When Kafka's hero Joseph K. in *The Trial* is stabbed to
death at the end of the novel by two anonymous men, his last
words are significant: " 'Like a dog!' he said. It was as if he meant
the shame of it to outlive him." The message is clear: the idea of
how he died should not be forgotten. Many more will die "like a
dog" unless we prevent it.

The Kafkaesque type of cruelty, cold-blooded, matter-of-fact, and merciless because feelingless, was not anticipated by any other writer—not Gorki, not Dreiser, not Barbusse. Scientific and psychopathological literature gave no such warning either. In the collected works of Freud, there is not a single line to indicate that the sheer quantity or quality of mass destruction of human lives was probable or even possible. And yet what happened to one of Freud's own sisters sounds as if it were directly and verbally taken from a Kafka story. Nobody but Kafka could have envisaged such a scene.

This sister, an aged lady, arrived at the death camp Treblinka with a document stating that she was a sister of Professor Sigmund Freud. She asked that in view of her impaired health she be assigned only lighter work. The deputy commander of the camp, Kurt Frank, enacted a scene of mock-deferential politeness. "Madam," he said (as was later testified in court), "is that really so? An error must have occurred, a terrible error. One will have to ask your forgiveness, my dear madam. And you don't have to work at all. At once you shall be taken back to Vienna. But before that, my dear madam, please go over there. There you will get a beautiful tub bath." He pointed to a building marked as a bathhouse, which was a gas chamber. That same day, she was put to death there, her hair was cut off for commercial utilization, and her clothes were carefully sorted out to be sent to Germany.

Antiviolence tendencies may, of course, express themselves in very different forms and ways in art and literature. There are many threads binding all the people of the world. Whatever strengthens them also counteracts the likelihood of any resort to violence. Social hostility in the form of national, racial, and religious fanaticism is amenable to alleviation by art. A good example of the deflation of prejudice in literature is the novel *Gora,* by Rabindranath Tagore. The hero, an extremist, intolerant student, believes himself to be a highborn Hindu but turns out to be the child of a British soldier who had been brought up by a Hindu family.

A great reservoir of antiviolence goodwill is in the folk art of practically all nations. It is an expression of the underlying abhorrence of violence. These are the feelings that Gandhi and Dr. Martin Luther King mobilized. They find artistic expression in simple but beautiful ways in the different branches of folk art—songs and tales, dances and paintings. This is true only of spontaneous, unadulterated creations of the people. Often folk art is not authentic, not a real expression of the feelings of the masses, but is contaminated by decadent content from other sources romanticizing violence and national strife.

"The walls of hostility," in Aleksei Remizov's phrase, that divide the nations are not erected spontaneously by the people. Contrary to the opinion of those who want to ascribe unbounded violence to the masses of people, as opposed to an elite, genuine folk art reflects strong and almost universal antiviolence attitudes. The people want to enjoy a modicum of freedom, live in harmony, and enjoy peace. The nineteenth-century American folk painter Edward Hicks, a representative of *peinture naïve,* left many paintings on the theme "The Peaceable Kingdom." They show wild animals and people living in perfect harmony and whites and Indians peaceably negotiating. Another example, typical and equally understandable all over the world, is the sentiment of the beautiful Spanish folk song from San Salvador recorded by the sociologist Alejandro Marroquín:

> *Noche de Dios, noche de paz*
> *Noche de paz, noche de amor.*

One of the tragedies of collective violence is the fact that it so often perpetuates itself and that the warring factions could do so much more for themselves if they were united and cooperated in a common goal. A modern epic of antiviolence devoted to this very theme is the novel *Masters of the Dew (Gouverneurs de la Rosée),* by the Haitian writer Jacques Roumain, translated by Langston Hughes. (A completed screenplay adaptation was left by Lorraine Hansberry at her death.) The hero of the novel returns to his village in Haiti after a long absence. He finds the fields burned by the sun, the river dried up, and the people living in poverty. He discovers a very productive spring in the woods. But all this water cannot be used for irrigation because the peasants are divided by a blood feud into two hostile camps. Between the feuds and the droughts, the community is destitute. Only the combined, whole population of the village can direct the water to the plain. With the greatest difficulty, the hero succeeds in uniting the villagers, and the irrigation project succeeds, to everybody's benefit. But the hero himself is killed in the process of saving his village.

## Pro-Violence Tendencies

Even sensitive modern poets inadvertently—but not unconnected with the spirit of the times—may occasionally become lyrical about cruelty. For example, Rilke in one of his poems describes the romantic, solitary melancholy of a Swedish king:

> And when this mood him overcame
> He took a girl and made her tame.
>
> .  .  .  .  .  .  .  .  .  .
>
> Then finds her lover and in the same breath
> With a hundred dogs hounds him to death.

Unfortunately a great deal of art and literature has used the power of aesthetic expression to make violence attractive or seductive. In the individual work, this may have been only incidental or entirely unintended. In addition to the artistic result, this has had an effect on thought, feelings, and attitudes, however. "The heart's grown brutal from the fare."

Often in the name of art, the Goddess of Violence has been venerated. We underestimate these subtle influences. Art predisposes us to something. The famous marionette-theater director Obratsov has made a point of having close contact with his audience. He writes in his autobiography: "It is very easy to do damage with art by arousing ugly emotions in the spectator, listener or reader. It is much easier than some painters, actors and writers think, because the effect of a work of art is often stronger than its author. Also the result of this effect is wider and more important than one perhaps assumes." This is especially true with regard to sadism and cruelty. Discussing pro-violence in a given work of art does not necessarily mean condemning it as a whole.

If a factory near a city pollutes its air, that does not mean that the factory is bad or that its products are no good. But it is a fact that should be given attention.

Uninhibited representation of violence has sometimes been deplored by critics, but it has hardly ever been analyzed. It is of more than purely theoretical interest. What Henry James said about sex—that the writers who insist that sex must have its place often find little place for anything else—is today even more true of violence. In the subliterature of sadistic magazines and pulp stories, this is obvious. But even in more serious fiction of our time, brutality and cruelty are a pronounced feature. The presentation of fornication may be more refined, but the treatment of killing is not.

It is the tragedy of violent art that the powers that be have been able to use art and literature to influence the public when they thought they needed violence. They could achieve this purpose just because they knew the value of art. And the artists, wittingly or unwittingly, have often failed to resist. What we are dealing with here is a circuit of subtle lines or streams of influence: the powers that be influence the artists, and the artists influence the public. Military art and intellectual militarization of a society are the clearest example. Two critics as widely separated in time and outlook as Sartre and Ruskin have objected to making light of massacres in art. Sartre has criticized Titian for flattering the great by painting "a massacre carried out on their orders." Few living writers have such a keen perception of both aesthetic and ethical values. In a similar vein, Ruskin, in his *Modern Painters,* criticized Raphael's *The Massacre of the Innocents* and wrote that slaughter should be avoided in painting unless out of the suffering comes a feeling of mercy. This may sound pedestrian or moralistic nowadays, for mercy is not presently popular in either life or art.

The graphic depiction of torture on the stage (or on the screen) always constitutes a pro-violence tendency. It blunts the sensibilities, provides a thrill for the sadistically inclined, and is an obstacle in the struggle for the abolition of torture in life. An example is the play *The Devils,* based on Aldous Huxley's novel *The Devils of Loudun* and produced in New York in 1965. In the last act the hero is tortured in full view of the audience; he shrieks wildly, then is carried around and his bloody garments displayed. Later, people are shown searching by torchlight for his bones, after he has been burned alive, and one bone is held up, discussed, and tossed into an ash can. How is such a play received? Evidently audience and critics have been so conditioned—in analogy with brainwashed, one is tempted to say heartwashed—that they accept it. The *National Observer,* although it records the detail that the hero is reduced to "a bloody pulp," calls the play "theater at its best," "rich and rewarding," and deserving "the loudest cheers." *The New York Times,* which mentions that the hero's "tortured, battered body is carried to the stake," speaks of the play as "one of the finest of our age" and "the most mature, integrated new drama of the season." The distinguished critic of the *Times,* Howard Taubman, who wrote this review, had written ten years before the memorable phrase "art cannot be above the battle." At present, the civilized world is waging a battle to abolish torture. We are not doing too well in that, as Algeria, Angola, and Vietnam have shown. If we want to banish torture in life, we must curtail it also onstage and on the screen. Representation and reality are not so totally separate.

Pro-violence tendencies consist not only in extravagant representation of violence itself, but in the presentation of the many factors that tend to make violence acceptable. That is often not clearly apparent and for that reason it is the more potent. One of the internationally most influential pro-violence writers was Nietzsche. He was not only a philosophical writer but, as far as style and expression are concerned, an excellent literary one. In the light of the history of the past few decades, it would be hard to conceive of a more mistaken message than the one insisted on very articulately and artistically by Nietzsche: that the greatest danger for mankind is that it will perish from too much softness of emotion, sympathy for suffering, and compassion for the weak. Millions have learned now that exactly the opposite is true, that untold suffering came not from excess but from lack of pity. Nietzsche influenced countless young people. Who can understand the bureaucrats of genocide if he does not realize that as youths they learned, in most attractive literary form, such lessons as that "we need a new terrorism," that "only the most noble-minded is really hard," that "the weak and misshapen have to perish," that "to achieve something great" one must "administer great pain," that man must be able to enjoy it when he himself causes suffering, that "he must be cruel with hand and deed and not only in his mind," and so on. The central message is that pity is weakness and cruelty is strength.

Another pro-violence idea sometimes expressed in art is that violence is an essential aspect of human life and that its presence is inevitable and immutable. For example, André Masson, writing about his painting, says that violence needs artistic expression because, along with hunger and love, it is "at the root of all human beings." A typical drawing of his, *A la Source la Femme Aimée,* is an agglutination of a landscape and a dismembered woman. Surrealist violence seems to have become a trend. A recent review in the journal *Les Temps Modernes* philosophically extols the painter Gastaud for showing "copulations where love takes on the face of death" and "monstrous actions which in implacable fashion link childbirth with infanticide."

Other pro-violence ingredients hidden in art and literature may take many forms. A lot of pain and suffering is caused by violence. Some artists idealize suffering and try to justify it. Others introduce violence into a plot as if it were one form of communication between human beings, when in reality communication is the opposite of violence. The violent do not communicate; they destroy. Again, we may find violence represented as an emotional adventure or thrill which the audience can enjoy, smug and comfortable, without the slightest implication or question of responsibility. Closely related to this type of representation are stories and plays which make it appear that the natural urge for action is the same as an urge for violence. Many young people confuse action with violence, and they are reinforced in this by otherwise artistic literary works or movies. Similarly, as the historian George Mosse has pointed out, violence explainable under extreme conditions may be so distorted that it appears as a great universal virtue.

Considerable harm in the direction of promoting mass violence has been done by gifted artists and writers who increase divisions among people by their works. An outstanding example is provided by the rightist brothers Jérôme and Jean Tharaud, who were both members of the French Academy. In a number of well-written and widely read books, they did more than their share of creating hate and hostility. This is a minor but not insignificant indication that seeds of violence reside in our institutions.

It is not easy to represent in art the true reality of modern violence. A high point in what may be called literary criticism in relation to violence is Mary McCarthy's discussion of John Hersey's book *Hiroshima*. This successful literary work filled an entire issue of the *New Yorker* magazine. It included accounts of colorful interviews with survivors, with many details of their experiences. Mary McCarthy's critique is a significant statement. In essence, it applies to many other works of art of totally different form and character in which violence plays a part. Hersey's book, she says, is not an indictment of atomic war. Its real effect is just the opposite. It minimizes it by presenting it as if it belonged to the familiar order of natural catastrophes like fires, floods, or earthquakes. This point is fundamental. The "human interest" stories do not elucidate the picture; they falsify it. They assimilate the mass killing as if it had been unavoidable and heaven-sent. The origin of the bombing becomes obscured, in Hersey's book, and those responsible appear to the reader completely inadvertent. We get no feeling that the bomb exploded not only in a city called Hiroshima but in our life and in our moral world as well. As Mary McCarthy remarks, if it had to be the interview technique, "Hersey would have had to interview the dead."

This critique goes to the heart of the matter. Hersey's book is not reality, although it claims to be. It is detached in a double sense. In fact, his approach is so detached that it arouses no strong feelings, no guilt, no shame, no condemnation, no resolution. And it detaches the bombing from the conditions that made it possible. If we leave out this context, nothing remains but the horror—and that is soon forgotten. Hersey's is not the real Hiroshima; it is part of the psychological fallout of the Hiroshima bomb.

War art and literature—that produced not during war, but between wars—often contains very definite pro-violence tendencies. Long before wars break out, their beauty and virtue are sung and praised in artistic creations. This is often done under a veneer of antiwar intent or sentiment, which functions as a disguise. The horrors of war are rendered, but in such a way that instead of causing revulsion they acquire a glamour of their own. Authors write about violence for nonviolence purposes just as militarists write about bombing for peaceful purposes. The authors who sensationalize war in one form or another may be called literary war profiteers. They may not bring about war, but they facilitate it. A lot of war stories are really advertisements for the next war. They are part of a kind of intellectual armament reaching into the arts which does not promote security but creates insecurity.

In the past, not only have military matters been made familiar in language and thought to idealistic youths, but the modern outrages and atrocities of war have been painted as natural and to be taken for granted. One telling example is the widely read novel *Partenau,* by Max René Hesse, which is still read and cited today. It was first published in Germany in 1929. The hero, Partenau, is described as a military genius. He advocates total war of conquest. According to his ideas, "conscience, regrets, morals" ought to be suppressed. A heroic picture of violence is conjured up. For Partenau's dreams and thoughts, the young friend of the hero says, "I would gladly die tomorrow." One of these thoughts of Partenau is that 35,000,000 Czechs and other non-Germanic people will be expelled from their native countries and transplanted to Siberia to make room for the superior German settlers. The novel was an artistic fantasy, but the later reality did not lag far behind. A little more than a decade later, Marshal Hermann Goering wrote in a top-secret directive: "Many tens of millions of people in this area will either die or have to emigrate to Siberia." The novel *Partenau* was taken seriously only by those who approved of it. The literary and social critics ignored its implications, just as we now do with the pro-violence literature of our time.

A significant progression—or rather regression—in style has taken place in war movies. In such classic films as *What Price Glory?* (1927) and *All Quiet on the Western Front* (1930), comic relief and humor were not absent, but the reality of war was presented in a sober mood. The treatment of death and suffering was decently serious. In recent movies the sober mood is lacking. War is presented as entertainment, as divertisement. It is all good fun. For example, *The Americanization of Emily,* which has a scene with the Normandy landing, is announced on the radio as "the wackiest war ever filmed." The chuckling-and-laughing-over-war school has found the ubiquitous behavioral scientist in the role of apologist. The head of the Columbia Universtiy Graduate School Deartment of Psychology told the public in 1965 that making fun of war "may in fact be the best, most normal way of response." You can guess the rest: "It gives people a chance to channel their emotions and tensions rather than bury them, thus being able to dissipate them." Clichés in defense of casualties! This is the same type of argument so widely used to justify sadism in the mass media.

A lot of violence-soaked literature, often well written, takes cover under the wide skirts of psychiatry. Or, rather, it is tucked away under what the authors think is psychiatry—a kind of instant psychiatry. Far more often than not, it is a contrived pseudo-psychopathology. Sorrow and suffering are put in psychoanalytic pigeonholes. Many modern writers think of human beings as problems. But we have to see human beings not as problems but as people.

Whatever brutality sadism, cruelty, or torture may be described, we are told by admiring critics that it is "clinically" correct. In the first place, it is usually *not* clinically correct. To try to find out why a person commits a murder is hard work and takes skill and time. In art as in life, it takes more than one or two childhood scenes to account for it fully. Human violence is not that simple. We need not only a depth psychology but also what may be called a breadth psychology.

In the second place, the artistic representation of violence cannot be strictly clinical. What should be human details in this treatment become formal symptoms. People are not white mice. If we misrepresent the mentality of violence, we lead people in the wrong direction: not against violence but toward it.

Some modern writers describe brutality with no holds barred under the smoke screen of psychology. They take a literary view of psychiatry and a psychiatric view of literature. It would be difficult to say what suffers most from this, art or psychiatry. The point is that violence is justified in fiction by recourse to psychopathology. In Norman Mailer's novel *An American Dream,* a man's murder of his wife is presented as a positive act in the development of his personality, as a liberation, a catharsis. After the murder, "illness" passes away from the murderer. This strikes one as a misunderstanding of psychotherapeutic principles.

An idea often expressed nowadays in artistic form is that all emphasis has to be placed on the violence in our own individual unconscious mind and that that will take care of the violent horrors of the contemporary world. For example, Hubert Selby's *Last Exit to Brooklyn* abounds in uninhibited, above- and below-the-belt brutality. Although it is very strong, one cannot call it unparalleled violence, because it is part of a trend in fiction today. How justify the detailed description of cruelties? Selby has written about this book: "Love could be possible between all men and all peoples if we could simply do away with our own deeply imbedded (unconscious if you like) violence." We have to "understand it for what it is; understand its source, etiology; understand that we all have this within us." "Simply"? The term "etiology" makes its sound clinical. But this is a purely speculative and unscientific psychology. How would it have helped the many millions who have perished from violence during the past few decades if they had first discovered these unconscious tendencies in their own minds?

Modern literature is rich in sadism. That is also rationalized and justified on pseudoclinical grounds. But the belief—often voiced—that representation of sadistic scenes prevents the execution of sadistic acts in life is superstition, not science. Fantasies in artistic form gain power over people. What authors who describe profusely the infliction of pain really give their readers has been put into words by one of the characters in a Mickey Spillane novel: "True violence isn't in the deed itself. It's the contemplation and enjoyment of the deed." Some writers savor sadism, then call their treatment of the subject scientific. But their approach is more culinary than clinical.

Sadistic literature may have a corrosive effect. When we are in what may be called an aesthetic mood, we are easily swayed, although we may not be conscious of it. One danger of this literature is its demagogic utilization by those who want to use violence. Undoubtedly this was a powerful factor in the Nazification of German youth in the previolence phase.

There is another aspect to the sadistic novel—its relationship to untoward trends in our intellectual life. Sometimes authors tell us about their theoretical ideas and what influenced them. *Ritual in the Dark,* by Colin Wilson, is a novel about a series of murders of women. It is the story of a Jack the Ripper of today. The author is mostly concerned with the mind of the murderer, who is seen not as ruthless but as disturbed, not cruel but compulsive. He satisfies something like a creative urge. The victims remain completely outside of any interest. The murderer is almost a hero; certainly all the others are unheroic.

In the essay "Crimes of Freedom—and Their Cure," Colin Wilson has explained his point of view. He writes: "The cause of most Western violence in this century is mental, not sociological." Twentieth-century violence is "definable largely in psychological terms." This exclusive emphasis on subjective psychology is one of the modern ways of supporting the status quo, the status quo which rests so much on violence. Leaving out sociology is as unrealistic and misleading as leaving out psychology. Is Auschwitz, Hiroshima, the murder of civil-rights workers, or even the assassination of President Kennedy "definable in psychological terms"? As a matter of fact, there is an interesting current sociological aspect to the real Jack the Ripper case. He is not only a legend but a tradition. He killed five or six prostitutes in Whitechapel in 1888. At present there is a series of murders of women in the Hammersmith district apparently even larger in number. That killer is also undetected. But whereas in 1888 there were worldwide interest and horror about the case which lasted for years, the present Hammersmith series of cases has aroused no great interest outside of England. We take these things in our stride. That is a sociological-historical frame of reference. "The heart's grown brutal."

Where do Wilson's vews of psychology come from? What theoretical influences was he exposed to? He has described that in the same essay. His ideas of psychology are based on a currently fashionable overindividualistic trend of academic psychology which postulates "self-actualization," an intense self-assertion, and so-called peak-experiences. Wilson believes that this type of psychology goes to "the very root of the problem of violence in our society." In peak-experiences, as they are defined, "there tends to be a loss even though transient . . . of inhibition . . . control . . . restraint." "The peak-experience [is] felt as a . . . self-justifying moment." This is more or less the same thing juvenile delinquents who had committed violent acts described to me as a thrill. It is disconcerting to see novelists agreeing with them.

Pro-violence tendencies are particularly difficult to assess in works of outstanding artistic quality. The film *The Collector* ranks as first-rate in all formal aspects—direction, acting, photography. It is suspenseful and captivating. A young man whose hobby is collecting butterflies kidnaps a pretty young girl, chloroforms her, ties her up, and keeps her as a prisoner in a secluded country house. The point is that he has her entirely in his power and she is completely helpless. There are strong erotic overtones throughout the entire story. The whole situation is clearly sadistic. In the end the girl dies in captivity. He goes after another girl.

This film—which is, after all, the story of a shocking, cruel, violent sex crime—was highly praised by reviewers. It is interesting how it is characterized. Most of the terms used are taken from psychopathology. So applied, these terms become mere clichés. The film is called "a basically sound study of abnormal psychology." It is not that at all. When one has examined many sex criminals, one finds that their thoughts, their problems, their acts are far more complex. But even if it were sound abnormal psychology, is that the overriding criterion for entertainment, aesthetics, or public information? Many of the terms and phrases loosely applied to *The Collector* contradict one another. Here is a partial list: "deep psychological intensity"; "maniacal reasoning"; "the psychology of the impotent"; "irrational hostility"; "a mind overthrown"; "a psychopathic personality"; "psychotic"; "death yearnings"; "obsessed" (the title of the film in the French version is *L'Obsédé*); "an introvert"; and so on. Do we know now why this young man does what he does? The psychopathology is not a discernment but a disguise. The sadism is the story.

The outline of the plot is a not uncommon morbid daydream. Some individuals have carried it out. I have examined a man who did exactly what the Collector did in the film. He abducted a good-looking young girl, kept her for days on end in his power in a deserted country house, fed her well, and finally killed her. His sadism expressed itself in overt action. He spanked the girl and made her do all kinds of sexual perversions. Another young man I examined had acted very similarly; he had kept the girl not in a house but in a secluded spot in a forest. In the end he also killed her.

In a film with this content, we have to supplement formal aesthetic judgment with an evaluation of the possible effects, both social and individual. A French review of this movie comments on the fact that the girl is treated like an insect: "Love becomes a department of entomology." Somehow the story of the butterfly-girl collection does not stand entirely alone. There exists in our world today what may be called an entomological view of human life. With chemical and other means, we can exterminate what one is actually tempted to term swarms of people in a manner and in numbers that make the Nazi gas ovens seem primitive.

Such a film has a potential effect on the susceptible individual. The review of the movie in the magazine *Time* ends by saying that it is "sure to quicken the pulse" of any girl who has to walk home alone. That is certainly true. But will it not also "quicken the pulse" of the boy who sees that girl walking home alone, the boy who may have daydreams of having a girl all alone in his power in some lonely spot where he can do with her what he wants? Any fourteen-year-old boy can see this film. In addition to all he knows about the birds and bees, it will instruct him about butterflies. By some ill chance it may, in young people, induce, fixate, or corroborate sadistic leanings. This is often denied, with reasoning that goes like this: if a patriotic film is shown, it makes for patriotism; if a religious film is shown it helps religiosity; if a communist film is shown, it spreads communism; but if a sadistic film is shown, it helps people to get rid of sadism.

The question remains: How can art in its future development help in the unmaking of violence? It would be futile to expect solutions from art and literature independent from life. Trees do not grow down from heaven to earth. But it would be equally wrong to assume that great historical changes occur without reflection in art. The belief that literature alone can effect basic social reforms—or retrogressions—is as untenable as the belief that they come about entirely independent of influences from art and literature. Whatever you may wish to think about their other ideas, Plato, Tolstoi, and Engels were certainly right when they said that literature has an important effect on social life. When we gave the Bollingen poetry award to Ezra Pound, who had used his gifts to stir up hatred and violence, we showed how much we respect art—and how little we respect human life. We acted as if art and life were entirely detached from each other. But history, and more especially the history of violence in fiction and in fact, teaches us that art and society, literature and life, form an organic entity.

Art can help us to rise above the cold violence of our time. Political-military strategists tell us that millions and millions of casualties are "acceptable." Slaughter has become merely a matter of statistics. Is it too much to expect from art that it will add compassion to computers? That can be achieved, however, only if artists realize the wider implications of their work. Even if violence is not their subject, they may inadvertently promote it. It is no longer possible to disregard social values. Instead of no values, false values develop under the surface. The writer may ignore politics, but politics does not ignore him. And if it seems to ignore him, it still does not ignore his readers.

Purely introspective, subjective art is not in tune with the best forward-looking tendencies of our violent times. That is especially so if the writers do not give us genuine psychological truths, but go by their pocket Freud, paperback Jung, loose-leaf Reich, and hard-cover Groddeck. They mistake scientific hypotheses for facts and present generalizations instead of the stuff of life. In a serious and well-written novel is this quotation from one of Dr. Georg Groddeck's writings: "Everyone is a sadist . . . everyone by reason of his nature must wish to give . . . pain." Exclusive emphasis on psychological and psychoanalytical frames of reference means erecting a barrier against the intrusion of the social realities of our time behind which sadism and cruelty can flourish.

Events today are so stark that the omission or misrepresentation of the sociological truth may have very harmful effects. It prevents people from understanding the nature of violence and makes them inadvertent and defenseless. In his *Incident at Vichy,* which deals with the greatest genocide in history, Arthur Miller makes an Austrian nobleman the hero who sacrifices his life to save a Nazi victim. We have no comprehensive sociology of National Socialism, but among the well-established sociological facts is the devoted participation of German and Austrian aristocrats in all the departments and activities of the Nazi movement, especially the most ruthless ones. As a group they were more involved than any other section of the population. Many aristocrats joined the SS, and a royal prince was commandant of the Buchenwald concentratration camp. Making a nobleman the hero in a play about Nazi genocide is historically misleading. Art may give us personal dreams, but it should not give us social illusions.

One great danger is the trivialization of violence and murder. This may take place in many—and often unexpected—forms. One example is *In Cold Blood,* by Truman Capote, the literary account of a murder case. Two young men learn from a third that a rich farmer, Herbert Clutter, keeps a lot of money in his house in Holcomb, Kansas. One night they go there, search for the money, and brutally kill the whole family: the man, his wife, a teenage son, and a teenage daughter. They did not find the money they expected because their information was wrong; the farmer did *not* keep money in the house. That is the naked plot: greed and the determination to eliminate all witnesses. To those who have studied murder and murderers in recent years, this has a familiar ring.

Capote, witness his novel *Other Voices, Other Rooms,* is an excellent writer. He tells the story well. But with all the details, a pattern is lost. The crime is described as an isolated phenomenon, as if as a whole it had no connection with anything else. What is its significance? We expect from the artist some illumination. He may claim the right to deny the wider social implications; he may possibly even ignore them. But he should not give us in the form of literary or reportorial objectivity a false steer, a false focus. The key sentence of the book, revealing its whole tenor, is this: "The crime was a psychological accident, virtually an impersonal act; the victims might have been killed by lightning."

Killing without mercy and brutal elimination of all possible witnesses have become a pattern both in fact and in entertainment stories. It is a part of the crescendo in the brutalization of American life. This pattern constitutes a real menace for many people in the future. Recently a man entered a loan-company office in Pennsylvania. He lined up the employees against a wall. Then after getting the money he wanted, he blazed away with a pistol. Two employees were killed, two others seriously wounded. Similar crimes occur in different parts of the country. Killing the witnesses is a stock in trade in countless current mass-media crime stories. If the criminal does not do away with the witness, that is an "error" which leads to his undoing. Not to kill has become the "tragic error." The murder of the Clutter family is part of a wave.

Looked at from the point of view of violence, Capote's book and its reception form a whole. It was one of the greatest instantaneous successes in the history of American publishing and received what *The New York Times* called "a nationwide chorus of admiration." Going over the reviews, we get the unique opportunity to study a phenomenon which may be summarized like this: the literary establishment looks at murder. We come to see that a society has become infected with a cliché-ridden complacence about violence that amounts to complicity.

What did the critics of the best newspapers and magazines get from this book about a planned, predatory, cruel murder? "The whole thing was insane"; "illuminates the interior climate of murder"; "it was meaningless"; "the senseless killing"; "they shot the family for reasons they could not really explain"; "this chaotic moment in our spiritual history"; "a classic"; "the tragedy was existential"; "two remarkable killers"; "mad, childish and ultimately pathetic"; "moral condemnation of them . . . is impossible"; "a major moral judgment"; "its refusal to make judgments"; "thoroughly warped by hideous childhood experiences"; "rushing toward some appalling, mysterious point of psychic infinity"; "the tragic patternings of life itself"; "murder was only incidental to the design"; "the chanciness of our individual existences"; "a grieving testament of faith in what used to be called the soul"; "the murders were almost totally irrational"; "such cosmic acts"; "multiple murder is one of the traditional expressions of youthful hostility."

A good deal of space in the book is given to psychiatric discussions. They are neither particularly sound in themselves nor pertinent to the issues. Just when we want to hear the artist with his artistic intuition, or the reporter with his factual background of similar happenings, we get verbatim the psychiatric jargon of the now so familiar speculative kind, with all its stereotypes. These psychological theories pretend to depth, but actually narrow the field of vision. They excuse but do not explain.

When we finally come to the graveyard scene, human sympathy has turned to sentimentality, literary skill to slickness. We have been transported not to Holcomb but to Hollywood.

*In Cold Blood* is hailed as a masterpiece. It represents an attitude about violence which some writers cultivate and which we, as the public, encourage. The measure of its success is the measure of our failure.

No one can tell an artist what subjects to choose or how to treat them. If one could, it would no longer be art. But the question of the role of art in relation to violence goes beyond the individual work of art or the individual artist. We can attempt to take a view of the whole and of the long-range direction of development. For example, there is a tradition of great artists writing against official mass cruelty. Mark Twain wrote about the Congo, Chekhov about the penal colony on the island of Sachalin, and Pierre Loti described the atrocities committed by the French in Annam (now part of Vietnam). What antiviolence writers are up against can be seen from the fact that the London *Times* at the time criticized Loti for making "the scene of butchery the subject of a literary sketch."

The tradition of such writing does not seem to be in flower at present. On the other hand, a central subject of violence, the death penalty, was for a long time greatly neglected in artistic literature. Legal executions occurred in the plots of novels and plays, the guilt or lack of guilt of individuals was dealt with, but the fundamental human problem of the justification of capital punishment has rarely found a place in works of literature. (Dickens' *Barnaby Rudge,* expressing his abhorrence of capital punishment, is an exception.) This is the more noteworthy because outside of artistic literature the problem was very seriously discussed for a long time. Cesare Beccaria (d. 1794) advocated the abolition of the death penalty; Kant, Hegel, and others debated it. Only in recent years, however, have writers like George Bernard Shaw, Sartre, Camus, and the Swiss Max Frisch attacked the death-penalty theme with artistic means.

The art of the future will have to rise to its new tasks in a violence-threatened world. Some of the lines of development are apparent now. In a negative way what will have to be avoided more and more are presentations which, in the words of William Cowper, sow "the seeds of murder in the heart of man." Constructively, we have to develop in art a heightened social consciousness, an enlarged sensitivity about the violence of the times. This will be something new, which can be achieved, however, only on the basis of the tradition of the best works of the past. Stendhal's *The Red and the Black* is an example. Stendhal was one of the first writers to recognize the dynamic significance of social forces in the life of an individual. He shows how the individual is formed by social conditions. Julien Sorel, the hero of *The Red and the Black,* his personal ambition frustrated, accepts the challenge and fights the good fight alone in and against his society. But through it all, he remains the individualistic hero, the heroic individualist. Such a description of the individual in relation to society was a great achievement in the art of the nineteenth century. Our time, with its back against the wall, confronted with institutionalized violence, demands something more. That is an overcoming of individualism and an integration of the fight with a truly social activity.

# CHAPTER FIFTEEN

# Man Against Murder

We have war because we are not sufficiently heroic for a life which does not need war.
—BARTOLOMEO VANZETTI

Of course, your youth will fight for you, but you, are you fighting for them?
—KJELD ABELL
(Danish playwright, d. 1961)

WHEN the statesman Ramón Narváez (d. 1868), who was Prime Minister of Spain several times, was on his deathbed, a priest asked him whether he forgave his enemies. Narváez answered, "I don't have to forgive my enemies. I had them all shot." This is one of many possible attitudes about violence. Can we hope to eliminate the causes of violence and change the attitudes favoring it?

The violence of our time is that point of intersection where the most primitive way of settling conflicts meets with the highest technological achievements. The tension at that point is overwhelming. In order to combat violence, two things are necessary. First, we need to have a proper long-range perspective, which means an understanding that eventually violence can be banished. Second, we have to learn—and, in the process of abolishing violence, learn over and over again—that it is not a thing apart but is linked by a thousand threads to the present fabric of our social and institutional life.

Can we arbitrarily set an unviolent world as a goal for human development? Is that not just a dream based on wishful thinking and good intentions? It is a part of my thesis that this goal is not just a vista from an ivory tower, but that it is based on objective evidence. It is the natural product of the historical development of society, and it has become an objective historical necessity. Our task is to obtain clarity about this goal. We can have a vision about this future without having illusions.

The idea of human progress is often declared untenable. It is a "Victorian belief," we are told, which in the light of recent history has become "absurd." Or it is said that the human mind "in conformity with its eternal nature" will always "relapse into violence":

Like to a wheel is our world, by fate driven upward and downward, So does the carpenter make for us equally cradles and coffins.

Sometimes when the idea of human progress is conceded, it is assumed to be so slow that it can hardly be taken into account for any goal-directed activity. For example, the psychoanalyst Theodor Reik stated that "it will take 100,000 years to change human nature." As against this, we need to consider that since the very first appearance of *homo sapiens* on earth, only some 30,000 or maybe 40,000 years have passed.

Progress, of course, is not automatic. It does not come to us as a gift. Nor is it inevitable. Serious reverses and reversals can and do occur. We deceive ourselves if we see only the great advances in the physical sciences and overlook the retrogressions of society. An increase in the rate of unemployment is as important a fact as an increase in the speed of jets.

Human progress is not an abstract concept but is a scientific fact. Disagreements are possible about the modes and mechanisms involved, but there can be no doubt that human societies have developed. The idea of science is inseparable from the idea of progress. As Engels pointed out, there has been progress in morality as in all other branches of human knowledge. In the field of violence, progress can best be compared to a road running upward over very many switchbacks. In the long view, every forward step in civilization was a step away from violence, although that was not always apparent. Sometimes even when the means were violent, the all but unconscious goal was in the direction of a higher stage of culture without violence. Of the fact of progress in this field there can be no doubt—despite the fearful reversals of genocide, atom-bomb killing, mass "euthanasia" of mental patients, and the starvation and murder of prisoners of war in the Second World War. We do not practice cannibalism any more, and it is characteristic that in our time only an insane person like Albert Fish would revert to it. We slaughter one another, but we do not devour one another. We also do not practice state- and religion-sanctioned human sacrifice any more. We know some of the stages by which this was overcome, as in prehistoric Greece, when goats were sacrificed to Dionysus as substitutes for the former human sacrifices of children and young men. The prohibition of homicide has been extended since early times so that the number of exceptions under which kings, slave owners, samurai, duelers, and so on, were permitted to kill has steadily decreased. On the whole—also with many reverses—our punishments of crime have tended to become less brutal and cruel.

In almost all present-day discussions of human progress, the great advances in scientific technology play a part. Two contrasting views have been expressed. Some people believe that modern technical achievements signify the domination of man by machines. They see in this a nihilistic force and regard it as a sign of a decline in civilization. In their opinion, modern science constitutes a menace. This view is reminiscent of some of the more dubious implications of Tolstoi's and Gandhi's teachings, namely, that a return to a technically more primitive life would be a step toward a more peaceful life. In reality, the greatest scientific achievements in the uses of atomic energy, rockets, the laser, and so on, open a way to a higher—and unviolent—stage of civilization.

The opposite view, that technical progress alone, far from being a menace, will guarantee social progress, is one-sided and misleading. For example, it is often claimed that the scientific advances in mass communications will by themselves do away with divisions and hostilities in the world. This is a dangerous and unrealistic notion. Machines can never be better than the men who use them. Mass communications as they function at present bear many signals of prejudice, suspicion, and hostility. We have become so accustomed to it that we take it for granted. Too often, both in their stories and in their news, they imply or espouse the law of the wilderness: kill or be killed. Mass media are not infrequently becoming a part of the machinery of hatred that fosters violence in our time. Like atomic energy, they should be used only for peaceful purposes.

The spirit of violence is penetrating deeply into the very citadels where violence is supposed to be prevented. Looking objectively at the world that confronts us today, the conclusion is inevitable that the traditional safeguards against violence in their present form are not sufficient. It is not enough to ban the tests; we must test the bans. Our capacity to destroy has become far greater than the efficacy of our social controls. Whatever these controls have accomplished in the past, the history of the past four decades or so shows that in their present stage they are not enough. There is an increasing gap between the power of the new destructive forces at our command and the attention being given to violence prevention in the respective fields of control.

A few examples illustrate this. Parliamentary democracy has historically achieved a great deal in reducing violence within and among nations. Its current role is not entirely in line with past achievements. Instead of increasing their power to declare or not declare war, parliaments have practically relinquished that power. Democracy has provided whole systems of safety measures, but they have proved not to be adequate for our time. Democracy has to find new ways of coping with present-day social tensions and hostilities. Some ask for a more "participatory democracy."

The very existence of modern weapons and the concentration of industrial-military power put a tremendous strain on democratic controls. At the time of the Cuban missile crisis in 1962, we came closest to World War III. In a speech at a university afterward, McGeorge Bundy, powerful special assistant to the President, in discussing "the practice of freedom and the theory of democracy," said about the crisis that the will of the people was "expressed in all the thousand voices of democracy." It was a poetical phrase. The prose of the facts was very different. The decision had been made entirely by a very small elite.

The law has historically been a most important instrument in counteracting destructive and violent tendencies. Legal prohibitions have long-range effects, but the traditional legal concepts have not caught up with the social realities. Modern mass violence represents something new and different, another order of magnitude, as the mathematicians say. The law is not prepared for these collective murder actions. They are qualitatively something different and cannot be measured within the same (individual) frame of reference. It is difficult enough in individual murder cases to distinguish between murder in the first degree, in the second degree, and manslaughter. In mass extermination the situation is far more complex. We cannot rationally fit the slaughter of men into the category of manslaughter. In the Auschwitz trial of 1965, one defendant was completely acquitted because he had shared only a "minor guilt." How much must a man participate in a mass-murder operation before the law can take cognizance? In the causation of violence the "minor guilt" is as important as the major guilt—and sometimes even more important.

The parallel phenomena of acquittal or mild sentences of mass murderers in Germany and of the blatant acquittals in civil-rights murders in the South have shaken the faith of millions in democratic law. Law without faith in it loses its effectiveness.

International law gropes with the problem of war. It aims to prevent world violence by world law. Under present circumstances it cannot achieve more than to postpone outbreaks. World law can be established only on the foundation of world planning. Law alone is not sufficient as a safeguard against war. How difficult that subject is can be seen from a statement by one of the judges in the Nuremberg war-crimes trial, Judge Winfield B. Hale of the Tennessee Court of Appeals. He said that legally there is no such thing as a "crime against civilization by initiating and waging wars of aggression." Such a statement has to be viewed in conjunction with the fact that a professor of international law at a German university, in a book called *The Nature of International Law,* has proclaimed that war is the social ideal.

Even in individual acts the law does not sufficiently differentiate between violent acts and others. In other words it does not take violence and the violent aspects of acts seriously enough in comparison with other transgressions. For example, although it may not be immediately directed against a person, arson is potentially a violent crime. In sexual offenses, those with violent components are not sufficiently singled out for attention as compared with relatively harmless ones. Although the law distinguishes rape in the first and second degree it nevertheless uses the term "rape" for two totally different offenses: violation of the female person by force and violence and sexual relations with a consenting girl under the age of eighteen. When the criminal law concerns itself with the areas of property ($p$), sex ($s$), and violence ($v$), it often has a Draconian attitude about crimes against property, a self-righteous harshness about sexual offenses, and what amounts to complacency about violent acts. This is not generally acknowledged, but it can be easily demonstrated by putting a large number of sentences together and comparing them according to the formulas $p:v$ or $s:v$ or $p:s:v$. In short, the law does not show a more rigorous attitude about violence than the prevailing social structure of which it is an integral part.

Education as a sufficient safeguard against violence is often taken for granted. Undoubtedly it does have an enormous influence and has helped to teach peaceable thinking to generations. But at present the educators have come up against a problem that education alone cannot solve. On the one hand, they want the pupil and student to find himself and develop his own capacities, his own individuality. On the other hand, they try to instruct him so that he can live and function according to the social norms in his environment. What do immature minds see as norms all around them with regard to violence? Air-raid drills before they can properly read, realistic toy guns and arms, thousands of homicides in comic books, on television, and in movies, glib talk about many millions of casualties in an expected war, and—as they get a little older—the mixture of snobbishness and sadism of James Bond. An experienced editor and writer, Richard Starnes, describes how he sees it: "We waste our finest young men on foreign beaches and in alien jungles, we kill our families by the tens of thousands on our highways, we sell soap and celebrate violence simultaneously on the great medium for mass hypnosis that television has become, we educate our children in brutal games of cops and

robbers and we don't tell them until too late that it is not always
the bad guys who get killed." The lesson, an all-around devaluation of human life, is clearer and more easily learned than those
given by formal education. Against this trend, modern education
has not been able to prevail.

Twenty-five years ago a question often raised was: Is religion
adequate to moderate and restrain violence? Today the question
is more often asked in the form: Why is religion not equal to this
task? We must, of course, to the extent that it is possible, distinguish among the religious sentiments and beliefs of the individual,
dogmatic religion, and the organized bodies of religion. Such facts
as that in Germany—for example, in Mainbernheim—the Nazi
swastika was mounted on a church steeple instead of the usual
cross have contributed to interfering with the image of organized
religion as an antiviolence agency. Religion, more in some epochs
than in others and more in some localities than in others, has played
an important role with regard to counteracting violence. At times it
has had both a strong immediate disciplining effect and a more
diffuse civilizing influence. But in recent eras, as pointed out by
William Bolitho, a keen student of violence, it is losing its efficacy
as a safeguard against violence. This is true both in the life of the
individual and as a social phenomenon.

The divisions among people fostered, encouraged, or created by
world religions have historically done much harm. The fact of this
separation of men is undeniable. We have not sufficiently learned
that intolerance in any form is a potent factor toward violence.
There is a serious aspect to the true story about the two clergymen, one of whom ends their discussion by saying, "We are both
doing God's work—you in your way and I in His." The advent
of the atomic era has been a severe test in all fields of human life.
That is the case also for religious influences. Just before the plane
carrying the atomic bomb took off for Hiroshima a clergyman
offered a solemn prayer in which he besought God's blessing for
those who were going into the heights of heaven to carry the battle
to the enemy and asked that they be kept under His protection
until their safe return. He said nothing about the victims. In a
recent book on atomic arms from a religious point of view this

passage occurs: "Nuclear weapons are here and will never again disappear from this earth. . . . They are irrevocably here." Such a view is not universally held, but it is by no means exceptional.

We need to examine not only general influences in our society, with regard to their efficacy in the prevention of violence, but also special agencies. For example, one agency put under very heavy strain by recent history is the International Red Cross. Of course, the Red Cross was up against gigantic tasks during the Second World War. But it would be ignorant not to realize how much it failed to perform the great function associated with its name. In reading the accounts of eyewitnesses and of survivors, we come again and again across anguished questions: "What has happened to the Red Cross?" "What about the International Red Cross?" "Where is the Red Cross?"

Whatever the Red Cross achieved in World War II, concern for the future does not permit us to overlook some important facts. We do not know the exact figures, but according to the best available estimates, of about 5,700,000 Russian war prisoners in Germany, only somewhat more than a million survived (Abendroth). These prisoners were inhumanly treated, with the rationalization that as Slavs and Asiatics they were inferior human beings. The Buchenwald death camp was visited by the Duke of Coburg, who was an SS officer, president of the Red Cross, and concurrently vice-president of the International Red Cross. He reported that rumors of maltreatment of inmates were wholly unfounded. The I. G. Farben slave-labor camp Monowitz was a component of the Auschwitz complex. Many thousands of prisoners died there as a result of their slave labor and hunger rations or in the death camps to which they were sent when exhausted. When the chairman of the board of the I. G. Farben industry was asked in court whether it was visited by the International Red Cross he answered, "Yes, it was visited and found good." In 1929 the Geneva Convention of the Red Cross had especially extended its protection to prisoners of war. In assigning responsibility, three elements have to be distinguished: the International Committee, the national societies, and the league of Red Cross societies through which the field-work of the national societies is coordinated.

Prevention without anticipation is not possible. To take the efficacy of the traditional, conventional safeguards against violence too much for granted has the serious effect of giving us illusions of safety. We behave as if violence were already almost abolished. That is one of the reasons why we are always surprised at a brutal murder, a massacre, a race riot, or

> When on a sudden, shrouded in poisonous smoke,
> They turn to slaughter amid the thundering rolls
> Of quick explosions, crumbling far and wide
> Imperial cities into dust again,
> And palaces, and farms of the countryside. (H. W. Nevinson)

Serious concern with violence, as well as the study of its prevention, is something new. For convenience' sake, one may speak of "violentology," meaning the study of violence from the point of view of its prevention. The term focuses attention on a phenomenon which people generally do not like to face in its stark reality, and it indicates that it is a special problem. The term enables us to say that a murder, a race riot, an assassination, or a war has been left unresolved "violentologically"—that is to say, from the strict point of view of the prevention of violence.

Violence occurs on very different levels. Individual and national action are governed by very different objective laws. But they have some things in common. For example, all violence unresolved will probably be repeated. In every violent act, four interacting forces are operative: the psychological tendencies for it, the psychological tendencies against it, the social forces for it, and the social forces against it. The field in which these forces operate is much wider than is usually considered. Violentological reasoning demands that we follow all the ramifications and connections.

From the point of view of the theory of science, violentology has to be based on the recognition of the widest interconnectedness between seemingly diverse phenomena, big or small. We have learned this primarily from five scientists in very different fields. Marx did *not* say that everything is economically determined. He did explain that there is a close connection between the economic factor and other areas. Freud did *not* teach that everything is sexual, but he did demonstrate that between the sexual attitudes and other life situations there is a close connection. Pavlov did *not* claim that all physiological behavior consists in conditioned reflexes. What he demonstrated was that "temporary connections" can play a decisive role in the activity of the organism. The atomic physicist Werner Heisenberg did *not* abolish the concept of causality, but he discerned the very closest connection between the observer and his measuring instruments and the observed particles of matter. Finally, Norbert Wiener in his cybernetics proved that there is an intricate connection between the outside influences impinging upon a system and the controlling forces operative within the system itself. No manifestation of human violence can be understood as a self-contained, isolated occurrence.

One feature that personal and national violence have in common is what may be called "violence-thinking." Violence-thinking is the readiness to see the solution of difficulties only in violent means and to invent all kinds of rationalizations to justify it. In individual psychology, that is well known. It occurs also on the social level. When we say that potential opponents understand only the language of force and violence, it shows what language we are thinking in and also that our imagination does not reach much further. We say freedom and mean power, we say power and mean violence. The atom bomb in the hands of violence-thinking statesmen is like a knife in the hands of a child.

There are two general theories about violence. According to the first, derived from Freud, man has an inborn instinct leading to it. In human nature, we are told, there is a fixed amount of aggression, and it has to express itself one way or another. We are born with that, and all we can study are what controls we can apply. Freud speaks in several places of "the ubiquity of aggression and destruction," of man's "inborn inclination toward evil, toward aggression, destruction, and with that also toward cruelty." He assumed that the instinct to destruction is derived from a general "death instinct" operative in every human being. That a psychologist in our time should get the idea that there is such a thing as a "death instinct" is really not astonishing.

The theory that violence is ingrained in man and is an intrinsic manifestation of human nature is very widely held. It has been qualified, mitigated, embellished, and camouflaged, but in one form or another, usually with the ambiguous use of the term "aggression," it dominates our intellectual life. The theory has been extended to war, which is supposed to be rooted in deeply embedded instincts rather than in social relations. For example, Dr. Edward Glover, in his book, *War, Sadism and Pacifism,* writes: "The first effective step toward abolishing war must be the investigation and the understanding of the nature of sadistic impulses." But the soldiers in modern wars do not fight because they have "sadistic impulses"; they fight because they have been drafted.

The term "aggression" is used to cover very different things. "One day in New York," the psychoanalyst Fritz Wittels wrote in the fall of 1940, "produces more aggression in the form of labor, business, professional activity, etc., than half a year of bombs over London." The cold war is also traced to instinctive aggression which does not have sufficient outlets. This overlooks the fact that the cold war comes from social conflicts. What we call the cold war is really a lukewarm peace.

The instinct-of-aggression theory makes violence a biological, natural phenomenon. That really legitimizes and rationalizes it. It is not an explanation but the evasion of an explanation. Human violence is not a product of nature, though; it is a product of society. It is socially conditioned and socially preventable. The analogy with the sex instinct is a false one. Of course, like all human behavior, violence has a biological substrate. But if we make that the cornerstone, we are leaving out what is truly human. The violent man is not the natural man with destructive aggressions but is the socially alienated man. We know, especially from the analysis of neurotic patients, that unconscious hostility based on buried emotional drives may lead to all kinds of eruptions. But to generalize this for social problems means to apply deep psychology in a superficial way.

The idea that we all have an aggressive-destructive instinct but different degrees of control or lack of control cannot do justice to the much more complex circumstances of violence causation and prevention. It unduly narrows down the whole question and assigns to the social environment merely a braking function. It makes of violence a problem that is personal and not sociological.

The instinct-versus-control formula is far too simple. It postulates that in everyone there is a struggle between darkness, *i.e.,* the aggressive instinct, and light, *i.e.,* control. It is a conception that is psychiatrically unclinical, philosophically unrealistic, and politically reactionary.

Reliance on the narrow frame of reference of a basic inborn instinct of aggression in human nature deprives us of an understanding of some of the most outstanding manifestations of violence in our time. The slave-labor-to-death camps which took hundreds of thousands of lives are an example. Which individual are you going to pick to analyze for the strength of his aggressive instinct or for the weakness of his control? The man who conceived it, the one who planned it, the one who organized it, the engineer who worked there, or the one who finally practiced it? The procedure has a prehistory in the colonies, where the same methods were used extensively—with the same cruelty and the same profits. It was a collective rapacity. The urge was not to kill but to make a killing. European parliaments did not object in the Congo colony, for instance. No instinct in an individual alone can explain it. In our time, it was free enterprise at its freest. The slave-labor-plus-killing methods were not just transitory eruptions of uninhibited instinct or hostility, but were fully integrated into the ordinary, successful, long-range industrial-commercial process. The shares of some of the firms which employed slave labor are internationally traded and are today higher than ever.

The second general theory of violence, suggested by violentological study, postulates that violence is not the explosion of any inborn instinct, but is always the result of negative factors in the personality development and in the social medium. Violence is a perversion of human relations. We overestimate the individual proclivity to destruction and underestimate the social permissiveness for destruction. The dynamics of violence cannot be understood on the basis of elemental biological drives in the individual, but only by reference to social forces. The anthropologist Margaret Mead has well expressed the contrast between the conceptions of an outbreak of innate hostility and the existence of social institutions which "generate" aggression. According to my analysis, violence is entrenched, built in, and deeply embedded in our institutions. We live in an atmosphere of institutionalized brutality which has affected both adults and children. An American child may not know for a long time how babies are made, but long before he can read he has learned how men are killed. He even gets a generous dose of the hate that goes with it.

The diffusion of violence in our society creates a different order of motivation. There are not only deep psychological but also deep sociological motives for it. Corresponding to this, there is not only one individual responsibility but a social responsibility, a coresponsibility. It is easier—and less controversial— to speculate on the violence in us than to analyze the violence around us. Many who have committed violent acts in our era have been encouraged, seduced, expected, or ordered to commit them. They are truly like marionettes. The threads on which they are suspended and which move them are invisible to the audience. To probe the mind of the modern mass murderer is like psychoanalyzing a marionette. The *Manchester Guardian* wrote some time ago: "The truth we are reluctant to face is that there is no depravity and no cruelty that is beyond the ingenuity of quite ordinary men who are otherwise amiable and even conventional." This is explainable only if we recognize the present-day institutionalization of cruelty and trace not only the personal but also the social roots.

Not far from the city of Prague was the concentration camp Terezin. It was a way station to death-factory camps. Fifteen thousand children under fifteen passed through this camp. All of them, with the exception of about a hundred, were killed. This is a key event in the history of modern violence. Violentologically, although they are of course all responsible, it is not enough to blame for this mass slaughter one man, one nation, one regime, one political party, or the many persons actually involved in the planning and execution. Nor is it correct to say that this was a reversion to a primitive state of mankind. To say that it is primitive and refer it to a mythical past means to try to explain it away and condone it. We cannot be "primitive." The fault is right here, buried deep in our time, our age, our civilization. It is part of a general devaluation and depreciation of human life; of the glib talk about "population explosions"; of the fact that in the United States, twice as many nonwhite infants die as white ones; of the battered-baby syndrome, which we have been so pitifully unable to control; of our pride in the advanced technology of mass killing; and of the "bloodless genocide" of millions of disadvantaged people which Dr. Fanon writes about.

Currently some widespread intellectual attitudes, far from counteracting violence, contribute to its perpetuation. Whatever attraction they may have and whatever role they may play in other spheres of life, violentologically they do not correspond to the reality of modern violence. And this reality is unforgiving.

One such attitude is represented by the idea that destructive aggression is an integral part of man's fate. We are told that this is an eternal problem of mankind, that it is part of the "total human predicament," that we must live with it as we have to with anxiety. The psychiatrist and existentialist philosopher Karl Jaspers declares that the "fight of man against man for life or death" is a "basic phenomenon of life." Pronouncements like that provide a convenient rug to sweep dust under. But violence is not human; it is inhuman. It is not an attribute of the human being as such, but of man-in-society. We may not know how human life will or should be, but we can be sure that certain things, such as cruelty, are wrong, and we can attack practically what we can attack. Instead of believing that violence will always be with us. we can try to reduce and eventually abolish it. One aim of violentology is to raise doubts about its eternal sway.

Closely allied to the belief in the eternity of human destruction is a pessimism, philosophically underpinned, that nothing fundamental can be done about it. If we analyze this pessimism and its academic supporting arguments, we find that it is essentially the expression of helplessness in the face of the pressures of a complex society. It is really a form of opportunism—an answer without facing the question. As opposed to this, we must arrive at the consciousness that man has the power to change and is not at the mercy of either his instincts or the forces operating in society.

A related, though in many ways different and more responsible, attitude toward violence is represented by the French writer Albert Camus, who has so influenced young people in Europe and the United States. This is a kind of nihilism. The London *Times* described it as "sophisticated despair." It is not insignificant that Camus regarded Nietzsche as the greatest European writer.

A widely extended attitude that is an obstacle in the struggle against violence may be called pseudohumanism. The term "humanism" has historically a serious forward-looking meaning, but it is apt to be misused, without regard to this meaning, as a conveniently abstract principle. In a variety of ways, it is asserted that if only we had more humanism, violence would cease. All sorts of social arrangements are supposedly enhanced or improved by adding the word "humanist." We may read, for example, about humanist colonialism. By adding this adjective, something is assumed to be something else.

How this abstract, literary humanism is to be translated into reality we are not told. Instead of the necessary analysis of concrete processes in concrete places, a simple humanism, with all its ambiguities and lukewarmness, is offered us. This has serious consequences. The truly humanist spirit is reduced to a kind of philanthropy, which in our time is not what those suffering most from violence and oppression want. These habits of thinking lead always to confusion about what is human and what is inhuman. It has become almost fashionable to deplore the use of computers and mathematics in human affairs as being "inhuman." But these scientific and technological advances are not inhuman. On the contrary, they will enable us to be more human than we were before. We need for that not less mathematics but more, not fewer computers but more and better ones.

The complacency about violence of those in authority, the decision makers, the opinion molders, the image builders, is one of the greatest problems. A nine-year-old boy was found hanging minutes after seeing a hanging scene on television. A pair of legs was shown on the screen dangling in the air. It was part of a scene in which the hero was working out a hanging mystery. The boy went to the hall to play with a rope. His teenage sister found him a few minutes later hanging inches above a chair by the hall stairs. There is not the slightest doubt that he died accidentally from his own experiment. A television executive made a statement about this that was reported in the press with the headline:

NO VIOLENCE

It read: "There was nothing violent in the episode of————, and it did not contain a sequence depicting a hanging. The hero did deduce from evidence that a dead man had been murdered and had not hanged himself. He proved his theory by reconstructing the scene and by demonstration in the broadest terms in a very general way." What is it in a man in a responsible position that causes such an uncaring attitude, which is indicative of so much violence in the world today? Edward R. Murrow, who was a great pioneer in electronic journalism, answered that question from his own experience: "If you sit and talk with executives of big corporations you find that as individuals they care about a hell of a lot of things that are not reflected in the programs they sponsor. There is often a complete divorcement between the individual and his corporate personality." Similarly, Freud spoke about lack of agreement or "estrangements" between two zones within the individual; and, interestingly, Marx wrote in almost the same words about "the division of the human being into a public and a private personality." It is especially in the field of violence that this side-by-side existence of two antagonistic ethical standards is manifest, one for the person himself and those near him, another for the rest of the people. Violence prevention demands an accounting between the two on a higher level, a protection for all.

We do not like to face the fact of violence and with it the simple main causes: greed, fear, power, hunger, prejudice, jealousy, clinging to privilege, revolt of the oppressed, revenge, rivalries, stirred-up hate. The methods of evasion are many. We look for murder in the dark recesses of the mind or the dark alleys of the cities. People are overoptimistic and regard murders as exceptions, race riots as exceptions, wars as exceptions. But near-murders, near-race riots, and near-wars are with us all the time. What is lacking is action in opposition. In this way, we remain enmeshed within the mentality of violence.

One reason for this is that we do not make sufficiently clear to ourselves what violence really is, what all its effects are, and what psychological associations it has. In the diary of a captured German flier in the Second World War was a note in which he complained that when he spent his furlough in Nazi-occupied Paris he found that the inhabitants looked surly. The diary added: "And we haven't even bombarded them!" In the same way, after I read a paper on the analysis of Richard Wright's *Native Son* before the American Psychopathological Association, I was asked by a Southern psychiatrist, "Why are Negroes so surly when I talk to them? I have observed it again and again," he went on, "and in our town we haven't had a lynching for years."

A whole army of experts—psychologists, sociologists, criminologists, political scientists—is ready for action to explain away every proffered cause of violence. Murder is not murder but always something else: an eruption of the unconscious, existential anxiety, natural need for aggression, senseless lust for destruction, frustrations of the infant in his crib, the hot weather, and so on. Whatever their conscious intention, these experts function as a Praetorian guard to preserve the status quo, violence and all. Of the rising juvenile violence, they say it does not really exist, but only seems to because the newspapers report it more; of sadistic mass media, that they are really good, for they prevent committing of sadistic acts; of a political murder, we are told that the murderer must have been insane and acting from a "compulsion" and that the surrounding hate and extremist agitation had nothing whatever to do with it; of a race riot, that it was really not a race riot, but merely a disturbance "triggered" (that convenient word) by a police incident and that some young people just wanted to plunder; of the now so typical callousness of witnesses who let a girl be killed within sight and hearing without even calling the police, that they acted like that because unconsciously they wanted to murder her too. (Since it is all "unconscious," it relieves us of elementary responsibility.)

Some of this has had a great effect not only on the ordinary man but on professionals and intellectuals as well. Often they write about violence with a kind of nervous conformity. What with all the violence around us, our conscience gets overburdened and is apt to fall asleep, especially if it finds such a comfortable bed. In this way, a violence-ridden nation becomes a violence-prone one.

Praetorian experts tell us that war is "obsolete." That is not science but wishful thinking. War is not obsolete. It is of the very essence of our time. The best intelligences are working on it. They devise ever-new methods of killing, not of preventing killing. Writers discuss peace in a military context and war in a psychological context. It is so much easier to trace the free flow of associations than to trace the free flow of credits. We cannot fight violence without taking up what people are violent about. Experts are especially anxious to convince us that the causes of war are not economic but are in "the structure of the psyche" or in ideologies. This is plainly contradicted by an official U.S. Government document given to the U.S. Senate Committee on Armed Services some time after World War II. It states: "Realistically, all wars have been for economic reasons. To make them politically and socially palatable, ideological issues have always been invoked. Any possible future war will undoubtedly conform to historical precedent."

Human violence is always a symptom. It is never an independent process. It indicates that there is something wrong. No single great cause is ever responsible without many little causes lending a hand. It is the small things, both in individual life and in our institutions, which foreshadow and help to facilitate or bring about the explosions of violence. These unspectacular facts, the *petits faits* of the French, often play a decisive role. Many murders were almost not committed, many wars almost not started. Just as the past has laid the groundwork for the cruelty of today, so today we are laying it for tomorrow. West German Minister of Justice Bucher said in a public statement in 1965, in commenting on the statute of limitations concerning war criminals, that "we must accept the fact that we may have to go on living with a few murderers." This was not only a local statement with local significance. Although not expressed openly and although we do not like to admit it, it applies in a larger sense also to us. Our attitude toward violence is so negligent that it amounts to "accepting" the fact of violence among us as a chronic symptom and a social climate. Careers like that of Albert Fish and the gangster Martin

Lavin or the murders in the South would not continue to be possible otherwise.

With regard to what can or should be done to counteract the permanence and spread of violence and war, two diametrically opposed views have been expressed. According to one, all efforts should be devoted to the struggle to prevent war. Endeavors for major social reforms and human progress should be entirely subordinated to this. The current world situation in which the most important thing seems to be to keep the balance of terror on one's own side, makes this argument very persuasive.

According to the opposing opinion, action against war and violence cannot be really effective unless social and economic conditions are changed first on a more or less global scale. The attainment of peace should be regarded as a result rather than as a primary aim.

Dispute about these two views has greatly hampered progress. But from a long-range, forward-looking point of view there is no real absolute contrast between them. The struggles for peace and for social betterment cannot be separated. No isolated solution is possible. We cannot have war abolished without very many other things having been changed too. That is why the call for a "world government," a "supernational authority," and so on, cannot be successful if raised without that. In the struggle against war, if it is seriously pursued, we inevitably learn about power conditions within our society; and in the struggle to improve social-economic conditions for all, we learn about the subsoil of war. In a thoroughly democratic society where "the thousand voices of democracy" *are* fully heard, the people do not want war. The objective situation is this: if we want to abolish war, we must bring about more democracy; and if we want to increase democracy, we must do away with war. Under the present world threat of armed conflict, democracy cannot fully flourish anywhere. Therefore it is necessary to perform both tasks without preconceived priorities.

There is a particular poignancy today in the remark made by the empire builder Cecil Rhodes: "I would annex the planets if I could." How can we curb individual and social-national predatoriness? There are no easy solutions. Nor can there at this stage be any panacea, blueprint, or over-all master plan. It has to be worked out phase by phase from the objective conditions and premises now in existence. We have the stones with which to build, but we must stop throwing them at one another.

More than 150 years ago the great natural scientist Alexander von Humboldt developed the thesis that man's highest development requires that we put the diversified resources of the earth into a common world stream of use. This is certainly a necessary condition if we want to lay a firm and lasting foundation for violence prevention.

In principle, violence is indivisible; but it has many faces. We have to pursue with the same fidelity both the general and the specific. The problem has to be attacked on all fronts. No area, however remote or trivial-sounding, can be neglected. It is like a ditch that fills up with water. If we just drain off the water, it may fill right up again. We may have to dig deeper at a distance to cut off the source of the water and keep the ditch dry. And with changing water-level conditions in the earth, even that may have to be repeated.

To make the world unviolent requires a greater state of disinterestedness than our everyday selves have. It cannot be done without sacrifices. Those who speak so much of an "open society" usually have a closed mind. An intimate relationship exists between individualism, selfishness, and latent violence. When—and wherever—we can, we must oppose hyperindividualism and hypernationalism, both of which seek satisfaction for themselves at the cost of others. An equitable social-economic structure of societies must be the basis for bringing about a universal revulsion against violence. If the individual—all individuals—and society become the integrated unity which they truly are in a fully developed civilization, motives for killing will yield to habits of nonviolence, and nobody will have to be afraid any longer of violent interference with his life or that of his children.

In our time the physical sciences have accomplished what countless generations have regarded as impossible. There is no valid reason to doubt that we can make the same progress in human relationships.

# Bibliography

ABENDROTH, W.: *Social History of the European Labor Movement,* Frankfurt, 1965.

ADLER, H. G.: *Theresienstadt 1941–1945: History, Sociology, Psychology,* Tuebingen, Germany, 1961.

ALEXANDER, L.: "War Crimes and Their Motivation," *Journ. of Crim. Law and Crimnology,* Sept.–Oct., 1948.

ALFRED, L., *et al.: Revolutionary Antimilitarism,* Metz, France, n.d. (about 1930).

ANDREEV, L.: *A Dilemma,* transl. J. Cournos, New York, 1926.

"Apartheid as Business," *Kursbuch,* No. 2, 1965.

BAUMGARTEN, A.: "Juridical, Sociological and Psychological Remarks on the Problem of War Prevention," in *Psychohygiene,* ed. M. Pfister-Ammende, Bern, Switzerland, 1949.

BENDER, L., and J. FROSCH: "Children's Reactions to War," in *A Dynamic Psychopathology of Childhood,* ed. L. Bender, Springfield, Ill., 1954.

————: "Children and Adolescents Who Have Killed," *Amer. Journ. of Psychiatry,* Dec. 1959.

" 'Benevolent' Weapon" (nonlethal gas), *Chemical Week,* Apr., 1965.

BENJAMIN, W.: *On the Critique of Violence,,* Frankfurt, 1965.

BOK, C.: *Star Wormwood,* New York, 1959.

BOLITHO, W.: *Murder for Profit,* Introd. by F. Wertham, Time Reading Program, New York, 1964.

BORN, M.: *Physics and Politics,* Goettingen, Germany, 1960.

BOSSCHÈRE, G. DE: "Direct Non-Violent Action," *Les Temps Modernes,* July, 1960.

BOWEN, C.: *They Went Wrong* (the Robert Brown case), New York, 1954,

BRAINES, S. N., *et. al.: Neurocybernetics,* Berlin, 1964.

BROMBERG, W.: *The Mold of Murder,* New York, 1961.

————: *Crime and the Mind,* New York, 1965.

BROWN, I.: *First Player,* New York, 1928.

BROWN, J. A. C.: *Techniques of Persuasion,* London and Baltimore, Md., 1963.

BURROW, T.: "Crime and the Social Reaction of Right and Wrong," *Journ. of Crim. Law and Criminology,* Nov.–Dec., 1933.

376 *A Sign for Cain*

BURTT, E. A.: "Theory of International Relations," *Journ. of Philosophy, 42,* 1945.

CAIRNS, H.: "The Humanities and the Law," *N.Y. Univ. Law Review,* Jan., 1952.
CALDER, R. L., and C. DARROW: " 'Is Capital Punishment Right?': A Debate," *The Forum,* Sept., 1928.
CARTHY, J. D., and F. J. EBLING, ed.: *The Natural History of Aggression,* London, 1964.
CHEVALIER, H.: *Oppenheimer,* New York., 1965.
CHITTAPRASAD, quoted by M. Krása in *New Orient,* Feb., 1961.
CLARK, L. D.: "A Comparative View of Aggressive Behavior," *Amer. Journ. of Psychiatry,* Oct., 1962.
COHEN, L. R., S. P. SEARS, and J. R. EWALT: "Observations on the Chapin Case and 'the Briggs Law,' " *Mass. Law Quarterly, XLI,* 1956. See also "The Kenneth Chapin Case," *Amer. Journ. of Psychotherapy,* Jan., 1957.
COMFORT, A.: "The Martyrdom of the House," *The Chimera,* Summer, 1943.
———: *Darwin and the Naked Lady,* London, 1961.
COOK, F. J.: *The Warfare State,* New York, 1962.
COOMARASWAMY, A. K.: *Am I My Brother's Keeper?,* New York, 1947.
———: *The Dance of Shiva,* New York, 1957.
CRAIG, E. G.: "On the Ghosts in the Tragedies of Shakespeare," in *On the Art of the Theatre,* Chicago, 1911.
"Criminal Responsibility," *Amer. Journ. of Psychiatry,* Feb., 1954.
CURRAN, W. J.: "A Psychiatric Report on Criminal Responsibility" (the Kenneth Chapin case), in *Law and Medicine,* Boston, 1960.

DALZIEL, M.: *Popular Fiction 100 Years Ago,* London, 1957.
D'AUVERGNE, E. B.: *Pierre Loti: The Romance of a Great Writer,* New York, 1926.
DAVIDSON, H. A.: "The Psychiatrist's Role in the Administration of Criminal Justice," *Rutgers Law Review, 4,* 1950.
———: "Rationalizations for Continued Smoking," *N.Y. State Journ. of Medicine,* Dec., 1964.
DAVIDSON, JUSTICE I. D., and R. GEHMAN: *The Jury is Still Out* (the Michael Farmer case), New York., 1959.
DAVIS, R. G.: "Art and Anxiety," *Partisan Review,* Summer, 1945.
DICKINSON, G. L.: *Appearances,* London, 1914.

"Documents About the Murders of Mental Patients," *Die Wandlung,* Mar., 1947, Apr., 1947.

DU BOIS, W. E. B.: "Does 'All Deliberate Speed' Mean 338 Years?", *Nat. Guardian,* Nov., 1957.

EAST, SIR N.: *Society and the Criminal,* Springfield, Ill., 1951.

EDWARDS, JUSTICE E.: "Judge, I Told that Boy . . . ," *New Republic,* Mar., 1960.

EHRHARDT, H.: *Euthanasia and Destruction of Life Devoid of Value,* Introd. by H. Hoff, Stuttgart, 1965.

ELLENBERGER, H., and M. DONGIER: "Criminology," in *Encyclopédie Médico-chirurgicale,* Paris, 1958.

ELLISON, J.: "Television: Stimulant to Violence," *The Nation,* Dec., 1963.

ENGELMANN, B.: "Himmler's Circle of Friends," in *Germany-Report,* Berlin, 1966.

"Euthanasia," in *Trials of War Criminals Before the Nuremberg Military Tribunals, I,* Washington, D.C., 1949.

"Euthanasia," *Der Spiegel,* No. 19, 1961; No. 8, 1964.

"The Extermination of Mental Patients Under the National Socialist Régime," *La Raison,* May, 1951.

FANON, F.: *The Wretched of the Earth,* Introd. by J.-P. Sartre, New York, 1963.

————: "On Violence," *Temps Modernes,* May, 1961.

FARRAR, C. B.: "Tests to Determine Responsibility for Criminal Acts," *Internat. Psychiatry Clinics,* Jan., 1965.

FEIFFER, J.: *The Great Comic Book Heroes,* New York, 1965.

FERRIER, J.-L.: "Gastaud and the Quest for Lost Spaces," illus., *Les Temps Modernes,* July, 1965.

FIEDLER, F.: *On the Unity of Science,* Berlin, 1964.

FORD, A.: *Edward Hicks: Painter of the Peaceable Kingdom,* Philadelphia, 1952.

FRANK, L. K.: "Toward a Projective Psychology," *Journ. of Projective Techniques,* Sept., 1960.

FRAZER, J. G.: *Psyche's Task,* London, 1909.

FREUD, A.: *Normality and Pathology in Childhood,* New York, 1965.

FRY, R.: *The Artist and Psychoanalysis,* London, 1924.

GAHRINGER, R. E.: "Punishment as Language," *Ethics: An International Journ. of Soc., Polit. and Legal Philosophy,* Oct., 1960.

GEHMAN, R.: *A Murder in Paradise*, New York, 1954.

GEISSLER, R.: *Decadence and Heroism*, Stuttgart, 1964.

GERBNER, G.: *The Literature on Violence and the Mass Media: A Bibliography*, mimeographed, University of Illinois, Urbana, Ill., 1963.

————: "Ideological Perspectives and Political Tendencies in News Reporting," *Journalism Quarterly*, Autumn, 1964.

*Germany—Reports of the Social-Democratic Party of Germany*, Vol. 6, Paris, 1939.

GIONO, J.: *The Dominici Affair* (the Drummond murders), London, 1955.

GLASS, H. B.: "The Scientist as Politician," *Johns Hopkins Magazine*, May–June, 1962.

GODWIN, G.: *The Trial of Daniel M'Naughton*, mimeographed, BBC, London, Oct., 1949.

————: *Criminal Man*, New York, 1957.

GORKI, M.: *On Children's Literature*, Berlin, 1963.

GOSHAL, K.: *People in Colonies*, New York, 1948.

GOULETT, H. M.: "The Insanity Defense in Criminal Trials," St. Paul, Minn., 1965.

GROHMANN, W.: *Art and Architecture*, Vol. III, Between the Two Wars series, Berlin, 1953.

GROTJAHN, M.: *Beyond Laughter*, New York, 1957.

HALL, J.: "Psychiatry and Criminal Responsibility," in *Studies in Jurisprudence and Criminal Theory*, New York, 1958.

————: "The M'Naghten Rules and Proposed Alternatives," *Amer. Bar Assoc. Journ.*, Oct., 1963.

————: "Psychiatric Criminology: Is It a Valid Marriage? The Legal View." Read at the American Psychiatric Association, May, 1966.

HALSEY, M.: *The Pseudo-Ethic*, New York, 1963.

HAMMERSTEIN, K. VON: *Reconnaissance Troop*, Stuttgart, 1963.

HAWES, E.: *Hurry Up, Please, It's Time*, New York, 1946.

HAYAKAWA, S. I.: "The Use and Misuse of Language: Thoughts on Thermonuclear Gamesmanship," *ETC: A Review of General Semantics*, May, 1962.

————: *Symbol, Status and Personality*, New York, 1963.

HAYS, H. R.: *In the Beginnings*, New York, 1963.

HENDERSON, SIR D. K.: *Psychopathic States*, New York, 1939.

————: *Society and Criminal Conduct*, Edinburgh, 1955.

HENDERSON, P.: *Literature*, XXth Century Library series, ed. V. K. Krishna Menon, London, 1935.

HENKYS, R.: *The National Socialist Crimes of Violence,* Stuttgart and Berlin, 1964.

HERZOG, H.: "On Borrowed Experience," *Studies in Philosophy and Social Science, 9,* 1941.

HESSE, M. R.: *Partenau,* Hamburg, 1952.

HILL, M. M., and L. N. WILLIAMS: *Auschwitz in England: A Record of a Libel Action,* London, 1965.

HOLITSCHER, A.: *Restless Asia,* Berlin, 1926.

HONAN, W. H.: "Toys and Christmas," *New Republic,* Dec., 1963.

———: "TV and the 'Bloody' Classics," *Quarterly Journ. of Speech,* Apr., 1965.

HONOLKA, B.: *Die Kreuzelschreiber: Euthanasia in the Third Reich,* Hamburg, 1961.

HOULT, T. F.: "Comic Books and Juvenile Delinquency," *Sociology and Social Research, 33,* 1949.

HSIAO CH'IEN: *Etching of a Tormented Age,* London, 1947.

HUGO, V.: "Speech at Centenary Celebration for Voltaire, May, 1878," in *Das Aktionsbuch,* Berlin, 1917.

HUIE, W. B.: *Three Lives for Mississippi,* New York, 1965.


*I. G. Farben, Auschwitz, Mass Murder: Documents on the Auschwitz Trial,* Berlin, 1964.

IRVING, D.: *The Destruction of Dresden,* New York, 1964.


JAECKEL, G.: *The Charité: The Story of the Most Famous German Hospital,* Bayreuth, Germany, 1963.

JAURÈS, J., and P. LAFARGUE: *Idealism and Materialism in the Conception of History: A Debate,* Paris and Lille, France, 1895.

JOCHMANN, W.: *In the Struggle for Power* (Hitler's speech before the National 1919 Club of Hamburg), Frankfurt, 1961. (Speech was delivered in 1926.)

JUNGK, R.: *Brighter Than a Thousand Suns,* New York, 1958.


KAPLAN, J., and J. R. WALTZ: *The Trial of Jack Ruby,* New York, 1965.

KEYSERLINGK, H. VON: *Alcoholism as a Social Problem,* Jena, Germany, 1961.

KING, M. L., JR.: *Stride Toward Freedom,* New York, 1958.

———: *Why We Can't Wait,* New York, 1964.

KINTNER, E. W., ed.: *Trial of Alfons Klein et al.* (the Hadamar trial), London, 1949.

KNEBEL, F., and C. W. BAILEY: "The Fight Over the A-Bomb," *Look,* Aug., 1963.

KOESSLER, M.: "Euthanasia in the Hadamar Sanatorium and International Law," *J. Crim. Law, Criminol. and Police Science, 43,* 1953.

KOGON, E.: *The SS-State,* Stockholm, 1947.

KOTHE, K.: "Case of a Juvenile Murderer," *Psychiatr., Neurol. and Med. Psychol.,* Jan., 1964.

KURZ, H.: *Anti-Dictator,* New York, 1942.


LA BOÉTIE, É. DE: *Discourse on Voluntary Servitude,* in *Complete Works,* Bordeaux and Paris, 1892.

LAFARGUE, P.: "The Origin of the Idea of Justice," in *Social and Philosophical Studies,* Chicago, 1906.

LANDAUER, G.: *Revolution,* Vol. XIII, Society series, ed. M. Buber, Frankfurt, 1907.

LANGE, J.: "Types of Lust Murderers," *Zeitschr. f. d. ges. Neurol, u. Psychiatr., 131,* 1930.

LANGER, S. K.: "The Social Influence of Design," *University* (Princeton), Summer, 1965.

LANTZ, P.: "Malthus and Marx or Scarcity Refound," *Les Temps Modernes,* Aug.–Sept., 1964.

LARSEN, O. N.: "Patterns of Violence: Controversies About the Mass Communication of Violence," *Annals of the Amer. Acad. of Polit. and Soc. Sci.,* Mar., 1966.

LASKER, E.: *The Philosophy of the Unfinishable,* Leipzig, 1919.

LEHMANN, DR. C., and PARVUS: *Hungry Russia,* Stuttgart, 1900.

LEIGHTON, G. R.: *Five Cities,* New York, 1939.

LEMMON, R.: "The Small-Fry Boom," *Saturday Evening Post,* Dec., 1964.

LESSING, T.: *Europe and Asia,* Leipzig, 1930.

LEVY, H., and H. SPALDING: *Literature for an Age of Science,* London, 1952.

LEWIS, W.: *Hitler,* London, 1931.

LIFSHITZ, M.: "Giambattista Vico," *Philosophy and Phenomenol. Research,* March, 1948.

LONDON, J.: "A Curious Fragment," in *When God Laughs,* New York, 1911.

LORENZ, G. W.: *Federico García Lorca,* Reinbek b. Hamburg, 1963.

LOWENTHAL, L.: *Literature and the Image of Man,* Boston, 1957.

LU HSUN: "The True Story of Ah Q," in *Selected Works of Lu Hsun,* Vol. I, Peking, 1956.

LUKÁCS, G.: *Turn of Fate*, Berlin, 1948.
LUXEMBURG, R.: Introduction to *V. Korolenko: The Story of My Contemporary*, Berlin, 1919.
————: "Tolstoy as Social Thinker," *Die Neue Buecherschau*, Sept., 1928.

MACALPINE, I., and R. HUNTER: *300 Years of Psychiatry*, London, 1963.
MACCHIORO, V. D.: *From Orpheus to Paul*, New York, 1930.
McDERMAID, G., and E. G. WINKLER: "Psychopathology of Infanticide," *Journ. Clin. and Experimental Psychopathol.*, Mar., 1955.
MACDONALD, J. M.: *Psychiatry and the Criminal*, Springfield, Ill., 1958.
————: *The Murderer and His Victim*, Springfield, Ill., 1961.
MANNES, M.: "The Conquest of Trigger Mortis," *The Reporter*, Oct., 1959.
MARROQUÍN, A. D.: *Panchimalco: A Sociological Investigation*, San Salvador, 1959.
MARTÍ-IBÁÑEZ, F.: "Bronze and Dream," *MD*, July, 1964.
————: "More Than a Man, a Castle" (Ortega y Gasset), *MD*, Nov., 1965.
"Martyred Poet" (Federico García Lorca), *MD*, Nov., 1959.
"Mask of Murder," *MD*, Aug., 1963.
MASLOW, V.: "On the Theory of History," *La Voz*, New York, Feb., 1963.
MASSIGNON, L.: "The Singular Exemplariness of the Life of Gandhi," *Esprit*, Jan., 1955.
MASSINGHAM, H. J.: *The Golden Age*, New York, 1928.
MASSON, A.: "Painting Is a Wager," illus., *Horizon* (London), Mar., 1943.
MAYER, J. P.: *Sociology of Film*, London, 1948.
————: *Alexis de Tocqueville*, New York, 1960.
MAYS, J. B.: *Crime and the Social Structure*, London, 1963.
MEAD, M.: "Recapturing the Future," *Saturday Review*, June, 1963.
MERLEAU-PONTY: *Humanism and Terror*, Paris, 1947.
MILLER, W. R.: *Nonviolence*, New York, 1964.
MITSCHERLICH, A., and F. MIELKE: *Science Without Humaneness: Medical and Eugenic Aberrations*, Heidelberg, 1949.
MORRIS, N.: "Daniel M'Naughten and the Death Penalty," *6 Res Judicatae*, Feb., 1954, pp. 304–336.
MOSSE, G. L.: *The Culture of Western Europe*, Chicago, 1961.
MOSSE, H. L.: "Aggression and Violence in Fantasy and Fact," *Amer. Journ. of Psychotherapy*, 2, 1948.

————: "The Misuse of the Diagnosis of Childhood Schizophrenia," *Amer. Journ. of Psychiatry, 104,* 1958.

————: "Psychiatry and the Law." *Amer. Journ. of Psychotherapy,* July, 1958.

————: "The Influence of Mass Media on the Mental Health of Children," *Acta Paedopsychiatrica, 30,* 1963.

MOSTAR, G. H.: "Insanity and Error" (the "euthanasia" trial in Grafeneck), in *The Wolfman,* Munich, 1963.

MUELLER, G. O. W.: "M'Naghten Remains Irreplaceable: Recent Events in the Law of Incapacity," *Georgetown Law Journ.,* Fall, 1961.

————: "Criminal Law," in *Annual Survey of American Law,* New York, 1965.

MUELLER-HEGEMANN, D.: "On the Influence of Eugenics on German Medicine," *D. deutsch. Gesundheitswesen, 14,* 1959.

————: *Modern Nervousness,* Berlin, 1961.

MURPHY, G.; "A Cross-cultural View of Ego Dynamics," *Bull. N.Y. Academy of Med.,* Mar., 1965.

MURROW, E. R.: Quoted in *Television,* Dec., 1959.


NANSEN, O.: *From Day to Day,* New York, 1949.

NEVINSON, H. W.: *Visions and Memories,* London, 1946.

NITSCHE, P., and K. WILMANNS: *The History of the Prison Psychoses,* Introd. by William A. White, New York, 1912.

NUSSBAUM, M.: *Togo: A Model Colony?,* Berlin, 1962.


"On the Pardon of Dr. Gorgasz," *Die Gegenwart,* Mar., 1958.

OSSIPOV, V. P.: "Malingering: The Simulation of Psychosis," *Bull. Menninger Clinic,* Mar., 1944.


PASOLINI, P. P.: *Vita Violenta,* Munich, 1963.

PLATEN-HALLERMUND, A.: *The Killing of Mental Patients in Germany,* Frankfurt, 1948.

PLAYFAIR, G., and D. SINGTON: *The Offenders,* New York, 1957.

PORTEUS, S. D.: *The Psychology of Primitive People,* New York, 1931.

PREOBRASHENSKI, E.: *Ethics and the Class Norms,* Hamburg, 1923.


REICHARD, S., and C. TILLMAN: "Murder and Suicide as Defenses Against Schizophrenic Psychosis," *Journ. of Clin. Psychopathol.,* Oct., 1950.

REINHARDT, J. M.: *The Murderous Trail of Charles Starkweather,* Springfield, Ill., 1960.

REMIZOV, A.: *The Fifth Pestilence,* transl. A. Brown, New York, 1928.

ROBINSON, J. S.: "Punishment of War Criminals," *Judge Advocate Journ.,* Fall–Winter, 1945.

ROCHE, P. Q.: *The Criminal Mind,* New York, 1958.

ROSS, S., and E. KIESTER: "Tomboys with Knives," *Parade,* Apr., 1955.

ROUMAIN, J.: *Masters of the Dew,* transl. L. Hughes, New York, 1947.

RUBINSTEIN, S. L.: *Being and Consciousness,* transl. H. Hiebsch, Berlin, 1962.

SACHS, W.: *Black Anger,* Boston, 1947.

ST. JOHN-STEVAS, N.: *Obscenity and the Law,* London, 1956.

SCHILDER, P.: *Psychoanalysis, Man and Society,* New York, 1951.

SCHNABEL, R.: *Might Without Morals,* Frankfurt, 1957.

SCHNEIR, W., and M.: *Invitation to an Inquest,* New York, 1965.

SCHWARTZ, H. (ed.): *The Evironmentally Injured Child,* Jena, Germany, 1961.

SCHWEITZER, A.: *Big Business in the Third Reich,* Bloomington, Ind., 1964.

SELBY, H., JR.: Discussion in *American Dialog,* May–June, 1965.

SELLIN, T., and M. E. WOLFGANG: *The Measurement of Delinquency,* New York, 1964.

SHAW, G. B.: *Crude Criminology,* London, 1950.

SHULTZ, G. D.: *How Many More Victims?,* Philadelphia, 1965.

SNOW, E.: *The Other Side of the River,* New York, 1962.

SOMMER, E.: *The Revolt of the Holy Ones,* Mexico, 1944.

SOREL, G.: *Reflections on Violence,* transl. T. E. Hulme, London, 1915.

STEFFENS, L.: *Moses in Red,* Philadelphia, 1926.

STEHLE, H.: "Euthanasia in the Hitler State: Documents of the Time," *Frankfurter Allg. Zeitung,* Dec., 1959.

"The Sterilization of Insane, Infirm and Poor: Documentation," *La Raison,* Nov., 1951.

STEVENS, H. B.: *The Recovery of Culture,* New York, 1949.

STUTTE, H.: "None of the Youths Looked Like a Murderer: Juvenile Criminals—Devastating Effects of Our Time," *Die Welt,* Apr., 1954.

SWADOS, F.: *House of Fury,* New York, 1941.

SWANN, M.: "What of the Future?", in *What the Human Race Is Up To,* ed. N. Mitchison, London, 1962.

SZASZ, T. S.: *Law, Liberty and Psychiatry,* New York, 1963.

THARAUD, J., and J. THARAUD: *When Israel Is King,* transl. Lady Whitehead (from the 64th French ed.), New York, 1924.

THOMSON, G.: *Studies in Ancient Greek Society: The Prehistoric Aegean,* New York, 1949.

THORWALD, J.: *The Century of the Detective,* New York, 1965.

TILLIM, S. J.: "Know You Right from Wrong?", *Nevada State Bar Journ.,* July, 1950.

TOLSTOI, L.: "What I Owe to Garrison," in Tchertkoff and F. Holah, *A Short Biography of William Lloyd Garrison,* London, 1904.

TWAIN, MARK: "King Leopold's Soliloquy," in *Mark Twain on the Damned Human Race,* ed. J. Smith, New York, 1962.

*The Unconquered Present: A Documentation,* Frankfurt, 1962.

VAN DAM, H. G., and R. GIORDANO, eds.: *Concentration Camp Crimes Before German Courts: Trial Documents,* Frankfurt, 1962.

VERCORS: *For the Time Being,* London, 1960.

WAGNER, G.: *Parade of Pleasure,* New York, 1955.

———: *Wyndham Lewis,* London, 1957.

WARSHOW, R.: "Paul, the Horror Comics and Dr. Wertham," in *Mass Culture,* eds. B. Rosenberg and D. M. White, Glencoe, Ill., 1957.

WEISS, J. M. A., J. W. LAMBERTI, and N. BLACKMAN: "The Sudden Murderer," *Archives of General Psychiatry,* June, 1960, and Mar., 1963.

WEIZAECKER, V. VON: "Euthanasia and Human Experiments," *Psyche,* No. 1, 1947.

WERTHAM, F.: "Forensic Neurohistology," in *The Brain as an Organ,* New York, 1934.

———: "The Catathymic Crisis: A Clinical Entity," *Archives Neurol. and Psychiat., 37,* 1937, and *Journ. Nerv. Ment. Dis., 86,* 1937.

———: *Dark Legend* (the Gino case), New York, 1941 and 1966.

———: "Medico-legal Report on a Deserter," *Amer. Journ. of Psychotherapy,* Apr., 1947.

———: "The Air-Conditioned Conscience," *Saturday Review of Literature,* Oct., 1949.

———: "Freud Now," *Scientific American,* Oct., 1949.

———: "The Road to Rapallo" (the Ezra Pound case), *Amer. Journ. of Psychotherapy,* Oct., 1949.

———: *The Show of Violence* (the Fish case, the Martin Lavin case, the Irwin case, etc.), New York, 1949 and 1966.

———: "The Psychiatry of Criminal Guilt," in *Social Meanings of Legal Concepts, 2,* New York, 1950.

———: "Psychological Effects of School Segregation," *Amer. Journ.*

of Psychotherapy, Jan., 1952. (Submitted to the U.S. Supreme Court, Washington, D.C., 1954.)

———: "Psychiatric Observations on Abolition of School Segregation," *Journ. Educational Sociol.*, Mar., 1953. (Submitted to the U.S. Supreme Court, Washington, D.C., 1954.)

———: "Trial by Violence," *The Nation*, July, 1954.

———: *Seduction of the Innocent*, New York, 1954.

———: Testimony on segregation in Chancery Court, Wilmington, Del., in H. Hill and J. Greenberg, *Citizen's Guide to De-Segregation*, Boston, 1955.

———: "Psychoauthoritarianism and the Law," *Univ. of Chicago Law Rev.*, Winter, 1955.

———: *The Circle of Guilt* (the Santana case), New York, 1956.

———: "The Jungle of Legal Insanity" (the Florence case), New York *Herald Tribune*, Oct., 1958.

———: "The First Step Towards a Complete Study of Insanity Plea Cases," *Journ. Amer. Judicature Soc.*, Oct., 1960.

———: "The Scientific Study of Mass Media Effects," *Amer. Journ. of Psychiatry*, Oct., 1962.

———: "Can Advertising Be Harmful?", *Amer. Journ. of Psychotherapy*, Apr., 1963.

———: "Society and Problem Personalities: Praetorian Psychiatry," *Amer. Journ. of Psychotherapy*, July, 1963.

———: "An Unconscious Determinant in Richard Wright's *Native Son*," in *Psychoanalysis and Literature*, ed. H. M. Ruitenbeek, New York, 1964.

———: "Can We Study Violence Scientifically?", *XXth Century* (London), Winter, 1964–1965.

———: "Mass Media and Sex Deviation," in *Sexual Behavior and the Law*, ed. R. Slovenko, Springfield, Ill., 1965.

———: Medicolegal reviews: *New York Times Book Review*, Jan., 1948; *Psychosomatic Med.*, *12*, 1950; *N.Y.U. Law Rev.*, *27*, 1952; *Buffalo Law Rev.*, *48*, 1953; *Northwestern Univ. Law Rev.*, *48*, 1954; *Univ. of Chicago Law Rev.*, Winter, 1955; *Amer. Journ. of Psychiatry*, *112*, 1956, *116*, 1959, and *117*, 1961; *Scientific Monthly*, *85*, 1957; *Amer. Journ. of Psychotherapy*, Oct., 1962.

WIDMER, K., and E. WIDMER, eds.: *Literary Censorship*, San Francisco, 1961.

WILDE, H.: *Political Murder*, Bayreuth, Germany, 1962.

WILLIAMS, R. F.: *Negroes with Guns*, New York, 1962.

WILSON, C.: *"Crimes of Freedom—and Their Cure," XXth Century* (London), Winter, 1964–1965.

WRIGHT, R.: "Psychiatry Comes to Harlem" (the Lafargue Clinic), *Free World,* Sept., 1946.

WYDEN, P.: *The Hired Killers,* New York, 1963.

WYRSCH, J.: "The Killing of Mental Patients," *Monatsschr. f. Psychiatrie u. Neurol.,* Nov., 1949.

# Index

# ABOUT THE AUTHOR

Fredric Wertham, M.D., is the author of *The Brain as an Organ, Dark Legend: A Study in Murder, The Show of Violence, Seduction of the Innocent,* and *The Circle of Guilt.* In addition to his books, he has written many articles for professional journals and such general magazines as the *Atlantic, Scientific American, New York Times Magazine, Reader's Digest, Ladies' Home Journal, Saturday Review, Harper's Bazaar, New Republic,* and *Redbook.*

Dr. Wertham received his medical training in Germany and England, and did postgraduate studies in France, England, and Austria. He has been chief resident psychiatrist at Johns Hopkins, senior psychiatrist at Bellevue Hospital in New York, and director of psychiatric services at Queens General. He is now consulting psychiatrist at Queens and also maintains a private psychiatric practice among both children and adults. Dr. Wertham has taught psychiatry at Johns Hopkins and New York University. He founded the first psychiatric clinic in Harlem (the Lafargue Clinic); directed the first psychiatric clinic in a major U.S. court in which all convicted felons were examined; was the first psychiatrist admitted to a federal court as an expert for the defense in a book-banning case, and has since appeared for the defense in similar cases. He was sole psychiatric consultant to the Kefauver Senate Subcommittee for the Study of Organized Crime and was the first psychiatrist to investigate the effects of school segregation by clinical psychiatric methods. His investigations were part of the case which led to the Supreme Court's 1954 decision abolishing school segregation.